P9-AGC-573

Understanding Reading Problems

Understanding Reading Problems

Assessment and Instruction

Second Edition

Jean Wallace Gillet

Charles Temple
Hobart and William Smith Colleges

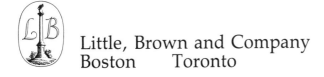

Little, Brown and Company
Boston   Toronto

Library of Congress Cataloging-in-Publication Data

Gillet, Jean Wallace.
  Understanding reading problems.

  Includes bibliographies and index.
  1. Reading—Ability testing.   2. Reading—Remedial
teaching.   I. Temple, Charles A., 1947–   . II. Title.
LB1050.46.G55   1986   428.4   85-24237
ISBN 0-316-31357-2

Library of Congress Catalog Card Number 85-24237

ISBN 0-673-39155-8

9 8 7 6 5

ALP

Printed in the United States of America

Acknowledgments
Page 22: Excerpt from P. D. Eastman, *Are You My Mother?* reprinted by
permission of William Collins Publishers Limited. *Pages 195–196*: Excerpt
from *Red Fox and His Canoe* by Nathaniel Benchley. Copyright © 1964 by
Nathaniel Benchley. Reprinted by permission of Harper & Row, Publishers,
Inc.

To the memory of George Edward Graham,
1946–1985

Preface

Understanding Reading Problems: Assessment and Instruction, Second Edition is intended as a primary text for preservice and in-service teachers in reading diagnosis and diagnostic-prescriptive reading courses. Moreover, it can be used as a guide or reference book for those who have already completed such a course and who are now working with children. Our purpose is to help teachers develop diagnostic insights and strategies so they can better meet their students' needs in reading.

Helping students become competent, effective readers is one of the challenges facing teachers. In addition to knowing how to use commercial reading programs and administer standardized tests, today's teachers must understand how reading skills normally develop and how reading problems can occur. They must also be able to carry out their own diagnostic procedures in the classroom, determine students' strengths and needs, and implement corrective instruction while maintaining responsibility for ongoing instruction and evaluation. To do this, teachers need diagnostic strategies and devices that yield qualitative information about students' reading performance and can be used during regular teaching activities. They need diagnostic tools that are flexible and practical, tapping the kinds of everyday reading tasks students must accomplish in and out of school. Such strategies and devices are the heart of this book.

Diagnosis is not the result of giving tests or compiling test scores. Rather, it is a kind of detective work requiring insight, imagination, and judgment. Since one cannot use a cookbook to develop these skills, this book presents no recipes for diagnosis. We have offered many suggestions, ideas, and models, but no step-by-step formulas. While conceptualizing and writing this book, we have proceeded from our belief that understanding why is as important as knowing how. Theory and practice are woven together as are diagnostic implications and suggestions for corrective instruction.

The concepts and principles that guided the development of the first edition have been strengthened and expanded in the second edition. In this edition we have concentrated on:

- □ updating and elaborating on important trends in inquiry and research;
- □ expanding coverage of instructional methods and materials; and
- □ including more coverage of the assessment and teaching of older poor readers.

This edition examines both traditional assessment topics and aspects of diagnosis and corrective instruction. In Chapter One we describe fundamental principles of diagnosis and assessment and offer an overview of the reading process from a perceptual and psycholinguistic perspective. Chapter Two describes in greater depth the development of cognitive and experiential concepts and operations fundamental to literacy, and reflects current trends and topics in reading theory and research. Chapter Three is devoted to assessing the concepts, skills, and print-related experience of prereaders and emergent readers, as well as ways to help these students acquire prereading competencies at home and school. Chapter Four deals with the assessment of reading skills and strategies by informal means, and demonstrates how to use scores, observations, and students' responses to determine their reading strengths and needs and to provide them with material of appropriate difficulty.

Chapter Five details how to use diagnostic findings to plan corrective instruction and describes corrective teaching methods in reading and listening comprehension, word recognition, word analysis, and reading fluency. Chapter Six extends the methodology of corrective teaching to subject areas in all grades and emphasizes the special diagnostic and instructional needs of older poor readers. Chapter Seven is devoted to assessing and teaching spelling and word knowledge, and clarifies the relationships between spelling, word knowledge, and reading. Chapter Eight describes formal assessment measures, including test and measurement concepts and vocabulary, descriptive statistics, and types and uses of norm-referenced and criterion-referenced reading tests. Chapter Nine deals with factors related to reading difficulties; intellectual, physical, and affective factors including intelligence and its assessment, capacity for reading improvement, learning disabilities and dyslexia, vision and hearing problems, self-concept, and attitudes about reading. Chapter Ten describes the consideration of the classroom and school as environments for reading success or failure and presents strategies for enchancing their effectiveness.

Features of the text include case studies and narrative descriptions of the problems and successes of many pupils with whom we have worked, chapter summaries, suggested activities to enhance and extend students' learning, suggested reading lists, and many illustrations. The accompanying Instructor's Manual lists a variety of demonstrations and other activities designed to involve students and help them gain experience and diagnostic insight.

As with the first edition we are indebted to many people for involvement, advice, and encouragement. Foremost among these are our colleagues who read and critiqued the manuscript for this edition: Camille Blachowicz, National College of Education; William Teale, The University of Texas at San Antonio; Page Bristow, University of Delaware; Larry Miller, Queen's University (Kingston, Ontario); and Donald O'Brien, State University College at Buffalo.

Again, we wish to acknowledge our first edition reviewers: Leo D. Geoffrion, State University of New York at Albany; Zelda R. Maggart, University of New Mexico; Janell Klesius, University of South Florida; Gary Anderson, Arizona State University; and David W. Moore, The University of Connecticut. Special thanks goes to those teachers who allowed us to do the photographic work in their classrooms: Marilyn Pope, Mary Stevens, and Ann Nesbitt in Victoria, Texas, and Dick Pronti and Midge Burns at West Street Elementary School in Geneva, New York. In addition we gratefully acknowledge our colleagues and students at the University of Virginia and Hobart and William Smith Colleges, our friends at other universities, those users of the first edition who sent us comments and students' criticisms, and Mylan Jaixen, Barbara Breese, and others at Little, Brown and Company. Finally, we offer our heartfelt thanks to our families for their limitless patience, encouragement and support of our work.

Brief Contents

Contents

Understanding Reading Problems

Chapter One

Introduction to Reading and Its Assessment

Whether you are preparing for a teaching career, are beginning your career with little prior experience, or have been teaching for some time, an important part of your responsibility will be to carry out much of the diagnostic assessment and corrective teaching of reading that your students will receive. Whether you are an experienced teacher or not, you may feel uncertain and unprepared for these responsibilities. We have produced this book to help you learn what to do and how to do it. We strongly believe that the more you learn about reading and about the ways students can encounter difficulty with reading, writing, and spelling, the more confident and effective a teacher you will become. And today we need informed, confident, and effective teachers more than ever.

In the sections that follow in this chapter we discuss some principles of diagnosis and assessment that underlie the diagnostic process and describe some important aspects of the reading process. These discussions serve as an introduction to the detailed explanations of theory and practice that follow in subsequent chapters. The principles of diagnosis that follow serve as a rationale for the approaches and methods which make up this book, and will help you put diagnosis and assessment into the larger context of teaching and learning.

Principles of Diagnosis

The range of techniques available for reading assessment is wide. While we have attempted to be comprehensive in our coverage of them, we have nevertheless proceeded from certain assumptions and beliefs about how assessment should be approached.

Diagnosis Is More Than a Testing and Measuring Process

Testing is a contrived activity. Children respond differently in testing than in their other schoolwork. Measurement assumes that there are arbitrary standards for performance in whatever is being measured. Placing a child in an inherently artificial learning situation and applying arbitrary standards to the performance yield a very restricted view of the child's behavior.

Diagnosis is a process of *becoming informed* about a child. This requires that we observe the child's responses and behavior in the course of natural everyday learning. We have to keep an open mind while observing so that we can be aware of and respond to unexpected behaviors and insights.

Any hypotheses made about a child should remain tentative until they are tested during actual instruction. Becoming informed means that we must reserve judgment until we have seen the student exhibit the same types of behavior in a number of instances rather than forming judgments on the limited sample of behavior that tests represent.

To assume that "diagnosis equals testing" implies that instruments can be selected that will provide answers to our questions on the basis of the test results. This is a very narrow view. We believe that diagnosis is a process requiring decision making by people, not instruments. It requires gathering many types of information, synthesizing this information, and creating informed hypotheses. Tests of certain kinds can provide some data for analysis, but the analysis and synthesis must be done by the human mind.

No Single Set of Diagnostic Procedures or Tools Can Be Used in Every Case

If diagnosis is viewed as a process of becoming informed about a child's reading, no single set of procedures would be sufficient unless: (a) all children learned in the same ways; (b) all children read by applying the same strategies; (c) all children read under the same conditions or for the same purposes; and (d) all teachers shared the same standards, biases, and teaching experiences. None of these four conditions is ever the case.

We know of practitioners who have a "kit bag" of tests they give every pupil they diagnose. Every time they test, such examiners analyze these same aspects of reading — but no other aspects. In effect, they ask the same questions in every case. Not surprisingly, they tend to come up with the same types of answers every time, and diagnosis then becomes the systematic compilation of largely the same data in every instance. This, of course, makes diagnosis a fairly simple process: ask these predetermined questions, get these answers, and form these judgments. After a while, the process can almost be done by rote.

This does not mean that there are no procedures or criteria that we can depend on for reliable information. If that were so, diagnosis textbooks would not be written. The point is that although procedures for diagnosis may not be infinitely variable, they certainly cannot be neatly set forth and adhered to in a set formula. The process of diagnosis must always be flexible, and practitioners must be able to apply different strategies "on the fly." In this book we have not only described many procedures that will help you gather information in most cases but also have supplemented these basic strategies with suggestions for additional strategies that may be helpful in other cases.

Diagnosis Means Looking for Strengths and Competence as Well as Needs and Difficulties

Many diagnosticians use their assessment procedures to determine all the things a student cannot do or does incorrectly. Remediation, then, becomes a "repair job," fixing up all those weaknesses and errors.

When viewed in this way, diagnosis is a dismally *negative* process. It is negative for the reader, who is faced with task after task ending in failure.

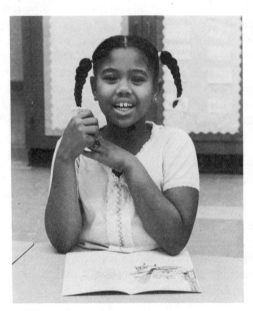

Every reader has different purposes for reading and different ideas of what it is about. Readers bring to reading all their prior experiences and expectations about print.

Such testing soon reaches the point where the student can no longer continue to work because the procedures dwell only on errors and weaknesses. No wonder many students who have been tested once have a fear of going through it again. The examiner is also affected negatively. Faced with a growing list of the things a student cannot do or does poorly, the examiner develops a view that is sharply skewed toward failure, and if the reading problem is a serious one, the teacher may feel overwhelmed by all the myriad weaknesses brought to light. Both student and examiner are left with the bitter taste of failure.

Diagnosis must be as much a process of locating *strengths* as of detailing weaknesses. It is only by knowing what the student already can do that we can begin to know how to attack the weaknesses instructionally. By learning what the child's strengths are, we can base remedial instruction on success rather than on failure. We can build instruction on the solid foundation of already acquired skills rather than on the sand of those yet to be mastered.

By looking first for strengths, then for problems, we can also make the diagnostic process a more positive one for everyone involved. When students are shown what they have done well, they approach other aspects of assessment with enthusiasm and persistence instead of fear and avoidance. The teacher, too, develops a picture of the student as a person who can do some things well and some things poorly, a more balanced and realistic view of the learner than that yielded by listing weaknesses alone. Those responsible for carrying out the remediation are also aided by knowing the areas of strength from which to teach, and they are reassured by knowing that the student is a person with recognized *abilities* as well as *disabilities*.

In this book we have attempted to show teachers how to look systematically for areas of strength and competence and to approach remediation as a way of building on these positive aspects. We have also included assessment of ways in which the home and school influence the student's reading, such as language development, experiential background, development of attitudes toward reading, and the profound influence of instructional programs. We have included an entire chapter on assessing classroom and school environments and their impact on reading success. We have done so because students do not learn to read, or fail to do so, in a vacuum. Diagnosis of the "whole child" means examining the reading environment as well as the reader.

Diagnosis Should Result in Instructional Change

To have value, diagnosis should result in more than labeling or categorizing problems. To know a problem is not to solve it. Diagnosis must point the way for instructional change and, through instructional change, to progress in learning. Diagnosis that results in labeling rather than in concrete direction for instruction is merely an academic exercise as well as a waste of time and resources.

Many teachers have experienced the frustration of requesting special testing for a student, waiting patiently for the results, and finally receiving a report that merely places the student in some category of disability. We have personally read numerous diagnostic reports from different sources that simply label the child's disability. Terms like "dyslexic," "learning disabled," "emotionally disabled," "culturally disadvantaged," "perceptually or neurologically impaired," "reading-retarded," and "motivationally dysfunctional" abound. All serve only to categorize the student, all imply specific meanings when few actually exist, and none serve to point the way for better instruction. Pedagogically they do little, if any, good and many even scare off the teacher because they imply grave disabilities or disturbances that the average teacher may feel unequipped to handle. Such labels have the same negative effect as the detailing of weaknesses described in the previous section. They can effectively hinder, rather than promote, the process of corrective teaching.

Unfortunately more time is often spent delving into the students' history for the precise cause of a disability than is spent determining what their present functioning levels are. Searching a child's past can be fruitful if it induces a present-day change that will help overcome the problem. Sometimes, however, nothing can be done to mitigate the effect of past events. Causative factors are often heralded as though they had some intrinsic value, but since we cannot undo the past, such findings are helpful only if they point the way to present-day change.

It is sometimes assumed that diagnosis results in final answers. This assumption could be true if children developed to some point and never changed thereafter, but teachers know that students of every age change and grow daily. Diagnosis, therefore, is a *continuous* process of asking, Where is the student *today* in his or her development, and where should we go at this time? There is no final answer to this question, for tomorrow's student will be different from today's. Diagnosis can never be a once-and-for-all event.

Informal Procedures and Instruments Can Be the Most Useful Source of Information about the Student's Reading

Standardized tests are administered under controlled conditions and yield numerical results that allow comparison of one pupil or group to others. These devices are widely used to assess achievement and to diagnose difficulties. They are adequate for the former purpose but have relatively little diagnostic usefulness. Numerical scores do not yield specific information about what the student can or cannot do. Test reading is not like reading for information or pleasure in the classroom or at home. It is usually the reading of single sentences or short passages under timed conditions and is constructed to test the recall of information rather than to inform or arouse interest. A student's reading tastes, interests, and purposes are relatively unimportant in test situations, although they are of great importance instructionally.

In contrast, informal assessment devices and procedures more closely resemble natural reading in the classroom and outside of school. Informal assessment means observing the student reading meaningful material for a variety of purposes and takes place during regular instruction or in an assessment setting that simulates the instructional environment. The informal approach to diagnosis looks at reading behaviors *qualitatively* rather than only *quantitatively*. Informal procedures are basically exploratory in nature since they allow the examiner to determine what a reader does and does not do during reading based on an in-depth, personal perspective. In informal diagnosis we are more concerned with determining what readers do during natural reading than in how their reading compares with someone else's reading. The rationale for this is our belief that in order to provide more effective instruction it is necessary to know with some precision what the individual can and cannot do in reading.

We have a definite bias in favor of informal assessment because we have found that such procedures yield the most useful information for direct teaching applications. Moreover, these procedures can be carried out during regular teaching activities with groups of students as well as with individual students. Other informal assessment procedures, even though they are more "testlike," also make use of typical classroom reading materials and simulate everyday reading and writing tasks. All such devices and procedures consider the whole child as he or she operates within the instructional setting. We prefer these means of assessment to more traditional standardized tests because they help us form a more realistic, accurate view of the way the reader functions.

In this book we have demonstrated how informal measures can be developed and used in the regular classroom as supplements to, or even in place of, standardized reading measures. We have consistently attempted to relate diagnostic findings to corrective teaching procedures and to illustrate the use of such methods in our case studies and examples. However, standardized testing is a fact of life in every classroom, and we have analyzed and described the major types of norm-referenced and criterion-referenced tests in a separate chapter. We hope that as a result teachers will be able to make qualitative judgments about students' reading by using informal classroom methods and that they will be able to evaluate and interpret more clearly the standardized measures they use.

We have placed the focus of diagnostic and corrective efforts within the regular classroom because we firmly believe that the teacher, not the outside specialist, has the greatest need for diagnostic information and data. Diagnosis of reading problems has often been invested with a false sense of mystery and complexity, which serves only to make teachers feel uncertain and ill-prepared. This need not be the case. The person with the fullest and clearest perception of the students is the one who works with them daily, not the specially trained expert who comes in to do the testing. In the final analysis it is the teacher, not the specialist, who will be responsible for the student's instruction. Diagnosis and corrective teaching are inextricably related, and both should be done within the regular classroom with the active involvement of the regular teacher.

Understanding the Reading Process

To understand and correct problems that occur as children read, and to develop diagnostic judgment, you must understand how reading normally develops and what readers must do to be able to read successfully. In the following discussion, we will describe some of the processes that make up successful reading for all learners.

Let's begin by defining what reading is: *reading is making sense of written language*. The most basic operation of the reading process is sense-making: getting and creating ideas, information, and mental images from print. Making sense is often referred to as *comprehending*. In order to comprehend, a number of processes occur, often simultaneously.

Visual Perception

One process involved in reading is *visual perception*, which means seeing and putting to use what we have seen. Seeing is a physical process, but using what we have seen is a mental, or cognitive, process. The two are inseparable, for what we have seen (called *visual information*) must be used by the brain or it is of no value to us. How the eyes and brain work together has been studied extensively for many years. In the later years of the nineteenth century, scientists became quite interested in studying the role of vision in reading. Some important studies in visual perception were conducted by Erdman and Dodge and reported by Edmund Burke Huey in his classic book, *The Psychology and Pedagogy of Reading*. These studies and their methods have often been replicated using modern technology.

They demonstrated that during reading the eyes do not move in smooth sweeps as the reader often assumes, but rather in short hops or jerks. The eyes appear to jump forward across a line of print, stop briefly, jump forward again, stop, and occasionally jump backwards (right to left) or back up to a previous line. The jerking movements are called *saccades,* the stops are called *fixations*, and the moves backwards are called *regressions*. (During fixations, the eyes appear to stop, but actually very small eye movements, detectable only by an eye camera, are present that activate the various visual reception cells in the retina.) Fixations, saccades, and regressions can be observed if you carefully watch the eyes of someone who is reading lines of print comfortably. You will be able to see the saccades, fixations and occasional regressions, but the reader will probably tell you that he or she felt as if the eyes were moving across the print in long smooth sweeps.

During the fixation, visual information is taken in by the eyes and sent to the brain by the optic nerves. During the saccades, when the eyes are moving to the next fixation, visual information is not taken in, because as the eye moves across the print, it would be seen as a blur. If visual information were sent to the brain during both the fixation and the saccade, what we would be aware of during reading would be a sequence of clear vision–blurring–clear vision–blurring, which would interfere with our processing of what was seen clearly and also probably make us feel slightly "carsick" as we read! Instead the brain processes, or uses in some way, the visual information taken in during the previous fixation. If what was seen can be made sense of, the eyes move forward; if it doesn't make sense, or if more visual information is needed before the brain can make sense of it, the eyes move back (a regression), and "take another look" at what was already read.

All this seeing, processing, and moving on takes a lot less time to do than it does to describe it! The eyes and brain are set up to make about *four fixations per second*. One fixation-plus-saccade takes, then, about ¼ second, or about 250 milliseconds (a millisecond is ¹⁄₁₀₀₀ second) on the average. The actual fixation, during which the eyes "see" what is in front of them, lasts an average of 50 milliseconds and the saccade, during which the information is mentally processed, takes the remaining 200 milliseconds. A variety of factors such as the reader's familiarity with words in the text, the grammatical and contextual complexity of the text, the purpose and context of the reading act, and others appear to affect the number and duration of fixations, but the foregoing figures are average rates that are predetermined by the working capacity of the human brain.

An important difference between unfluent and fluent readers is not how long their fixations take, but *how many* fixations per line of print they need to make and how often they make regressions. To explain this, we must turn our discussion to how the brain works as it directs the eyes during reading.

Cognition and Memory

How much visual information is taken in and processed during a fixation-and-saccade depends more on how well the brain *recognizes* the information than on how well the eyes function. The brain can process more information and do so more efficiently if what was seen is familiar and easily recognizable than if it is highly unfamiliar. To understand this, try this experiment with a partner.

Use the visual arrays in Figure 1.1 and two small cards or pieces of paper. Cover the first line completely, than *very briefly* uncover it and cover it again, as your partner looks at the array. Your partner should immediately jot down everything he or she remembers seeing in that "flashed" exposure. Continue through all six lines in the array.

FIGURE 1.1. Visual arrays.

---

1. ⟋ᵒᶜ₃ ˎ₁ ⁊ ⊥ ᶜ⟋ ᶜ⟋ᴸᵔ₁
2. pnsrvntcb
3. larmorkle
4. Washington
5. cranked squirm call rash sugar do
6. the boy was hungry because he hadn't eaten

Ordinarily, people will be able to write down from two to five of the "squiggles" in line 1, some incorrectly. Subjects usually write down from three to six of the random letters in line 2, most of the letters in the nonsense word in line 3, the whole word in line 4, three or four of the words in line 5, and most or all of the sentence in line 6.

In each case, usually between three and six *items* are recalled, but the nature of the items changes. The first line contains marks that are parts of printed letters, but they are not immediately recognized as such. In line 2 the same marks are combined into letters, which are more quickly recognized than the letter parts, so by recalling three to six real letters, more letter parts are recalled than in line 1. In line 3, letters are arranged in a wordlike sequence, so more letters are usually recalled than when they were arranged randomly. The same is true for line 4, which contains a real word rather than an unfamiliar nonsense word. Hence most subjects recall all the letters in *Washington*. Likewise, in line 5, real words are arranged at random, and three or so of them are usually recalled, but in line 6 real words are arranged in a meaningful sentence, and more words from the sentence are usually recalled than from the line of random words.

In each case, a maximum of five to seven items are usually recalled, but whereas only a few letter parts are recalled, as the arrays become progressively more meaningful and thus more easily recognized by the brain, by line 6 as many as seven or eight entire words may be recalled. This demonstration shows how recognition and recall are profoundly influenced by the material itself — what is seen. The more meaningful and familiar the material is, the more the eyes can take in and send the brain in each fixation.

Short-term Memory. Even when the visual array is meaningful and easily recognizable, however, there is a limit to how many items can be perceived: five to seven items or "bits" of information is the maximum. This visual information is processed during the following saccade. During this processing, the information is sent to a sort of "mental waiting room," which is called *short-term memory*.

Short-term memory may be thought of as a sort of holding area for bits of information that are about to be processed more fully and possibly stored in our long-term memory, but that are being temporarily "held" so they can be related to other bits of information which are acquired in successive fixations. When the presently held bits of information (e.g. syllables, words, and phrases) can be related to others so that ideas and mental images are created, these ideas are sent to long-term memory for what we think of as remembering. But they must be held, for the moment, to wait for other bits of information as they come in.

It is in short-term memory that the limit of five to seven items is imposed, for this "mental waiting room" can only receive so much information at one time. Its limits are *finite* in both capacity and duration: five to seven items can be received at one time, and they can be held there for only about 5 to 7 seconds (without conscious rehearsal). If the information received in one fixation cannot be related to other bits and made into a phrase, idea, or image that makes sense to the brain within about 7 seconds, these items are dropped from short-term memory; they are forgotten. Information can only be stored in long-term memory or forgotten; it cannot be stored in short-term memory indefinitely (Smith, 1978).

To illustrate this point, look again at the arrays in Figure 1.1. Imagine that you were trying to read and make sense of (i.e., remember) line after line of letters randomly arrayed, as in line 2. In one fixation you would send, say, three or four letters to short-term memory, then take in a few more in the next fixation, and so on. If, however, you were unable to perceive any pattern in the arrangement of the letters, such as that the same letter occurred in each group of four or that the sounds they represented sounded like a word, you would find that after several fixations, the letters you first looked at were forgotten. You would be able to remember those seen in the last one or two fixations, but not those seen 7 or more seconds previously. Because the brain was unable to find a way to relate the letters and thus send them to long-term memory, they simply were pushed out of short-term memory by new bits of information coming in.

We can see this same phenomenon going on as an unfluent reader tries to read material in which he or she cannot recognize many of the words. After stumbling through a sentence or paragraph at a painfully slow rate, an unfluent reader may have no idea of what he or she read! This is not because the reader didn't "try hard enough," pay attention, or comprehend: it is due to the processing limit of the brain and its memory capacities.

Long-term Memory. On the other hand, when visual information can be taken in and sent to short-term memory in "large" bits, like groups of several words instead of single letters or syllables, it is much more likely that they can be related to other bits of information in idea groups, and sent to *long-term memory*. When this occurs, we understand and remember them. Long-term memory is like a huge warehouse of memories. In fact, it has seemingly limitless capacity and duration.

The limitations of long-term memory are not in capacity or duration, but in the means by which information is stored and retrieved. In both storage and retrieval, or learning and remembering, the critical process is *associating*.

Information must be related to, or associated with, other information to proceed from short- to long-term, and it must be retrieved by the same means by associating it with other information. Random or meaningless information will not be stored in long-term memory, but will be forgotten.

"Chunking" Information

Another key to remembering is what we referred to earlier as "large" bits of information, such as the word groups you were able to perceive in one fixation in the visual arrays. When what is seen is highly familiar, as we demonstrated, more visual information can be taken in each fixation. This is called *chunking*, or taking in information in large chunks. For the unfluent reader we described earlier, chunking was impossible because the words on the page were not quickly recognizable. Chunking, which maximizes the brain's capacity to make sense of information and store it permanently, depends in part on the ability to recognize whole words immediately, which is called *sight recognition*.

The Fallacy of Eye Movement Training

We have already described how readers can take in more visual information in each fixation if they can recognize most or all of the words on sight than if they have to examine and figure out many words in the passage. When the words are highly familiar, which is the case when reading comfortably in material that is not too difficult, most readers make from three to five fixations per line of print. Print is typically arranged in books in lines of ten to twelve words each, so this means that most readers see two to four words in each fixation. This allows the reader to effectively chunk information, maximizes comprehension, and makes successful reading fairly rapid. Unfluent readers who have only a small vocabulary of words recognizable at sight, or readers trying to read material that is too difficult in vocabulary or content, will necessarily make more fixations per line than fluent readers. Because more fixations mean less information perceived in each one and reading at a slower rate, what is perceived may also make less sense, and more regressions may occur as the brain sends the eyes back again and again to take another look.

In the sixties and early seventies, it was thought that unfluent readers made more regressions and fixations because of "inefficient eye movements" or bad habits related to their eye movements. Often, unfluent readers were subjected to exercises intended to "train" their eyes to make fewer, more rapid fixations and to eliminate regressions. Special machines were used that in some cases exposed only a portion of a line at a time, and in other cases used a "pointer" or similar device for the eye to follow across a line. These machines could be gradually speeded up in an effort to help these students sweep their eyes more quickly across a line, and move only left to right and top to bottom. Some students were also subjected to similar methods designed to "strengthen eye muscles" so that eye movements would become faster and more regular during reading.

The obvious flaw in these techniques is that they concentrated on the eyes, instead of the brain, as the critical element in reading. They were developed on the assumption that the eyes move in some standard, regular ways and at the same rate no matter what is being read, no matter what the reader's purpose is for the reading, and no matter what the reader already knows. We know today that these assumptions are false. The eyes move in reading as they are *directed* to move by the brain, based on what the brain can recognize, make sense of, and store in long-term memory. Frequent regressions and fixations are not a symptom of inefficient eye movements or bad reading habits. They are the natural result of the brain's inability to recognize what is on the page and make sense of it. Such eye movements cannot be corrected by exercises or by artificially manipulating text with bands of light or pointers. They will become more efficient when readers read text at a comfortable level, where both the words used and information conveyed are familiar and can be recognized quickly.

Prediction and Cues

Another cognitive process related to chunking is *prediction:* that is, the forming of tentative hypotheses about what new information is coming, based on what has already been taken in. When readers are reading material in which most of the words are recognizable at sight, they can take in chunks of several words and short phrases in each fixation. These chunks are more meaningful than groups of letters or syllables, so they make more sense right from the start. The brain gets a head start on relating these large chunks of information by forming hypotheses, or predictions, about what words and phrases will most likely follow in successive fixations. When these predictions are borne out, the ideas flow quickly into long-term memory, comprehension results, and the reading goes smoothly on. When, occasionally, what follows does not fit with a prediction, the brain may direct the eyes to move backward and look again at already-read words, or to stop and look again at the new words. This explains why regressions occur in everyone's reading.

Let's look now at how readers use the process of prediction to make sense of what they read. Let's say, for example, that you read this portion of a sentence before it ended at the bottom of a page:

The sprinter settled into a crouch and waited for the . . .

Before you turn the page and read the next words, you have probably already formed a prediction about the words to follow. Your prediction is based on several kinds of *cues*, or signals, available to you from the previous words.

One cue is related to *syntax,* or grammar: what kind (or class) of words usually follows *the?* Not usually verbs, prepositions, or other articles, but almost exclusively nouns, and descriptive words followed by nouns to complete a noun phrase.

But you're not expecting just *any* modifiers or nouns to follow: you'd probably be surprised if you read on to find that the sprinter waited for the *yellow school bus,* the *total eclipse of the sun,* or the *refrigerator door to open.*

Why would you be surprised? Because phrases like this work grammatically (syntactically), but they don't make sense. *Semantics,* or meaning, is another crucially important cue. The meanings you associate with the words "sprinter," "settled into a crouch" and "waited for" and the mental image they combine to convey, can only be completed by a noun or noun phrase. Sensibly, what might a sprinter crouch and wait for? Of your 20,000-plus words and thousands of noun phrases, only a very few work semantically:

> starting gun
> race to begin
> signal to start

and a few others associated with the beginning of a foot race.

Of course, additional cues are available to you, but in this example they would only be available *after* you turned the page and actually looked at the next words. These cues involve the letters, or *graphemes,* in the words and the speech sounds, or *phonemes,* letters and letter groups represent. Therefore, these cues are called *graphophonic.* Because you would have to look at the word to use them, graphophonic cues would not be involved in the prediction you began to form before you turned the page, in this example, or before you began to study the unrecognized word you may encounter in other running text. But graphophonic cues too have their place in the prediction process, because they help to further reduce the number of alternatives that the unrecognized word may have.

Thus, to complete our example, let's say that you read *"the sprinter settled into a crouch and waited for the . . . ,"* and used both semantic and syntactic cues to predict that the next words would be *"race to begin."* But when you turned the page and glanced at the beginning of the next word and saw the letters *st,* your prediction would immediately change to accommodate this additional information: "starting gun," "starter's gun," or "start of the race" would be logical alternatives. The briefest glance at the actual words on the page would suffice to complete your prediction and send you on to subsequent words and phrases.

Effective reading, comprehending, and making sense of written language relies on just such prediction strategies, repeated over and over within each sentence and sentence group. These predictions are made subconsciously and very rapidly: remember that fixations are occurring at about a 4/sec rate. We don't consciously ask ourselves, "What will probably occur next?" and read on to find out, but we certainly do it subconsciously when we are actively engaged in understanding what we read. However, this critically important aspect of comprehending depends on our ability to recognize the words on the page rapidly and accurately.

We'll develop this idea of predicting during reading later. But before we leave the idea here, we need to detail one more aspect of the reading process, one of the ways prediction and word recognition interact.

Prediction, Cues and Miscues

As we are engaged in chunking information and in a rapid cycle of predicting, reading successive word groups and confirming our predictions (and occasionally regressing when our predictions are not borne out), we are engaged in *constructing for ourselves what the writer meant*. One way that we can examine this process of constructing meaning and consider the reader's prediction strategies is to consider the kinds of divergences from the text that the reader makes while reading orally.

In the sixties Kenneth and Yetta Goodman and their colleagues (Goodman, 1967, 1969; Goodman and Burke, 1972) demonstrated that all readers make occasional *divergences from the written text during oral reading*. Goodman et al. called these divergences *miscues*. Their findings challenged the long-held notion that "good reading" was totally accurate in word recognition and that only poor readers used words different from those on the page. Miscue researchers, instead, demonstrated that all readers occasionally miscue when reading aloud and probably do so when reading silently, but that their miscues differ in type from those made by less-fluent readers. Fluent readers are likely to make minor slip-of-the-tongue miscues, which they correct spontaneously, and to make miscues that mean about the same thing as the printed word, such as "the *runner* settled into a crouch . . ." for "the *sprinter* settled . . ." or "Sally and her *daddy* . . ." for "Sally and her *father* . . ." Unfluent readers are likely to make more uncorrected miscues than their fluent peers and to make miscues that violate the author's message, such as "the *spinner* settled into a crouch . . ." or "Sally and her *famous* . . ."

The insights from miscue research made educators reexamine their attitudes about oral reading errors, but what seemed then like entirely new insights had actually been proposed some fifty years before. Edmund Burke Huey did more than just report on eye movement research in his 1908 book: he predated many of the most important insights of cognitive psychologists and reading experts of the next fifty years. One of the topics he addressed was the tendency for readers to substitute words of their own for words on the page during oral reading. Huey saw immediately that such reading behaviors must be related to the readers' attempts to make sense of what they were reading. In fact, he actually encouraged teachers and parents not to be overly concerned about word substitutions *when they made sense in context*. He wrote:

It is not indeed necessary that the child should be able to pronounce correctly or pronounce at all, at first, the new words that appear in his reading. . . . If he grasps, approximately, the total meaning of the sentence in which the new word stands, he has read the sentence. . . . And even if the child substitutes words of his own for some that are on the page, provided that they express the meaning, it is an encouraging sign that the reading has been real, and recognition of details will come as needed. (1908/1968, pp. 348–349)

Huey's thinking, so far ahead of its own time, has come to mirror the insights we have carefully developed in the past twenty years and now hold to be correct.

Some Conclusions about the Reading Process

We have described the variety of visual and cognitive processes that go on during reading. We do not believe, as some do, that reading is an abstract, complex mass of skills and processes that only a scientist could understand or describe. It is certainly a complex of interrelated processes, but many young children learn to read successfully and enjoyably without direct instruction, in much the same way that they learn to talk. However, we also do not mean to oversimplify what is involved in learning to read.

Reading is much more than recognizing words, or sounding them out, or any other single process. Rather, it is an active process of getting and constructing meaning from print, involving word recognition, memory processes, sense-making strategies, and the use of context, vocabulary, and prior information to form predictions about what is coming. At all points along the way, the brain directs the eyes to move in particular ways during reading so as to provide the brain with the most possible information on which it can act.

In every act of reading the same visual perception, cognitive, and memory processes are used, but readers apply different strategies at different times as they read. This is so because all human brains are essentially very similar, but all readers are different and unique in their prior experiences, expectations, purposes for reading, and use of language. Each reader develops a repertoire of strategies to use and approaches to reading, but these are applied individually. Though a whole group may be taught the same things, each member of the group may learn and apply them somewhat differently at different times.

This is why the process of identifying reading problems and discovering an individual reader's strengths and needs must be a flexible, ongoing process of inquiry and deduction. It is why one set of measures, strategies, or diagnostic devices will not serve all our needs or those of all our students. In the chapters that follow we will describe both the ways that children are often similar in their reading and the ways in which they differ, and we will offer you a wide variety of devices, strategies, and processes for exploring your students' reading and for teaching them effectively. We hope that in the process you will come to share some of our curiosity about reading, our awe at the incredible power of children's thinking, and our excitement about the processes of diagnosis and teaching.

References

Goodman, Kenneth S. "Reading: A Psycholinguistic Guessing Game." *Journal of the Reading Specialist* 6 (1967): 126–135.

Goodman, Kenneth S. "Analysis of Oral Reading Miscues: Applied Psycholinguistics." *Reading Research Quarterly* 5, No. 1 (1969): 9–30.

Goodman, Yetta and Burke, Carolyn. *Reading Miscue Inventory.* New York: Macmillan, 1972.

Huey, Edmund Burke. *The Psychology and Pedagogy of Reading.* Cambridge, Mass.: MIT Press, 1968 (originally published 1908).

Smith, Frank. *Understanding Reading,* revised ed. New York: Holt, Rinehart & Winston, 1978.

Chapter Two

Foundations for Literacy

It is pointless to talk about reading problems without first knowing how normal reading works. Reading problems are not diseases; they are patterns of behavior that children use when they encounter print. Sometimes they are on the way to becoming the right patterns — they just haven't matured yet. But sometimes the patterns are on the wrong track altogether, so that poor readers are practicing behaviors over and over that take them further away from skilled reading. In this chapter we will lay out a collection of behaviors that research and experience suggest make up the ability to read; that is, when these behaviors come together properly, children usually learn to read. When children aren't making adequate progress learning to read, something like an explanation — and a solution — can often be found by examining the behaviors we are setting out here.

Of course, you *could* say that when a child doesn't make expected progress in learning to read that that child simply has a reading problem. But big problems usually turn out to be made up of collections of little problems, just as smoothly orchestrated complex behaviors — such as hitting a baseball — can be envisioned as several smaller moves done together. That's an apt example, because it leads us to a caution: You probably couldn't think consciously about all of the discrete moves that go into batting — tracking the ball, gripping the bat, pivoting at the waist, and swinging the arms — and ever hit a baseball. Likewise, even though reading problems can be reduced to smaller parts, we must be careful not to get too fond of thinking of reading as discrete skills, lest the parts add up to something other than fluent reading.

So what *is* involved when children learn to read? We can advance two kinds of explanation. The first kind focuses on the social circumstances that make it natural for a child to become a reader. In this view we might describe a child's family, what they read, and how her mother and father read to her. We could catalogue all of the print she saw around her — on cereal boxes and drink cans; flashed up on the TV screen; on signs identifying fast-food chains. We could talk about her early attempts to be a reader, as she paged through favorite books and recited the remembered story to herself. We could extend this account into school, where direct teaching would enter the picture — nevertheless, we would have to see her school learning as a continuation of what had begun long before at home; as a kind of bargained outcome in which her already strong ideas of what reading is, come together with what her teacher and reading program say reading is. By fourth grade or so, it is likely that her progress or lack of progress as a reader will be a natural outgrowth of her earliest encounters with literacy — at home. We could call all this a *social learning view* of reading. Social learning is the transfer of patterns of behavior from the group to the individual, a process that seems invisible, that seems to work almost by osmosis. A lot of reading is learned that way.

The more detailed skill-by-skill look we can call the *psycholinguistic view*.

Psycholinguistics concerns itself with the psychological process by which language is learned, and with a detailed study of exactly what is learned when one learns language. A psycholinguistic view of Sherry's learning to read will focus on her knowledge of language itself: the words she knows and their meanings, the rules she has learned on an unconscious level that enable her to speak and understand grammatical sentences; her concepts about written language — the ways letters are different from pictures, and eventually, what the letters are; how the letters combine to make words; how words combine in message frameworks to make stories and other discourse forms. We will talk about this aspect of her reading skill in detail in this chapter.

Outline of a Social Learning View of Reading

After reading the research on the connection between social class and learning to read (see, e.g., Seitz, 1977), a pessimist could conclude that learning to read is hereditary. Not in a real genetic sense, of course, but somehow parents who read pass on this practice to their children, while parents who don't read often have children who don't read — in spite of what teachers do in schools.

Those who are not pessimists have begun to take some good hard looks at the beginnings of literacy in the home before schooling, asking such questions as:

- □ when do children begin to get really engaged in literacy?
- □ do all parents who read to their children do the same things?
- □ are children whose parents don't read to them deprived of all exposure to print?
- □ how much do children learn about reading (and writing) before they reach school age?
- □ do children from different social backgrounds have different conceptions of what literacy is and what it is for?
- □ how do different home experiences with literacy prepare or fail to prepare children for reading instruction?

What all of these questions eventually lead us to is the question,

> Assuming that reading instruction is presently more successful with children from some social backgrounds than others, what else can we do in schools to make reading and writing natural pursuits for *all* children?

Early Exposures to Print

In a middle-class family, a newborn daughter is brought home to her nursery. Her crib is hung with brightly colored mobiles. The wallpaper is decorated with nursery rhyme motifs: a cow jumps over a moon; feet protrude from a haystack. These pictures make no sense without reference to stories from a literate tradition (Heath, 1983). During the first six months of this baby's life, the mother plays face-to-face interaction games with the girl and sings songs to her. By the eighth month, the girl has some words. Her mother is reading to her, and the reading episodes, like the face-to-face games, are highly interactional:

MOTHER: Look.
CHILD: (Attends to picture.)
MOTHER: What's that?
CHILD: Cow!
MOTHER: Yes, it is. (Teale, 1984, p. 111)

This interactional reading gradually gives way to a more one-sided affair in which the mother reads the story through and the child listens.

Researchers have found much variety in reading-to-children episodes after the second year. Some parents read the story straight through, even discouraging interruption from the child. Other parents ask for commentaries from the child:

"What's that?"
"Isn't that scary?"
"Do you think she should go *in* there?"
"What's going to happen now?"

Does it matter which way parents read to their children? It very well might. Years ago, the Russian psychologist Lev Vygotsky suggested that much of what eventually becomes thought is actually the internalization of social relationships. This bears thinking about: it means that the conversations that parents invite as a text is read are gradually turned into patterns of thought by children — they are the lines of thinking the children will use when responding to a text on their own (Vygotsky, 1978, 1981).

Vygotsky's is a hypothesis not accepted by everyone. But we can see clear evidence that many of what Teale and his colleagues call "literacy events," the things that happen as an older person and a younger person read together,* are picked up and imitated by children. By three years old, after having been read a favorite book several times by an older person, a child will "read" a book to himself. The example in Box 2.1 has David, who has just turned two, leafing through the pages and "re-enacting" (Holdaway's term) the text of P. D. Eastman's *Are You My Mother?* The original text is written on the left. David's version appears on the right.

---

*In their research, Teale and his associates use this definition of literacy event: "any action sequence involving one or more persons in which the production or comprehension of print plays a significant role." (Anderson and Stokes, 1984, p. 16).

BOX 2.1. Sample of a reading re-enactment

PAGE	TEXT	RE-ENACTMENT
3	A mother bird sat on her egg.	The mummy bird sat at an egg.
4	The egg jumped. "Oh oh!" said the mother bird. "My baby will be here! He will want to eat."	Ow ow! A bumble bird baby here. ('Bumble' is a regressive form of 'Mummy' in David's speech.) Someping a eat. ('a' always used for 'to' and 'for').
6	"I must get something for my baby bird to eat!" she said. "I will be back." So away she went.	Must baby bird a (i.e. 'to') eated. Dat way went. Fly a gye (Fly to the sky).
8	The egg jumped. It jumped, and jumped, and jumped! Out came the baby bird.	Ig jumped and jumped. Out baby bird!
10	"Where is my mother?" he said. He looked for her.	Whis my mother? She look a her and look her.
12	He looked up. He did not see her. He looked down. He did not see her.	Her look up, look down, see her — [plus shake of head.] (Perhaps meaning, 'She can't see her'. Throughout, David shows no surface language for negation, yet operates meaningfully on what must be a comprehended deep structure.)
14	"I will go and look for her," he said. So away he went.	Look down. *Look* her! Way went. Way went. (The second 'look' is signalled by intonation to mean, 'I will look for her' — a typical syntactic elision by babies — cf. 'kiss' meaning 'give me a kiss'.)
16	Down, out of the tree he went. Down, down, down! It was a long way down.	Down, down, down, down, went. Down, down, down the bay went.
18	The baby bird could not fly. He could not fly, but he could walk. "Now I will go and find my mother," he said.	Could fly. Could walk. ('Could fly' turned into a syntactic negative by a violent shake of the head!) Now fin find mother (a self-correction).

SOURCE: Don Holdaway, *The Foundations of Literacy*. (Gosford, N. S. W.: Ashton Scholastic, 1979). Reprinted by permission of Ashton Scholastic. Excerpt from P. D. Eastman, *Are You My Mother?* reprinted by permission of William Collins Publishers, London.

Older children whose language has elaborated further give richer reenactments, of course, but David's transcript is already full of elements of literacy. He is able to produce language outside of the context of a conversation; that is, he recognizes that reading books is an occasion to produce language that, unlike normal language use, may be unrelated (some say "disembedded") to whatever or whomever shares space with the child. It is clear that he understands the story, that he follows the sequential building of events, and appreciates (on some level, at least) the drama of an infant's searching not only for its own mother, but for a mother of its own kind. What is more, he uses the *language* of books: "Ow ow! I(t) jumped and jumped. . . . Down, down, down, went." He even demonstrates the behavior of self-correction: "Now he could *fin find* mother. . . ." That is, he knew when his production of a word did not make sense in that context and spontaneously corrected himself. As we shall see, this is a sophisticated and necessary part of reading ability.

Three years from now, when he enters kindergarten, David will very likely be ready to read. We can see that his readiness is not simply the result of his having passed some invisible milestone in the course of maturation. It is rather the experience of thousands of literacy events and much internalized reflection and activity on David's part, all of which have combined to give David what Holdaway calls a "literacy set": ". . . a formidable range of early skills and attitudes . . . (which enable children) . . . to operate immediately and automatically in appropriate ways whenever they are faced with print" (Holdaway, 1979, p. 49).

Social Group Differences in Preparation for Literacy

We might conclude that children who come to school with a "literacy set" have the equivalent of several years more schooling than their classmates who have missed the same early exposure to literacy. But things are not so simple. Some children whose parents rarely read to them during their preschool years do not lag behind children whose parents did read to them and become fine readers in first grade. This was a finding of Teale's research (1984), though, on the whole, he felt that reading to children certainly helped. Then there is Shirley Brice Heath's finding (1983) that some children who were read to consistently during their preschool years failed to achieve independent literacy after they entered school. These were not isolated cases, either, but rather the children from a whole social group that had particular ways of raising their children, and particular ways of reading to them. Fortunately, Heath got to know these children and their families intimately over a 10-year period and was able to write a detailed account of the progression of their language and literacy experiences from birth through the primary grades.

One of the groups she studied was composed of white Southern textile mill workers. These families made a great fuss over their babies. They had brightly decorated nurseries for them, many toys — especially those that were advertised as "educational" — and they read to them. What was wrong? To put it simply, the parents themselves were not readers. They paid lip-service to the importance of reading — they subscribed to magazines, talked about the need to read in this modern world, and dutifully read to their children. Yet the magazines piled up unread on the coffee table while the parents watched television; and when they wrote letters to distant relatives, these were stiff and formulaic — real news was shared on the telephone. Even when they read to their children, there was a forced quality to the interaction. Children were made to pay attention, to talk only about the text being read, but not to embellish upon the reading with imaginative responses. The parents seemed concerned that they "get it right." In the mill, the parents' employers complained that the adults could not read written instructions and follow them. In school, the teachers complained that the children were "word callers" — they could read the words on the page but the words did not appear to move them. They showed poor comprehension and little imagination. Heath thought the shortcomings of the parents were reflected in the shortcomings of the children: in spite of serious efforts to prepare their children in the home for literacy, the parents could not make their children into the literate people they themselves were not. Perhaps Vygotsky was right.

But there is more to it. The parents were not simply failed literates. It seems that they lived in a community that was strongly centered around the church. At the church, scripture was read, but the congregation was admonished not to come up with their own ideas about what it meant. Only the preacher could do that. The congregation was supposed to receive the Word, but by rote, without discussion. There were parallels in everyday speech: there was a *right* way to talk; *right* words to say for every situation. Among the things that were not right was the practice of telling stories. Children were expected to tell the truth, not blur the truth with fictions. Hence, in school, these children wanted to "get it right," not find things out for themselves. Such activities as asking why something happened, or predicting the ways a story might end, generally useful reading practices, were discouraged by their parents: it was not for the children to question motives or to decide how the story might end. They must be quiet and listen. Strangest of all, when the teacher invited them to "write a story," the children perceived that she had asked them to do something dishonest!

Heath goes on to tell about the teachers in those schools and how they went out of their way to learn about their children's homes and cultures, how they set up classrooms that did not stop at teaching reading, but also immersed children in a literate environment at the same time the teachers reached out to the parents to forge two-way connections between the literate culture of the school and that of the home. Few miracles. Some successes. Much hard work.

We present this account as one example of how cultural differences in children's experiences with literacy can have deeper implications than the choice of teaching method. We also leave the reader with a question phrased by Deborah Brandt (1985, p. 129) in a recent review of Heath's book:

> Do cultures, subcultures, even individuals differ merely in the uses they make of reading and writing, or must we more accurately say that they develop different literacies, complete with different frameworks for thinking about written language and about what it means to read and write?

What Makes a Reader? A Psycholinguistic View

We call the close-up view of learning to read the *psycholinguistic* perspective, because a large share of the insights into these component abilities have been generated by the *psychological* study of reading as a *linguistic* process. The sections of the chapter devoted to psycholinguistic studies of reading cover many more pages than the previous discussion of reading from a social learning perspective — reflecting fairly well the greater use, currently, of psycholinguistic insights in understanding reading problems and helping students who have them.

In the following pages, we will look first at the language abilities that help a person become a reader. Then we will talk about the language of books and the structure of text — these are language forms that readers must understand. In fact there is even a language about language, called *metalanguage*, that good readers seem to use more easily than poor readers. There are strategies for taking from the text cues to its meaning. These fall under the general headings of word recognition and comprehension, though each subsumes many other abilities. We will begin with language abilities.

Vocabulary

In colonial times students learned to read in whatever book their parents had at home. This was usually the Bible or John Bunyan's *Pilgrim's Progress*. After rudimentary instruction in the sounds made by the letters of the alphabet, these youngsters were force-marched through text that drew from vocabularies of many thousands of words. The task was made easier, we presume, by the fact that many times they had heard the same books read aloud well before they undertook to read them. This archaic example points out how far we've come. Most modern reading methods use books prepared especially for students or generated by students (as in the Language-Experience Approach) that have far fewer words in print than children use in their speech.

But several cautions are in order with regard to vocabulary and reading: first, the vocabulary load in texts increases sharply after the first two years. Second, some words are learned orally later than others and may give children trouble when they encounter them in print. Third, children do not acquire vocabulary at the same rate, and there are some children for whom vocabulary (invariably in conjunction with other aspects of language) delays their entry into reading.

It appears that most children enter kindergarten or first grade with sizable vocabularies. One count of the development of children's vocabulary size — an old study, but one still widely reported — was done by M. E. Smith in 1926 (Dale, 1976; Gibson and Levin, 1975). Smith's findings, presented here in Table 2.1, show a surge in vocabulary acquisition in the middle of the third year, and growth beyond the 2000 word mark by age five. Other sources put the numbers much higher. Cuff (1930) estimated that third graders have a vocabulary of around 7425 words, and later Seashore and Eckerson (1940) put the third grade figure at 25,000 words. The differences in the estimates arise both from sampling difficulties and disagreements over precisely what constitutes a separate word: if "run" is a word, is "running" another? What about "runner"?

A more important problem for teachers is what it means to "have" a word. A child may use a word in speech yet not have in mind for it the full range of meaning an adult does. Linguists have noted that preschool children sometimes use words to refer to *more* than their normal range of inclusiveness: for example, they might use the word "dog" to refer to dogs, cats, sheep, and goats. This usage is called *overextension* (Bloom, 1973). A

TABLE 2.1. Vocabulary growth as a function of age

AGE (YEARS, MONTHS)	NUMBER OF WORDS	INCREMENT
0;8	0	
0;10	1	1
1;0	3	2
1;3	19	16
1;6	22	3
1;9	118	96
2;0	272	154
2;6	446	174
3;0	896	450
3;6	1222	326
4;0	1540	318
4;6	1870	330
5;0	2072	202
5;6	2289	217
6;0	2562	273

SOURCE: Adapted from M. E. Smith, "An Investigation of the Development of the Sentence and the Extent of Vocabulary in Young Children," *University of Iowa Studies in Child Welfare*, 3, No. 5. (1926).

child might go the other way and use a general term to stand for only one particular instance of a class: Bloom (1973) reported that at nine months her daughter used "car" to refer only to vehicles seen moving in the street below her apartment window, not to cars that she rode in or to those parked on the street.

Sometimes it appears that children's early use of a word refers vaguely to a range of meaning, and gradually becomes specific as children add *semantic features* to the word in their memory storage (Eve Clark, 1973). Thus *tall* is used first to mean *large* (including the feature *fat*, but possibly also *short*), and only later narrowed down to the vertical dimension we normally mean by our use of *tall*. We adults are sometimes this imprecise ourselves. We may know, for example, that *chiaroscuro* has something to do with shading in paintings, but not be able to picture what it looks like.

The relation between words and the concepts they stand for is controversial. Most psychologists who follow the Piagetian school of thought hold that children will not learn a word before they have developed the concept underlying the word, normally through active nonlinguistic means. Followers of Lev Vygotsky, on the other hand, maintain that language exposure itself contributes to the formation of concepts (Bartlett, 1981). Vygotsky held that children's first concepts — he called them *spontaneous concepts* — are rather haphazardly organized. The word *dog,* for example, can refer to a chain of associations that cut across categories normally held by adults: meaning at once the family beagle, the scratchy feeling of having one's hair brushed, a furry rug, or even a ripe olive (for the resemblance to the family dog's nose) (de Villiers and de Villiers, 1979). It is only through exposure to the language of adults around them that children are able to rework these spontaneous concepts into the common hierarchically arranged concepts adults hold — which Vygotsky calls *scientific concepts* (Vygotsky, 1962). Whether we talk about underextensions, overextensions, semantic features, or spontaneous concepts, it is clear that skillful observation in a broad context is needed to determine if children use words with their normal range of meanings. It is just as clear that children need plentiful opportunities to work with people and things, to act on their environment, but especially to do so in the presence of a fluent adult speaker who will both model precise language and encourage children to accompany their actions with words.

In considering children's vocabulary development, it is important to note not only the connection between words and underlying concepts, but also the fact that some common words may stand for concepts that are quite complex. Concrete nouns such as *dog* and *tractor* are learned early and easily, as are vivid action words such as *fall down* and *eat.* More difficult are words for time relationships — *before, after, early,* and *late.* Many words have no stable referent, but have meanings that are situationally determined: *then, next, another, his,* or *yours.* Difficult, too, are some verbs that stand for a combination of actions: consider *promise*, which means not only to tell someone something but also bind to oneself to a future deed. Contrast *promise* with *order:* to tell someone something that binds that person to an immediate or future action. "Accuse," "borrow," "lend," and "buy" all have complex underlying meanings. Carol Chomsky's research has shown that many children do not have full control over these complex verbs until the age of nine or ten (Chomsky, 1969).

Children, as we have seen, normally enter school with a vocabulary of several thousand words (though their understanding of these words may not be fully developed). Early reading books typically have vocabularies limited to fewer than 1000. After third grade, however, the vocabulary load of school textbooks increases dramatically. Nagy and Anderson (1984) recently estimated the number of distinct words students are likely to encounter in "printed school English," by which they mean the language in textbooks used between grades three and nine. The total came to 88,500! These authors went on to report that structured programs to teach students new vocabulary require enormous repetition — one such program required between 26 and 40 repeated exposures to achieve a learning rate of 86 percent. Devoting half an hour per day to vocabulary instruction, the program could cover only 400 words per year. In 10 years' time such a program could make only a tiny dent in the total number of words students must learn.

Because good students *do* learn vocabularies approaching 88,000 words, it is clear that learning new words directly from reading is not only possible, but the only feasible answer for students who must cope with the enormous vocabulary burdens of upper-level text. A critical aspect of vocabulary skill in reading, then, will be the ability to discern word meanings from text. We will discuss means for developing these skills in Chapter Six.

Syntax

When children *do* have trouble understanding words, sometimes the problem is not that they have an inadequate vocabulary, but that the sentences in which the words appear are structured in a fashion too complex for them. What the students experience as a confusion over individual words is in fact a confusion over *syntax* (Reid, 1984).

Syntax, sometimes called grammar, can be described as the set of rules we know that enables us to string individual words together into meaningful phrases and sentences. The rules work in two ways. First, they control *word order*, as in —

> The woman bites the dog.
> The dog bites the woman.

In these sentences, the order of nouns and verb signal the difference between biting and being bitten. Word-order patterns are powerful clues to the meanings of English sentences. And there are few enough of them for the patterns to be immediately recognizable to mature speakers. Most linguists, in fact, identify not more than five *basic sentence patterns* that form the core of most of the sentences we speak or write. The following five are taken from Constance Weaver (1979):

1. *Noun Phrase/Subject + Intransitive Verb + (Adverb)*
   The football player sobbed uncontrollably.
2. *Noun Phrase/Subject + Transitive Verb + Noun Phrase/Direct Object + (Adverb)*
   Amy tilled her garden all weekend.
3. *Noun Phrase/Subject + Transitive Verb + Noun Phrase/Indirect Object*
   The teller gave him the money.
4. *Noun Phrase/Subject + Linking Verb + Noun Phrase/Predicate Noun*
   You may already be a winner.
5. *Noun Phrase/Subject + Linking Verb + Adjective/Predicate Adjective*
   The witch became furious.

Basic sentence patterns such as these are usually learned by the age of five years (Loban, 1976). However, some language-delayed children may not control the whole set by the time they have reached school age. Marie Clay and her associates have created a simple diagnostic device for identifying the basic sentence patterns that children do and do not control. Their *Record of Oral Language* is described in Chapter Three.

Another aspect of sentence patterns that tends to come under children's control later than the basic sentence patterns is *sentence transformations.* Sentence transformations are the conversions that speakers apply to the basic sentence patterns to make the sentences passive, interrogative, imperative, complex, ellipsoid, and so forth:

Basic pattern:	Helen dumped the trash.
Passive sentence:	The trash was dumped by Helen.
Interrogative sentence:	Who dumped the trash?
Ellipsis:	Helen did.
Adjectival:	The trash that Helen dumped was old.

Some transformational forms are not normally used by children until they reach school age. Language-delayed children will only begin to use structures expected of preschool children after they have entered first or second grade. A useful progression of sentence structures is provided in Table 2.2. Adapted from the work of Ursula Bellugi (1971) and Carol Chomsky (1969), this list of sentence structures is presented in the order that most children learn to use them. The last three normally do not come into use until school age.

As anyone who has studied a foreign language will know, it is easier to understand the sentences someone else speaks than it is to speak your own.

TABLE 2.2. Syntactic forms acquired in early and middle childhood.

1. SUBJECT/VERB/OBJECT ORDER
   John greeted Sarah.
   Sarah greeted John.

   Does the child understand that the first-mentioned person is the doer and the second the receiver of the action?

2. PLURALS OF NOUNS
   Show me the monkey.
   Show me the monkeys.

   Does the child understand that the s on the noun means "more than one?"

3. POSSESSIVES OF NOUNS
   Show me the child's mother.
   Show me the mother's child.

   Does the child understand the relationship of possession denoted by the inflection 's?

4. NEGATIVE AND AFFIRMATIVE STATEMENTS
   The boy is sitting.
   The boy is not sitting.

   Does the child understand the significance of *not*?

5. SINGULAR AND PLURAL VERBS
   The girl walks.
   The girls walk.

   Does the child understand that the s on the verb indicates the number of the subject?

6. MODIFICATION OF NOUNS
   The little dog has a big bone.
   The big dog has a little bone.

   Does the child correctly use word order to match the attribute with the correct noun?

7. NEGATIVE AFFIXES
   The blocks are stacked.
   The blocks are unstacked.
   The blocks are not unstacked.

   Does the child understand the meaning of the negative affix *un*?

8. REFLEXIVE PRONOUNS
   Sheila painted her.
   Sheila painted herself.

   Does the child understand to whom each pronoun refers?

9. PASSIVE SENTENCES
   The car hit the truck.
   The car was hit by the truck.

   Does the child understand which was hit?

10. SELF-EMBEDDED SENTENCES
    The boy that the girl knew fell down.
    The cat that chased the dog was out of breath.

    Which one fell down?
    Which was out of breath?

11. COMPLEX VERBS
    Sam promised Mary to bake cookies.
    Sam told Mary to bake cookies.

    Who was to do the baking?
    Who was to do the baking?

It is easier to read a foreign language, too, than to speak it. So we must be careful not to assume that children will have difficulty reading sentence forms that they cannot yet use in speech. Thus it is worthwhile to note which children do not have control over syntactical patterns such as transformations that may show up in the books they read. Devices for measuring children's understanding of syntax, including sentence transformations, are described in Chapter Three. (For further discussion of sentence patterns see the Suggested Readings at the end of this chapter.)

Besides word order and transformations, another aspect of syntax we use includes *inflections*, the particles of words we add to show such features as plurality, past tense, and comparative quantity:

> The boys run.
> The boy runs.

Most children learn these elements before school age. They learn them gradually, and — curiously enough — most children learn them in roughly the same order, though not at the same rate (Brown, 1973).* For example, Brown and Bellugi found that the learning of the following syntactical elements proceeded in the order presented here:

1. Present progressive   *-ing*   Him sing*ing*
2. Plurals of nouns   -s   Two shoe*s*; two knee*s*
3. Irregular past   I *went*; you *saw*
4. Possessive   -'*s*   Kitty'*s* tail; John'*s* book
5. Articles   *the, a*   That's *a* dog
6. Regular past   -*ed*   She shout*ed*; they play*ed*
7. Third person singular   -s   She talk*s*; it run*s*

Most children use all of these forms confidently by the time they are four years old. However, some children may be delayed in mastering these forms until after the age of school entry. Moreover, speakers of certain dialects such as Black English may not use these syntactical forms in everyday speech and hence have difficulty when they encounter them in print. Marie Clay and her associates have created a simple procedure for assessing children's control over grammatical inflections. They call it *Biks and Gutches.* We describe it in Chapter Three.

We have pointed at several syntactic elements that are normally developed in children by school age. But to what extent are reading problems traceable to deficits in syntactic ability? A straight answer is hard to come by. Several investigators have reported that poorly developed knowledge of syntax was involved in reading difficulties. Clay (1975), for example, suggests that an assessment of children's syntactic abilities can spot kindergarten and first-grade children who are at a high risk of having an unsuccessful

*SOURCE: Adapted from Roger Brown, *A First Language* (Harvard University Press).

experience in beginning reading instruction. However, other researchers (e.g., O'Donnell, 1963) have found that the relationship between reading ability and syntactic knowledge was not strong enough to warrant direct teaching of syntax. Syntactic knowledge is too deep-seated to respond well to direct teaching anyway (Braine, 1971).

The authors have worked with children who were nonreaders with poorly developed syntax. A six-year-old first grader from a Mexican-American family comes to mind. She spoke in whispers, and her sentences rarely exceeded four words in length. Another was a fourth-grade boy in rural Virginia, the child of a pulpwood cutter and his wife. While his sentences were longer than hers, they were devoid of most inflections and many transformations, and they made use of many nonstandard vocabulary items. It seemed to us that language was intimately involved in these children's difficulty in learning from reading instruction, since neither could adequately comprehend grade-level material when it was read aloud. There was simply too much difference between the language each child spoke and the language each was expected to learn to read.

Part of the difference lay in syntax, in the structures of sentences and the uses of grammatical inflections. But the differences lay in other areas, too: in vocabulary, and in two areas of language development we will discuss presently: the elaborate use of language and the "language of books." Corrective teaching strategies that were outlined for both these children were built around stimulating experiences, encouraging talk about those experiences with peers and with fluent adult speakers, listening to stories, learning poems and songs (and later following along with the written versions of them), and writing down and reading back their own accounts of exciting happenings. Clearly, syntax is developed in the course of carrying out such activities, but so are other inseparable language skills.

Elaborated Use of Language

Although a limited command of syntax can translate into a limited potential for reading comprehension, there is more to language development than syntax. Two learners may have a roughly equal command of syntactic forms, yet one may be decidedly better equipped linguistically to read.

The difference lies not only in the syntactic forms the learner has mastered, but also in the degree of *elaboration* used. Elaboration in language reflects how much we let the extralinguistic circumstances (our surroundings, our gestures, and the knowledge that we and our listeners share) speak for us, and how much we actually encode our messages into words. In speech, the choice to use elaborated language or not is often influenced by whom we're with and the setting of the conversation. When, for example, we are in a familiar situation with someone we know intimately, talking about something well known to both of us, then the verbal part of the messages that go back and forth between us may be quite reduced.

Oral language fluency is a stepping stone to reading for most children. A puppet theater provides a stimulus for much oral language development as children make up stories, act them out, and discuss each others' productions.

Imagine a husband offering his wife coffee at the breakfast table:

HUSBAND: Want some?
WIFE: Lovely.
HUSBAND: Enough?
WIFE: Um hm.
HUSBAND: Sugar?
WIFE: Unh unh.

Five words and two grunts are adequate for the messages intended.

Notice what happens, however, when someone not familiar with the topic is involved in the conversation. Imagine that the wife recounts this scene later to a friend:

WIFE: My husband is so sweet.
FRIEND: Why?
WIFE: Well, since he got this new job, he doesn't have to go to work until an hour after I do.
FRIEND: So?
WIFE: Well, now he's the one who gets up and fixes the coffee.
FRIEND: That's nice.
WIFE: Yeah, you should see the old bear. Bumping around the kitchen in his ratty blue bathrobe, eyes half shut. But he makes good strong coffee.
FRIEND: I like it that way.
WIFE: Funny thing, though. We've been married five years and he still can't remember I don't take sugar!

In this example, scores of words were required for adequate communication. The language used in the two scenes represents two very different styles of talking that have been termed *restricted* and *elaborated codes* (Bernstein, 1966). The restricted code is used by all of us when we and the people we are talking with both presume that there is no need to "spell things out." The restricted code is telegraphic; we use gestures, grunts, and a lot of unspecific references like "it," "that," "this thing," and "here." The restricted code is used when we talk about concrete things in the here-and-now: we are more likely to use it when serving each other breakfast than when speculating on the nature of the lost continent of Atlantis.

The elaborated code, on the other hand, is what we use when we do have to spell things out, when the topic or the audience requires it. We might be forced to use the elaborated code if we were serving coffee to a Buddhist monk who had never had coffee before; we certainly would use it to explain photosynthesis to a class of children. Language in the elaborated code is less dependent on the setting of the communication or the shared understandings of the communicators to get the message across. It takes few shortcuts. It is richer in explanations, more complete, more precise.

Most adults shift back and forth between restricted and elaborated codes many times a day, depending on their perception of the information needs of the people they are talking to. Children begin to develop the ability to differentiate their speech for different audiences before school age, though they continue to develop this ability in the elementary years (Ervin-Tripp and Mitchell-Kernan, 1977; Ochs and Schiefelin, 1979).

Some children, however, apparently cannot use the elaborated code. These children may have had parents who did not use the elaborated code themselves or who, through harsh financial circumstances, were forced to leave the children in the company of other young children who were not speakers of elaborated codes. Whatever the circumstances, some researchers have maintained that children who have not had fluent adult models to listen to, who have not been listened to and had their thoughts drawn out themselves, have not had their questions entertained and had the world explained to them through language — never develop the use of the elaborated code.

There has been a great deal of research in England on the relationship between social group membership and people's use of the elaborated code. Basil Bernstein (1966) put forward the idea that restricted and elaborated codes are used differently by different social classes. The working class, he found, tended to use the restricted code, while middle-class and professional people tended to use the elaborated code. According to Bernstein, the restricted code suffices for people's communicative needs within working-class communities. Members of these communities have contacts that are limited mostly to each other; thus they tend to share experiences and attitudes. With so much in common, there is little need to spell things out. The difficulty comes, of course, when children who speak in restricted codes arrive at school. In school, the elaborated code is used heavily, as often as teachers and students find it necessary to discuss things precisely and in detail.

Bernstein's theories have been controversial, since they seem to support views based on racial or class prejudice that one group's language could be "better" or "worse" than another's. Such was never his intention when he advanced his theory. Rather, as a sociologist, he was trying to deduce why working-class children with apparently normal intelligence performed less well in school as a group than other children. He was also trying to suggest a solution: by identifying school failure as a language problem, he was pointing the way for educators to develop language-based remedies for school failure (Halliday, 1980).

More recent approaches to the problem of restricted language have improved on Bernstein's work, first by prudently avoiding any attribution of language type to social classes, and, second, by specifying in much greater detail the subtypes of language that could be restricted or elaborated. One such approach is Halliday's (1975) description of language as a collection of *functions.* Halliday has suggested that children first learn language for what they can do with it. According to his research, language is useful for several different purposes, and children learn to use language for each of the following seven functions as their experiences make each function necessary.

1. "Gimme!" *(the instrumental function)* Language is used as a tool to get something for the speaker.
2. "Stop that!" *(the regulatory function)* Language is used to control another's behavior, though not for the direct benefit of the speaker.
3. "What's that?" *(the heuristic function)* Language is used to find things out: to ask questions, assess answers, and formulate new questions.
4. "How are you doing?" *(the interactional function)* Language is used to build a "we-ness" between the speaker and the listener.
5. "I'm scared." *(the personal function)* Language is used to explore and communicate the speaker's feelings and his or her point of view.
6. "Twinkle, twinkle, little star." *(the imaginative function)* Language is used purely for the fun of combining new words and ideas, or repeating old ones to amuse and entertain.
7. "It's snowing!" *(the representational function)* Language is used to represent reality and convey information about it to others.

Recently, Joan Tough (1982) has also put forth a system of language functions. Hers have the advantage over Halliday's of being derived from extensive observation of three- through six-year-old children, while Halliday's seven functions grew out of a study of his son, Nigel, before the latter reached the age of three. Tough's categories of language function are presented in Table 2.3.

The categories of language described by Tough are presented in roughly the order in which children learn to use them. These categories are to be used by teachers to assess an individual child's language. Tough's approach is pursued further in Chapter Three.

How do these uses or functions of language relate to reading? The written language we read is, in Bernstein's terms, an elaborated code. In Halliday's terms, it is representational, imaginative, and regulatory; and in Tough's terms, reading uses language for reporting, for logical reasoning, for predicting, projecting, and imagining. To understand the language of books, children must have a working knowledge of these codes and functions of language.

Reading and Bilingualism

The teacher who develops special skills in teaching reading is often called upon to help children with a host of different learning problems. In recent years, one of the most interesting challenges many reading teachers (and other classroom teachers) have undertaken is to help children who are not

TABLE 2.3. Joan Tough's categories of language functions.

USE OF LANGUAGE AND SUPPORTING STRATEGIES

1. Self-maintaining

Strategies
1   Referring to physical and psychological needs and wants
2   Protecting the self and self interests
3   Justifying behaviour or claims
4   Criticizing others
5   Threatening others

2. Directing

Strategies
1   Monitoring own actions
2   Directing the actions of the self ——
3   Directing the actions of others
4   Collaborating in action with others

3. Reporting on present and past experiences

Strategies
1   Labelling the components of the scene
2   Referring to detail (e.g. size, colour, and other attributes)
3   Referring to incidents
4   Referring to the sequence of events
5   Making comparisons
6   Recognizing related aspects
7   Making an analysis using several of the features above
8   Extracting or recognizing the central meaning
9   Reflecting on the meaning of experiences, including own feelings

4. Towards logical reasoning*

Strategies
1   Explaining a process

2   Recognizing causal and dependent relationships
3   Recognizing problems and their solutions
4   Justifying judgments and actions
5   Reflecting on events and drawing conclusions
6   Recognizing principles

5. Predicting*

Strategies
1   Anticipating and forecasting events
2   Anticipating the detail of events
3   Anticipating a sequence of events
4   Anticipating problems and possible solutions
5   Anticipating and recognizing alternative courses of action
6   Predicting the consequences of actions or events

6. Projecting*

Strategies
1   Projecting into the experiences of others
2   Projecting into the feelings of others
3   Projecting into the reactions of others
4   Projecting into situations never experienced

7. Imagining*

1   Developing an imaginary situation based on real life
2   Developing an imaginary situation based on fantasy
3   Developing an original story

*Strategies that serve *directing, reporting* and *reasoning* may serve these uses also.
SOURCE: From Joan Tough, *Listening to Children Talking* (London: Ward Lock Educational Co. Limited, 1976). Reprinted by permission.

native English speakers. Working with non-English speaking children used to be the preserve of teachers along our southern border with Mexico, in southern Florida, in Alaska and northern Canada, Hawaii, and in the largest North American cities. However, in recent years large groups of political refugees from Asia, Haiti, Cuba, and Central America have come into the United States and Canada, and with the help of sponsoring church and civic groups, are being resettled in communities that have rarely hosted non-English speakers. In the 1980s, children who do not speak English are walking through the doors of schools all over North America. These children need thoughtful help both in coping with schoolwork in a language that is strange to them and in learning that language.

Reading in bilingual education has a troubled history. Many Mexican Americans in their thirties and even twenties can remember being disciplined for speaking Spanish on the school grounds. When a friend of the authors was six years old, she was taken aside by a teacher and told that she better learn English in a hurry or else she would be a worthless Mexican like the rest of her family. Navajo children in reservation schools were beaten for using their native language, not very long ago. Few who were victims of such experiences find it easy to talk without emotion about the use of native languages in schools. Language is intensely personal. Perhaps more than any other issue in education, language policy strongly affects children's and whole communities' sense of being welcome in school.

Some groups have argued, understandably, that their children's native language should be honored in the school. But not all groups feel that way. Numbers of recent Asian immigrants have actively opted to learn English and things American. The Goodmans (1978) report on Arabic families that have moved into the Detroit area and have made the same choice: America is their new home, and their highest expectation of the schools is that they teach their children to speak, read, and write English. Some ethnic groups, the Navajos in particular, discourage the use of the written form of their language. Literacy for them is literacy in English (Goodman, Goodman, and Flores, 1978). Finally, there is the bilingual movement in Canada, in which English-speaking parents are sending their children to special schools where they use nothing but French for the first three years and then use both languages. It is difficult, then, to make generalizations about what English or non-English language instruction means to everyone who is affected by the choice. The one thing certain is that the question evokes very strong feelings.

When Should English Language Reading Instruction Begin?

Standard practice over the past decade has been to teach children to read in their native language first while developing children's spoken fluency in English. This practice seems to have arisen as a reaction to the harsh denial of native language use in schools. Pedagogically, it seems to have been based on three assumptions:

1. children can only read a language they know well, which, at first, is their native language;
2. children shouldn't try to learn to read two languages at once, lest the two somehow interfere with each other;
3. good spoken fluency in English is the necessary base on which reading that language must be built.

Barrerra (1978, 1983) and others (Goodman, Goodman, and Flores, 1978) have challenged all three assumptions. First, in some cases, parents and children may not desire literacy in the native language, at least not until children have mastered English. Often there will not be a person available who can teach reading in the first language, or if there is, this teacher may not be skillful. As the Goodmans argue, reading instruction carried out by a native speaker who is not an experienced teacher or by an experienced teacher who is not a skillful user of the second language is bound to be poor reading instruction. Workbooks and heavily programmed procedures — unsupported by listening to stories, by writing, singing, acting out, experiencing and discussing — are unsatisfactory means of learning to read in any language. It cannot reasonably be argued that such instruction could both teach children to read in their first language and form the basis for later learning to read in a second language as well.

Second, there is little evidence that learning to read in two languages sets up serious problems of interference. The psychological process of reading, of getting meaning from written symbols, is the same, regardless of language (Gray, 1955). People can learn to read in one language and apply the same process to another language. Language learners are remarkably skillful at keeping their language codes separate; they recognize when text is written in a different language. They do not attempt to read Spanish as if it were English.

Third, it may not be necessary for children to develop oral fluency in English before they can begin to read it. Learning written language, Goodman argues, is like learning spoken language. We learn by being exposed to written language in meaningful contexts: by being read to, by reading labels of things that are significant. We also learn written language by trying to use it ourselves. As Bruner and Ninio (1981) have shown, episodes of being read to, along with their accompanying discussion, are central events for learning to talk in a first language. There is every reason to believe this is true in a second language as well. Reading need not wait until oral language is mastered. The two abilities can be learned at the same time.

There is an important distinction to be made between our *receptive* use of language and our *productive* use of language. All of us can understand language more easily than we can speak it. This can be especially true in a second language. Children may comprehend language that they hear or read in a second language, but be unable to express the meaning adequately in that language. A teacher who assumes that the hesitant speaker of English is not ready to understand that language in print is likely to be wasting valuable time: the capacity to comprehend may already be there. As an example, consider the following retelling of a passage that this Arabic-speaking fourth-grade boy has just read:

> They were working at to plant something and his father always pulled the polo and it was very hard. Salom tried to get the donkey and tried to pull it, but the donkey couldn't. . . . And then he tried the camel to pull it and he couldn't and then they both push the solo and it worked and it went deep under the earth and it went just straight. (Goodman, Goodman, and Flores, 1978, p. 33)

Does this boy understand that the passage was about *plowing?* He misread the word twice *(polo, solo)*. The researcher asked him, "What's a solo?" The boy replied,

> Well, it's a thing with two handles and something pointing down. You got to pull it, but they don't push it with a camel; they push it with a cow. When the cow moves, the one who's pushing it gotta push on it so it . . . so it goes deeper in the underground. (Goodman, Goodman, and Flores, 1978, p. 33)

How Should Beginning Reading Be Approached for Bilingual Students?

The Goodmans have several recommendations for approaching beginning reading with bilingual students that are good enough to pass on:

A Comprehension-Centered Curriculum. The Goodmans' first premise is that the aim of reading instruction is not developing skills, but rather getting meaning from text. We should read texts that mean something, and our strategies should all be directed toward getting that meaning. Since meaning is largely personal, ways must be found to work reading into the day-to-day aims and aspirations of the students. Reading should be part of the curriculum: we read to get things done, to find things out, to learn how to do something else.

A Biliterate Environment. First-grade classrooms for English speakers have labels on everything: the clock, the window, the door, the bookshelf. This practice of labeling can be made bilingual as we label the same items in English and the children's native language. The same goes for bulletin boards, articles in classroom newspapers, and learning centers.

Integrate Language Arts and Other Content. If language arts skills of discussing, writing, acting out, and reading can be combined with meaning-filled activities in social studies, science, health, and other subjects, the students' language use is given a context that makes it more natural and sensible: they learn faster than from workbook exercises. These language practices give children several avenues, also, to the meaning in these subject areas, and they are not limited to just reading.

Read to the Children. Reading to children helps monolingual children develop the same receptive use of language they will later exercise in reading on their own. It offers the same benefits to bilingual children. They hear the language structures, see the pictures, talk about the developments in the story, poem, or other nonfictional work — and they gradually learn language forms they will put to use when they read themselves.

Have the Students Write. Writing is one of the best forms of practice for what we know about written language. Elsewhere in this chapter and in Chapter Seven we discuss the importance of writing for children learning to read. Writing is helpful for bilingual students as well.

Use Meaning-Seeking Reading Strategies. A reader who is learning the English language will not know all of the words she or he encounters in a passage or perhaps even a line of English text. To stop and ask about or look up every unknown word only breaks up the reader's overall sense of the passage: she gets the word but loses the meaning of the paragraph. The reader must develop strategies that make heavy use of prediction and confirmation, constructing for herself a general sense of what a passage is about, confirming and, as necessary, modifying that sense as new information is encountered in the text. When students develop such strategies, they find they can guess at the meanings of unknown words and still get a fairly accurate sense of the passage. They may also find that they have figured out the approximate meaning of an unknown word, once they have a sense of the whole context.

Teaching strategies that help children make predictions include the *directed reading activity* and *directed reading-thinking activity*, and the *cloze procedure* described in Chapters Four through Six.

Approaches for helping older non-English speaking students are discussed in Chapter Six.

The Language of Books

Listen as Jean-Paul Sartre tells of the first time his mother, Ann Marie, read to him:

> Ann Marie sat me down opposite her, on my little chair. She bent forward, lowered her eyelids, fell asleep. From that statue-like face came a plaster voice. I was bewildered: who was telling what and to whom? My mother had gone off: not a smile, not a sign of complicity. I was in exile. And besides, I didn't recognize her speech. . . . A moment later, I realized: it was

a book that was speaking. Frightening sentences emerged from it: they were real centipedes . . . Sometimes they disappeared before I was able to understand them; and other times I understood in advance; and they continued to roll nobly to their end without sparing me a single comma. That discourse was certainly not meant for me. . . .

After a while, I took pleasure in that sudden lift which took me out of myself. . . . I grew sensitive to the rigorous succession of words. At each reading, they returned, always the same and in the same order. I awaited them. (1964, pp. 28–29; quoted in Cazden, 1981, p. 136)

Sartre's great strength is his ability to make the familiar strange and make it teach us. His mother's eerie transformation into an entranced figure uttering words from somewhere else invokes the awe that our illiterate ancestors must have felt as they stood in temples or shrines or cathedrals and heard the medieval priests intone holy words from a book. We quickly forget how different the language of reading is from our everyday talk. As Sartre suggests, while the differences may partly reside in curious words and uncommon sentences, perhaps the strangest quality of this language is its ability to stand on its own, to keep coming out whether we have anything to say to it or not.

Written language can stand on its own, independent of the context in which we read it, because it uses devices that knit its parts together into a meaningful structure. There are two kinds of such devices. The first kind joins individual sentences one to another by means of words that refer to other words, words that link phrases, omissions that make us recall words previously stated, and clusters of words that are commonly considered as a group. Collectively these are called *cohesive devices* (Halliday and Hasan, 1976). The other kind of devices relate groups of ideas to some large function, making them a story or an explanation or an argument, or a description. These are called *text structures*. Text structures and cohesive devices are important because they knit sentences together. But even more important, they help us understand the text.

Cohesive Devices

Consider this passage:

As I was driving toward the beach one day I came upon a man and a woman standing dejectedly near a stalled car. She had black grease from her fingers to her elbows and a big smudge across her forehead. Even her clothes showed signs of intimate involvement with an automobile engine. He, however, looked as natty as a London banker as he stood, arms folded, at some distance from the car. It struck me that he was unsure whether to stay with her, or flag me down and leave her and the motor to their conversation.

Here, many cohesive devices not only knit the sentences together, but also help the reader interpret unclear words. The first sentence introduces *a* man, *a* woman, and *a* car. The indefinite article *a* suggests that we haven't met these before, and they are named explicitly as *man, woman,* and *car.* Already in the first sentence there is cohesion: we cannot understand *dejection* without relating it to the *stalled car.* Cohesion between sentences starts in the second sentence: who is *she?* This is a *reference* to the woman previously mentioned. In the same sentence there is an *ellipsis,* a cohesive device that leaves out words understood from a previous phrase: ". . . and _____ a big smudge across her forehead." What word goes in the blank? "Had," from the previous phrase. "Even her clothes showed signs . . ." What does "even" mean here? It suggests that in a previous sentence we have heard that one thing was so, and now we are about to hear that, rather surprisingly, another similar thing is so. This is cohesion by *conjunction,* the use of words like *even, although, also,* and the like to relate sentences. There is *lexical cohesion,* the use of words whose meanings relate them, between the "stalled car," "black grease," and "intimate involvement with an automobile engine." (The last phrase in the passage, about the conversation between the woman and the motor makes no sense without lexical cohesion to these same elements.)

A reader of the passage who lacks a working knowledge of cohesive devices would be confused in many places, just as surely as if that reader lacked vocabulary or knowledge of the syntax. Because the phenomenon of cohesion is not widely understood among reading teachers or even among publishers of reading materials, children are rarely exposed to the workings of cohesive devices in any careful way. Materials that teach reading one sentence at a time are almost devoid of them. Dictated experience accounts, used in the language-experience approach, may use few cohesive devices if the sentences are dictated one at a time by children who do not tie their contribution to what was said before.

Children who have been read to seem to develop an instinctive understanding of cohesion and carry that understanding into reading tasks. Children without much prior exposure to literature may experience difficulty with cohesion by second grade, when reading books introduce connected text with fewer restrictions on passage simplicity.

We suggest ways to find out if children's difficulty understanding what they read involves difficulty with cohesion. The first is to use the *cloze procedure* (described in Chapters Four and Five). This activity, which essentially has readers fill in blanks left at regular intervals in a long passage, tests readers' ability to use the information in previous sentences to pinpoint what a deleted word might be. Though many kinds of information besides cohesion are employed, cohesion is often an important cue. As an instructional device, the cloze procedure leads readers to practice using context to identify words, practice that works on their sense of cohesion among other language cues.

The second suggestion for investigating difficulties centering around cohesion is to be mindful of it when you are reading with a child. When a reference using a pronoun is encountered, you may ask, " 'Who is *she*' in this sentence?" Likewise, when a word is left out in an ellipsis, ask if the reader can fill it in. All five types of cohesive devices can be investigated in this way. If the child is uncertain about some of them, you can discuss their meaning, perhaps by writing out a passage in two versions — one with cohesive devices and one without — and having the child compare them.

Text Structure

In addition to cohesive devices, a text also has an overall structure that makes it possible for readers to see how each part relates to the whole, and gives readers a sense of what the parts should add up to. Knowledge of text structure seems to be closely related to children's ability to comprehend what they read (Rumelhart, 1975; Mandler and Johnson, 1977; Stein and Glenn, 1978; Meyer, 1976; Marshall and Glock, 1978).

Text structures have been identified for a range of written materials, including writing that explains, gives directions, describes, persuades, expresses the author's personal feelings, or tells stories. By far the most thoroughly studied kind of text structure is the last mentioned: the structure of stories.

Story Structure

What exactly is story structure?

> It happened that a fox was ambling along a country lane when he spied a bunch of ripe grapes hanging from a vine high above his head. Hungry as he was, the fox determined to have those grapes for his dinner. He stood tall on his hind legs, but could not reach the grapes. He leapt high in the air, but missed the grapes and fell painfully onto his back. He was too sore to make a further attempt at the grapes, so he sighed and turned away down the road. "Well," he said to himself. "The grapes were probably sour anyway."

The reader will immediately recognize this group of sentences as a story. If you compare the number of lines of the story with the same number of preceding lines in this book, you will discern a pattern of organization or structure that is quite distinct from the other lines of writing. How would you describe the structure of the story? What are its parts? What are the relationships between the parts?

The answers different readers bring to those questions may vary. However, most would probably include a *character*, a *setting*, a *problem*, an *attempt* to overcome the problem, and a *conclusion*. Some would add a *motive*, a *cause and effect* relationship, a *theme*, and perhaps other elements. Researchers on story structure have found that virtually all stories told in Western culture share these elements in some combination (Greimas, 1971; Propp, 1968). There have been several interesting attempts to describe the essential components and structures that stories have in common. Notably,

Rumelhart (1975), Mandler and Johnson (1977), Thorndyke (1977), and others have each developed *story grammars,* elaborate sets of rewrite rules modeled after transformational grammar or computer programs. These grammars can account for the structures of a variety of different types of stories, and they impress us with the complex nature of the knowledge children must have in their minds that enables them to understand and to create stories.

Below we give a much simplified account of some key elements that most story grammars employ. For each element an illustrative passage is supplied from *The Fox and the Grapes.*

1. *A setting* — the protagonist is introduced in some place and time.
   It happened that a fox was ambling along a country lane. . . .
2. *An initiating event* — either an action or an idea that strikes someone and sets further events in motion.
   . . . when he spied a bunch of ripe grapes hanging from a vine high above his head.
3. *An internal response* — the protagonist's inner reaction to the initiating event, as a part of which he sets a *goal,* a desired state of affairs.
   Hungry as he was, the fox determined to have those grapes for his dinner.
4. **An attempt* — the protagonist makes an effort to achieve his goal.
   He stood tall on his hind legs. . . .
   He leapt high in the air. . . .
5. **An outcome* — an event or new state of affairs that directly results from a given attempt.
   . . . but could not reach the grapes.
   . . . but missed the grapes and fell painfully onto his back.
6. *A consequence* — an action or state of affairs that follows from the protagonist's success or failure to achieve the goal.
   He was too sore to make a further attempt at the grapes, so he sighed and turned away down the road.
7. *A reaction* — an emotion, an idea or a further event which may express the protagonist's feelings about his success or failure to achieve the goal, or relate the events in the story to some broader set of concerns.
   "Well," he said to himself. "The grapes were probably sour anyway."

*Note that *attempts* and *outcomes* may come in groups, as they do in *The Fox and the Grapes.*

Theorists of story structures (Applebee, 1978, 1980; Stein, 1978) claim that ideally the story structure resides both in the story itself and in the mind of the listener. People who can comprehend stories have some sort of internalized idea of story structures in their minds, and they use these structures to comprehend and remember stories (Bartlett, 1932). Because of the internalized structures, actual stories may lack one or more elements of structure and still be comprehended, because listeners or readers are able to supply the missing element or the missing relationship.

How Do Children Learn Story Structures?

Children's use of story structures is a deep-seated psychological process and not something they can readily talk about. Terms like *initiating event* and *internal response* mean nothing to a six-year-old child and little to most adults. Yet it is clear that learners do develop a sense of story structure from their early experiences in listening to stories.

Consider pupils who hear stories read aloud or told again and again. Although the stories differ in particulars, such as who the characters are and what specific events take place, they are similar in their structure. They all have some kind of setting, initiating event, a goal, attempts at the goal, and so forth. More often than not, stories present these elements in the same sequence. Slowly but surely, students' expectations are shaped by encounters with these stories. When they hear a new story, they will be ready to assign someone to the role of character and an incident in the story to the role

Readers develop a sense of story structures by listening to stories told and read aloud. A sense of how stories are structured helps readers to predict what comes next and remember story events.

of initiating event, and they will comprehend the character's attempts to achieve a goal. Thus they can use story structures to understand a story, even though they may not be able to talk about the structures explicitly.

Children may have a well-developed sense of story structures yet be unable to describe directly what these structures are or how they are used. We can *infer* their use of such structures, though, by observing some of their interactions with stories.

Making Predictions

One way that we can see the use of story structures demonstrated is to ask students to predict events as yet unheard or unread, on the basis of the parts of the story that have already been revealed. Suppose, for example, we were reading the story "The Dog and His Shadow" to a class.

THE DOG AND HIS SHADOW

Once there was a big brown dog named Sam. One day, Sam found a piece of meat and was carrying it home in his mouth to eat. Now on his way home, he had to cross a brook. He looked down and saw his own shadow reflected in the water beneath. He thought it was another dog with another piece of meat, and he made up his mind to have that piece also. So he made a snap at the shadow, but as he opened his mouth, the piece of meat fell out. The meat dropped into the water and floated away. Sam never saw the meat again. (McConaughy, 1980, p. 158)

When we read the sentence "He thought it was another dog with another piece of meat . . ." we would stop and ask the class, "What do you think Sam the dog might do now?" Here are some responses we might get:

1. "I don't know."
2. "Jump in after the other dog."
3. "Keep on walking."
4. "Go sit and eat the meat."

Which of the responses reveals a better sense of story structure? With 1 we cannot be sure what the student thinks, except that he or she may not have realized that predicting what might come next is an important part of understanding a story; 3 seems to be based on everyday reality, as does 4, but neither recognized the initiating event that will shape succeeding events in the story. Only 2 does this. Even though it is not a correct prediction, 2 reveals a better sense of story structure than the other three predictions.

Remembering Stories

Another indication of the use of story structure lies in the way students *retell* a story they have heard or read. When asked to retell a story, the student should pick out several of its important elements for inclusion in the retelling.

Here are different versions of "The Dog and His Shadow" as recounted by two fifth-grade children:

1. "There was a dog that found a piece of meat and he went to some water and he saw another piece of meat and he opened his mouth and the piece fell out and he never saw it again."
2. "A dog tried to get another piece of meat and lost his" (McConaughy, 1980, p. 158).

Both accounts include the setting, the character, the initiating event, and the reaction. The first account includes attempts and outcomes but omits the internal response and the goal. The second includes the goal but omits attempts and outcomes. Both retellings are skeletal versions of the original. Not all the information is retold, but the parts included are important ones. The first retelling is more elaborate and explanatory than the second; it also demonstrates more awareness of story structure than the second.

Another aspect of remembering stories can be demonstrated by using a deliberately "scrambled" story. By changing the logical order of story parts and asking students to retell the story, we can see whether they use a logical sequence in the retelling. Two interesting things usually happen, depending on how distorted the story sequence is.

When events in a story are only slightly disordered, say by placing an attempt before an initiating event that sets the stage for the attempt, even young children will correct the order. Although the story was originally told with the order of events violated, their retellings will usually conform to the normal structure of stories.

If, however, the structure is seriously violated, with several key aspects out of order, the retellings suffer. The amount of information included is seriously reduced compared with the retellings of normally ordered stories (Stein, 1978). These findings give considerable weight to the contention that story structures help learners remember the stories they hear or read.

While story structure is an important cue to meaning and a valuable basis for making predictions about what one is likely to encounter in written text, it is possible to read without making use of story structure. Some beginning reading materials limit the writing to simple phonogram patterns without any real story structure, as shown by this "story" from the Merrill Linguistic Reading Program, 1975:

A cat sat on a mat.
Pat the cat.
Is the cat Nat?
The cat is fat Nat.
Pat Nat on the mat.
(*I Can*, p. 10)

In sentences like these there is no story structure to employ, and real comprehension is necessarily minimal since there is little to comprehend.

The use of meaning cues such as story structure varies from learner to learner, as their individual reading strategies differ. Some students read clearly structured stories without relying on the structure to organize their comprehension. Many beginning readers do rely on story structure to guide their comprehension, and probably all efficient mature readers do (Marshall and Glock, 1978–1979). Those who develop early reading strategies without building in higher-order meaning cues like story structure often show up later in a special reading class with comprehension problems.

In summary, the use of story structures in reading depends on:

1. assimilating a sense of story structure from encounters with stories learners have heard read aloud to them;
2. recognizing that it is important and beneficial to use story structures to predict what is coming next in a story;
3. having access to reading materials that are written around perceivable story structures rather than those that are written solely to conform to readability formulas or phonic patterns.

Knowledge of story structures is widely shared in our culture and, it is sometimes argued, in all cultures. By the age of five, most children can use story structure in retelling a story they have heard. The same cannot be said about other forms of text structures, however.

Other Text Structures

By the time they enter third grade, children have begun to encounter reading matter other than stories. Some readings will describe things while others will explain how certain things work or how to carry out a procedure. Later readings will give opinions and try to persuade the students to adopt certain attitudes and beliefs, while the students' own writings will still largely take the form of expressions of their personal feelings. Each of these purposes of writing tends to have its own structure, and each structure has a name. Material that describes is called *descriptive* writing. Writing that explains or gives directions is called *expository.* Writing that persuades is variously called *argumentative* or *persuasive.*

Far less research has been focused on these other text structures, but it is clear that

☐ knowing nonfictional text structures helps readers understand nonfictional text (Meyer, 1977).
☐ students who don't have a sense of these structures cannot comprehend text as well as those who do (Marshall and Glock, 1979).
☐ many older students lack an adequate sense of nonfictional text structures and hence do not know how to read nonfiction text (Marshall and Glock, 1979).
☐ many students who can read adequately in fictional text begin to founder at about fourth or fifth grade when the diet of nonfictional text is

increased dramatically as reading is relied upon more heavily as a medium for learning other content (Jill Richards, 1978).

Problems in reading nonfiction text are most acute in the context areas — science, social studies, health, and the rest — where students are expected to read nonfiction text and learn from it. We will devote a large portion of Chapter Six to these problems, so our present discussion will be left very brief.

Concepts of Written Language

Children who grow up in families in which the parents read and write know a lot about written language before they actually read and write themselves. In fact, as Yetta Goodman (1984) has suggested, we could never possibly tell children all they must know in order to read. Nevertheless, we often find children in our classes without rich backgrounds in literacy. When we do, many subtle points about literacy of which *we* may have been unconscious now must be made explicit to these children. Let us look at three important areas: the purposes of reading, language about language, and concepts about print.

The Purposes of Reading and Writing

We learn to do things more easily when we know what we're trying to get done. If we want to teach someone a new game, the first thing we usually do is to tell the player what the object of the game is. If we know the overall goal, the steps of play begin to make sense, and we can learn these steps more efficiently because we know how they fit together in an overall strategy.

A few years ago a teacher in Scotland (Reid, 1966) wanted to see if her first graders knew the object of the "game" of reading. "What are we trying to get done when we read?" she asked. The children weren't sure. Since then, that question has been raised again and again with children in other parts of the world. The rather startling answer has often been, "We don't know."

Downing and Oliver (1974) investigated children's understanding of the reasons for reading and also of the "parts": what a letter is, what a word is, what "sounding out" means, and so on. They found that those who knew the most about what reading was for, and what the terms used in reading instruction meant, were performing more proficiently than other children when their reading was measured some months later. Downing and Oliver called the concepts of these higher achievers *cognitive clarity*. Students who have cognitive clarity about reading take to beginning reading instruction more successfully than those who do not have it.

What sort of confusion arises in early reading? Many students are not convinced that reading is for finding things out, whether it is finding out what happens in a story, how a lima bean grows, or how to make tacos. Such confusion is found not only in young children, who have not yet had much experience with print, but also in older nonreaders who have had little experience learning anything positive or interesting from print.

Many students think the end product of reading is to render print out loud. Hence they develop superficial strategies that ignore story structure, syntax, and even meaning as they render print into sound. Beginning readers whose experience with reading has been entirely oral frequently do this. They quickly figure out that *reading* must mean *saying*, and they concentrate on pronouncing letter sounds correctly rather than on understanding what the words mean.

Many young prereaders confuse the roles of print and pictures in text. Kita (1979) showed that they thought the pictures in storybooks told the story and that printed words simply embellished the pictures.

Some prereading youngsters have had little contact with print outside of school, have heard few stories read aloud, and have not observed adults reading very often. Such students rarely have an adequate idea of why one would want to read. If they have not explored storybooks and other print with someone who can already read, asking questions about print and trying (or pretending) to produce print themselves, they rarely have much of a concept for the terms we use frequently in beginning reading instruction: *word*, *letter*, *sound*, *sentence*, and *line*.

Language about Language

Does language exist? Is it a thing that we can talk about and learn about? Clearly, for us it is. Teachers of reading regularly use words like *story*, *sentence*, *sound*, *word*, *phrase*, and *paragraph*, all of which refer to language as if it existed and could be discussed. It is rather startling, then, to realize that for many people, language is invisible — it is not something they can separate from themselves and talk about. An anthropologist who has long studied the differences between literate and nonliterate cultures found that among the LoDagaa it was believed that while cooking and farming were skills that could be taught, language was something that developed, like walking and running. They had few words for talking about language, and most conspicuously lacked a word for *word*. (Goody, 1982; in Olson, 1984). Heath (1983) discovered similar attitudes toward language development along the residents of Trackton, a low-income black millworkers' neighborhood in the Carolinas. Said one woman with regard to her grandson:

> He gotta learn to *know* 'bout dis world, can't nobody tell him. Now just how crazy is dat? White folks uh hear dey kids say sump'n, dey say it back to 'em, dey aks 'em 'gain and 'gain about things, like to 'posed to be born knowing. You think I kin tell Teegee all he gotta know to get along? He just gotta be

keen, keep his eyes open, don't he be sorry. Gotta watch hisself by watchin' other folks. Ain't no use me tellin him, learn did, learn dat; what dis? what dat? He just gotta learn, gotta know; he see one thing one place one time, he know how it go, see sump'n like it again, maybe it be the same, maybe it won't. He havta try it out. If he don't he be in trouble; he get lef' out. Gotta keep yo' eyes open. Gotta feel to know. (Heath, 1983, p. 84)

Olson (1984) has suggested that children who are raised by highly literate parents learn a different attitude toward language from the very beginning. A child in a parent's lap sees the parent point to a picture and say, "What's that? Can you say *cow? C-o-w?* Say c-o-w. . . ." Before she's a year old this child is thinking about words. She can slow them down, pull them out of the context of a sentence, apply them deliberately as names for things in the world. By school age she can reflect on language, and she has most of the words used to talk about language, *sentence, story, word,* and so on. Those she does not have she has the concepts for. The discussion that surrounds reading instruction will make good sense to her.

On the other hand, contrast those children who do not have this background. They lack many of these terms, and in some cases, may not have the concepts about language that underlie them. Note the following example from Marie Clay's work:

> Suppose a teacher has placed an attractive picture on the wall and has asked her children for a story, which she will record under it. They offer the text "Mother is cooking," which the teacher alters slightly to introduce some features she wishes to teach. She writes:
>
> Mother said,
> "I am baking."
>
> If she says, "Now look at our *story,*" 30 percent of a new entrant group will attend to the *picture.*
> If she says "Look at the words and find some you know," between 50 and 90 percent will be looking for *letters.* If she says, "Can you see Mother?" most will agree that they can, but some *see* her in the picture, some can locate *M* and others will locate the word *Mother.*
> Perhaps the children read in unison "Mother is . . ." and the teacher tries to sort this out. Pointing to *said,* she asks, "Does this say *is?*" Half agree that it does because it has *s* in it. "What letter does it start with?" Now the teacher is really in trouble. She assumes that the children *know* that a word is built out of letters, but 50 percent of children still confuse the verbal labels *word* and *letter* after 6 months of instruction. She also assumes that the children know that the left-hand letter following a space is the "start" of a word. Often they do not. (Clay, 1975, pp. 3–4)

Since the percentages used by Clay derive from her research with children in New Zealand, they may not translate exactly to the case of American children, but clearly the trend is the same with our own children.

Other Concepts about Print

In addition to appreciating the purposes of reading and being able to think and talk about language and its parts, several other concepts about print may be troublesome to some children (we will talk about these in greater detail in Chapter Three in the discussion of testing procedures for concepts about print.)

Directionality and Page Arrangement. English writing is organized left to right and top to bottom. Hence when we are talking about the *beginning* of a story, we mean the upper left-hand word. Some children do not know this.

How Written Words Represent the World. For children whose more familiar means of representing the world may be pictures, the question of exactly what written words do may be a tough one. Emilia Ferreiro (1983) found as Kita (see above) did that children may first think of writing as a sort of embellishment on a picture. When four-year-olds are asked to add a caption to a picture, they often make the letters border the picture, as in Figure 2.1. Later they may think that words stand for things in their own right, but on a very peculiar basis: when Papandropolou and Sinclair (1974) asked a four-year-old to think of a "long word," he said, "a train." When they asked for a short word, he said, "a caterpillar!" Similarly, Ferreiro found that children would write a lot of letters to stand for a big object, and a few letters to stand for a small one even though the words for these objects may have been short and long, respectively.

Taking Meaning from the Act of Reading

In the earlier sections of this chapter we have been looking at the language skills a child must have in order to learn to read. We've seen that readers must have a spoken language that is roughly congruent with the language of the books they must read: in vocabulary, in syntax, and in elaborative style. We've seen, too, that a child must also learn several elements that are unique to the language of print, including cohesion, text structure, and the terminology that describes reading and writing.

Having all of the preceding language skills in place, however, still does not make a person a reader. A reader must employ some specific strategies in order to take meaning from print. In the present section, we will explore strategies in the two areas of *word knowledge* and *comprehension*.

Word Knowledge

At the threshold between what an author says and a reader understands is the ability to recognize written words. We will use for this ability the term *word knowledge,* because it is broad enough to stand for some abilities other than word recognition itself that are necessary for a person to come to

FIGURE 2.1. This child is beginning to separate pictures and print.

SOURCE: From Emilia Ferreiro, "The Underlying Logic of Literacy Development," in Hillel Goelman, Antoinette Oberg, and Frank Smith, eds., *Awakening to Literacy* (Portsmouth, N. H.: Heinemann Educational Books, 1984). Reprinted by permission.

recognize words. Among these are the *concept of word,* or the realization that language comes in units of individual words; *the ability to segment phonemes,* that is, to break a word down (mentally) into its constituent sounds, and *orthographic awareness,* the knowledge of the spelling patterns out of which English words are built.

The Concept of Word

An anthropologist working in a village where no one had ever learned to read had her curiosity aroused when she found that the villagers' language had a word for *a saying,* but no word for *word.* She wondered if they had a concept for a word — that is, if they thought of words as the building blocks of language as we do in literate societies. She devised an experiment to find out. After locating an adult volunteer, she explained that she wanted to see how he would break up sayings into smaller parts. He was to tap a stick on the table once for every part of a sentence she spoke. He agreed, and the experiment proceeded to an interesting conclusion: sometimes he tapped his stick to phrases and sometimes to syllables — but never to words. Of all the villagers she could get to try her experiment, not one could tap the stick in time to the words (Scribner and Cole, 1981). Thinking about words, being able to manipulate these units of language in our minds, is apparently not a skill that comes automatically with knowing a language, but must come from experiences with print.

Just like these villagers, most five-year-olds and many six-year-olds lack a working concept of words as language units. So what? As it turns out, they need to have this concept in place before they can learn to recognize words in print, to amass a sight vocabulary — in short, to learn to read. Consider, for example, a child who has memorized a poem, "Twinkle, twinkle little star." Now her teacher writes these words on newsprint, and, after telling the child that the words say the poem she has just learned, asks her to read them. If the girl lacks a concept of word, she is likely to look at the first *T* and say "twinkle," look at the *w* and say "twinkle" again, look at the *i* and say "little," look at the *n* and say "star" — then wonder what's going on. Or she may look at *Twinkle* and read "twink," look at the next *twinkle* and read "-kle," and so on.

Although the activity in this example — writing down phrases a child already knows so she or he can see the words in print — often helps children build a repertoire of words they can recognize, it won't lead quickly to that result in this instance because the child is not accurately matching the units of language on the page with corresponding units of language in the mind. Before children can learn to recognize words, then, or add new words to their sight vocabularies, they must develop a *concept of word.* In Chapter Three we will present a technique for assessing children's knowledge of the concept of word, and methods for helping them develop it.

Phonemic Segmentation

People who can't speak pig Latin have trouble learning to read (Savin, 1972). The connection between these two seemingly unrelated skills lies in the ability to break a word down into the sounds that make it up — its *phonemes*. Saying "Ig-pay Atin-lay" requires as a first step that we be able mentally to break off the first phonemes from the words. Figuring out the unknown word *can* from the known word *man* involves the same skill. We must first recognize the stem they have in common (*-an*), then break off the first phoneme of *man*, replace that letter with the phoneme spelled by the letter *c*, and finally pronounce the result.

In order to develop a full-grown ability to recognize words a person must be able to separate ultimately not just the first but all the other phonemes in spoken words from each other, a process called *phonemic segmentation*. Only when the phonemes have been segmented can the reader find a match between the sounds in the spoken word and the letters and letter clusters in the printed one. Hence phonemic segmentation has been found to be closely related to early reading ability (Liberman et al., 1979).

Phonemic segmentation is difficult for many children, however. While most kindergartners can break a word down into syllables when asked to tap a stick on the table for the number of syllables they hear in a spoken word, few can do the same for phonemes. Most children cannot segment phonemes until they are in first grade, and those who are delayed in their ability to segment phonemes are also delayed in their progress in word recognition (Liberman et. al., 1980).

What is difficult about phonemic segmentation? Those of us who can read are usually blinded by our own familiarity with print to the difficulty experienced by nonreaders with phonemic segmentation. We have seen that written words are made up of letters and find it an easy step to the realization that spoken words are made up of smaller units that correspond to letters. It's not surprising to us that *c-a-t* contains three separate sounds. But in fact, spoken words are not so easy to divide into distinct phonemes as they may seem.

Evidence from acoustic phonetics shows that the sound we hear in speech comes in units that are closer to syllables than to phonemes. The phonemes are produced all run together in larger units by a process called *coarticulation*. Evidence for coarticulation in the production of speech can be seen in graphic recordings of speech sound frequencies as shown in Figure 2.2. It is impossible to locate visually any distinct break between one phoneme and another. In fact, the same consonant phoneme, the sound /b/ in Figure 2.2, consists of vibrations that vary greatly as the /b/ sound is paired with different vowels.

FIGURE 2.2. Spectrograms, or graphic renderings of the syllables [ga], [ba], and [pa], show no clear break between consonants and vowels.

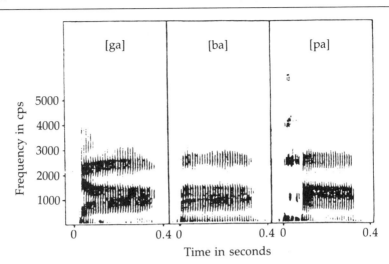

SOURCE: Jill de Villiers and Peter de Villiers, *Language Acquisition* (Cambridge: Harvard University Press, 1978), p. 12. Reprinted by permission.

Another kind of evidence that phonemes are not easily separated is found in experiments in which people listen to physically isolated phonemes. Words such as *cat* can be recorded onto a tape, which can then be cut into strips in an effort to capture individual phonemes. When these strips are played to listeners, however, a strange thing happens: the vowels are correctly heard, but consonants are described as sounding more like birds chirping than human speech sounds and are not recognized at all! (Liberman, et al., 1967) In a concrete sense, phonemes really do not exist in isolation from each other, any more than the color green exists as other than an attribute of things that are green. When we say we hear three sounds in *cat*, we are actually imposing our own mental abstractions of phonemes on the speech signal we hear.

The ability to segment words into phonemes comes primarily, or perhaps exclusively, from the experience of exploring written language. In one study, when adults in a nonliterate society were given the "tap-test" to segment phonemes, they performed no better than American preschoolers (Morais, 1978).

Phonemic segmentation is not always taught directly in reading instruction. Still, it is wise to make sure that younger delayed readers can segment phonemes. Though we will discuss techniques for exploring and enhancing children's ability to segment phonemes, we can note now that this is a point of contact between early reading and early writing. The practice of *invented spelling* (see Chapters Three and Seven) exercises very directly children's phonemic segmentation ability in a context that most children find interesting and meaningful (Temple, Nathan, and Burris, 1982; Calkins, 1984).

Orthographic Awareness

Read these words:

> glarm   flose   ranction   blanagrity   dwarge

Good readers can read *pseudowords,* words like these that look like English words but are not, much more proficiently than poor readers can (Shankweiler and Liberman, 1972). If good readers can read pseudowords with hardly a pause, they must have in their minds some general set of spelling rules or patterns that enable them to go from combinations of letters to sounds. For years, research and teaching experience have shown us that the ability to pronounce a word from its spelling is critically important to reading. This ability is quite often the main difference between good and poor readers (Liberman et al., 1980; Stanovich, 1982; Perfetti and Lesgold, 1979). The crux of that word recognition ability is the awareness of the spelling structure or the orthographic structure of words.

How spelling structure is used in reading is not fully clear. Some psycholinguists have argued that normal fluent reading cannot depend on the sounding out of individual words, because this would occupy so much brain capacity as to reduce the amount left for comprehending higher-order information. Theorists such as Smith (1978) and Goodman (1976) suggest that readers use their expectations, the context of the reading matter itself, as well as syntactic cues to aid in "guessing" what words are without having to scrutinize them closely (and hence without tying up limited mental attention in doing so). They assert that it is possible for readers to proceed directly from the recognition of a word to meaning without first having to pronounce it to themselves either aloud or in inner speech.

There are some difficulties with this position: experiments have shown that when readers are shown target words in print and then exposed to other words spoken to them at the same time, they are far more likely to be confused by words that sound the same (such as hearing *log* while reading *dog*) than they are by hearing words that sound different but have related meanings (hearing *pet* while reading *dog*) (Baddeley, 1966; Conrad, 1972). Also, as we have mentioned, proficient readers simply turn out to be better at recognizing words, both real words and pseudowords that follow English spelling patterns. If the ability to decipher spelling patterns were not important in reading, it is not obvious why fluent readers should be so much better at it than disabled readers.

There is good evidence that children do not use spelling patterns in their earliest word recognition. Youngsters first recognize certain words as wholes: their own names, or the names of fast-food restaurants, breakfast cereals, and other brand names are good candidates for first words read first. In many of these, the graphics or other concomitant visuals (golden arches, colorful red *K*'s, etc.) make these words as recognizable as faces (Y. Goodman, 1984). Later, perhaps toward the end of first grade for many, children begin to pay attention to the ways words are spelled and begin to be able to determine the pronunciation of an unrecognized word from the similarity of its spelling with that of a word they know: they can read *get* and *low*, so they can figure out how to read *let*.

Still, questions remain about the amount of spelling knowledge that is required if children are to decipher words. Research in the 1960s showed 100 or more rules were needed to account for the pronunciation of even 80% of the words found in an elementary textbook, and the 20% that did not fit the rules were mostly the highest-frequency words (Clymer, 1963). These rules, however, were based on the pronunciation of single letters. Using syllables and meaningful word units *(morphemes)* as his unit of analysis, Venezkey (1967, 1970) found a few dozen spelling patterns and a coherent web of spelling rules that accounted for virtually all of the 20,000 most frequently used words in English. English spelling is not so irregular as we thought, and children are capable of putting together for themselves language rules of incredible complexity (on a tacit, working level, though: they are not aware of and cannot talk about the rules as such). These were two big discoveries of the linguistics-inspired reading research of the 1960s and 1970s.

When it comes to the spelling structure of words, children find it easiest in the beginning to divide words into only two parts: a beginning consonant or consonant cluster (if either occurs) and everything else (Henderson, 1982). Thus *boat* is divided into *b* and *-oat, coat* into *c* and *-oat*, and so on. This is fairly natural activity for children; it is the basis of rhyming and other word games. For example, a favorite game of some four-year-olds we know is a variation of the old rhyme, "Ding, dong dell/ Kitty's in the well." When we say the first line they have to come up with the second, like this:

us: "Ding, dong, dink"
THEM: "Ummm . . . Kitty's in the sink."
us: "Ding, dong, dimming pool"
THEM: "Kitty's in the swimming pool!"

It is a straightforward matter to group words by their right-hand element: *light, sight, tight, might,* and so forth. Word-sorting activities (see Chapter Five) work on this principle.

After children can easily make the division of the first element from the rest of the word, they can be led to vary the final element, too. If children think of *-oat* words as a group, we can change the final consonant or consonant cluster and invite them to study the result:

$b+oat \rightarrow m+oat \rightarrow moa+n$. Once they can vary the first and last elements in a one-syllable word, readers are ready to attend to the vowel pattern in the middle. See, for instance, how the previous example cast the *oa* pattern into relief.

Short vowel patterns, as in *cat, crab, lad, hat,* and *had,* are spelled with fewer variations than long vowels (the "long A" sound may be spelled *eigh* as in *eight* and *freight, -ea* as in *break* and *steak, ai* as in *laid* and *paid, a/e* as in *cake* and *rake, ey* as in *hey,* or *ay* as in *say*). It is, perhaps, simpler to start with the short vowels — but if students are examining words that they already know for their spelling patterns, it will not be possible to put off looking at long vowel patterns indefinitely. As the discussion of "Word Study" in Chapter Five will make clear, it may be best to have students form at first one general category for "short A" words (or "words that sound like *cat*") and another general category for "long A" words (or "words that sound like *rake*"). Later this second category can be broken down further, after students find within the large category numbers of words that have their own spelling, such as "-ai" words, "eigh" words, and so on.

When students have become able to identify several patterns of spelling for similar sounds, it can be useful, particularly with older poor readers and spellers, to look more deeply at the spelling patterns to find out where they came from. Venezkey (1967) is a rich source of such information. He tells us, for example, that there is an *alternation rule* in English spelling that says, in effect, "Y may not come in the middle of a word, and I may not come at the end; so Y must change to I in the middle of a word, while I must change to Y at the end." Thus, *pay* is allowable, but **payed* is not. The Y must be changed to I to give us *paid.* This rule holds up fairly well: consider say/said, fry/fried, boy/boil, toy/toil. G. H. Vallins' *History of English Spelling* (1954) is another good source of insights into English word construction and the historical reasons for it. Of course, if students are encouraged to examine words to find patterns for themselves, they will discover many of the same principles that are described in these authorities.

A final note on spelling structure and reading: the pattern of learning we have described here — beginning with whole words, then dividing the first element from everything else, then dividing off the last element and studying the vowel spelling patterns — is the normal sequence both for young beginning readers and for older disabled ones. Both the sequence of the study and the word study activities themselves have worked well from the first-grade to senior high school level — with, you can imagine, some interesting adaptations for each age level.

Recognition of Written Words

As the ability to match spoken and printed words develops, the person learning to read comes to locate printed units quickly and confidently as the corresponding words are spoken and eventually begins to recognize written words as individual entities. Words located over and over begin to look different from all others, and characteristics of the appearance of individual words begin to appear obvious. When the same words occur frequently and in a context that gives them meaning, they become recognizable with very little examination needed. Only a glance suffices to recognize a familiar word, just as only a glimpse is necessary to let us identify a very familiar face in a crowd. The learner has begun to recognize written words, a basic competency underlying the ability to read. Recognizing a word automatically, as soon as it is seen, is called *sight recognition*. A word so familiar that it is recognized instantly is called a *sight word*. Sight words are necessary for all reading. When nonreaders have sufficient experience with print that they begin to develop sight recognition of some words spontaneously, they are learning to read.

Sight words serve as stepping stones in a line of print. If readers recognize a few of the words in the line as sight words, they can often make an educated guess about what the other words are; they can begin to use syntax, picture clues, letter-sound clues, and any other means they can to make sense of the text.

Sight words also serve as anchors for the neophyte reader who practices making the speech-to-print match. Let's suppose, for example, that Becky knows what the following line says, as she would if she had dictated it or heard someone read it aloud:

Becky brought her rabbit to school today.

If Becky recognizes her own name and *school* as sight words, then she will discover a mismatch if she reads *rabbit* as *rab* and *to* as *bit*. By this strategy, *school* should be read *to*; but Becky knows this is not right, because she recognizes *school* as a sight word. Then she will be led to reexamine the print to the left of *school* to find a better fit for her words.

Until a child has accumulated enough sight words to encounter two, three, or more in each line of print, smooth reading will not be achieved. Without sight words the child has no basis on which to activate meaning cues and is thus dependent on phonic decoding, but decoding every word is far too burdensome for anyone, especially a beginner. Besides, the speech-to-print match is not likely to be fully developed before some sight words are learned, so the reader may not be able to apply decoding strategies to the right units of print! The acquisition of some sight words precedes real reading, whatever methods of instruction one undertakes.

Let us clarify a point that is sometimes confusing. The term *sight word* is used by different authors to refer to somewhat different concepts. In its broadest sense, the term means any printed word a person can immediately recognize with no analysis or aid needed. Some authors, however, use the term *basic sight words* to refer to a special collection of words a reader should recognize on sight. Numerous lists of this kind have been compiled, such as the Dolch Word List (Dolch, 1955). Most lists contain the same 100–200 words.

The basis for such lists is quite logical. Numerous studies have been undertaken to determine how frequently different English words normally occur in print. These studies have shown that some words are used frequently and some infrequently. Durr (1973) analyzed 80 juvenile trade books and found that 10 words occurred so frequently that the reader encountered one of the 10 in every 4 or 5 words, on the average. Durr further found that 188 words accounted for only 6 percent of the different words used in the 80 books he studied, but those same 188 words occurred so frequently that they made up almost 70 percent of the running text. Ekwall (1976) cited studies showing that 200 words accounted for nearly 70 percent of the words in easy reading materials. Thorndike and Lorge (1944) assessed and classified the frequency of 30,000 words in adult reading material, and their frequency ratings are still used to construct school materials.

There is clear justification for the development of these basic sight word lists: beginning readers who could quickly and accurately recognize such words would find a number of ready stepping stones to help them get across any line of print. Most commercial lists feature largely the same words, so it doesn't matter much which list is mastered. The words are frequently taught *in isolation*, however, so their meanings can't be used as a recognition clue, which is a very poor instructional practice.

Selected lists of basic sight words and the groups of words children actually acquire on their own usually overlap (Henderson, Estes, and Stonecash, 1972), but they don't overlap entirely, and for a good reason. Basic sight word lists are mostly composed of the grammatically necessary but nondescript words such as articles, conjunctions, pronouns, and prepositions that bind together the real information-bearing words in a sentence. The lists sometimes include a few nouns, adjectives, and verbs in their ranks, but these are used so generally that their meanings are not precise, and the words are not very memorable.

A child could know all the basic sight words in a sentence, however, and still not approach the meaning. As an example, here is a passage with only the basic sight words left in. We took out all the words that Ekwall (1976, p. 70) did not designate as basic for preprimer, primer, and first grade levels:

_____ _____ and his _____ _____ _____ in the _____. They _____ in green. They _____ the _____ for _____ with their _____ and _____.

Could you make any sense of this passage? All the meaningful and memorable words have been left out. There is not much left to carry the meaning of the sentences.

Now here is the same sentence with the basic sight words left out and the less frequently encountered words restored:

Robin Hood _____ _____ Merry Men lived _____ _____ forest. _____
dressed _____ _____. _____ shot _____ deer _____ food _____ _____ bows
_____ arrows. (Manning-Sanders, 1977, p. 1)

It is easier to guess the basic sight words if we know the low-frequency
words than it is to infer the low-frequency words when we know the basic
sight words.

Words like *Robin Hood, Merry Men, shot, bow,* and *arrow* become sight
words more readily than the basic sight words simply because they are more
vivid and interesting. The less memorable words must be recognized too,
but they are most easily learned and recognized when taught in the context
of sentences rather than in isolation.

Reading Comprehension

When we sit down beside a struggling reader and wonder at the nature
of his problems so we can help him over them, besides listening to him read,
we virtually always have to take some measure of his understanding of what
he has read. Sometimes we are surprised: there is the occasional reader who
badly misreads the words yet gives a fair account of the meaning afterwards.
Then there are the others who recognize most of the words, though seeming
to name them rather than read them, but who show very little understanding when questioned later.

Normally, recognizing the words and understanding the text are closely
related. Word recognition rates predict understanding fairly well. In fact,
several quick reading placement tests measure word recognition alone.
Also, understanding a passage makes word recognition easier — a person
who can recognize only 75 out of 100 words shown to her one at a time can
recognize as many as 90 when they appear in connected text. The meaning
supplied by context makes word recognition easier.

With many students, nevertheless, understanding falls behind word
recognition. Or, to put it another way, many students fail to make good use
of the information they gain from their ability to recognize words. The four
reasons that usually explain a person's comprehension falling behind his or
her ability to recognize words are:

- □ *background concepts:* the student doesn't have sufficient background
  knowledge of the subject in the text to make sense of it;
- □ *text structure:* the student can't follow the arrangement of the information in the text;
- □ *metacognition:* the student isn't actively using his or her background
  knowledge or knowledge of text structure;
- □ *problems of measurement:* sometimes our means of measuring comprehension fail to tell us what a student really understands from her or his
  reading.

Text structure has been considered already in this chapter. Next we will explore the three other important issues in comprehension (background knowledge; metacognition, or comprehension monitoring; and the problem of measuring comprehension).

Background Knowledge: Schemata and Reading Comprehension

Suppose a person can accurately read all the words in a passage. Does it follow that this person will understand the passage? Not necessarily. An understanding of what we read is not the simple sum of individual word meanings, or even of successive sentences added together.

We can demonstrate that understanding consists of more than the meanings of individual words or sentences using the following passage and questions:

> Johnny was nearly in tears. It was his classmate Susan's birthday, and he'd forgotten to tell his mother. After school she hadn't been home, so Johnny had to come to the party empty-handed. Here he was, standing a little behind a cluster of children who were greeting Susan at the door. Inside beyond the door he could see the cake on the table, and brightly colored paper decorations taped to the wall and hanging from the ceiling.
> The other children now had moved inside. Susan turned and saw him.
> "Oh, hello, Johnny," she said. "I'm glad you could come."
> "Hi, Susan." Holding his hands behind his back he stepped forward, feeling his face blush bright red.

1. Retell this story in your own words without looking back at it.
2. See if you can summarize the story in one sentence.
3. What is Johnny so upset about?
4. Why is he empty-handed?
5. Describe the cake he saw inside on the table.

In answering the first four questions, most skilled readers would mention a birthday present. Johnny had come to his friend's party without one, because he'd forgotten to ask his mother to get it or to help him get it — we're not told which. That seems to be the point of the story, so far. Asked to describe the cake, many readers will fill in details: candles, icing, with words written in gooey lines of bright, contrasting colors.

A quick rereading will show that *none of the answers to these questions were stated in the passage.* We are told that he was empty-handed but not what he should have brought in his hands. We are told that his mother was unavailable but not what she was unavailable to do. We are certainly not told what the main point of the passage was or even that the cake on the table was a birthday cake. Nevertheless, we had to know these things to understand the passage. How did we know them?

If you were to ask another reader to read this passage line by line, saying aloud the thoughts that occur to her after each phrase or sentence, very likely it would turn out that the reader would say early on, "Ah, it's about a birthday party." Your reader would search through her own experiences to find some overall explanation of what was going on in the passage, a framework of ideas that would help her make sense of the details she encountered. Moreover, since she would supply this mental framework herself, you might find as she talked about the passage that she had added some details that were not present in the passage.

Finding an overall mental framework for interpreting a text, and supplying for ourselves those details that "round out the picture" for us, are both common starting points in comprehending. We use them every time we read. Sometimes the mental framework might relate to a baseball game, a religious ceremony, a murder plot, or even directions for assembling a Japanese bicycle. Whatever the text is about we must summon up a mental frame that lets us make sense of the details that occur in the passage, and fill in for ourselves those details that the author does not supply.

These overall frameworks for understanding text have been called *schemata* (the singular form is *schema*), and they form the center of an explanation for understanding text that has been called *schema theory* (Minsky, 1975; Collins, 1977; Anderson, 1984). The account of the reading act that schema theory provides runs essentially as follows: as people have experiences in the world, they store in their minds the knowledge they gain, in the form of mental frameworks called schemata. All the experiences they have modify and develop their schemata. When a new event is encountered, whether in real life or in literature, the reader summons up appropriate schemata. These schemata will help a person make sense of the information supplied by the event, at least partially, by filling in details not present in the event itself.

As Jean Piaget has shown us with his description of *assimilation* and *accommodation*, two things happen when we summon up schemata to make sense of experience. First, the information in our own schemata color greatly the experience we have, so that a person with more elaborate schemata will get more out of the experience than a person with less elaborate schemata. Second, by interpreting a new experience in light of our existing schemata, we ever so slightly modify and enrich those schemata. We encounter a lhasa apso and expand our schema for dogs. We meet a melancholy fat person and revise our old schema that says "all fat people are jolly." This is how we learn, whether in real life or in reading. We learn when a new experience catches our attention and challenges us to examine and revise our old ways of thinking.

In reading, having background schemata for the topics we are reading about is all-important. We cannot understand something we know nothing about, because understanding requires that we relate new information to knowledge structures we already had. For instance, readers who are not familiar with the area of linguistic theory known as generative phonology will not be much informed by the following passage:

> 2.6.1 *Acoustico-articulatory data*
> The segment /r/ is simply a voiced apicoalveolar flap. We may confidently assign to it at least the features [+vocalic, +consonantal, -obstruent, +voiced, +coronal, +anterior, -strident], and with only slightly less confidence, [+continuent, -tense]. (Harris, 1969, p. 46)

This passage will not make sense to most readers because they have no relevant schemata to which to assign new information and out of which to fill in the gaps. What are the features Harris is talking about? What manner of beast is an apicoalveolar flap? We have to know something about a topic in order to understand what we read about it.

Comprehension Monitoring

A reader can have background knowledge necessary to understand a piece of text, be familiar with the type of discourse the text represents and conversant with the patterns in which the ideas are organized, and still not comprehend it. In fact, this is what happens to us at those times late at night when we find our eyes at the bottom of the page of an assigned textbook, unable to remember anything written on the previous several pages. It is not enough to have the background schemata and know the text structure; we must also actively pursue meaning in what we read. If we do not, what we take away from our reading ranges from nothing at all to a collection of jumbled details that refuse to add up to anything meaningful.

Happily, each of us has a facility that usually keeps us using what we know in order to take meaning from text. This facility goes by several names. It is sometimes referred to as if it were a thing, such as the "executive system of the mind" (Anderson, 1975), and other times as if it were an activity, as in "metacognition," or *comprehension monitoring*, the term we shall be using in this book.

Comprehension monitoring consists of a range of activities, from the almost reflex phrase-by-phrase checking that alerts us if we read a word improperly ("there was a bear in the refrig — no, sorry — there was a *beer* in the refrigerator . . .") to the more conscious and deliberate setting of expectations of what we will find out in a piece, with subsequent checking to see if we are finding out what we expected to. ("Hmm. . . . This article is about boat building in plywood. Let's see if the author is onto the new techniques for preventing dry rot. If not, I won't bother to read on. . . .")

Comprehension monitoring of the reflexive type first described leads readers to make *spontaneous corrections* when they read words incorrectly. Children who are just learning to read show signs of this kind of comprehension monitoring, as Marie Clay (1982) and Don Holdaway (1979) both have pointed out. In fact, when children do not spontaneously correct their errors, there is cause for concern, as this suggests that they do not expect their reading to make sense — or that they are so far from understanding a particular passage that they do not know what sense it should make. Clay and Holdaway advise teachers to look for signs of spontaneous correction when they observe children reading and to remind students repeatedly that they need to ask themselves if what they are reading makes sense, especially at those times when they are unsure what a word is.

On a more deliberate level, comprehension monitoring may include setting purposes and expectations for what we are about to read and checking periodically to see if these are being met as we go through the text. This kind of comprehension monitoring does not come naturally to all readers. Far more typical is this pattern:

1. start right in reading
2. get fidgety
3. get distracted
4. lose your place
5. give up
6. not remember what you read

Deliberate strategies for setting purposes and monitoring comprehension can be taught. They constitute one area of reading ability that can profit tremendously from direct teaching. The Directed Reading-Thinking Activity or DRTA (see Chapter Five) is a teacher-led reading experience that leads students to set purposes before reading and to see afterwards if their purposes have been met. In the DRTA, the teacher prepares the students just before reading by asking very general questions that invite the students to examine their own prior knowledge about a topic, set their own questions, and raise detailed expectations about what they might get out of a reading passage.

"What is this reading passage about?"
"What do you already know about the topic?"
"What do you *not* know that you may find out?"

The aim of teacher-led lessons like the DRTA and other similar activities such as reciprocal teaching (see Chapter Six) is for the students to form habits of self-questioning, purpose setting, and comprehension monitoring that will stay with them when they read on their own. In Chapters Five and Six we will discuss strategies that are designed for these ends. In the present section, where our purpose is to point out the many abilities that make efficient reading possible, it is enough to say that students who do not adequately monitor their own comprehension, whether at the reflex word-by-word level or at the more deliberate purpose-setting level, should be identified and helped.

Measuring Comprehension

At the beginning of this section we listed four common reasons why some readers' comprehension may lag behind their ability to recognize words. The first three were *a dearth of background knowledge or schemata related to the topic of the reading, a lack of familiarity with the structure of the presentation of the material,* and *a failure to read actively and monitor one's comprehension.* We come now to the fourth reason: *the great difficulty in telling with any certainty what someone has comprehended from reading.*

We haven't always recognized the difficulty. Only a few years ago, our notions of what constitutes comprehension were far simpler. Many theorists assumed that the meaning of a piece of writing lay fully in the writing and that experts could agree on the meaning. The task of measuring comprehension was easy. First, you determined the meaning of the text. Next, you had students read it. Finally, you asked them questions to find out if they understood the meaning. If they answered the questions in the way you expected, they understood. If they answered the questions differently from what you expected, they did not understand.

This way of proceeding is still very much with us, but the theoretical grounds for it have been shaken. Schema theorists tell us that the reader's experience of meaning is constructed by the reader, on cues from the author. Since readers' schemata, their mental frameworks for understanding and their mental images, are derived from their own life histories, it follows that no two readers could possibly have exactly the same experience in reading a text. It follows further that there is never an absolute meaning of any text, no certain standard against which to measure a reader's comprehension.

In recent years, literary critics have reveled in the maneuvering room afforded them by relativist views of meaning. Primed with Freudian psychology, the psychoanalyst Bruno Bettelheim (1976) has shown that for children, fairy tales can help them work out deeply rooted problems of living, all on a subconscious level that is not apparent to adults. The critic Norman Holland (1968) has done the same for adult fiction, arguing that what a book means to us depends upon our psychic make-up. Feminist theorists have studied literature for the ways that it both reveals and distorts the lives of women (Donovan, 1975). Marxist theorists have examined the economic implications of the ways literature and other media shape and channel people's consciousness (Eagleton, 1976). Finally, the comprehensive literary critic Northrup Frye teaches us that all literature has a common source: the striving of humanity to overcome a sense of a long-past fall from paradise and to be restored to a status of unity with nature and the universe. All literature, according to Frye, is one fabric, woven together around this common theme and joined by patterns of allusion from one work of literature to another. Because this is so, argues Frye, and because it is also true that we experience each new piece of literature through eyes that are experienced with what we have read before, it follows that students should be given rich experiences with literature: Bible stories, myths, folktales, and great works of tragedy, comedy, irony, and romance.

It is difficult to say how far we should take the idea that the meaning of a text is dependent upon the reader. We can argue just as strongly that readers gain similar experiences from what they read. That is why it is possible to discuss a book with others. If there weren't *some* predictability in readers' responses to reading, there could be no craft of writing. Perhaps the best way around the problem is to say that within any community of people, there are culturally agreed-upon meanings that lead to common ways of experiencing (Berger and Luckman, 1966). One of the traditional purposes of public education has been to create a sort of national culture and community, by exposing people to the same ideas so that they can experience things in a similar way. Television and other mass media also have the effect of creating "national schemata," so that diverse people experience things similarly.

With respect to reading, however, real differences in interpretation — in the individual's experience of meaning — are common. In measuring or estimating comprehension, we have to assume that meanings are shared, but we also must be alert for individual interpretations.

Summary

Diagnostic judgment is built on an understanding of how reading normally begins and develops, and this chapter has examined the most important competencies underlying the ability to read.

Before students can learn to read their language, they must be able to understand it. We looked at three aspects of language ability: *vocabulary, syntax,* and the *elaborate use of language.* Vocabulary knowledge involves having a set of concepts as well as the words to go with them. Young children's words may not match concepts in the same way adults' words do, but rather refer to a more extensive range of meaning *(overextensions)* or a more restricted one *(underextensions).* People learn vocabulary by having opportunities to act on their environment in the presence of a good language model.

Syntax refers both to the ordering and inflections that enable words to combine meaningfully into sentences. Though most children have developed a control over most syntactic structures by school age, there are many structures — notably *transformations* — that do not come under control until the age of nine or ten. Children who are delayed readers may lag behind other children in their control of syntax.

The *elaborated use of language,* the third aspect of language ability covered, relates to the degree to which speakers spell things out. Researchers have found that individual speakers or whole speech communities may tend to use restricted forms of speech — forms that are adequate in informal speech situations but inadequate as a basis for learning to read, because the language of print is elaborate. Both Michael Halliday and Joan Tough have proposed a set of *language functions* that teachers can use to pinpoint more precisely which aspects of language children can use elaborately.

Many language conventions are specific to print. For example, the quality of *cohesion* (a quality of relatedness between two or more sentences) was a set of conventions we saw as well as the *structure of text*. Structure refers to the overall plan that relates beginning, middle, and end and provides the reader a basis for following what is happening and for predicting what will happen. *Story structure* is the most widely studied variety of text structure, but there are discernible structures that hold together descriptive, expository, and argumentative writing as well. Understanding text structure is important in reading comprehension.

More specific conventions about print that children must know about in order to learn to read include the language that is used to talk about reading (*word, sentence, beginning, end,* etc.) as well as a sense of what reading is for, and how and why one does it.

Under the heading "strategies for taking meaning from the reading act," we grouped together two very sizable chunks of understanding and ability: *word knowledge* and *comprehension.* Word knowledge is not a single skill. It consists of knowing what a word is, having a *concept of word.* It also includes being able to *segment phonemes* — that is, knowing that *cat* has three sounds in it, and being able to "pull apart" those sounds. Too, it includes *orthographic awareness,* a knowledge of the system of rules that relate spelling to sound. These rules are complex, but they are knowable. Children pick them up by exposure, apparently, although they can rarely talk about them. We will look at orthographic rules in more detail in Chapter Seven. *Sight words* are another aspect of word knowledge, coming into play as children begin to store up words in memory that they can recognize immediately.

Comprehension is not a simple thing, either. At a minimum it involves *background concepts* or *schemata.* These are structures of our knowledge of the world that enable us to make sense of the things we encounter, either in the real world or in print. Because texts are never totally explicit, some filling in of information from our own schemata is always necessary in comprehension. *Text structure* got another mention in this context, because an important part of comprehension is the ability to follow a story or an argument, or a set of instructions. We couldn't follow very well without a knowledge of text structure. We *wouldn't* follow very well without using what is variously called *metacognition* or *comprehension monitoring.* Both terms refer to the activity of paying attention to our own understanding of what we are reading, so that we will know if we misread a word, if we are not understanding an argument, or if we are otherwise not meeting our purposes for reading.

With the final aspect of comprehension, the question of measuring what is understood, our discussion took a philosophical turn. Measuring comprehension is not strictly possible, because meaning is ultimately a private affair involving the reader's own schemata (which in turn, derive from her or his unique experiences) and the cues that are in the text. It is healthy to recognize the mutability of meaning, because it suggests that measuring comprehension is more a process of comparing interpretations than of counting right answers. Of course some interpretations are more plausible than others. Still, as Bruno Bettelheim has eloquently argued, even fairy tales have meanings for children that are far deeper and more profound than the children can express. And it would be wrong to expose children to literature that had only immediately obvious and therefore easily tested meaning.

Extension Activities

1. Discuss with a nursery school or kindergarten teacher the role of oral language development in learning to read. How do average children differ in their syntactic development and elaborateness of oral language? How does the teacher aid children who lag behind in these abilities?

2. Discuss the same issues with a teacher of nonreaders who are older students or adults. Are there particular characteristics of the oral language of older nonreaders? What role does the teacher believe oral language facility plays in reading improvement? How does the teacher improve a student's oral language?

3. Talk to some young children who have not yet begun to read and then to some older nonreaders. What do they believe reading and writing are for? If they could read (or read more easily), what could they do that they cannot do now? How are the responses similar or different, in respect to the respondents' age?

4. Find a simple story with an obvious structure, like a short fairy tale, folk tale, or fable. Revise it so that one or two events are slightly out of sequence. Read or tell the story to some young children individually and ask each to retell the story. Do they correct the order of events? Do they realize that anything was wrong with your version? What aspects of story structures does each include in the retelling?

5. Teach a young prereading child a jingle, nursery rhyme, or short poem. Recite it with him or her until the jingle has been memorized. Then show the rhyme in print and ask the child to recite the words and point to the written words at the same time. Observe the pointing: can the student do the task easily? If not, what units does the child point to while reciting? Where does the process seem to break down? If you show the student how to do it, can he or she then do the task correctly?

Suggested Readings

Clay, Marie. **Reading: The Patterning of Complex Behavior, 2nd ed.** *Exeter, N.H.: Heinemann Educational Books, 1980.* An unusually detailed account of what a child must perceive, comprehend, and do in order to become a reader, along with suggestions for helpful teaching.

de Villiers, Peter, and de Villiers, Jill. **Early Language.** *Cambridge, Mass.: Harvard University Press, 1978.* A very readable introduction to the psycholinguistic study of children's language.

Goodman, Kenneth, Goodman, Yetta, and Flores, Barbara. **Reading in the Bilingual Classroom: Literacy and Biliteracy.** *Rosslyn, Va.: National Clearinghouse for Bilingual Education, 1978.* A well-detailed introduction to the issues and strategies of bilingual reading instruction, with good references for further help.

Heath, Shirley Brice. **Ways With Words** *Cambridge, England: Cambridge University Press, 1983.* A sensitive and eye-opening account by a teacher-turned-anthropologist of the effects of social group-based child-rearing patterns on children's orientations to literacy.

Holdaway, Don. *Foundations of Literacy.* Exeter, N.H.: Heinemann Educational Books, 1978. A wonderful blend of child-watching and teaching strategies. Wise and inspiring.

Tough, Joan. *Listening to Children Talking.* Exeter, N.H: Heinemann Educational Books, 1982. A very readable presentation of a functionalist approach to children's language development, complete with assessment strategies and language samples on which you can develop your analytic skills.

References

Adams, Marilyn, and Collins, Allan. "A Schema Theoretic View of the Learning To Read Process", in *New Directions in Discourse Processing,* Roy Freedle, ed. Norwood, N.J.: Ablex, 1979.

Aitchison, Jean. *The Articulate Mammal.* London: Hutchison and Company, 1976.

Anderson, Alonzo and Stokes, Shelley, "Social and Institutional Influences on the Development and Practice of Literacy," in Hillel Goelman, Antoinette Oberg, and Frank Smith, eds. *Awakening to Literacy.* Exeter, N.H.: Heinemann Educational Books, 1984.

Anderson, Barry. *Cognitive Psychology: The Study of Knowing, Learning, and Thinking.* New York: Academic Press, 1975.

Anderson, Richard. "Role of the Reader's Schema in Comprehension, Learning, and Memory," in Richard Anderson, Jean Osborne, and Robert Tierney, eds. *Learning to Read in American Schools.* Hillsdale, N.J.: Lawrence Erlbaum Associates, 1984.

Applebee, Arthur. *The Child's Concept of Story.* Chicago: University of Chicago Press, 1978.

Baddeley, Allen. "Short-term Memory for Word Sequences as a Function of Acoustic, Semantic, and Formal Similarity." *Quarterly Journal of Experimental Psychology* 18 (1966): 362–365.

Baker, Linda and Stein, Nancy. "The Development of Prose Comprehension Skills," in Carol Santa and Bernard Hayes, eds. *Children's Prose Comprehension Skills.* Newark, Del.: IRA, 1981.

Barrera, Rosalinda. *Analysis and Comparison of First-Language and Oral Reading Behavior of Native Spanish-Speaking Mexican-American Children.* Doctoral Dissertation, University of Texas at Austin, 1978.

Barrera, Rosalinda. "Bilingual Reading: Some Questions About Some Questionable Views and Practices," in Teresa Escobedo, ed. *Early Childhood Bilingual Education: A Hispanic Perspective.* New York: Teachers College Press, 1983.

Bartlett, Elsa. "Selecting an Early Childhood Language Curriculum," in Courtney Cazden, ed. *Language in Early Childhood Education.* Washington, D.C.: NAEYC, 1981.

Bartlett, Frederick. *Remembering: A Study in Ex-*

perimental and Social Psychology. Cambridge, England: Cambridge University Press, 1932.

Berger, Peter and Luckmann, Thomas. *The Social Construction Reality*. Garden City, N.Y.: Doubleday, 1966.

Bernstein, Basil. "Elaborated and Restricted Codes: Their Social Origins and Some Consequences," in George Smith, ed. *Communication and Culture*. New York: Holt, Rinehart, and Winston, 1966.

Bettelheim, Bruno. *The Uses of Enchantment*. New York: Vintage, 1977.

Bloom, Lois. *One Word At a Time: The Use of Single Word Utterances Before Syntax*. The Hague: Mouton, 1973.

Braine, Martin. "The Acquisition of Language in Infant and Child," in C. E. Reed, ed. *The Learning of Language*. New York: Appleton-Century-Crofts.

Brandt, Deborah. "Three Books on Literacy: A Review." *College English*, 47, No. 2.

Brown, Ann, and Smiley, Susan. "The Development of Strategies for Studying Texts," *Child Development*, 49 (1978): 1076–1088.

Brown, Roger. *A First Language*. Cambridge, Mass.: Harvard University Press, 1973.

Calkins, Lucy. *Lessons from a Child*. Exeter, N.H.: Heinemann Educational Books, 1984.

Cazden, Courteney. "Language and Reading," in Courtney Cazden, ed. *Language in Early Childhood Education*. Washington, D.C.: NAEYC, 1981.

Chomsky, Carol. *The Acquisition of Syntax in Children from 5 to 10*. Cambridge, Mass.: MIT Press, 1969.

Clark, Eve. "What's in a Word? On the Child's Acquisition of Semantics in His First Language," in T. E. Moore, ed. *Cognitive Development and the Acquisition of Language*. New York: Academic Press, 1973.

Clay, Marie. *Reading: The Patterning of Complex Behavior*. Exeter, N.H.: Heinemann Educational Books, 1972.

Clay, Marie. *Observing Young Readers*. Exeter, N.H.: Heinemann Educational Books, 1982.

Clymer, Theodore. "The Utility of Phonic Generalizations in the Primary Grades," *The Reading Teacher*, 16 (Jan. 1963): 252–258.

Cuff, N. B. "Vocabulary Test." *Journal of Educational Psychology*, 21 (1930): 212–220.

Dale, Phillip. *Language Development: Structure and Function, second edition*. New York: Holt, Rinehart and Winston, 1976.

de Villiers, Jill, and de Villiers, Peter. *Language Acquisition*. Cambridge, Mass.: Harvard University Press, 1978.

de Villiers, Peter, and de Villiers, Jill. *Early Language*. Cambridge, Mass.: Harvard University Press, 1979.

Donovan, Josephine. *Feminist Literary Criticism*. Lexington, Ky.: University of Kentucky Press, 1975.

Eagleton, Terry. *Criticism and Ideology*. London: Verso Editions, 1976.

Ferreiro, Emilia. "The Underlying Logic of Literacy Development," in Hillel Goelman, Antoinette Oberg, and Frank Smith, eds. *Awakening To Literacy*. Exeter, N.H.: Heinemann Educational Books, 1984.

Frye, Northrup. *On Teaching Literature*. New York: Harcourt Brace Jovanovich, 1972

Gibson, Eleanor and Levin, Harry. *The Psychology of Reading*. Cambridge, Mass.: MIT Press, 1975

Ginsburg, Herbert, and Opper, Sylvia. *Piaget's Theory of Intellectual Development, second edition*. New York: Prentice-Hall.

Goodman, Kenneth and Goodman, Yetta. "Learning to Read Is Natural," in Lauren Resnick and Phyllis Weaver, eds., *Theory and Practice of Beginning Reading*. Hillsdale, N.J.: Lawrence Earlbaum Associates, 1976.

Goodman, Kenneth, and Goodman, Yetta. *American Children Whose Language Is a Stable Rural Dialect of English or a Language Other Than English* (Final Report, Project NIE 00-3-0087). Washington, D.C.: U.S. Department of Education, 1978.

Goodman, Kenneth, Goodman, Yetta, and Flores, Barbara. *Reading in the Bilingual Classroom: Literacy and Biliteracy*. Rosslyn, Va.: National Clearinghouse for Bilingual Education, 1978.

Goodman, Yetta. "The Development of Initial Literacy," in Hillel Goelman, Antoinette Oberg, and Frank Smith, eds. *Awakening to Literacy*. Exeter, N.H.: Heinemann Educational Books, 1984.

Goody, Jack. "Alternative Paths to Knowledge in Oral and Literate Cultures," in David Tannen, ed. *Spoken and Written Language*. Norwood, N.J.: Ablex, 1982.

Greimas, A. J. "Narrative Grammar: Units and Levels," *Modern Language Notes*. 86 (1971): 793–806.

Halliday, Michael. Personal communication, May 5, 1980.

Halliday, Michael, and Hasan, Ruquaya. *Cohesion in English*. London: Longman, 1976.

Harris, James. *Spanish Phonology*. Cambridge, Mass.: MIT Press, 1969.

Heath, Shirley Brice. *Ways With Words*. Cambridge, England: Cambridge University Press, 1983.

Henderson, Edmund. *Learning to Spell and to Read*. DeKalb, Ill.: Northern Illinois University Press, 1982.

Holdaway, Don. *The Foundations of Literacy*. Exeter, N.H.: Heinemann Educational Books, 1979.

Holland, Norman. *The Dynamics of Literary Response*. New York: Oxford University Press, 1968.

Kita, Jane. "Children's Conceptions of Reading and Writing." Paper presented at the annual meeting of the National Reading Conference. San Antonio, Texas, November 1979.

Liberman, Alvin, Cooper, Frank, and Studdert-Kennedy, Michael. "Perception of the Speech Code." *Psychological Review* 74 (1967): 431–461.

Liberman, Isabelle, and Shankweiler, Donald. "Speech, the Alphabet, and Learning to Read," in Lauren Resnick and Phyllis Weaver, eds. *Theory and Practice of Early Reading*. Hillsdale, N.J.: Lawrence Erlbaum Associates, 1979.

Liberman, Isabelle, Liberman, Alvin, Mattingly, Ignatius, and Shankweiler, Donald. "Orthography and the Beginning Reader," in James Kavanaugh and Richard Venezkey, eds. *Orthography, Reading, and Dyslexia*. Baltimore: University Park Press, 1980.

Loban, Walter. *Language Development*. Urbanna, Ill.: NCTE, 1976.

Mandler, Jean, and Johnson, Nancy. "The Remembrance of Things Parsed." *Cognitive Psychology* 9 (1977): 111–151.

Manning-Sanders, Ruth. *Robin Hood and Little John*. London: Methuen, 1979.

Marshall, Nancy, and Glock, Melvin. "Comprehension of Connected Discourse," *Reading Research Quarterly*. 16 (1979): 10–56.

McConaughy, Stephanie. "Using Story Structure in the Classroom," *Language Arts* 57 (1980): 157–165.

Minsky, Marvin. "A Framework for Representing Knowledge," in P. H. Winston, ed. *The Psychology of Computer Vision*. New York: McGraw-Hill, 1975.

Myer, Bonnie. "The Structure of Prose: Effects on Learning and Memory and Implications for Educational Practice," in Richard Anderson and Rand Spiro, eds. *Schooling and the Acquisition of Knowledge*. Hillsdale, N.J.: Lawrence Erlbaum Associates, 1977.

Nagy, William, and Anderson, Richard. "How Many Words Are There in Printed School English?" *Reading Research Quarterly*, 19 (1984): 304–330.

Ochs, Elinor, and Schieffelin, Bambi, eds. *Developmental Pragmatics*. New York: Academic Press, 1979.

Olson, David. " 'See Jumping!' Some Oral Antecedents of Literacy," in Hillel Goelman, Antoinette Oberg, and Frank Smith, eds. *Awakening to Literacy*. Exeter, N.H.: Heinemann Educational Books, 1984.

Perfetti, Charles, and Lesgold, Allan. "Coding and Comprehension in Skilled Reading and Implications for Reading Instruction," in Lauren Resnick and Phyllis Weaver, eds. *Theory and Practice of Early Reading*. Hillsdale, N.J.: Lawrence Erlbaum Associates, 1979.

Propp, Vladimir. *The Morphology of the Folktale*. Austin: University of Texas Press, 1968.

Reid, Jessie. "Learning to Think About Reading," *Educational Research* 9 (1966): 56–62.

Richards, Jill. *Classroom Language: What Sorts?* London: Allen and Unwin, 1978.

Rumelhart, David. "Notes on a Schema for Stories," in D. G. Dobrow and A. Collins, eds. *Representation and Understanding*. New York: Academic Press, 1975.

Sartre, Jean-Paul. *The Words*. New York: Fawcett, 1964.

Savin, Harry. "What the Child Knows About Speech When He Starts To Learn To Read," in James Kavanaugh and Ignatius Mattingly, eds. *Language By Ear and By Eye*. Cambridge, Mass.: MIT Press, 1972.

Scribner, Sylvia, and Cole, Michael. *The Psychology of Literacy*. Cambridge, Mass.: Harvard University Press, 1982.

Seashore, R. H., and Eckerson, L. D. "The Measurement of Individual Differences in General English Vocabularies," *Journal of Educational Psychology*. 31 (1940): 13–48.

Seitz, Ruth. *Social and Ethnic Group Differences in Reading*. Newark, Del.: IRA, 1977.

Shankweiler, Donald, and Liberman, Isabelle. "Misreading: A Search for Causes," in James Kavanaugh and Ignatius Mattingly, eds. *Language By Ear and By Eye*. Cambridge, Mass.: MIT Press, 1972.

Singer, Martin, and Stanovich, Keith. *Competent*

Reader/Disabled Reader. New York: Academic Press, 1982.

Smith, Frank. *Understanding Reading*. New York: Holt, Rinehart, and Winston, 1978.

Smith, M. E. "An Investigation of the Development of the Sentence and the Extent of Vocabulary in Young Children," *University of Iowa Studies in Child Welfare* 3, No. 5 (1926).

Stein, Nancy. "How Children Understand Stories." Urbana, Ill.: University of Illinois Center for the Study of Reading, Technical Report No. 69, March 1978 (ERIC: ED 153 205).

Teale, William. "Reading to Young Children: Its Significance for Literacy Development," in Hillel Goelman, Antoinette Oberg, and Frank Smith, eds., *Awakening to Literacy*. Exeter, N.H.: Heinemann Educational Books, 1984.

Temple, Charles, Nathan, Ruth, and Burris, Nancy. *The Beginnings of Writing*. Boston: Allyn and Bacon, 1982.

Thorndike, Edward and Lorge, Irving. *The Teacher's Word Book of 30,000 Words*. New York: Teachers College Press, 1944.

Thorndyke, Perry. "Cognitive Structures in Comprehension and Memory of Narrative Discourse," *Cognitive Psychology* 9 (1977): 77–110.

Tough, Joan. *Focus on Meaning: Talking to Children to Some Purpose*. London: Allen and Unwin, 1973.

Tough, Joan. *Listening to Children Talking*. Portsmouth, N.H.: Heinemann Educational Books, 1983.

Venezkey, Richard. "English Orthography: Its Graphical Structure and Its Relation to Sound," *Reading Research Quarterly*, 2 (1967): 75–106.

Venezkey, Richard. *The Structure of English Orthography*. The Hague: Mouton, 1970.

Vygotsky, Lev. *Thought and Language*. Cambridge, Mass.: MIT Press, 1962.

Weaver, Constance. *Grammar for Teachers*. Urbana, Ill.: NCTE, 1979.

Chapter Three

Assessment of Prereading Competencies (Readiness)

Two six-year-old girls sit beside each other in a first-grade reading group. One of them matches each point of the teacher's instruction with two leaps forward of her own. The other is taught and retaught with much practice and encouragement but makes little progress. By December of the first-grade year, the first child is reading fluently but the second is not.

Teachers of young children are aware that their young students differ considerably in their *readiness* for reading instruction. The little bit of encouragement that is necessary to start one youngster reading seemingly has no effect on another. It is now standard procedure in schools to assess children to determine which ones are ready to read and which ones are not.

Recently, however, the concept of readiness has been criticized because the term carries the connotation that children become ready for reading in the same mysterious way that flowers become ready to bloom. This concept implies that readiness is more dependent on biological maturation than on experience. In contrast to this view, recent studies have shown that reading readiness may consist of several prereading competencies, such as familiarity with story structure, concepts about print, the concept of what a word is, or about what reading is and what it is for. Children must reach a certain level of maturity before they can acquire these competencies effectively, but maturity alone is not the issue. Many reading experts prefer the term prereading to reading readiness because prereading and the competencies that it consists of suggest a more active agenda for teachers than the term readiness. Whether children profit from beginning reading instruction may not be so much a matter of whether they have become somehow ready to read but rather whether they have had the requisite prereading experiences. And if we look at the problem this way, then it is easier to see a course of action for the teacher whose students need to develop prereading competencies.

In Chapter Two of this book we discussed in detail the factors we think are most necessary for learning to read. In this chapter we discuss ways of assessing the prereading competencies we consider to be essential:

- □ oral language fluency
- □ sense of story structures
- □ the speech-to-print match
- □ print orientation concepts
- □ sight word recognition
- □ letter recognition

In the pages that follow, we present techniques for investigating children's development in each of these areas, along with suggestions for helping them grow. The techniques center mostly around observing children as they are engaged in talking, and in reading or reading like tasks, and most require no more special equipment than illustrated reading books, paper and pencil (supplemented, perhaps, by a tape recorder) for taking notes, sharp eyes, and keen ears. For investigating some prereading abilities, commercially published materials exist that in our view simplify or add power to the teacher's unaided observations. We describe these materials and provide sources for them where appropriate.

Also in this chapter, we meet the first of our case studies.

Case Studies

LISA

Lisa entered first grade at the age of five years, eight months, one of the youngest in her class. The previous year she attended kindergarten, where she did not experience noticeable difficulty, although she was somewhat shy and often played alone. When she began first grade Lisa was tiny, spoke softly, and was somewhat timid about joining in group activities. She rarely volunteered a response in discussions and at times seemed overwhelmed by the activity around her.

As the first weeks of school went by, Lisa made very little progress in learning to read, and her teacher, Betty Decker, was puzzled by her erratic performance. Lisa seemed to learn something one day only to forget it the next. Or, she would have two or three "good days," when she was able to remember the letters and words in her lessons and could apply what she had learned, but then she would forget it all again. At times she would stare at a letter she'd known for days just as though she'd never seen it before. It was as though every time Lisa learned something new, she'd forget something that had come before.

Ms. Decker paced the lessons in the basal series more slowly for Lisa's reading group and took advantage of every practice activity in the manual as well as making up her own. The other children in Lisa's group benefited from all the additional practice, but the teacher suspected they could move forward a bit more quickly. Lisa, however, needed enormous amounts of practice and still was not very successful. Ms. Decker hesitated to remove her from the reading group because she felt that the group interaction would be helpful in drawing shy Lisa out of her shell. After six or seven weeks of instruction, however, Lisa was becoming discouraged. She seemed more withdrawn than ever, was easily discouraged, rarely finished her independent seatwork, and several times had broken into tears after minor mishaps. Ms. Decker knew that these were behavioral signs of Lisa's frustration and unhappiness, but *why* was she having such difficulty learning to read?

KATIE

Betty Decker often sought advice from her friend Myra Whittier, who taught second grade next door. As Ms. Decker described some of Lisa's problems, Myra Whittier's thoughts turned to Katie.

Katie was almost nine years old in October of second grade; she had been retained in first grade the year before. Katie was a tall, athletic girl with a sunny nature and sweet personality. She gloried in the responsibility of running small errands and helping the teacher and could always be depended on in this role. She took an almost maternal interest in the welfare of her younger classmates and would ignore her own work to help others if allowed to. Ms. Whittier often thought fondly of Katie as her "mother hen."

Katie's sweetness and helpfulness could not hide her slow academic progress, however. After two years in first grade she could just barely read at a primer level and was always in the lowest reading group. Although her work was always done with painstaking care, it could take her all morning to complete a workbook page or dittoed exercise. She worked diligently and never got discouraged, but her progress was painfully slow. It seemed so unfair, mused Ms. Whittier, that a child so industrious, responsible, and motivated should have so little success in reading. Katie tried so hard and yet moved forward so slowly. What would happen if she lost that enthusiasm and began to give up? How could her progress be enhanced?

Assessing Oral Language Fluency

Reading is an exercise in language use, and successful reading draws heavily on what children know about language. A reader needs to associate ideas with words, to use language elaborately to express fine shades of meaning that go beyond informal conversation, and to recognize the effects of grammatical structures on the meaning of word strings. In this section we describe two procedures that allow teachers to assess the oral language fluency of children in the context of activities that teach as well as test. The first is the *dictated experience account*, an activity that we will return to throughout this chapter because it offers other diagnostic insights beyond the assessment of oral language fluency. The second of these procedures is *echo reading*, a sentence imitation task based in the language of books. Next we will describe two more assessment approaches, each with a more limited focus. Marie Clay and her associates' *Record of Oral Language* (1982) deal with syntactical knowledge; Joan Tough's observational procedure identifies the functions to which children are able to address their utterances.

Dictated Experience Accounts

These accounts are told aloud by a child and printed, exactly as spoken, by another person. One child can dictate a complete account, or a group can collaborate with several children or each child contributing individual sentences.

Dictated experience accounts are a part of the language experience approach to beginning reading (Stauffer, 1980). Language experience is

Dictated experience stories are an aspect of the language-experience approach to beginning reading. They can be useful in assessing children's oral language fluency.

usually thought of as an instructional method, but dictations and rereadings have considerable value as a diagnostic technique for a small group or an individual child.

MATERIALS

1. Individual account
   a. a stimulus (a hamster, arrowhead collection, picture book, or other concrete object or actual experience the child has just had)
   b. paper and pencil
2. Group story
   a. a stimulus (concrete object or event the group has just experienced together)
   b. an experience chart (a pad of large newsprint)
   c. a felt pen or crayon

PROCEDURES

Whether with an individual or group, the dictated experience account starts with a concrete stimulus, which the children experience directly. The stimulus should be out of the ordinary enough to (a) give the children an urge to talk about it and (b) enable them to remember it two or three days later when the dictation is reread.

After the experience has been enjoyed and discussed, sit down with the students and explain that together you are going to write an account of what has happened. You can begin by having the children talk about the stimulus and writing down some key words they use. Then ask each child to tell something about the experience and write down each one's contribution, including the child's name, like this:

THE STRIP MINE

John said, "We went and saw a strip mine."
Avery said, "It was real deep."
Sheila said, "I was scared we would fall in."
Bobby said, "They dig up coal with big machines."
Sue said, "My daddy works on a strip mine."

Be careful to write down exactly what the children say, regardless of whether the sentences are complete or have errors in syntax, so as to preserve the integrity of their language. When it is all written up, read the whole account aloud two or three times, rapidly pointing to each word or line as it is read. Then ask the children to chorally read the piece with you. The idea is to have them memorize it so that the sentences become firmly anchored in their minds. When they have choral-read it twice or more, and seem confident, ask for volunteers to come forward and read a sentence, or the whole piece, if they can do so. As they recite the sentences, they should point to or underline individual words they know.

You can then make up a duplicating master of the group account and reproduce a copy for each child. These can be illustrated, reread many times, and as additional single words are recognized they should be underlined. Many children collect these accounts in booklets.

The dictated experience account can be done with one child, a small group of children, or a whole class. For diagnostic purposes it is best used with an individual or small group.

The activity can be spread over a number of days: the dictation one day, the choral and individual reading on the second day, and the distribution of copies to the children for individual reading on the third day.

What to Look for in Dictated Experience Accounts. When a child dictates an experience account, the teacher can get an indication of the child's fluency as a language user. Some aspects to consider are:

☐ Does the child speak in sentences, or in single words and word clusters?
☐ Does the child use descriptive names for objects and events or many ambiguous terms like "it," "that," "this thing"?

□ Does the child speak slowly and distinctly, repeating as necessary for the teacher to take the dictation, or blurt out or mumble sentences and then forget what was said?

□ Does the child provide information that a reader who had not experienced the stimulus would need in order to reconstruct the event or assume that everyone has the same information about the event?

The more precise their terms are, the more inclusive their sentences, the more their speech takes into account the listener's informational needs, then the more we would say that they are speaking in an elaborated code. As we learned in Chapter Two, this speech style is closest to the language of books. Children who speak in an elaborated code will learn to read that language more easily than children who speak in a less elaborated code. Perhaps the best summary of the expressive use of language is this: a dictated experience story is "talk written down" (Allen, 1976); nevertheless, the more children's talk sounds like book language, the better their oral language prepares them for learning to read.

Echo Reading

In Chapter Two we noted that language fluency has two aspects that are especially important. One, expressive use of language, can be informally examined by using the dictated story. The other aspect, development of syntax, can be examined by using an *echo-reading* procedure.

We are not speaking here of a reading activity in the traditional sense, for of course we are assessing *prereaders!* In echo reading, the teacher reads a sentence aloud and the child repeats or *echoes* the teacher's words, verbatim if possible, while looking at the line of print. The reading is not independently done but is accomplished in a highly supportive setting. What we are interested in is the precision with which the child can echo the teacher's words.

Syntax, you will recall, is a system of ordering and inflecting words within sentences and ordering sentences within utterances. The intuitive understanding of syntax helps in constructing and understanding sentences with many components. Syntax is a complicated topic, but in the present context of reading diagnosis we are concerned with only a minor aspect of it — namely, that syntactic development can limit the number of words a child can speak in a single sentence, which in turn can hinder the child's reading and discussion of written language, so it is a matter of concern in diagnosis.

 Ordinarily by the time children are about five years old, their utterances are complex and lengthy, and counting the number of words in their sentences has ceased to be a worthwhile enterprise, as it was when they began talking. Some children, however, are still limited in the number of words they can comfortably handle in one sentence when they reach first or second grade. When this is the case, it is sometimes hard to spot, since the paucity of speech may be mistaken for shyness. If the teacher does have a child who is a reluctant speaker, using echo reading is a fairly straightforward means of deciding if there is a lack of syntax.

The procedure for echo reading is as follows:

MATERIALS

Select an eight-line passage from a book written at approximately a first-grade level. To record the echo reading, make a copy of the lines. To keep records on several students, type the lines, triple spaced, and duplicate a copy for each student.

PROCEDURE

1. Sit down with one student at a time in a place that is relatively free of distractions.
2. Explain that you will read the lines aloud and that as you do so you want the student to repeat the words you just read, exactly as you read them.
3. Read a line clearly, stop, and have the student echo it.
4. Repeat for each of the eight lines.
5. As the student echoes, record his or her words on your copy. You may find it convenient to tape record these sessions and score the echo reading later.

Code the echo reading as follows:

1. Place a check mark (√) over each word repeated correctly.
2. Circle words, word parts, or phrases that are omitted.
3. Write in words substituted for those in the line and draw a line through the words that were not repeated.
4. Write in words inserted in the line; use a caret (∧) to indicate where the insertion was made.

Here are some examples.

My new red wagon has four shiny red wheels. (correct and omission)

My brother and I pull things in it. (correct, substitution, and insertion)

Why is the ability to repeat sentences important? It is a curious fact of language development that children cannot accurately repeat a sentence that is more syntactically advanced than one they can produce spontaneously.

If you ask children to repeat a sentence more complicated than one they can produce themselves, they will normally simplify the sentence in the repeated version (Slobin and Welsh, 1971). Here, for example, are some sentence repetitions by young children between two and four years.

1. Adult: Look at the doggy.
    Child: Doggy.
2. Adult: This boy is all wet.
    Child: Boy all wet.
3. Adult: The new bikes and roller skates are over there.
    Child: A new bikes are there and a skates are over there.

The link between children's ability to imitate sentences and the limits of their syntactic ability is fortuitous for language assessment. It enables us to get an idea of the limits of the complexity of their sentences by asking them to repeat sentences we read to them. Thus the method of echo reading can indicate whether a child's syntax is sufficiently developed to encompass the sentence patterns encountered in reading books written on a given level. Experience tells us that if the language patterns of a book do not lie within the children's control, they will be at a disadvantage in reading that book. And occasionally, reading teachers encounter children whose syntax is not adequate for any but the simplest books.

What to Look for in Echo Reading. One or two words deleted or substituted per sentence are not a cause for alarm, especially if the child substituted a familiar for a less familiar word such as *store* for *shop*. Similarly, if the child leaves off grammatical endings, plural markers on nouns, or tense markers on verbs, it is considered normal if he or she belongs to a dialect group that usually omits these endings. If, however, the child regularly leaves out important words or rewords whole phrases, it is more serious. In the examples above, 1 and 2 show important elements omitted.

If children have a great deal of trouble with a basal reader, it is helpful to find out what they *can* successfully echo-read. It is easier to echo-read material written with predictable patterns of language, such as nursery rhymes and simple poems and jingles. If the children are still having trouble even with this kind of material, you should observe whether or not they are taking advantage of the rhythm of the sentences. Do they repeat the sentences rhythmically? If not, make them tap their hands on the table along with you as they recite. Getting into the rhythm of the language will often help them repeat longer sentence patterns.

The important thing here is to find out what the children *can* do once the limits of their syntactic development have been found — that is, the length and type of sentence where their repetition falls below about 80 percent of the words, dialectical variances excluded. In these cases, their language in response to books will have to be drawn out before reading instruction can successfully proceed. Songs, poems, rhythm games and chants, and dictated experience accounts should all be used lavishly, as well as any simple books with a pattern (a rhyming or rhythmic element, as many books for young children have).

A Structured Sentence Imitation Task: The "Record of Oral Language"

While the level of difficulty of the echo-reading task (see above) can be set to any level of text by the selection of the sentences out of which it is constructed, a more standardized version of the same task assigns kindergartner and first graders as having high, average, and low levels of syntactical development. This device, *The Record of Oral Language* by Marie Clay and associates, also has provisions for pinpointing the kinds of sentence constructions (the *basic sentence patterns*), as well as specific transformations of these patterns (including *passives, imperatives, interrogatives,* and several types of *imbeddings*).

The *Record of Oral Language* is based on the same principle as echo reading. The groups of sentences to be repeated are carefully controlled for their form and their complexity, however, and they are arranged in three levels of difficulty. This test comes bound in book form (the pages can be reproduced) with clear instructions for administering the test and scoring the children's responses. Also provided is a detailed discussion of the syntactic structures being tested, the origins of the test, and the average scores of large groups of students for purposes of comparison. Because these students were all in New Zealand, however, it is inadvisable for American teachers to use these data *verbatim* in judging the performance of their students. A safer approach will be to administer the test to one or more whole classes of students and determine the range of scores that emerge (see Chapter Eight for a discussion of ways of setting up and interpreting test norms).

A sample page from the *Record of Oral Language* is found in Figure 3.1.

Biks and Gutches

Knowledge of syntax has two aspects: the ordering of words in sentences and the inflections added to words that signal information (e.g., person, number, and tense of verbs, plurality in nouns, and comparatives in adjectives). The *Record of Oral Language* tests primarily the first sort of syntactical knowledge: sentence structure. Marie Clay and her associates have developed another test to investigate the second aspect of syntactical knowledge, word inflections. This test, derived from a famous experiment into children's knowledge of word inflections by Jean Berko (1958), is administered orally to one child at a time by the teacher, who reads an opening sentence that sets up a meaningful context, then pauses at a point where the child must supply a version of a word with its proper inflection (see Figure 3.2 for examples).

There is solid research evidence that the ability to use word inflections

FIGURE 3.1. Sample page from the *Record of Oral Language*.

Class: ....   School: ....   Child's Name: ....
Date of Birth: ....   Date: ....   Age: ....
                                                            Recorder: ....

The Levels Sentences

Level 2 Part 1.
TYPE
A   *That big dog over there is going to be my brother's.*   ☐
B   *The boy by the pond was sailing his boat.*   ☐
C   *The bird flew to the top of the tree.*   ☐
D   *For his birthday Kiri gave him a truck.*   ☐
E   *Can you see what is climbing up the wall?*   ☐
F   *Here comes a big elephant with children sitting on his back.*   ☐
G   *My brother turned the radio up very loud.*   ☐

Level 2 Part 2.
Type
A   *That old truck in there used to be my father's.*   ☐
B   *The cat from next door was chasing a bird.*   ☐
C   *The dog ran through the hole in the fence.*   ☐
D   *For the holidays Grandpa bought us a ball.*   ☐
E   *The boy saw what the man was doing to the car.*   ☐
F   *There is my baby riding in his pushchair.*   ☐
G   *The girl threw her book right across the room.*   ☐

Total for Level 2 ☐

Enter 14 on the next page if all Level is credited.

SOURCE: Marie Clay et al., *The Record of Oral Language and Biks and Gutches* (Auckland: Heinemann Publishers Ltd., 1982), p. 20. Reprinted by permission.

grows steadily along with, and can be an indicator of, general language development (Dale, 1972; Selby, 1972; Kirk and McCarthy, 1966). However, the authors of *Biks and Gutches* report that the scores on their test vary widely with the size of the groups to which it is given and the dialect group to which the subjects belong. Rather than supply norms against which an individual child's performance should be judged, Clay et al. suggest that the test be used experimentally for the various purposes of gaining insight into this aspect of children's language growth in general, determining if children are making progress in language growth (which assumes the test will be given

FIGURE 3.2. Sample questions to test syntactical knowledge.

Biks and gutches

11 This is a bik and here is another bik.
   There are two ____.   (biks)
12 There is a gutch and here is another gutch.
   There are two _____.   (gutches)

Open the door

The children said to the lady, 'Open the door.'
4 The lady is _____ the door.   (opening)
5 But she is careful when she _____ it.   (opens)
6 Yesterday she nearly knocked the little girl over
   when she _____ the door.   (opened)

SOURCE: Marie Clay et al., *The Record of Oral Language and Biks and Gutches* (Auckland: Heinemann Publishers Ltd., 1982), pp. 58, 59, 62, 63. Reprinted by permission.

repeatedly at intervals throughout the year) and investigating how well speakers of other languages or dialects are acquiring the inflections of standard English.

The Range of Children's Language: Joan Tough's Approach

There is much more to language than syntax. In Chapter Two we investigated Bernstein's notion of the restricted and elaborated codes, Halliday's seven functions to which children put language, and Tough's extension of Halliday's work, in which she identified a rather different set of seven uses of language, each with a subset of "supporting strategies" (see page 37 in this book). Tough developed an extensive assessment program to investigate children's growth in each of the areas she identified (see her book *Listening to Children Talking*, available from Heinemann Educational Books, 4 Front Street, Exeter, New Hampshire 03833).

For each of Tough's subcategories of language use (e.g., *directing: monitoring own actions*) sample children's sentences are provided to make the category clearer (e.g., for the above, "Turning it 'round. The lorry's going 'round," p. 82), as well as extensive discussion of what is meant by the category. There are exercises for the teacher to practice categorizing samples of children's speech using Tough's system, and whole transcripts of children's speech for the teacher to analyze using the categories.

Tough's assessment system employs a series of action-filled drawings accompanied by a set of questions for the teacher to use in eliciting children's commentary on the pictures. The questions are chosen to draw out language from the whole range of uses in Tough's system.

Tough's categories of language use are well thought out. It is possible to use them during informal observations of children's language; however, the series of pictures enables the teacher to observe a far wider range of language use in a shorter time. Because her book is so well illustrated and because the pictures are such a valuable assessment device, we recommend the purchase of this book to anyone wanting to go more deeply into the assessment of children's language.

Assessing the Sense of Story Structures

A sense of story structures is an important aspect of prereading competence. Children should recognize a main character when one appears, sense a complication when one arises, and actively wonder how the main character will overcome the problems of the story. Children with a sense of story structure can make the most of the information that a story presents them. Those without this sense will not be able to tell an important event from a minor detail and may have little comprehension of a story even after hearing and understanding all of the words.

We suggest two procedures for assessing a sense of story. The first is a predictive questioning procedure known as the *directed listening-thinking activity*. The second is the *oral retelling of stories*.

The Directed Listening-Thinking Activity

This procedure, developed by Russell Stauffer (1980), is another assessment activity that also teaches, and the predictive questioning it employs fits well into the classroom instructional routine.

MATERIALS

You need a storybook or picture book that has a good, strong plot with the elements of story structure described in the preceding chapter.

PROCEDURE

The teacher reads the story aloud in parts, pausing several times just before some important event to ask the students to predict or guess what they think might happen next in the story, to summarize what they have found out in previous sections, and to determine what they still need to know. The aim is to get them to hypothesize about what *might* occur and what seems *most likely*. All predictions are accepted noncommittally regardless of whether they turn out to be correct.

The directed listening-thinking activity may be done with an individual, small group, or whole class. The spirit of friendly give-and-take and the proliferation of ideas the children generate make a group session preferable to an individual session.

What to Look for in the Directed Listening-Thinking Activity. Reading a story with the predictive questions of a directed listening-thinking activity demonstrates two aspects of children's orientation to stories. First is their attitude toward them; second is their sense of story structure.

1. When you announce the activity, which children come quickly and enthusiastically to the circle? Which ones do not? Over a number of trials, this is an indicator of expectations and attitudes toward books and reading.
2. When shown the cover or illustration of a book, do the children expect the cover to contain clues to the story? Do they expect the title to contain clues? Do they expect the pictures to give information? Their comments and predictions will reveal whether they have such expectations.
3. After a part of the story has been read and they are asked to make predictions:
   a. Do they make any predictions at all?
   b. If so, are their predictions:
      1. wild and random?

2. based on what might happen in real life?
3. based on story logic and story structures?
c. Can they give a reason or justification for their predictions?

These questions reveal their ability to sense the structure of a story and use it to predict upcoming events. As we have seen, this is an important component of prereading.

Oral Retelling of Stories

Another probe of children's awareness of story structure is to ask them to retell the story in their own words. Their retellings can be compared with the original for completeness and also analyzed for their story structure.

We can expect a youngster's retelling to have many of the structural elements of the original story: the setting, the initiating event, the goal, one or more attempts, or the resolution.

One retelling, however, is not an accurate measure of sensitivity to story structure. A child may not like a certain story or feel like saying much on a given day. On the other hand, if a child on two or more occasions leaves out most of the structural elements in the retelling and does not venture good story-based predictions in the predictive questioning activity, it indicates that this child has not yet learned to function well with stories.

Happily, the solution follows the same process as the assessment: read and talk about lots more stories! It is through rich exposure to stories read aloud that youngsters abstract these structures and develop expectations about stories. Nothing can substitute for being read to daily. The predictive questioning group activity just described is an excellent vehicle for bringing children and stories together and helping them to develop a sense of story structure and language.

Assessing the Speech-to-Print Match

As described in Chapter Two, the speech-to-print match refers to one's ability to match spoken words with the same words as they appear in print. Children gain this ability only after they have acquired the following concepts about written language: (a) words are separable units; (b) printed words have spaces on either side that separate them from other words; and (c) words and syllables are not necessarily the same things. Therefore, dividing a line of writing up into its audible syllables or "beats" will not necessarily be an accurate way to separate the line into words (Morris, 1979).

The speech-to-print match can be assessed by informal means, either in a special *voice-pointing* procedure or as a follow-up to a dictated experience story.

The Voice-Pointing Procedure

This technique is best carried out by the teacher with one child at a time, although good results can be obtained with two or even three children at once.

MATERIALS

You will need a short poem or a very memorable story, four lines long. A nursery rhyme, jingle, verse from a simple song, or similar material is perfect. Print or type the lines on paper or tagboard and triple space the lines. If large type is available, use that, because it helps the children to locate the printed words.

We have found that rhythmic children's stories like Martin and Brogan's (1971) *Instant Readers* work well with prereaders. These little books come in sets that include titles like *Brown Bear, Brown Bear, What Do You See?* and *Whistle, Mary, Whistle,* which have just the right elements of rhythmic, repetitious language and strong picture clues to make the lines easy to memorize and repeat. It is necessary for the child to learn to recite the lines confidently before the procedure begins, so choose some easily memorized text. Be sure that within the four lines you choose there are at least two words of more than one syllable.

Make a set of eight word cards, which you can use to see if the child already knows how to read any of these words from the text. For the word cards, choose two words from the beginnings of lines, two words from the ends of lines, and four words from the middles of lines. Two of the eight words chosen should be longer than one syllable. For example:

> *Twinkle,* twinkle little *star,*
> How *I* wonder *what* you are.
> *Up* above the *world* so high,
> Like a *diamond* in the *sky.*

PROCEDURE

1. Use the word cards to pretest recognition of the words.
2. Recite the lines until the child has memorized them but has *not yet* seen them in print.
3. Read the lines aloud, pointing to each word as you read.
4. Have the child recite the lines and point to the words while doing so.
5. Read selected words aloud and ask the child to point them out.
6. Use the word cards to posttest recognition of those words; the child may now recognize some or all of them as a result of the activity.

The first and sixth steps, using the word cards, are intended to show if the child already knew any of the words before the exercise and if any of those selected were learned during the exercise. You should take note of the number of words recognized, if any, during steps 1 and 6.

The second step, memorizing the lines, is not timed or scored. It is important not to show the child the printed lines until after this stage is completed. Later on you will want to see how easily he or she can form associations between spoken words and printed ones, so it is important not to teach these associations inadvertently at this stage. Make sure that the child knows the lines before going on, inasmuch as children differ in how many repetitions they need to memorize the lines.

In the third step, you model the voice-pointing procedure. Read each line at a normal speed and point to each word as you read but make sure that the child is watching your finger. Then, in step 4 ask the child to do the same thing, one line at a time. As each line is recited and pointed to, observe how accurately the child matches the spoken and printed words.

It is easier to keep track of the child's performance in step 5. This time you should call out the eight words that you put on the word cards, one at a time, and ask the child to point to them. It is to be expected that children will have to recite the entire line to themselves while searching for each word, so do not show them the word card but just pronounce the word and see if they can "count" across or between lines to find it. Keep track of how successful each child was in this search.

In the last step, scramble the order of the word cards and see if any of the words are now recognizable in isolation. Keep track of the child's performance on this posttest step.

At the conclusion of this activity, you should have:

□ pre- and posttest scores of the child's recognition of words from the text in isolation
□ observations of the child's voice-pointing performance
□ a score of the number of spoken words he or she could identify in the context of the printed lines

What to Look for in the Voice-Pointing Procedure. This procedure directly tests three important components of beginning reading:

1. the concept of the word as a written unit in print;
2. the ability to recognize words in a meaningful context;
3. the ability to learn new words from a supported reading activity.

Research with this procedure by Morris (1979), who developed it, has indicated that children tend to fall into three groups by their responses:

1. One group of children perform poorly on word recognition and on the voice-pointing procedure. Their posttest scores show little or no improvement over their pretest scores. They cannot yet reliably match speech to memorized print, and they are not able to learn to recognize words even in a repetitious and highly supportive learning context like

this activity. Until they develop a concept of word through more exposure to and experience with print, they will probably not profit from beginning reading instruction. The best program for these children is to read to them a great deal, to have them memorize rhymes and poems and practice the read-and-point routine.

2. Another group knows some words in isolation. These children can eventually identify words in context after they have learned to count through the line to the target word, reciting as they go. Their posttest score on word recognition in context is higher than their pretest score.

   These children show some proficiency at pointing to words in a line, but two-syllable words usually throw them, which indicates an unstable word concept. Their word recognition in isolation posttest shows some improvement over the pretest, but they do not get more than half the words right.

   This performance indicates that these children are making progress toward developing a concept of a word in print but that they need more practice at tasks similar to the testing procedure to help them develop this concept. You can accomplish this with any easily memorized text: dictated stories, poems, jingles, nursery rhymes, and songs.

3. A third group of children may miss the words from the story on the pretest of word recognition in isolation. Their voice pointing will be nearly perfect, however, and they will be able to correct any errors in voice pointing very quickly and confidently. Their posttest recognition of words in isolation is nearly perfect, which shows that they have learned several new words from this brief reading activity.

   The children in this group are ready to begin formal reading instruction. The practice of reading new material with the support of a meaningful context produces new words for these children and rapidly expands their vocabulary in each new encounter with print. As they begin reading simple basal stories, they should have frequent experience with dictated stories and simple poems in order to reinforce their expectation that print matches speech and is predictable.

Using Voice Pointing with a Dictated Experience Story. Dictated experience stories provide excellent opportunities for teachers to test and develop a child's speech-to-print match. Earlier in this chapter we introduced the dictated story of "The Strip Mine" in which John dictates a sentence and the teacher reads the passage twice and then chorally reads it with the children. There is a good probability that John will remember his sentence, because he just said it: "John said, 'We went and saw a strip mine.' " He probably can recognize his own name, too. If the teacher asks him to read the sentence aloud he will be able to do so, perhaps even with his eyes closed! If the teacher asks him to point to his name, *John,* he should be able to do it. If she asks him to point to each word in the sentence as he says it, he probably will do so even though he may be a little hesitant. Now the question is: Can he point to a single word like *mine* or *saw*? If he can, he is showing signs of the speech-to-print match. He can recognize that bound configurations on the page correspond to spoken words in his head. This is how the sixth word, for example, in his spoken sentence comes to match the sixth word in his written sentence.

Assessing Phonemic Segmentation by Means of Invented Spelling

As we noted in Chapter Two, an important prerequisite for learning to recognize words is the ability to segment the word into its smallest constituent sounds, or *phonemes* (see pages 56–58). While a few words can be used as whole words before a child can segment phonemes, in order to begin to form generalizations about the ways groups of letters represent sounds — the basis of the *orthographic knowledge* we described in Chapter Two), a person must first be able to break a word up into its constituent parts.

The most natural way to observe whether or not a child has this ability is to ask him or her to spell words that he or she does not already know. By asking words the child does not know, we ask the child to rely upon his or her *invented spelling,* the inner capacity to forge connections between letters and sounds. As we shall see in Chapter Seven, children have an amazing intuitive ability to invent spellings, and we can learn very much about their word knowledge by looking at their invented productions.

A procedure for testing phonemic segmentation, then, is to have the child spell a list of words that you call out. Try a list such as the following:

bite	(three phonemes)
seat	(three phonemes)
dear	(three phonemes)
bones	(four phonemes)
load	(three phonemes)
fold	(four phonemes)
race	(three phonemes)
roar	(three phonemes)
beast	(four phonemes)
groan	(four phonemes)

Explain to the child that you want to see how he or she believes words are spelled. You're going to ask him to spell some words you know he doesn't know how to spell. After you call out each word (at least twice, and as many more times as the student requests), ask the student to try to spell each sound in the word. If the student says he can't, ask him to listen to the way the word begins. What sound does it start with? He should write down a letter for that sound and letters for any other sounds he can hear. If the

student is not sure how to spell a sound, he or she may write a little dash
(—).

After reading all ten words (fewer, if the test seems too arduous for a
particular child), count the number of letters the child wrote for each word,
and compare that to the number of phonemes in the word. A child who
consistently writes three or four letters that show some reasonable connection to the sounds in the word appears able to segment phonemes. A child
who writes nothing or strings together many letters indiscriminately is not
yet able to segment phonemes, while a child who writes one or two reasonable letters per word is just beginning to segment phonemes. See Chapter
Seven for further information about invented spelling.

Assessing Print Orientation Concepts

Marie Clay's *Concepts About Print Test* (1972) assesses a number of aspects of a
child's orientation to books and to written language that are not dealt with
elsewhere. This test is highly recommended for kindergarten and primary
grade teachers as well as for reading clinics. It comes with one of two
reusable books and is available from Heinemann Educational Books, 8 Front
Street, Exeter, New Hampshire 03833.

The aspects of the Concepts About Print Test that are especially relevant
to the present discussion of prereading competencies are:

☐ book orientation knowledge
☐ principles involving the directional arrangement of print on the page
☐ the knowledge that print, not the picture, contains the story
☐ understanding of important reading terminology like *word, letter, beginning of the sentence, top of the page,* and so on
☐ understanding of simple punctuation marks

The assessment of orientation concepts about written language can be
carried out by using a simple illustrated children's book, one that the child
being tested has not seen before. *The Concepts about Print Test* has two
specially made books (*Sand* and *Stones*) but teachers can get much of the
flavor of the procedure with a book of their own choosing. The following are
some concepts that can be tested and the procedures for them:

1. Knowledge of the layout of books. Hand the child the book, with the spine
facing the child, and say, "Show me the *front* of the book." Make a note as to
whether the child correctly identifies the front.

2. Knowledge that print, not pictures, are what we read. Open the book
directly to a place where print is on one page and a picture is on the other
(you should make sure beforehand that the book has such a pair of pages,
and have it bookmarked for easy location). Then say: "Show me where I
begin reading." Observe carefully to see whether the child points to the print

or the picture. If the pointing gesture is vague, say, "Where, exactly?" If the child points to the print, note whether or not the child points to the upper left-hand corner of the page.

3. *Directional orientation of print on the page.* Stay on the same set of pages and after the child points at some spot on the printed page, say, "Show me with your finger where I go next." Then observe whether the child sweeps his or her finger across the printed line from left to right or moves it in some other direction.

Then ask, "Where do I go from there?" and observe whether the child correctly makes the return sweep to the left, and drops down one line.

Note that a correct directional pattern is like this:

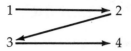

If the child indicates some other directional pattern, make a note of it.

4. *Knowledge of the concepts of beginning and end.* Turning now to a new page, say, "Point to the beginning of the story on this page," and then "Point to the end of the story on this page." Observe whether the child interprets both requests properly.

5. *Knowledge of the terms top and bottom.* Turning to another pair of pages that have print on one and a picture on the other, point to the *middle* of the printed page and say, "Show me the bottom of the page," and then "Show me the top of the page." Then point to the *middle* of the picture and say, "Show me the top of the picture," and then "Show me the bottom of the picture." Note whether or not the child responds accurately to all four requests.

6. *Knowledge of the terms word and letter.* Now hand the child two blank index cards and say, "Put these cards on the page so that just *one word* shows between them," and then "Now move them so that *two words* show between them." "Now move them again so that *one letter* shows between them," and then "Now move them so that *two letters* show between them." Make note of the child's response to all four requests.

7. *Knowledge of uppercase and lowercase letters.* On the same page, point to a capital letter with your pencil and say, "Show me a little letter that is the same as this one." (Beforehand, make sure that there is a corresponding lowercase letter on the page.) Next point to a lowercase letter and say, "Now point to a capital letter that is the same as this one." (Again, make sure that there *is* one.) You may repeat this procedure with other pairs of letters if the child's response seems uncertain.

8. *Knowledge of punctuation.* Turn to a page that has a period, an exclamation point, a question mark, a comma, and a set of quotation marks. Pointing

to each one in turn, ask, "What is this? What is it for?" Note whether or not the child answers correctly for each of the five punctuation marks.

In order to follow this assessment procedure efficiently, you will have to choose a book carefully and practice using the assessment questions enough times to become proficient. The procedure is easily carried out with Marie Clay's own test booklet, which is well worth the nominal cost.

The Concepts about Print Test was extensively reviewed by Yetta Goodman (1981), who has long been interested in what young children know about print and who has suggested several perceptive adaptations to the test. She recommended using a trade book relevant to the experience of the children rather than using Clay's *Sand* or *Stones*, which accompany the test. Goodman felt that the particular children pictured and their particular activities might not be culturally relevant to all. She also urged that teachers read the entire book to the children before asking the orientation questions because she found that some of the children she worked with became impatient with the interruptions of the story for the questioning.

It is advisable to make up a record sheet that provides for the quick recording of information yielded by the assessment. Clay's own test is matched with a scoring system. We believe, however, that it is sufficient simply to make a list of those print orientation competencies the children do or do not have. Then, as you work with them in simple trade books and basals, with dictated stories and by reading aloud to them, you can begin to draw their attention to the concepts they have not yet mastered: the direction of print, capital and lowercase letters, periods, and the like.

Teaching Print Orientation Concepts

How do we help children develop print orientation concepts? Don Holdaway (1979), a careful reader of his compatriot, Marie Clay, has tackled this problem for us. He begins by noting that there are practical problems to be overcome in teaching groups of children about print. Books, after all, are usually just big enough to be read by one person. If a teacher tries to point out features of print to a group of children sitting around her, it's not likely that they will be able to see, say, the spaces between words if she uses a textbook to point them out. Besides, if she sits so that she is facing them, her book will be oriented upside down to them unless she holds it up upside down to her.

The solution, Holdaway proposes, is the "big book:" a giant, three-foot-high version of the readers the children are using (see Figure 3.3). The teacher can place a big book on a chart stand where it can be readily seen by a group of children and have them read along with her as she points out features of print: where the text begins on a page; the left-to-right direction of reading; the return sweep; the spaces that demarcate words; and punctuation.

The Concepts about Print Test helps reveal young readers' ideas about books and print. *Above,* Jessica points out the bottom of the printed page of a book with elements such as upside-down prints and pictures and scrambled words.

In New Zealand, these big books are usually made by the teacher or a parent volunteer. They might be chosen to accompany a reading series of which the children have copies; that way the children can look for the features on the page in front of them that the teacher points out in the big book. Big book versions are also made up from favorite trade books. When children already know and are excited about the story line, they can more easily pay attention to the way the print portrays the text, which is the point of this sort of lesson. In Canada, Holt, Rinehart and Winston, Ltd., publish big books to accompany their basal series. They have also recently added big book versions of Bill Martin, Jr.'s, *Instant Readers.* We are told that these books will soon be marketed in the United States as well, but they can now be ordered from Holt, Rinehart and Winston (Canada), Ltd.

Sight Word Recognition

Before children can read independently (i.e., before they can make sense of text they have not dictated or heard read aloud), they must accumulate a number of sight words. Words that children recognize immediately are

FIGURE 3.3. Teaching print orientation concepts using the "big book."

SOURCE: Don Holdaway, *The Foundations of Literacy* (Gosford, N.S.W.: Ashton Scholastic, 1979), p. 65. Reprinted by permission.

stepping stones that help them get through text that contains unknown words. Without sight words, reading is reduced to word-by-word decoding, and while this resembles reading in some superficial ways, it is not reading in a meaningful sense.

It is therefore important to see if children have begun to acquire some sight words. We cannot productively ask them to name all the words they can recognize in print, however. We must instead construct a sample list of words they are likely to encounter in beginning reading, test them on those, and estimate from their performance what proportion of typical words they are apt to recognize as sight words in other contexts.

A *sight word inventory* can be made up by the teacher from early reading material. Here are the steps:

MATERIALS

1. Get a copy of the earliest reading books that have simple sentences. These are usually preprimers and primers. You probably can omit the commercial readiness books, as they usually feature only single words.
2. Open the first book to a page approximately a third of the way through.
3. Select the fifth word on that page and every fifth word thereafter until ten words have been selected.
4. Eliminate any repetitions of words already selected and replace them by the sampling method in step 3.
5. Select ten words from each of the next readers, using the process outlined in steps 2 through 4.
6. Type or print (in large letters) each group of five words together on a piece of tagboard, arranging them in columns like this:

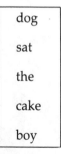

dog

sat

the

cake

boy

Don't label the lists according to the reading level; just arrange the lists in order, beginning with the easiest.
7. Make a ditto master of the word list and run off a copy for every child to be tested.

PROCEDURES

This procedure is used with one child at a time. If you are right-handed, sit with the child on your left. Put the tagboard with the word list in front of the child and a duplicated copy of the list by your right hand. (If you are left-handed, the placement is reversed.) Using two index cards, frame one word at a time to the child, asking, "What is this word?" "How about this one?" Put a check mark ($\checkmark$) on your sheet next to every word the child recognizes. You can put an X next to any word the child did not know at sight but was able to figure out. Continue until all the words have been exposed unless the student becomes frustrated or unhappy with this experience, which may happen if the child knows only a few sight words. Use your judgment and stop if the child gets discouraged.

Record the percentage of correct identifications for each list on the score sheet, along with the date and child's name, and keep the paper for later reference. As sight vocabulary grows, so will reading proficiency.

Basal readers differ quite widely in the number of new words introduced at each level, the number of times they are repeated, the syntactic complexity of the sentences, and the degree to which the sentences sound like natural language. Some primers use forty or fewer words arranged in short, repetitious sentences; others have fewer vocabulary controls and feature a hundred or more different words and fairly lengthy sentences. Some basal series teach a core of ten to twenty basic words at the end of the readiness level so that children using preprimers have a few sight words established; in other series, the first words are introduced in the preprimers. Consequently, what constitutes an adequate score on the sight word inventory depends on what program you are using and where in the program the child is. We're not hedging; hard-and-fast criteria for everyone just cannot be established.

The best procedure is to look at your own students and their books. Try out the inventory with a number of children from all ability levels. Include some children you are sure can already read a little and compare their performance with the nonreaders. Using other informal assessments as well, determine what range of scores on the sight words is associated with each group of children: those who have begun to read, those who seem to be about ready to begin, and those who are not ready to read at all even with help. Normally, children who have begun to read and are comfortable in preprimers and primers will recognize about 90 percent of the words in these books; those just beginning to read with help will identify about 70 percent of the words; and those who are not yet ready will identify fewer than 50 percent even at the earliest levels.

Letter Recognition

Everything in reading education is controversial, even the teaching of the alphabet. Most educators, however, believe that children who do not know the letters of the alphabet are usually at a disadvantage when it comes to learning to read. If your students do not have the ability to read, it is a good idea to verify with an alphabet inventory whether or not they can identify all the letters, both upper- and lowercase.

There are two reasons to go to the trouble of making up a special assessment device for the letters of the alphabet. The first is to test their recognition out of the order in which they are usually recited. The *abcdefg* . . . routine is strong enough to cue an unknown letter by a known letter occurring before or after it. The *a-b-c* order, however, isn't very helpful when the letters are in words, and if a true test of letter recognition is to be made, the letters must be presented out of the normal order.

The second reason for preparing a special letter recognition inventory is to test children's ability to recognize different typefaces. The lowercase letters a and g have alternate forms ɑ and ɡ, respectively, and children will sometimes fail to recognize both forms. Also, delayed readers have trouble associating handwritten letter forms with their printed counterparts. If this is suspected, then the teacher can prepare a different version of a letter recognition inventory that mixes handwritten and typed forms of the same letters.

MATERIALS

To prepare a letter recognition inventory, type a set of letters on sturdy paper with a triple space above and below each letter. Then prepare a duplicator master of the same list. Score sheets can be run off from the master. (These could be combined with the sight word inventory to make up a single test.)

Here is a randomly ordered list of letters that can be used for testing:

d	f	t	g	n	b	e	h	l	v	o	y	m	ɑ
a	r	c	q	z	u	s	j	p	i	x	k	w	ɡ

F	W	D	T	N	R	A	C	G	Z	B	Q	E
V	J	O	I	Y	P	M	X	K	H	L	S	U

PROCEDURES

As you proceed from left to right across the line, point to each letter and ask the child what it is. You may wish to enter on the record sheet only a notation of what letters were misidentified or unnamed.

Many beginning readers will have difficulty recognizing Z, Q, V, and perhaps one or two other letters encountered out of sequence. Difficulty with b, d, p, q, and g is also common because of directional confusion. Children who confuse these letters in isolation may still read them correctly in words, though they will be more uncertain than those who do not confuse them. Children who have difficulty identifying letters other than these are not likely to begin reading soon. They will need more experience with print and letters before reading instruction can begin.

Cognitive Maturity

When we have taken into account all of the factors we have associated with the readiness to learn to read — oral language fluency, familiarity with books and the purposes of reading, the sense of story structures, the speech-to-print match, print orientation concepts, sight word recognition, and letter recognition — is there not still some other underlying factor whose presence makes a child ready to read? If so, the best candidate would seem to be a maturing of the mind. Child developmentalists such as Elkind (1973) have argued that a child must be capable of what Piaget called *concrete operational thought* before the several demands reading makes on the mind come within her power. We would not quarrel with that claim. Surely when a child grows in all of the areas we have explored in this chapter, she has grown mentally. But growth in the particular is easier to nurture than growth in general. We can stimulate children's language, and give them daily rich experiences with stories and with print; and after months, perhaps many months, we can watch them grow to the point when they begin to read.

Case Studies

LISA

Lisa was the small, shy first grader who was having little success learning to read in Ms. Decker's first-grade class. Her performance was erratic, she was unable to remember new material, and after six weeks of instruction she grew discouraged. Her cohorts in the low reading group were capable of making faster progress than Lisa, but Ms. Decker didn't want her to miss out on the group interaction.

Ms. Decker discussed with her supervisor the possibility that Lisa was unready for first-grade work. Several things pointed to this immediately: she was still only five when she began first grade; she was somewhat undersized; she was shy and timid; and she seemed overwhelmed at times by the demands of first grade. A meeting with Lisa's kindergarten teacher confirmed that she had been a pleasant, compliant child in kindergarten but that she had been shy and made few friends that year. The kindergarten teacher's judgment, however, was that Lisa would probably "grow out of her shyness" in first grade and that there seemed to be no reason for holding her in kindergarten.

Ms. Decker had been gathering various kinds of informal information about Lisa's abilities since the first weeks of school. She summarized it as follows:

1. Oral language. Lisa was adequately developed in this respect, but she rarely spoke spontaneously and sometimes had to be "really pulled" to get her to talk.

Lisa had dictated a number of group and individual experience stories, and although her language was complete and well formed, it was "terse"; one or two sentences were all she would produce. She always had great trouble memorizing dictated stories, and she rarely remembered one for more than a few days. She could echo-read a dictated story with little difficulty but had trouble repeating the longer sentences found in library books. After echoing a few sentences she usually wanted to stop.

2. *Sense of story structures.* This ability was somewhat hard to judge. In a directed listening-thinking activity, Lisa would rarely offer a prediction. She enjoyed listening to stories but never volunteered a prediction and usually said "I don't know" if asked directly. When Ms. Decker tried this activity individually with Lisa, she did offer a few simple predictions, but her guesses were very tentative and didn't always make sense. Her retellings of stories she had heard were always very brief and lacked main events as well as supporting detail.

3. *Speech-to-print match.* In dictated stories, Lisa had much difficulty with voice pointing even after many repetitions. She would get off the track when she came to words of more than one syllable, and she would reach the end of a sentence in print before she had said all the words in the sentence. She also had trouble remembering the sentences and often stumbled in reciting them. After much practice, Lisa did learn to recite and voice-point in two very simple repetitious trade books. She enjoyed rereading these books to herself and pointing to the words, but she preferred to practice reading these two books rather than trying new stories.

4. *Print orientation concepts.* Lisa was fairly well developed in this capacity. She knew which way print went, what letters and words were, and how books were laid out. She could discriminate between capital and lowercase letters but when she wrote she produced both at random.

5. *Word and letter recognition.* Lisa had a lot of trouble remembering the names of all the letters and more trouble remembering their sounds. She learned to recognize only her own name in print, which she often wrote as LIAS or LIA. In spite of much practice, she was unable to remember for very long the letters or the sounds she had been taught and was nowhere near learning to decode words yet.

When all the evidence was weighed, Ms. Decker and her supervisor could see that in almost every important way, Lisa was not ready for beginning reading instruction. She had just barely acquired but had not yet mastered the basic prereading competencies. She needed a great deal more experience with books and print, as well as greater socialization and oral language fluency, before beginning reading instruction could be a successful venture.

It was recommended that Lisa be returned to kindergarten for the rest of the school year and begin first grade the next fall. Her parents were uncertain at first, but they had noticed her growing unhappiness, and they reported that she had asked several times if she could just stay at home and not go to school anymore. They needed little convincing to see that Lisa was unready for the demands that had been placed on her and that she needed another year of growing up.

Certain other recommendations were made to ensure that Lisa got the experiences she needed:

1. Parents and teachers should read stories to her several times daily, sometimes asking her to guess about upcoming events. Some stories

should be read uninterrupted, just for enjoyment so that she would be encouraged to retell stories as fully as possible.

2. Oral language should be developed as fully as possible by encouraging Lisa to tell stories, give descriptions and explanations, and recount stories for dictation. Her kindergarten teacher was encouraged to make use of a commercial self-awareness program for young children and to make sure that Lisa was included in it.

3. Several times weekly, Lisa should dictate a story at home or school, practice voice pointing, retell the story in other words, and identify letters and words within the story. Not much emphasis should be placed on her learning new words, but the dictation should be used to build her experience base with print.

After a few weeks in kindergarten, Lisa's parents reported that she seemed to be much happier and more relaxed now that she had less tension, and she began to make progress again.

KATIE

Katie was the second grader who had been retained in first grade and was now almost nine. She was a sweet, cheerful child who enjoyed helping her teacher and the other students. She never got discouraged in spite of her slow progress, but in October of second grade she was barely holding her own in a primer.

Given Katie's age and her retention the year before, Ms. Whittier knew that transfer to a lower grade was not a good alternative. The school psychologist gave Katie an intelligence test, and since she scored at the low end of the average range, it was recommended that she stay in the regular classroom rather than going into a special education class. Ms. Whittier knew it was up to her to help Katie learn to read successfully that year.

Myra Whittier reviewed with her supervisor what was known of Katie's ability and background. She was the oldest of the girls in her family and several of her older brothers had also experienced reading problems. Little reading was done at home and school achievement was not emphasized. Her hours after school were usually spent caring for the younger children.

In both her years in first grade Katie was well liked by teachers and peers but made little academic progress. She had almost no prereading experience with books or print and was slow to learn letters, sounds, and words. Although her oral language was underdeveloped at first, much work had been done in this area in the past two years, and now her oral language was normally developed and she expressed herself freely and fully.

By fall of second grade Katie was operating with print much like a normally developing first grader. Her oral language was adequate. She had now heard enough stories read to have some sense of story, and she made enthusiastic and logical predictions in directed listening-thinking activities, which she loved. She was particularly apt at remembering and retelling stories and often told these stories to her young charges at home to entertain them. Katie knew all the letters, uppercase and lowercase, and had all her print orientation concepts mastered. She knew a lot of letter sounds and could recognize about forty to fifty different words in print. She could read simple sentences using high-frequency words if there were picture clues to follow, and she could do some rudimentary decoding of simple words.

Myra Whittier and her supervisor agreed that Katie was a normal child who had reached a level of prereading competence later than many other children. Coming to school with very little preliterate experience with print, it had taken her the last two years to acquire the necessary competencies and experiential background to begin reading. The fact that she could read some material and was acquiring sight words indicated that she had acquired sufficient experience for reading to commence.

Her best assets were her persistence, diligence, and optimistic nature. Ms. Whittier felt that these personal qualities should be nurtured by giving Katie every possible success and many opportunities to gain status in the eyes of others.

Katie's most serious problem was that everything came to her so slowly. In the immediate future her reading progress would probably remain slow and would have to be accompanied by much practice. Most important, she needed to be in a language-rich environment where she would be constantly surrounded by print and oral language.

Ms. Whittier and the supervisor agreed on a two-part plan to enrich Katie's experience with print and provide active support and encouragement. In the classroom, her primer-level instruction was extended to daily use of dictated experience stories. She began compiling and illustrating a collection of stories, mostly retellings of stories she heard read in class, which she could read to her little siblings at home. She worked assiduously at memorizing and learning to reread her dictated stories for this purpose. Without much ado, Ms. Whittier began focusing on helping Katie to recognize individual words from these stories so that she could expand her sight vocabulary. She also did echo reading from a storybook Katie chose until Katie could read it smoothly on her own. Then she arranged for Katie to visit the kindergarten and share her story. Katie was delighted at this responsibility, and it became a regular part of her program.

At home, Katie was encouraged to read to the other children. Ms. Whittier also helped her to make up some simple card games with the alphabet letters and some simple letter sounds to entertain her younger siblings. Ms. Whittier knew that these activities would provide needed practice for Katie without her really noticing it.

Through these procedures, Ms. Whittier tried to enrich Katie's experience with print, increase the amount of contact she had with print, support her emotional need to feel competent and responsible, and make productive use of her after-school hours.

Katie responded well to these efforts. As she worked at polishing her reading for the younger children, she began to recognize more words in other contexts. Since the younger children gave her positive reinforcement for being able to read, she worked even harder and began to feel more confident. The more time she spent in contact with print, the more she gained. Although reading never came easily to Katie, and she was still reading below grade level at the end of second grade, she was getting the extended print experience she needed, and for Katie that made all the difference.

Summary

In this chapter the term *prereading competencies* has been offered as a replacement for *reading readiness*. To look at the growth that must occur in particular areas before a child is ready to read does more to provide a clear agenda for teaching than does the more general concept of reading readiness. In this chapter we discussed the assessment of these competencies: *oral language fluency, a sense of story structures, the speech-to-print match, print orientation concepts, sight word recognition, and letter recognition.*

Oral language development can be measured by several means: the two tests by Marie Clay et al., *The Record of Oral Language* and *Biks and Gutches*, devices dedicated to the assessment of children's oral language fluency, were described in this chapter. Joan Tough's checklist of children's ability to use language for different functions was shared as well. We would suggest that a teacher who is not adept at assessing children's language ability orient himself to the task by using one or more of these devices. Once he knows what he is looking for, he may be able to assess language ability informally while he is teaching: we suggested ways that the *Dictated Experience Story* might be used for this purpose.

A child's *sense of story structures* can be inferred in at least two ways. One method is the *directed listening-thinking activity,* in which children listen to a portion of a story and are asked to predict what might happen next. The predictions and comments can reveal whether a child has certain expectations about the structure of stories. Another method is to have children *retell stories* they have heard read aloud. Retellings can be analyzed to see if critical elements of stories were included in their proper order.

The child's ability to make the *speech-to-print match* in a memorized written sequence can be assessed by using the dictated experience story or some other easily memorized material. The *voice-pointing procedure* is used with either type of material to determine if children can match spoken and written words in a familiar portion of text and if a supported rereading activity helps them to recognize new words in print.

A *phonemic segmentation task using invented spelling* was described for the purpose of investigating children's ability to divide words up into their smallest sound units, a necessary part of word knowledge related to the application of phonics.

Print orientation concepts can be assessed by using the *Concepts About Print Test* or by adapting this procedure in minor ways, such as varying the questions asked and the text used. The *Concepts about Print Test* represents a real reading experience with prereaders. It helps the teacher learn what a child knows about book orientation, directionality of print and pages, concepts of letters, words, spaces, and punctuation marks, and the communicative nature of print and pictures.

Big books, recently brought back into popularity by New Zealander Don Holdaway, were suggested as an excellent aid for teaching print orientation concepts, since they enable children to read along with the teacher in a favorite story and notice features of the print as they do so.

The *acquisition of sight words* can be informally assessed by using a *sight word inventory* made up of words frequently occurring in beginning reading materials. Words are presented in isolation, but the presentation is untimed. A similar inventory can be used to examine the *recognition of letters,* uppercase and lowercase.

Extension Activities

1. Using the procedures described on pages 98–101 of this chapter, make up a sight word inventory from the preprimer through first-reader levels of a recent basal series. Then try out the inventory with several children from first or second grade. From the results, determine which level would contain material that could be read comfortably by each child. Compare your estimate with the basal level in which each child is currently placed.

2. Conduct a directed listening-thinking activity (see pages 89–90) with a small group of young children. (Try to get at least two and not more than ten children.) Choose a well-illustrated children's book appropriate to their age level. Plan two or three "stops" for predicting and place them just before some critical event happens. Accept all predictions as possible, but ask children to tell why they guessed as they did. (Review the procedures described in this chapter beforehand.)

   A little later, read the same story to a group of children of the same age but omit the predicting. Just read the story straight through. Which group seemed more interested in and curious about the story? Why do you think this was so?

3. Make up an alphabet inventory or a simple game involving matching and naming of letters on cards. Visit a kindergarten, assess the letter recognition of a number of children, and rank-order them according to their letter recognition. Then ask their teacher to tell you which children he or she thinks are at or closest to readiness, and why. Does your ordering roughly correspond to the teacher's? Why or why not? What factors does the teacher believe are more important in judging readiness?

4. Try a dictated experience story (see pages 79–82) with a kindergarten or a first-grade child. Using a concrete stimulus, elicit four or five sentences and print them exactly as spoken. Choral-read the story completely several times until the child can recite it confidently.

Now try the voice-pointing procedure (see pages 91–94) by modeling how to read and point for each line and see if the child can successfully make the speech-to-print match. If he or she can do this easily, use a simple primer or very easy book to see if the child has begun to read yet. If there is difficulty with the voice pointing, where does the trouble occur? Can the first and last word in the story be located? As the child recites, what elements are pointed to? Letters? Whole words for single syllables? After a number of tries, can the child do it correctly or is the process still too difficult? Make a judgment about the child's state of readiness and compare your judgment with that of the child's teacher.

5. With three kindergarteners and three first graders, try the echo-reading procedure found on pages 82–84. Work with the children one at a time. Were there more differences among children within a single grade or between the two grades? If you rank-order their performances within each grade, do your orderings match the teacher's judgment?

Suggested Readings

Allen, R. Van, and Allen, Claryce. **Language Experiences in Early Childhood.** *Chicago: Encyclopedia Brittanica, 1969.* A wealth of ideas and techniques, most of which are relevant to prereaders.

Clay, Marie M. **The Early Detection of Reading Difficulties, 2nd ed.** *Exeter, N.H.: Heinemann Educational Books, 1979.* An excellent guide for screening and helping young problem readers.

Pflaum, Susannah. **The Development of Reading and Language in Young Children,** **2nd ed.** *Columbus: Charles Merrill, 1978.* Summarizes a number of important concerns as well as useful procedures for dealing with prereaders and beginning readers.

Tough, Joan. **Focus on Meaning: Talking to Children to Some Purpose.** *London: Unwin Educational Books, 1973.* Applies Halliday's and Bernstein's research to preschool and primary grades and describes techniques for helping those who most need to develop oral fluency.

References

Allen, R. Van. *Language Experiences in Communication.* Boston: Houghton Mifflin, 1976.

Clay, Marie. *Concepts About Print Test, Sand, and Stones.* Exeter, N.H.: Heinemann Educational Books, 1972.

Goodman, Yetta M. "Test Review: Concepts About Print Test." *The Reading Teacher* 34, No. 4 (Jan. 1981): 445–448.

Martin, Bill Jr., and Brogan, Peggy. *Bill Martin's Instant Readers.* N.Y.: Holt, Rinehart & Winston, 1971.

Morris, R. Darrell. "Beginning Readers' Concept of Word and Its Relationship to Phoneme Segmentation Ability." Paper presented at the National Reading Conference, San Antonio, Nov. 1979.

Slobin, Daniel I., and Welsh, Charles A. "Elicited Imitation as a Research Tool in Developmental Psycholinguistics," in Celia J. Lavatelli, ed. *Language Training in Early Childhood Education.* Urbana, Ill.: University of Illinois Press, 1971, pp. 170–185.

Stauffer, Russell G. *The Language Experience Approach to the Teaching of Reading,* revised ed. N.Y.: Harper & Row, 1980.

Chapter Four

Informal Measures of
Reading Ability

In this chapter we discuss reading assessment with students who have already begun to read or who have been reading for some time. The main questions we address are the following:

1. What sorts of things can go wrong in reading development and how can we tell when they do?
2. How do we judge the level of reading materials in which a child should be placed?
3. How do we "get inside" children's reading and determine what strategies they used?
4. How can we tell if children are reading as well as their potential indicates they should?

In order to answer these questions, we need assessment devices and techniques that will help us to observe students reading real text in a natural situation. We want to be able to analyze aspects of their sight vocabulary, word analysis strategies, skill in understanding and remembering main ideas, details, and vocabulary items, and the ability to make inferences and judgments about what they read. We don't want to get bogged down, however, in giving separate tests for every possible reading skill, which would take more time than the average teacher has.

Moreover, it would break up or "partition" the reading process to the point where the wholeness of the process would be lost. If we wanted to study the architecture of a building, we would not knock it down and study each separate brick and board. Something would definitely be missing from such an analysis! Likewise, our aim is to study aspects of reading within the context of real reading, not as isolated components of a complex process. Therefore, we need assessment devices that will have students read the kind of text they must read in school and at home. Only then can we draw meaningful conclusions about various important reading skills.

We also want assessment devices that will yield more than just numerical scores. In order to provide just the right materials and instruction we need to learn more than just the reading levels of our students. We also have to know what they do well and what needs improvement so that we can discern patterns of strength and weakness. Therefore, we want reading tests that will give us *qualitative* information as well as *quantitative* information.

A reading assessment procedure that combines all these features is the *informal reading inventory* (IRI) (Betts, 1957), which has been around for many years. There are numerous commercial IRIs, and many basal series also supply their own. Some of them, however, are flawed by poor questions or overly short, dull passages, and some teachers prefer to construct their own IRIs, drawing material from their basal readers or content area texts. Many IRIs are also coupled with an informal *word recognition inventory* (WRI). This device, which also may be teacher-made, examines both of the aspects of word recognition previously discussed: recognizing words immediately and figuring them out from their letters and parts. The WRI tests are constructed for many different levels of difficulty.

Cloze and *maze procedures* are also useful devices for determining whether particular materials are easy, comfortable, or too difficult for particular readers or groups. These teacher-made devices help us learn more about students' comprehension of text and use of context by requiring students to read and complete text in which words have been systematically deleted.

In the following sections, we will explain:

□ how to select a commercial IRI
□ how to administer an IRI and WRI effectively
□ how to score the instruments and determine the levels on which the child is reading
□ how to use quantitative and qualitative analyses to determine what strategies the reader has used and where strengths and weaknesses lie in silent and oral reading and word recognition
□ how to construct your own IRI and WRI
□ how to develop, administer, and use cloze and maze procedures

Case Studies

JERRY

Jerry, a twelve-year-old fifth grader, took little interest in school and moved passively through each school day. He was a quiet boy who avoided contact with adults when he could and never drew attention to himself. He did little real work, just enough to get by, and much of what he produced was poorly done. He never volunteered a remark in discussions and although he never overtly refused to do his work, he was adept at stalling and other strategies to avoid reading and writing tasks.

Jerry was a year older than his classmates because he had been retained in second grade. His reading and general school achievement were low, and he never had a really successful school year. Each year he did just enough to be promoted but was always in the lowest reading group and his school record showed consistently low achievement. Since his retention in second grade, he had received remedial reading instruction in addition to language arts in his regular classroom, but the remedial work never did much to help him improve in reading.

As the end of Jerry's fifth-grade year approached, his teachers were faced with the dilemma of making recommendations for the next year. If he were promoted to sixth grade, he would go to the middle school where he would have five academic subjects and a different teacher for every class. Should he go on to middle school, they wondered? Could he handle the work? Was he too old for another retention? If he were to go on, what support would be available to him?

Jerry's teachers knew that his passivity and disinterest were the usual cover of a student who reads very poorly. At the end of fifth grade he was able to read comfortably at only an early second-grade level. For her lowest readers, Jerry's teacher used a supplementary basal series written for older poor readers, and Jerry's reading group was working in a book of second-grade difficulty. In remedial reading Jerry worked with "high-interest, low-vocabulary" books for teen readers and did individual work from skills kits.

Other than these materials, he read very little. His math, social studies, and science textbooks for fifth grade were much too hard for him to read himself. His reading teacher let him listen to tapes of these books, so he did learn something about these subjects, and sometimes his mother read his homework assignment aloud to him. He never read library books, however, or even comics. When his class did sustained silent reading he sometimes fell asleep, and when his teacher pressed him to read something he would idly flip through a magazine. It was apparent that print had little importance in his life. His teachers knew his unwillingness to read and his slow progress in reading were related, but they just couldn't spark any interest on Jerry's part.

His teachers were gravely worried about his academic future. How does a twelve-year-old student with a second-grade reading level cope with the many social and academic demands of middle school? At the middle school Jerry would attend, the reading teachers faced the common dilemma of having large numbers of students in need of special reading help, many with severe reading problems and chronic school failure. Reading classes of less than ten students were an impossible luxury.

Because of Jerry's age and social development, the decision was finally made to promote him to sixth grade and try to provide as much specific information about his reading as possible. His teachers began drawing up a descriptive profile of his strengths and weaknesses in reading and an accurate assessment of his reading level so that they could make recommendations for support at home and instruction at his new school.

BRIAN

Brian, a small wiry boy who was a fine athlete, entered fourth grade with a record of excellent school achievement and high standardized achievement test scores. Because of his "late birthday," Brian was only five when he began first grade. Although he was usually the youngest child in his classes, he was always described as "mature." In many ways, he was a model student: a diligent worker whose work, if not always correct, was always neatly and promptly completed. He was a conforming student who observed the rules and valued his teacher's praise very highly. He was popular with his classmates, a leader in group discussions, and a fierce competitor on the playing field.

Brian's parents were highly educated professionals who closely supervised his school achievement, urged him to participate in a number of group sports, and rewarded him for good grades with money, toys, and privileges.

His fourth-grade teacher expected that he would experience the same pattern of achievement as in earlier grades, so she was surprised when, as the autumn wore on, he began to have more and more difficulty with his work. His oral reading was rapid and highly accurate, although he did not read with much expression. In activities dealing with word analysis skills and vocabulary, he was a star. In discussions of what was read, however, Brian often could not recall important events or ideas, and in comprehension activities he made what his teacher thought were "careless mistakes." She frequently had to caution him to be more careful and think harder.

Brian's conformity gradually gave way to a growing tension. His teacher noticed that he was becoming restless, bit his nails, hummed and whispered to himself, and began to ask if he were right more and more often. He became almost obsessively neat in his written work, often erasing over and over again before he was satisfied. Eventually he refused to turn in written work, saying he'd "messed it up."

By late winter of fourth grade, Brian's achievement seriously declined. He was falling behind in his work, he showed more anxiety and restlessness, and his achievement test scores plummeted. Faced with these problems, his parents realized that they had to confront his difficulty and arranged a school conference. His teacher, unable to understand why such a capable and willing student would begin to fail so rapidly, sought the help of a reading specialist and an elementary school counselor to determine the causes of his decline.

Levels of Reading Ability

Parents, teachers, and students alike are concerned about reading levels, which are often linked to issues of retention, promotion, and graduation. Usually the statements and questions we hear about reading levels assume that a reader has one single reading level, but this is an oversimplification. Most readers who have progressed beyond beginning reading have three reading levels, each appropriate for reading of different kinds of text for different purposes.

The Independent Level

At this level of difficulty the student can read text *easily*, without help. Comprehension of what is read is generally excellent, and silent reading at this level is rapid because almost all the words are recognized and understood at sight. The student has to stop rarely, if at all, to analyze a new word. Oral reading is generally fluent, and occasional divergences from the written text rarely interfere with comprehension.

The Instructional Level

At this level the material is not really easy but is still *comfortable*. Here the student is challenged and will benefit most from instruction. Comprehension is good, but help is needed to understand some concepts. The silent reading rate is fairly rapid, although usually slower than at the independent level. Some word analysis is necessary, but the majority of the words are recognized at sight. Oral reading is fairly smooth and accurate, and oral divergences from the written text usually make sense in the context and do not cause a loss of meaning.

The Frustration Level

Here the material is *too difficult* in vocabulary or concepts to be read successfully. Comprehension is poor, with major ideas forgotten or misunderstood. Both oral and silent reading are usually slow and labored, with frequent stops to analyze unknown words. Oral reading divergences are frequent and often cause the reader to lose the sense of what was read. Because of this difficulty, it is frustrating for students to attempt to read such material for sustained periods of time, and their efforts often fail. This level is to be avoided in instruction.

Table 4.1 shows the characteristics of each level and some typical kinds of reading a student might do at each level.

TABLE 4.1. Functional reading levels.

	CHARACTERISTICS	TYPICAL READING
INDEPENDENT LEVEL Easy	Excellent comprehension Excellent accuracy in word recognition Few words need analysis Rapid, smooth rate Very few errors of any kind	All pleasure reading All self-selected reading for information Homework, tests, seatwork, learning centers, and all other assigned work to be done alone
INSTRUCTIONAL LEVEL Comfortable	Good comprehension Good accuracy in word recognition Fairly rapid rate Some word analysis needed	School textbooks and basal reader Guided classroom reading assignments Study guides and other work done with guidance Forms and applications
FRUSTRATION LEVEL Too hard	Poor comprehension Slow, stumbling rate Much word analysis necessary	No assigned material Reading for diagnostic purposes Self-selected material where student's interest is very high in spite of difficulty

The instructional level, where the student is comfortable yet challenged and will benefit most from instruction, is the level we usually mean when we refer to a student's reading level. The other two levels, however, are also very important. At the independent level we want students to read for pleasure, information, and enrichment. Reading assignments such as homework, tests, and seatwork should also be at the independent level so that they can complete it alone.

We want to be able to place a student at the instructional level with regard to materials for direct instruction, such as basal readers, other textbooks, study guides, workbooks, skills activities, and worksheets that are to be read in class where the teacher can provide help and guidance.

It is necessary to determine what material represents the frustration level even though trying to read these passages on an informal reading inventory is difficult for the student. Unless we explore the outer limits of the student's reading ability, we will not know how far he or she can go. The teacher has to see what strategies students can use when pushed and what strategies continue to serve them well. After the frustration level has been determined, a reader should *never be assigned* to read material that difficult.

The Informal Reading Inventory

An informal reading inventory consists of text passages corresponding in difficulty to basal and textbook materials at grade levels from primer through secondary school, and sets of questions for each passage intended to test readers' comprehension and recall after reading. Passages and their questions are arranged in order of difficulty from easiest (primer and primary grades) to hardest (usually ninth grade or above). IRIs usually also contain a word recognition inventory, or lists of individual words arranged in levels like those of the reading passages, and many commercial IRIs have supplementary tests such as phonics inventories, cloze tests, and spelling inventories.

Many basal reading and language arts series provide an IRI to be used for placement within that series and for diagnostic use. There are also a number of commercial IRIs, most of them essentially similar, and a list of those follows at the end of the next section, Selecting a Commercial IRI. IRIs can also be made up by teachers, and instructions for doing so are included in the section Constructing an IRI at the end of this chapter.

Teacher-made IRI passages are selected from basal readers or other school texts while commercial IRIs have passages that are selected from many types of trade books or that are specially written for the test. Usually they are only 50 to 250 words long and can be comfortably read in a few minutes. An IRI consists of a student's booklet of the reading passages and an examiner's copy of the instrument. The examiner's copy contains the reading passages and the corresponding comprehension questions with their correct answers.

So that an examiner can assess oral and silent reading separately, a good IRI should have two or more different passages at each grade level. The passages should be from different stories but comparable in difficulty. To be most useful in testing children of various abilities and ages, the grade levels represented should range from preprimer or primer through at least sixth-grade text, preferably through ninth- or even twelfth-grade material.

Figures 4.1 and 4.2 show a student page and corresponding examiner's page from a commercial IRI (Bader, 1983).

Commercial IRIs have both advantages and disadvantages. They offer the teacher a complete set of word lists, passages, and questions already compiled and ready to reproduce and use. They feature multiple forms at each grade level, which allow the teacher to assess oral and silent reading or to retest later with new material. They are inexpensive and widely available.

They do have shortcomings, however. IRIs that accompany a basal reading series are made up of passages from that series, and the students being tested may have previously read one or more of the stories from which the passages came. Therefore, their comprehension scores on those passages may be falsely inflated. Other commercial IRIs have passages that are specially written to conform to readability levels or passages selected from sources other than basal readers, but the quality of such passages varies widely. Also, some tests use short passages, which severely limit the number of ideas available to the reader and the number of questions that can be asked.

In addition to these disadvantages there are several others: particularly at the lower levels, some passages are written in short stilted sentences that don't sound much like real language. Some portray males and females in very stereotyped ways or contain derogatory comments about females.

FIGURE 4.1. Commercial IRI pupil page.

JAMES' CUT

It was after lunch when James cut his finger on the playground. He was bleeding and he hurt a little, too.

He went inside to find his teacher. He showed her his cut finger and asked for a Band-Aid. She looked at it and said, "Well, it's not too bad, James. I think we should wash it before we bandage it, don't you." James did not want it washed because he thought it would sting. But he was afraid to tell Miss Smith. He just acted brave.

When it was washed and bandaged, he thanked Miss Smith. Then he rushed out to the playground to show everyone his shiny new bandage.

SOURCE: Reprinted with permission of Macmillan Publishing Company from *Bader Reading and Language Inventory* by Lois A. Bader. Copyright © 1983 by Lois A. Bader.

FIGURE 4.2. Commercial IRI examiner's page.

Here is a story about a boy named James.

JAMES' CUT

It was after lunch when James cut his finger on the playground. He was bleeding and he hurt a little too.

He went inside to find his teacher. He showed her his cut finger and asked for a Band-Aid. She looked at it and said, "Well, it's not too bad, James. I think we should wash it before we bandage it, don't you?" James did not want it washed because he thought it would sting. But he was afraid to tell Miss Smith. He just acted brave.

When it was washed and bandaged, he thanked Miss Smith. Then he rushed out to the playground to show everyone his shiny new bandage. (111 words)

UNPROMPTED MEMORIES

Please retell the story.
____ James cut finger
____ on playground after lunch
____ bleeding and hurt
____ went to teacher, showed finger
____ asked for Band-Aid
____ she looked and said wash first
____ then bandage
____ James didn't want it washed
____ he thought it would sting
____ acted brave when washed and bandaged
____ said thank you, went back to playground
____ showed his new bandage

COMPREHENSION QUESTIONS

____ What happened to James? (cut his finger)
____ When did he hurt himself? (after lunch)
____ Where did the accident happen? (on playground)
____ Where did James go when he cut his finger? (inside school to find teacher)
____ What did the teacher say? (they should wash it)
____ Why didn't James want it washed? (he thought it would sting)
____ How did James act when he was getting his finger washed? (brave)
____ What did he do after it was bandaged? (said thank you)
____ (went back to playground)
____ What did he show his friends? (new bandage)

Interpretive question: Why didn't James want to tell Miss Smith he was afraid to have his finger washed.

Acceptable answer: ____ Yes ____ No

SOURCE: Reprinted with permission of Macmillan Publishing Company from *Bader Reading and Language Inventory* by Lois A. Bader. Copyright © 1983 by Lois A. Bader.

Some carry on the same story from passage to passage, making it difficult to omit the lower levels or move from a higher to a lower level during administration. Some are taken from the middle of a story, but no introduction is provided to help the reader understand what preceded the passage. Some have fairly interesting passages but use factual recall questions almost exclusively while ignoring other aspects of comprehension.

For these reasons, students in reading diagnosis and assessment courses sometimes are taught to make up and evaluate their own IRIs. This is an extremely helpful practice, but making up an IRI is a challenging and time-consuming task. When teachers opt to buy a commercial IRI, they must use judgment and care in evaluating these instruments. The following section will help you consider the most important aspects of commercial IRIs.

Selecting a Commercial IRI

To choose the best IRI for your use, you must examine and compare several, then select the one you believe has the most strengths and will serve your diagnostic needs best.

We believe that the following aspects are of critical importance in choosing an IRI:

1. literary quality of reading passages
2. clarity and relevance of questions
3. balance of question types, including a range of comprehension skills and both convergent and divergent questions
4. convenient format
5. complete instructions, including examples

Literary Quality of Passages. The heart of an IRI is the reading passages. When you consider an IRI, *read the passages.* Are they generally interesting, with topics that many children will likely know something about and be interested in? We cannot expect good comprehension of dull text.

Does the language sound natural? When there is dialogue, do the speakers sound like real people? Are descriptive passages colorful and memorable? At the upper levels and in nonfiction passages, is the language clear and straightforward? Are sequences and cause-effect relationships presented clearly? Are the words and ideas in the passages appropriate for the grade levels and ages for which they are intended? In the primary levels, is there some story or sequence of events present? If there are illustrations, are they necessary to an understanding of the passages? Keep in mind that all information should be presented in the text, not in the illustrations.

You may not expect brilliant prose in an IRI, but do look for one that has consistently interesting, clearly written, straightforward passages with natural-sounding dialogue, colorful descriptions, and topics that a wide range of students can recognize and understand.

Quality of Questions. Most often, the questions we ask are the primary means we have of assessing comprehension. (Retelling, or spontaneously recalling what was read, is another useful means that will be described later.) If the IRI questions we use are confusing, picky, or limited in the thinking skills they require, we will not get an accurate picture of the reader's comprehension. To get good answers, we must ask good questions.

Good questions should be clear and simple, should follow the organization of the passage, should tap the most important information conveyed, should call on a variety of comprehension skills, and should be answerable only after reading the passage, not by general knowledge, prior experience, or illustrations. They should require elaborated responses, should call on both convergent and divergent thinking, and should not be answerable by yes or no without explanation or elaboration. They should not be repetitious. Vocabulary questions should feature a passage-based context for the word; for example, "In the sentence 'Jim put the package on the bar,' what did *bar* mean?" is a better question than "What did *bar* mean in this story?" or "What is a *bar?*"

Format and Instructions. In order for you to assess oral and silent reading comprehension separately, the IRI you use should have two different passages of equivalent length and difficulty for each level. Most commercial IRIs have three equivalent forms, which allows you to use a third passage for retesting or for assessing listening comprehension. The instrument's format should make it easy for you to locate and use the appropriate passages and questions during testing.

Are the different forms and grade levels clearly labeled and easy to locate? Are pupil pages coded in some way so that the grade level of the passage is not apparent to the student? Is a record or summary sheet provided to help you summarize your observations, findings, and conclusions?

Are the directions for administering the IRI clear and concise? Are there directions for interpreting findings? Are there examples of students' responses for you to study and practice interpreting?

All of these features will make it easier for you to use an IRI correctly and effectively.

Some commercial IRIs are:

Bader, Lois A. *Bader Reading and Language Inventory.* New York: Macmillan, 1983.

Burns, Paul C., and Roe, Betty D. *Informal Reading Assessment.* Chicago: Rand McNally, 1980.

Ekwall, Eldon E. *Ekwall Reading Inventory,* 2nd. ed. Boston: Allyn and Bacon, 1985.

Johns, Jerry L. *Basic Reading Inventory*, 2nd ed. Dubuque, Ia.: Kendall-Hunt, 1981.

Johns, Jerry L. *Advanced Reading Inventory*. Dubuque, Ia.: William C. Brown, 1982.

Silvaroli, Nicholas J. *Classroom Reading Inventory*, 4th ed. Dubuque, Ia.: William C. Brown, 1982.

Woods, Mary Lynn, and Moe, Alden J. *Analytical Reading Inventory*, 2nd ed. Columbus, Ohio: Charles C. Merrill, 1981.

The following sources will give you additional information and guidance in evaluating commercial IRIs:

Jongsma, Kathleen S. and Jongsma, Eugene A. "Test Review: Commercial Informal Reading Inventories." *The Reading Teacher* 34, No. 6 (March 1981): 697–705.

Kavale, Kenneth. "Selecting and Evaluating Reading Tests," in Robert Schreiner, ed. *Reading Tests and Teachers: A Practical Guide*. Newark, Del.: International Reading Association, 1979.

McKenna, Michael C. "Informal Reading Inventories: A Review of the Issues." *The Reading Teacher* 36, No. 7 (March 1983): 670–679.

Pikulski, John J., and Shanahan, Timothy "Informal Reading Inventories: A Critical Analysis," in John J. Pikulski and Timothy Shanahan, eds. *Approaches to the Informal Evaluation of Reading*. Newark, Del.: International Reading Association, 1982.

Schell, Leo M., and Hanna, Gerald S. "Can Informal Reading Inventories Reveal Strengths and Weaknesses in Comprehension Subskills?" *The Reading Teacher* 36, No. 3 (December 1981): 263–268.

If your basal reading series includes an IRI, you should examine it critically before you use it, just as you would if you were choosing a commercial IRI. Basal series IRIs have an important advantage in that they often closely match the kind of text students read every day. This is because the IRI passages are usually taken directly from the reading books. However, this can have a negative effect too; if the student being tested has previously read the material in class, his or her comprehension may be falsely inflated. The ideal basal IRI would feature test passages very similar to the text material in difficulty, quality of writing, and topical interest, but not taken directly from the basal readers.

Other factors, if present, may limit a basal IRI's usefulness. Story passages should be long enough to be fairly complete in themselves (not always the case when a portion of text is lifted from a longer story or account). Questions should be asked by the examiner and answers recorded; students should not be given questions to read and answers to mark or write. As with all IRIs, questions should relate directly to the reading passage, not to illustrations or to information contained in the longer book passage.

Administering the IRI

Giving an IRI takes about thirty to fifty minutes, depending on the student's reading ability, and it does not all have to be done in one sitting. Often teachers giving an IRI in class during regular instruction time break up the testing into a number of short sittings, with the student reading one or two passages at a time, and finishing the IRI over a period of several days. This allows you to give an individual test without taking too much time away from other students or activities. You will need a student copy of the passages or the appropriate books, an examiner's copy for recording, and pencils.

It is not necessary to begin with the lowest level passages. If you are testing to see whether a particular book or other material would be comfortable reading, begin there. If the student is successful, you may proceed to higher levels or stop. If he or she is unsuccessful, you should drop down to an easier level.

If your diagnostic purpose is more general, begin two or three grade levels below the student's present grade. For primary graders, begin at primer or first grade. If the student is not reading easily and experiencing immediate success at that level, drop back. If the first passage seems easy, go on to higher levels.

Steps to Follow. These detailed steps will make IRI administration most effective.

1. Start where you think the student will be able to read easily. (If you overestimated, you can drop back to lower levels.) Some authorities advocate giving the word recognition inventory (WRI) first in order to find out where to begin the IRI. This practice is discussed in Administering, Scoring, and Interpreting the Word Recognition Inventory.

2. Give the oral reading passage at that level first. Show the student where to begin reading and where to stop and say, "Please read this passage out loud to me. When you are finished, close the book and I will ask you some questions about what you have read."

3. Follow the reading on your copy and carefully mark down the responses that diverge from the text. These divergent responses, which happen naturally when we read aloud, have been termed *miscues* by researchers who have studied oral reading behaviors systematically (Goodman, 1970; Goodman and Burke, 1972). These miscues will be analyzed later in order to provide detailed information about the reader's use of phonic and structural analysis, syntax, and word meanings during oral reading. The marks used to code oral reading miscues are listed and discussed in Marking Oral Reading Miscues.

4. When oral reading is completed and the passage is removed, ask the

comprehension questions. Jot down key words or phrases from the student's answers. Don't hesitate to probe for more information or ask a student to explain or justify an answer.

5. Give the silent reading passage for that level. Show the student where to begin and stop reading. Tell him or her to read silently and close the book (or turn over the card) when finished. Then ask questions after the reading is completed.

6. If the student answered 60 percent or more of the comprehension questions correctly, proceed to the next level. (The scores may rise again at the next level.) If oral comprehension scores are low but silent comprehension is still above 60 percent, discontinue the oral reading but continue silent reading at higher levels until these scores also drop below 60 percent and remain there. If the student shows poor silent comprehension but oral comprehension scores are still above 60 percent, continue oral reading.

Assessing Comprehension with Retellings and Reinspection. Most often, readers' comprehension of IRI passages is assessed by asking comprehension questions and by expecting unaided recall (i.e., answering without looking back to the passage). There are several problems inherent in this approach:

1. When reinspection is not allowed, both recall and comprehension are being tested. Readers may comprehend but fail to recall information, resulting in our underestimating their comprehension (Baker and Stein, 1981).

2. Readers may fail to include information in a response because, to the reader, it appeared obvious, redundant, or secondary to other information. Reinspection tends to encourage more complete answers.

3. Recall without reinspection is more a test-taking skill than an everyday reading strategy. In classroom reading students usually discuss material and answer questions with the material before them rather than with books closed.

Another issue involves the use of questions alone, rather than allowing students to retell or describe in their own words what they remember from passages. By the very act of asking questions, we shape students' comprehension, cuing them to what we feel is important for them to remember and include in their answers. Because of this, an effective way to learn more about students' comprehension is to ask them to retell what they have read, and either record what each student tells you or use a checklist of all of the information in a passage, allowing the student to use his or her own words in recalling these items.

Few commercial IRIs have yet incorporated retellings in their comprehension assessment. The Bader Reading and Language Inventory (Macmillan, 1983) is one that does, and Figure 4.2 shows a page from this inventory. You will see that both a checklist for retelling and a set of questions is included for each passage. Students are asked to "retell the story" without prompting or probes, before questions are asked. Retellings are not scored quantitatively, but are rated as to whether the retelling was "organized" or not.

If you are using an IRI that does not include retellings, you may create lists of the type used in the Bader inventory (Figure 4.2) to help you assess these retellings. You can informally assess retellings without such lists, but you will have to keep careful track of the information the student does provide. Tape recording the retellings is extremely helpful.

The issue of whether or not to allow reinspection in an important one, and you can incorporate reinspection fairly easily into standard IRI administration. To do so, you should direct the reader to look back to the passage and locate some specific information after the retelling and questioning. Again, some commercial IRIs have so-called "reinspection items" included in the comprehension questions, but many do not. It is a simple procedure to direct the reader to "Look back and find the place where it says that . . ." or the like, noting which item is being used for reinspection, and take note of whether the reader is able to scan for the desired information or must begin reading all over again, and whether the information can be located successfully.

We typically include one reinspection item for each IRI passage and do one or two retellings at levels where we feel the reader is reading comfortably while we are giving an IRI. Both procedures lengthen the amount of time it takes to give an IRI, but both provide valuable and often-overlooked information about a student's comprehension.

Marking Oral Reading Miscues. While the student is reading the appropriate passages aloud, you must mark all of the *oral divergences from the text*, or *miscues*, on your copy of the passage. Miscues are analyzed to determine what strategies the reader used to figure out unknown words during the oral reading.

Here is a simple coding system that will allow you to record all miscues accurately:

Substitution of a word or phrase: the student's word written over a word in text

dog
The doll fell from the shelf.

Insertion of a word not in text: a word written in over a caret or small arrow
down
The doll fell⌃from the shelf.

Omission of a word, word part, or phrase: the omitted element circled

The (big) dog ran away.

A word given by the examiner: parentheses placed around that word

The climbers were assisted by (Sherpa) tribesmen.

Such marks will be used to calculate the student's *quantitative* accuracy in oral reading when the IRI is scored. These are called *scorable miscues*. There are a few other miscues the reader may make that will not be included in the accuracy score but will provide additional *qualitative* information about the oral reading:

Miscue spontaneously corrected by the reader: check mark next to original coding

doll ✓

The big dog ran away.

Repetition of word or phrase: wavy line under repeated element

Once upon a time a wizard . . .

Reversal of order of words: proofreader's symbol for inversion used

"Let's go," (shouted Sally)

Pauses longer than normal: slashes to indicate long pauses (one per second)

The // controversial theory was discussed. . . .

Figure 4.3 shows a sample passage with miscues coded.

Assessing Listening Comprehension. When the student reaches a level of 60 percent or lower comprehension, functional reading has broken down. One very important aspect remains to be tested, however: the student's *listening comprehension*, sometimes referred to as *hearing capacity*. The listening comprehension level, the highest level of text a reader can comprehend when listening to another read aloud, provides a rough estimate of one's potential for reading improvement. It is of great help in forming reasonable expectations for growth in reading and is quite easy to determine.

When reading comprehension scores indicate that the reader has become frustrated (scores of 60 percent or less), read either of the next level passages aloud to the student and then ask the comprehension questions. Before you read, say: "You've worked hard and the last story was difficult.

FIGURE 4.3. Miscue coding.

(158 words, .63 percent per word)

FIRST, ORAL

Each and All, p. 94

Sheep dogs work hard on a farm. They must learn to take *the* sheep from place to

place. They must see that the sheep do not run away. And they must see that the

sheep are not lost or killed.

Sometimes these dogs are // trained to do other kinds of farm work.

They // earn the right to be called good helpers, too.

Can you think of one other kind of work dog? He does not need a coat or strong

legs like the sheep dog's. He does not learn to work with a sled in the deep, cold

snow. He does not learn to be a farm worker.

He learns to help the man who cannot see. This dog must be kind and wise. He

must help the man do many things. He must stay right beside the man day and night.

He must learn to see for the man. Sometimes he must learn for the man, too.

SOURCE: *Each and All Read*, Level E (New York: American Book Company, 1971), p. 94. Reprinted by permission of D. C. Heath & Company.

This time I want you to listen carefully while I read the story. Afterward I'll ask you questions as I did before." Read normally rather than too slowly or with exaggerated expression. If the student gets more than 60 percent of the questions correct, read a passage from the next level. Proceed until you reach a level where the student gets 60 percent or fewer of the questions correct, and then stop.

To summarize, the steps in administering an IRI are as follows:

1. Begin the IRI two or three levels below present grade or at a level you think the student can read comfortably.
2. Administer the first oral reading passage and code the miscues. Tape record oral reading, if possible, for greater accuracy. Ask comprehension questions and record the gist of the answers.
3. Administer the first silent reading passage. Ask comprehension questions and record the gist of the answers.

4. When silent and oral comprehension scores drop to 60 percent or less, read one of the next level passages aloud and ask questions as before.
5. When listening comprehension drops lower than 60 percent, stop the IRI.

Scoring an IRI

Scoring procedures for an IRI are quite simple. Accuracy in oral reading and comprehension is scored by percentages, which help the teacher determine the student's independent, instructional, and frustration levels.

Because IRIs are often used to determine a student's independent and instructional levels, the criteria for setting these levels are very important. IRIs have been widely used since the 1940s, when Betts (1941, 1957) and others popularized their use and the criteria for setting levels were derived largely from clinical experience (Beldin, 1970). For many years the minimum instructional level criteria attributed to Betts (95 percent oral reading accuracy and 75 percent comprehension) were widely accepted.

Today many authorities still use the Betts criteria, although 70 percent comprehension is most often used. The oral reading accuracy criteria, however, have been challenged as too stringent (Powell, 1970, 1971; Powell and Dunkeld, 1971). Powell (1970) presented convincing evidence that primary grade readers can read effectively at the instructional level with about 85 percent or better accuracy, and third to sixth graders with 90 percent or better accuracy. He later (1971) stated that in easier material a higher level of miscues could be tolerated than in more difficult materials. From our experience we concur that 95 percent is too high, and we use 90 percent as the lower end of the instructional range for oral reading accuracy.

Oral Reading Accuracy. For each oral passage of the IRI used, score the oral reading accuracy by counting the number of *uncorrected* substitutions, omissions, insertions, and words provided by the examiner ("aid miscues"). These are the scorable miscues, the first four listed on pages 124–125. Remember that we will not count any miscues the student corrected, whether the correction occurred immediately or after reading on a bit. (Sometimes a reader must read on a bit before realizing that, based on what follows, a miscue has been made.)

If you tape recorded the oral reading passages, as well as marking miscues as they occurred, you will find it very helpful to replay your tape, perhaps several times, as you follow along in the passages and mark any miscues that you did not catch the first time. Tape recording the oral reading is an excellent practice, particularly when you are learning to give an IRI. When you have done this many times you may not need this "backup."

As you count the scorable miscues, you may find it helpful to write in the margin at the end of each line of print the number of miscues you will count in that line. This helps you gain greater accuracy and aids in checking your work. Remember that although you marked corrections, long pauses, repetitions, and any word order reversals, you will not count those toward the accuracy score at this time. We will use them, however, in analyzing the miscues later. To obtain the gross accuracy score, or the percentage of words called accurately during oral reading without taking the quality of the miscues into account, you will need to know not only how many miscues occurred but also the number of words in the passage, and how much each word is worth in percentage terms. In other words, what percentage of the total words does each individual word contribute?

This figure is called the *miscue deduction*, and it is expressed in a decimal number. It is necessary for you to determine an accuracy score in percentage points.

To do so, count the number of total words in the passage. Then divide 100.00 (or 100%) by the total number of words. For example, the passage in Figure 4.3 has 158 words:

$$158 \overline{) 100.00}^{.63}$$

Each of the 158 words in that passage accounts for .63 percent, or a little more than ½ percent, of the total. For each scorable miscue, then, .63 percent will be deducted from the score.

Some commercial IRIs have the miscue deduction already figured for you, and listed at the top of each passage along with the total number of words. Some only give you the totals, but not the miscue deductions. In the latter case, you must go through your IRI and figure the miscue deduction for each passage and write it on the examiner's copy of the passage. After you have done this once and written it down, you will not need to do it again. It will only take you a few minutes with a calculator.

When you know the miscue deduction for the passage, the rest of the scoring is easy. Count up the scorable miscues and multiply this number by the miscue deduction for that passage. In Figure 4.3, nine scorable miscues were recorded:

$$\begin{array}{r} .63\% \\ \times \quad 9 \\ \hline 5.67\% \text{ (rounded off to 6\%)} \end{array} \qquad \begin{array}{r} 100\% \\ -\quad 6\% \\ \hline 94\% \end{array}$$

By making nine scorable miscues in a passage of 158 words, the reader made 6 percent miscues and, by subtraction, read with 94 percent accuracy.

When you are calculating these accuracy scores, round off the percentages of accuracy to the nearest whole number, as we did above to arrive at the 6 percent figure.

Write the percentage of accuracy on each oral passage, or on a sheet listing all scores at each level. The oral accuracy scores derived so far will be used to determine whether each successive grade level represents the student's independent, instructional, or frustration level for oral reading.

The score criteria for oral reading accuracy are:

Independent level: 97% or higher
Instructional level: 90–96%
Frustration level: below 90%

These criteria may still seem very high, but remember that the context of a sentence provides a powerful word recognition aid. In sentences, words are constrained by their grammatical usage and meaning. An unknown word in a sentence does not appear there arbitrarily, as in a list, but because it fits grammatically and semantically. The number of alternatives for any individual word is therefore small, and it is easier to recognize words in context than in isolation.

Reading and Listening Comprehension. Score the silent and oral reading comprehension questions separately for each passage and determine the percentage of questions answered correctly. Enter the scores on the record sheet. Repeat the same procedure for all passages read to the student. The generally accepted criteria for reading and listening comprehension scores are:

Independent level: 90% or higher
Instructional level: 70–90%
Frustration level: below 70%

(In our discussion of administering IRIs, you were told to continue testing until 60 percent or less was attained. By doing so we can be sure that the frustration level has been reached.)

Keeping Track of Scores. After you have derived scores for oral reading accuracy, oral and silent reading comprehension, and listening comprehension, enter the scores on a record sheet, which can be stapled to the front of the examiner's copy of the student's IRI. Having all the pertinent scores and observational notes you made during the testing on one sheet aids in interpreting the student's performance. (Interpreting IRI results is discussed in the next section.)

A model score record sheet is included on page 146 as Figure 4.6. On this sheet are spaces for recording all scores from the IRI, notes and observations, information about the student such as age and grade, and scores from the word recognition inventory (discussed later in this chapter). Look ahead at Figure 4.6 now, and read more about it in the next section.

Interpreting the IRI

As with all assessment procedures, the IRI scores are not an end in themselves. They should be interpreted and then applied in instructional planning. To do so, the student's functional reading levels must be determined.

Establishing Reading Levels. The scores derived from the oral reading and comprehension measures are used to determine overall levels. Scores for both oral reading and comprehension areas should meet the criteria for the instructional level in order to be sure the reader will be comfortable at that level. The necessary scores are:

	ORAL READING	COMPREHENSION
Independent level:	97%	90%
Instructional level:	90%	70%
Frustration level:	below 90%	below 70%
Listening comprehension level:	—	above 70%

The child in Example 1 is reading comfortably at the preprimer (PP) level with accurate word recognition, excellent comprehension, and scores at the independent level.

At the primer (P) level, her oral reading accuracy is still good although she made more miscues, and comprehension is good in both oral and silent reading. Primer level is a good instructional level for this youngster, but beyond primer, both word recognition and comprehension break down. The first-grade level represents her frustration level.

The listening comprehension score of 80 percent at second grade shows that this youngster's potential reading level is second grade, which corresponds with her grade placement. She has the potential, represented by her listening comprehension, to read at second-grade level but presently is able to read only primer level material, about two levels below her potential at this time.

The student in Example 2 read the IRI passages at second-grade level because of his age. If his performance at second grade had not been good, we could have moved back to lower levels. His scores at second grade on oral reading and both oral and silent comprehension show that he can read

EXAMPLE 1. Scores for eight-year-old student, second grader (in percentages).

GRADE	ORAL READING	COMPREHENSION		
		ORAL	SILENT	LISTENING
PP	97	100	100	—
P	94	75	80	—
1	88	60	50	—
2	—	—	—	80
3	—	—	—	60

EXAMPLE 2. Scores for eleven-year-old student, fifth grader (in percentages).

		COMPREHENSION		
GRADE	ORAL READING	ORAL	SILENT	LISTENING
PP	—	—	—	—
P	—	—	—	—
1	—	—	—	—
2	99	100	90	—
3	94	85	80	—
4	91	70	70	—
5	86	50	55	—
6	—	—	—	90

material through the second grade independently. His scores on all measures at the third and fourth grades fall within the instructional range, and consequently we can say that fourth grade represents his highest instructional level. His instructional reading level includes both third- and fourth-grade material.

With all fifth-grade scores falling in the frustration range, we can conclude that fifth-grade material is too difficult for this youngster to read, but the 90 percent listening comprehension score at sixth grade shows his ability to deal successfully on an auditory basis with material above his present grade. A fifth grader with a fourth-grade instructional level is probably not experiencing serious difficulty in his present grade, but this youngster's listening comprehension score shows that he has the ability to read at least sixth-grade material. Thus he is not functioning at his full potential.

Deriving percentages of correct responses and using these scores to determine reading levels is called *quantitative analysis*. It shows *how many* correct and incorrect responses the reader has made. Although this analysis is useful, it is incomplete because it lacks the essential element of in-depth analysis of the student's responses. In order to determine what the reader knows and where help is needed, we must determine the strategies underlying the correct and incorrect responses. We have to look for patterns of strengths and weaknesses. From this perspective it is not so important *how many* correct responses the student made but rather *which* responses were right and *why*. This assessment is termed *qualitative analysis*, because it focuses on the quality of responses and the strategies the reader demonstrated. Quantitative analysis will aid us in determining the levels of difficulty of text the reader can deal with successfully. Qualitative analysis aids us in determining what the student has mastered and what skills and processes are lacking. Only when both kinds of analyses are accomplished can we develop a prescriptive program for a reader.

Analyzing Oral Reading. The context in which a word appears is a powerful aid to word recognition, but context is provided only by connected text. When we code the responses during the oral reading of IRI passages, we can analyze word recognition within the real act of reading. Thus accurate coding and analysis are important.

In oral reading, even the most fluent adult reader will occasionally say something a bit different from the precise words on the page. Any well-read adult who has made minor slip-of-the-tongue errors while reading aloud knows this, and we are usually unaware that what we said was not precisely what was written. These divergences can hardly be called errors. In fact, they are not even noticed when the syntax and meaning are perfectly preserved. While some miscues change the meaning very little, if at all, other miscues can change the author's message and interfere with comprehension. Consider the following examples.

Two young readers encounter this sentence in print:

My father and I went fishing.

One reader says, "My *daddy* and I went fishing." The other reader says, "My *fatter* and I went fishing." Each youngster made one divergent oral reading response, both on the same intended word. Are the young readers alike in their reading strategies? Not at all! The first reader shows much greater reading power because this miscue preserved the author's intended meaning. "Daddy" is an acceptable synonym for "father," particularly in some widely used Southern and Western dialects.

The second reader's miscue, however, did not preserve the author's meaning. "Father" and "fatter" do not have the same meaning, nor do the two words function similarly in text; they are different parts of speech — one is a noun and the other is a comparative adjective. Therefore, both meaning and syntactic continuity are broken. What has the second reader used to produce this miscue? Apparently, letter sounds. The initial and final sounds in "father" and "fatter" are alike, although the first-syllable vowel sound and medial digraph are not; also, both words have two syllables and look very similar. While the printed word and the miscue look and sound somewhat alike, the miscue violates both syntax and meaning within the sentence. The first reader's miscue was not serious, but the second reader's miscue was.

We can ask ourselves four basic questions about any oral reading miscue that involves the substitution, insertion, or omission of a word or phrase in text:

1. Does the miscue *mean* about the same as the word(s) in the text? Is the message radically altered?
2. Does the miscue *function* syntactically in nearly the same way as the word(s) in the text? Is the miscue the same kind of word (part of speech)?

3. Does the miscue *look* or *sound* much like the word(s) in the text? Are the number of syllables, general configuration, or letter sounds largely preserved?
4. If the reader is a dialect speaker, does the miscue make sense within his or her dialect?

A reader can use meaning, syntax, and letter sounds to identify unknown words without radically changing the author's message or the syntax. In the foregoing example, the substitution of "daddy" for "father" preserves both meaning and syntax. This is qualitatively the "best" kind of miscue, for there is little or no loss of comprehension. Because meaning and syntactic function are so closely related in language, qualitatively "good" miscues often reflect both semantic and syntactic similarity to the author's usage. However, syntax can be changed somewhat without necessarily changing the meaning. A reader might change the tense of a verb or change an adverb to an adjective and still preserve the author's intended message. Thus a qualitatively "good" miscue can preserve the meaning even if the syntax is altered.

The least productive strategy, exemplified by the miscue "My fatter and I . . .," is the use of letter and letter-sound cues exclusively, without regard for the word's meaning or function. When a student tries to read words letter-by-letter or syllable-by-syllable, the meaning is frequently lost because a letter-by-letter or part-by-part strategy slows down the reading of the text too much for comprehension. It also fragments meaningful units to the point where their meaning is lost. A reader who uses both letter sounds and context clues to analyze an unknown word has the best chance of producing a miscue that will not interfere with comprehension.

Let's review the more common types of miscues and how they are coded on the IRI. (Figure 4.4 summarizes the miscue types and the coding system we introduced earlier in this chapter.)

Our previous example of miscue coding, Figure 4.3, illustrates how miscues would be analyzed qualitatively. Some of the miscues in Figure 4.3 occur singly, some in phrases. We will consider those that occur in phrases and meaningful units together, because here we are not concerned with how many miscues there are, but whether there is a change in meaning as a result of them.

First, let's compile a list of the miscues, showing what the text said on one side and what a young boy said on the other. Our list would look like Table 4.2.

Included in this list are the two spontaneously corrected miscues, which are marked "optional." Some practitioners analyze corrected miscues, others do not. What is important is the fact that the reader did correct them. When meaning was being interfered with, the meaning loss was caught and corrected. For analysis we will look at corrected and uncorrected substitutions, insertions, and omissions, but we will not analyze regressions or words the examiner supplied. Table 4.3 shows eight uncorrected and two corrected language units involving one or more miscues. How many, and which ones, changed the author's meaning significantly?

Let's look at each miscue, compare it with the author's construction, and place a check next to each miscue that significantly alters the author's message.

It may be argued that the author's message *is* altered by such changes as "*a* farm" to "*the* farm" or "*one* other kind" to "*another* kind," but such alteration is exceedingly small, and it is doubtful that the overall facts or tone of the passage are at all modified by such minor semantic adjustment. It is

FIGURE 4.4. Miscue types and miscue coding system.

Substitution of a word or phrase: student's word written over word in text

$$dog$$

The doll fell from the shelf.

Insertion of a word not in text: Word written in over a caret or small arrow

$$down$$

The doll fell ∧ from the shelf.

Omission of a word, word part, or phrase: Omitted element circled

The (big) dog ran away.

Examiner aid given to student: Parentheses placed around word

The climbers were assisted by (Sherpa) tribesmen.

Spontaneous correction: Check mark next to original coding

The (big)✓ dog ran away.

Repetition of word or phrase: Wavy line under repeated element

Once upon a time a wizard . . .

Reversal of order of words: Proofreader's symbol for inversion used

"Let's go," shouted Sally.

Pauses longer than normal: Slashes indicate long pauses (one per second)

The // controversial theory was discussed . . .

TABLE 4.2. List of miscues.

TEST	READER
. . . on a farm.	. . . on the farm.
. . . sheep do not run away.	. . . sheep don't run away.
And they must . . .	They must . . .
. . . sheep are not lost . . .	. . . sheep do not get lost . . .
. . . one other kind . . .	. . . another kind . . .
. . . kind of work dog?	. . . kind of sheep dog?
. . . in the deep, cold snow.	. . . in the cold, deep snow.
optional: . . . a farm worker.	. . . a worker. (corrected)
optional: . . . dog must be kind . . .	. . . dog must be king . . . (corrected)
. . . help the man do many things.	. . . help the man to do many things.

TABLE 4.3. Miscues and original text phrases.

TEST	READER	MEANING CHANGE?
on a farm	on the farm	
sheep do not run away	sheep don't run away	
And they must	They must	
sheep are not lost	Sheep do not get lost	
one other kind	another kind	
kind of work dog	kind of sheep dog	√
deep, cold snow	cold, deep snow	
a farm worker	a worker (corrected)	√
must be kind	must be king (corrected)	√
help the man do	help the man to do	

very interesting to note that in this passage only one meaning-change miscue occurred that was not corrected. The correction on the other two meaning-change miscues indicates that although this reader's oral rendition does not precisely match what appears on the page, he was sensitive to and was monitoring his own comprehension and in two of three cases was aware of his more serious miscues and reread to correct himself. The other miscues, which preserved the author's message, were ignored (uncorrected). In spite of the inaccuracies, this reading was qualitatively good, because there was only one uncorrected meaning-change miscue.

Recall that in the section Scoring an IRI, when we counted the gross number of uncorrected miscues in the passage to determine the quantitative percentage of accurate word recognition in context, we counted nine scorable miscues: five substitutions, two insertions, one omission, and one word given by the examiner. In our qualitative analysis, we did not include the "examiner aid" but did include the two-word reversal of word order. If we simply count the number of miscues, the student had 94 percent accuracy in the oral reading. When we look at the quality of each miscue, however, the 94 percent figure is somewhat misleading because only the substitution of "sheep dog" for "work dog" changed the meaning of the sentence.

We could carry our analysis one step further. Since we have calculated a *gross* oral reading accuracy score for all uncorrected miscues and evaluated each miscue for its degree of meaning change, we could now score the word recognition in context by including in the count only the uncorrected miscues that caused a meaning change. In this way we could derive a *net* oral reading accuracy score. In the "sheep dog" example (Figure 4.3, page 126) the reader's gross accuracy was 94 percent and the net oral reading accuracy about 99 percent, since for each uncorrected miscue we deducted .63 percent. The difference in these two scores, according to the criteria for independent and instructional levels, means that this material is appropriate for this student's instructional level if great oral reading accuracy is required. It is appropriate for independent level reading if the teacher tolerates a number of miscues or if the material is to be read silently.

Few teachers today require nearly perfect oral reading at sight, which is a demand few, if any, readers can fulfill. Miscue research has repeatedly shown that no one consistently reads aloud without miscuing, and most teachers tolerate miscues that do not change the author's meaning. In such a miscue-tolerant setting, the student could be given this material or comparable material to read independently for pleasure and information, homework, extended direct instruction, or a research project. Although the oral reading was not perfect, the miscues were qualitatively good and rarely caused his comprehension to suffer. The miscues indicate that this reader understands more than his oral reading accuracy suggests.

Informal analysis of the miscues in an oral reading passage sometimes reveals that, unlike this student, a reader's miscues do contribute to comprehension loss. These miscues are easily spotted when a meaning-loss checklist is made, like the list in Table 4.3. In this case, both the gross and net oral reading accuracy percentages will be similar.

When miscue analysis reveals that many of the miscues are significantly different in meaning from the words in the text, then the material should not be used for instruction even if the gross oral reading score is within the instructional range. The reader will need not only to be placed in somewhat easier material, but also to be taught how to use context more effectively as a word recognition cue as well as decoding.

An effective way to teach this process to students is to use a method Holdaway (1979) refers to as "confirmation," in which text is placed on a transparency and a mask is used to uncover successive parts of the story or passage. Salient words are left covered while the children are encouraged to guess at several alternatives that would make sense in the context; then the first letter or first few letters are uncovered to allow readers to select their most likely alternative or come up with another guess.

In Chapter Five, we will describe in detail how this method is used as well as the instructional use of the cloze procedure. The point to be made here is that it is not only possible but very important to systematically teach youngsters to use context and sense-making strategies *along with* decoding strategies when they are reading (both orally and silently) so that when miscues occur, as they do in everyone's reading, the miscues will change the meaning as little as possible.

Another important issue to keep in mind in analyzing miscues is the reader's use of self-correction. We have already seen that we do not count corrections the reader makes when we derive the oral reading accuracy score, but we need to do more than just give credit for corrections. For corrections reveal to us whether or not the reader is monitoring his or her own comprehension and whether or not the reader is willing to back up and take another look when something doesn't seem to make sense. Self-corrections occur when the reader considers what he or she has said (read aloud) in light of further information (Cohen, 1975). Thus they indicate an ongoing attempt to understand and make sense during reading.

Dialects and Oral Reading. Standard English written text may differ in a number of subtle ways from the grammar of a reader's nonstandard oral dialect. When the dialect speaker reads aloud, *dialect miscues* may result. These miscues occur when the dialect speaker translates standard English syntactic forms into the slightly different, predictable syntactic forms of his or her dialect.

For example, a speaker of Black English may oral-read

"This is my mother," Rose said.

as

"This my mother," Rose say.

or

He has ten cents.

as

He got ten cent.

Because the conventions of Black English may include omission of auxiliary verbs in particular semantic contexts, use of *be* in place of *am, is,* and *are,* and omission of some noun plural and verb tense markers, the miscues in the preceding examples represent dialect translations rather than word recognition errors. The oral reading does not correspond precisely with what is written, but meaning is not lost. The miscues represent the reader's translation of standard English syntax into his or her oral dialect.

During the 1960s and 1970s it was proposed that because many poor readers were also dialect speakers, the apparent "mismatch" between their dialects and written standard English was a major cause of reading failure. This *dialect interference theory* led to the creation of beginning reading material in Black English and other largely unsuccessful remedies. Subsequent research has failed to show, however, that dialect causes reading failure (Lass, 1980; Schwartz, 1982 and others). In listening comprehension tasks, young Black English speakers have been shown to comprehend standard English stories better than those in Black English (Branisel, 1977; Cagney, 1977).

It is important not to confuse dialect miscues with true word recognition problems, for such confusion can result in falsely underestimating the word recognition abilities of dialect speakers, applying remediation when it is not needed, and undermining the self-confidence of dialect speakers.

In order to distinguish dialect miscues from word recognition problems, you must be well informed about and familiar with the range of standard and nonstandard forms your students use, and with the grammatical regularities of dialects in your area. If you are unsure whether the miscues a student produced are dialect translations, ask him or her to explain the point in other words, or somehow demonstrate what was read. Dialect miscues may not sound exactly like what was on the page, but if the dialect speaker can demonstrate that the text was comprehended, the miscues are of relatively little significance.

Analyzing Comprehension. By looking at oral and silent reading comprehension scores across several grade levels, we can determine if the reader has a marked strength or weakness in comprehension during either oral or silent reading and whether this pattern is consistent with what others of the same age do. We can also spot a pattern by looking at responses to the different types of comprehension questions within a grade level and across levels that tell us whether the student has particular strengths or weaknesses in recalling main ideas or details, forming inferences, and other comprehension skills required by the questions.

Oral versus silent comprehension. If readers consistently show better comprehension performance with oral reading and lower comprehension scores with silent reading, we can conclude that they have to hear themselves say the words aloud in order to understand. Such readers process print as though they were processing speech. They translate or recode print into speech sounds and derive meaning from the spoken words. This is fairly typical of beginning readers, especially those whose initial reading instruction has been primarily oral. Often these beginning readers literally cannot read silently; they mumble, whisper, or hunch over their books and continue reading aloud, but softly. When forced to read silently, they sometimes lose their places because they do not have their voices to help "anchor" them in the print. It is not surprising when they read aloud and show consistently better oral than silent comprehension, since oral reading is still so widely used in primary classrooms. If, however, we see a student older than about eight or nine reading this way, it is a matter of great concern. Reading aloud, even softly, is not mature, adult reading — silent reading is. Beyond the primary grades, emphasis quickly shifts to rapid, silent reading for meaning. An older student who has to read audibly may have much trouble reading the volume of material required in upper grades.

Also, silent reading is much faster than oral since it has almost no maximum limit. Speed readers can often read 1000 words a minute, and most fluent-reading adults can zoom through interesting material for pleasure at 400–600 words a minute. Speed is certainly not everything, but it is important because of the limits of short-term memory. Poor readers who must claw their way across a line of text, suffering from Smith's metaphorical "tunnel vision" (1978), may find it virtually impossible to grasp the meaning of what is in front of them. Most fluent-reading adults can read popular adult materials silently at roughly 300–500 words a minute, perhaps faster when interest is high. On the other hand, oral reading, even when it is rapid, is limited to the normal speed of speech. Because of our articulatory limitations, we can be clearly understood only if we read no faster than 200–300 words a minute. In oral reading, even when the eyes are leaping ahead, the mouth must necessarily lag behind. Thus the speed factor is another reason why mature reading is silent rather than oral.

Most experts agree that oral reading is somewhat more difficult than silent, except perhaps for the very beginning reader. For everyone who already knows how to read, oral reading is a two-step process (getting meaning plus proper pronunciation with expression) while silent reading omits the pronunciation step.

It is therefore a common finding that as children approach the end of the primary grades, somewhere between the second and the fourth grade, they begin to shift toward more silent reading and characteristically show better comprehension after silent than after oral reading. This is a normal developmental finding; it certainly does not indicate that these older students show an oral reading weakness or that they should begin a lot of remedial oral reading! On the contrary, it should be deemphasized and silent reading emphasized in the upper grades.

Comprehension skill patterns. If we go back to the comprehension questions following the IRI passages, and if we included a notation of *what kind* of question each one was, we can discern whether there was a particular type that gave a student consistent difficulty. Now we can see the great usefulness of notations like (V), (F), and (MI) next to each comprehension question. By systematically looking from one grade level to another, we can see what, if any, pattern emerges. Was there a kind of question, for example, inference questions, that repeatedly gave the student difficulty at different levels? Was there a type of question that the student consistently answered correctly across several grade levels? A typical pattern might be one where they always got the main idea questions correct but had great difficulty with recall of important details; another might be that they showed much ability to remember factual, explicitly stated information but had difficulty arriving at conclusions or forming inferences based on implied information. Looking for individual patterns in comprehension responses allows us to design appropriate comprehension activities for students according to their individual needs.

However, in order for us to interpret that a reader's patterns in responding to questions indicate strengths or weaknesses in comprehension, we must be quite certain that the questions really tap the comprehension skills they purport to. Schell and Hanna (1981) argue that too often comprehension questions on commercial IRIs "... are not always objectively classifiable and that the meaning of the various subskill groups may not be uniformly clear . . ." (p. 264). In other words, do IRI questions labeled as "main idea," for example, clearly and discretely call for comprehension of the main idea? Hanna and Schell demonstrated that even experienced teachers attempting to classify comprehension questions by type often classified questions quite differently from the authors of a particular IRI.

Unquestioning acceptance of IRI question classifications, and indeed unquestioning acceptance of all IRI questions as "good questions," just because they appear in a published IRI, is unwise. But comprehension patterns can often be discerned, and helpful teaching strategies devised from these judgments *if* teachers continually use critical judgment when they use IRI questions.

Our best advice to you is, don't take either the quality of questions or the way the author classified them on faith. Read the passages and each of the questions, and consider carefully whether you think the questions are appropriately labeled by type. Then, if you discern a consistent pattern in a student's response to particular question types, consider your judgment as a "working hypothesis" about the student's needs.

Begin instruction, based on your hypothesis that a student needs practice in particular areas, but continue to evaluate based on how the student responds to that instruction. Further teaching may reveal that what looked like a comprehension skill weakness on the IRI did not persist or that what looked like an area of strength did not continue to be a strength for the reader beyond the IRI, in real text. Only further teaching will reveal whether your judgments were accurate.

Patterns in listening comprehension. If students achieve 70 percent or better on the comprehension questions after listening to a passage read aloud by the examiner, we assume that they can deal successfully with similar concepts and vocabulary on an auditory basis, although they cannot read that level of material for themselves. We refer to the highest grade level at which the student had 70 percent or better as the student's listening comprehension level, or hearing capacity level. This level is important because it helps us determine what we can *expect* this student to achieve and thus makes it possible to set reasonable instructional goals.

Most students who are not fluent, mature readers can listen to someone else reading aloud and understand material they cannot yet read successfully because most of them, especially the younger ones, are still learning and developing as readers while they have been competent listeners and language users for a lot longer. Most students who are still developing as readers can grasp the meaning from oral language (including print read aloud) more easily and efficiently than from written language. Therefore, their hearing capacity levels are somewhat above their instructional reading levels, which is predictable, for it shows that they are not yet able to read as well as they can think.

Some youngsters will have instructional reading and listening comprehension levels that are the same. Material too difficult for them to read is also too difficult for them to understand on an auditory basis. This is fine. What it shows is that they are reading just as well as they can and that at the present time there is not much room for improvement. These pupils are reading right at their potential, using all their ability to read as well as they do. They need support and further instruction, but if they are poor readers, they will probably make steady, but not spectacular, gains in reading. The listening comprehension level represents a sort of overall goal in reading improvement. If all conditions were ideal (which they never are, of course) readers might be expected to be able to raise their instructional levels up to their listening levels. If these levels already match, then for the present time they are doing as well as we could expect.

The listening comprehension level is dynamic, not fixed or static. As children grow older and their experiences burgeon, they can understand more and more difficult material. The average seven-year-old can listen to and understand stories appropriate for second or third graders and understand them, but ninth-grade material would be too difficult conceptually. By the time the child is twelve or thirteen, however, ninth-grade material may well be comprehensible because vocabulary, store of concepts, and experiences have grown in those five years. The listening capacity level represents an estimate of *present* functioning. Just as we would expect a child's instructional level in June to be somewhat higher than in the previous September, we would expect his or her listening capacity level to have advanced somewhat through a school year. Establishing a student's capacity level once and using it as an ongoing standard, however, is no more appropriate than expecting last year's instructional level to be the same next year.

The capacity level should never be equated with or confused with I.Q., but it does give us some rough indication of whether a child's verbal intelligence is about average, or somewhat above, or somewhat below. Children with average verbal intelligence will usually have listening capacity levels at or very near their present grade placement. Here are three examples, all second graders:

Jenny's listening comprehension level is late second grade. Since she is in second grade, we infer that her verbal intelligence is roughly average for her age and that she has the necessary concepts and vocabulary to learn to read second-grade material successfully, although at the present time she has a first-grade instructional level. Although her instructional level is low, she can improve her reading with appropriate instruction and support.

Matt has a listening comprehension level of sixth grade. He has the concepts and vocabulary to listen to and understand very advanced material, and he is obviously very bright. In spite of his potential, he is achieving at grade level, and has an instructional level of late second grade. Thus his achievement is average for his grade, although he has the potential for higher achievement. The finding that Matt is not performing at his full potential is not necessarily negative. If he is comfortable, motivated, and interested, there is no need for concern. If he appears apathetic, bored, or frustrated, then he certainly needs greater intellectual challenge.

Sandy has an instructional level of first grade, and his listening level is also first grade. Although Sandy's achievement is below grade level, it is in line with his present potential. Sandy may be a slow learner or of below-average verbal intelligence; he may have learned to read later than others, or may be disinterested in high achievement or in the materials he works in. At any rate, his performance and potential appear to be in line at the present. Sandy needs much support and instruction, and as he becomes a more proficient reader, his listening capacity level will increase. This in turn will make greater reading improvement possible.

Constructing an IRI

Creating your own IRI is a very challenging task. Selecting good passages and creating thoughtful, challenging questions will help you become much more aware of the comprehension process and become a more discerning user of all tests. However, it is not a task we recommend you undertake without a great deal of help and supervision. A team of teachers working together with the help of an experienced clinician or instructor is the best way to attempt such a task.

Constructing an IRI consists of two stages. The first is developing the material themselves: selecting reading passages and creating comprehension questions, retelling outlines and cloze procedures for each passage, and making up both a reader's copy and examiner's forms. The second stage, often omitted in directions for IRI construction, is critically important: try out and evaluate your instrument before you use it to make decisions about a student's reading. Commercial test makers call this "field testing," and it is as important for you to field test your own IRI as it is for the biggest commercial test maker.

Creating IRI Materials. The following steps will help you complete the first stage of IRI construction.

1. *Select passages for reading and listening comprehension for each book level, primer (or preprimer) through ninth grade (or above).* Most often, passages are selected from current basal readers. We recommend using a series other than the one you use for your ongoing reading instruction, because if you use passages from stories your students have already read, their performance may be inflated. Use an alternate series that is similar in format and difficulty to the one in current use; *don't* use an old, outdated series, for it may be considerably easier than the one you use.

Select three different passages at each grade level, so you can assess silent and oral reading and listening comprehension separately. Choose passages (parts of longer stories, if necessary) that are typical of that grade level in content and subject matter. Avoid passages with many unusual proper names, words in another language, or unusual or technical topics. Keep all the passages at each grade level consistent in length: 100- to 200-word passages are best, with primary-grade passages shorter than higher-level ones. Avoid using the middle of a longer story, for important information may be lost by omitting the beginning. Do not use one long passage divided into two or three parts, as some experts recommend, for whatever is understood (or not understood) from one passage will necessarily affect comprehension of the subsequent parts.

Always recheck the difficulty level of passages using a readability formula. Don't assume that a publisher's statement of the reading level of a book necessarily holds for a particular passage, since different stories in any basal may vary widely in readability level. Readability formulas are easy to compute by hand and many are available as software programs for personal computers. (Ask your librarian or reading specialist if your school has such a program available for assessing readability of books.)

2. *Write comprehension questions for each passage.* There is no "best" number of questions for a passage; the number of questions depends on passage content. Begin by reading each passage and creating a list of information you recall from the passage. Then develop a set of questions that tap this information, including not only direct recall of stated information but also questions that call for interpretation and evaluation. Main ideas, important supporting details, sequences, cause-effect relationships, inferred information, understanding of vocabulary, and interpretation of characters' feelings and motives are all aspects of comprehension. Figure 4.5 shows sample questions that call on a variety of comprehension abilities.

Include a reinspection item for each passage so you can observe how successfully a reader can scan for and locate specific information after an initial reading.

Here are a few guidelines that may be helpful in writing comprehension questions:

FIGURE 4.5. Sample comprehension questions.

Literal Comprehension

(Answers to questions explicitly stated in passage)

Main idea: What event was this story about?

What might make a good title for this story?

Important detail: What kind of animal was Nitwit?

What did Bob do as soon as he got home?

Sequence: What happened after Jill heard the window break?

Where did the children go first?

Characterization: What did Ms. Willis do that showed she was angry?

How did Bruce act when he saw Jamie again?

Reinspection: Find the sentence that describes Ben's new bike and read it to me.

Find the place in the story where the children began to argue, and read it out loud.

Interpretation and Judgment

(Answers to questions not explicitly stated in passage)

Inference: Why do you think Jim spoke roughly to the dog?

What makes you believe Cathy might enjoy flying?

Vocabulary: What did Rita mean when she said "I'm simply green"?

What is a "chopper" in this story?

Prediction: What might happen if the delivery boy loses the package?

If Shana runs away, where might she go?

---

a. Make sure every question can be answered or inferred from the selected passage.

b. Do not make all the questions literal comprehension questions; about half is sufficient.

c. Formulate questions for each passage that require interpretation and judgment as well as literal comprehension (see Figure 4.5). However, you need not include every type of question for every passage.

d. Frame questions that call for understanding the most important events or concepts in the passage. Ask yourself, "What is the student most likely to remember after reading this passage?" Don't ask for unimportant details.

e. Keep the wording simple. A long, involved question can preclude a correct response.

f. Avoid yes-no and either-or questions. They can be answered correctly 50 percent of the time by guessing. "Did Bob go to the zoo?" or "Did Bob go to the zoo or to the park?" are poor questions. A better question would be "Where did Bob go?"

g. Avoid questions that require only one-word answers; encourage the reader to respond and explain in natural language.

h. Ask the questions in the order in which the information appeared in the story. If you don't, one question can give away the answer to a subsequent one.

For additional information about informal reading inventory questions refer to Johnson and Kress (1965); Pearson and Johnson (1978); Peterson, Greenlaw, and Tierney (1978); Pikulski (1974); Pikulski and Shanahan (1982); Schell and Hanna (1981); Stauffer, Abrams and Pikulski (1978); and Valmont (1972).

3. *So that you can use retelling as a comprehension check as well as questions, create a retelling outline for each passage.* Refer to Figure 4.2 for an example. A checklist format is easy to use. Include all the important information in phrases, in the order in which the information occurred in the passage. (Use your own recall to help you include the most important information.)

4. *Make up a student's copy of each passage.* You will use this copy over and over, so you only need one copy of each passage. Carefully type each passage on a separate sheet of paper, double spacing for clarity. For primary-grade children, type the primer and first-grade passages using a large-type or primer typewriter. Check and recheck for typing errors! For greater durability, laminate pages or glue them to tagboard sheets. Put the passages in order and place them in a binder or notebook.

5. *Make up examiner's pages for each passage.* Double space each passage so you have room above each line to write in miscues. Include at the top of each passage the title, book, and page number and series from which the passage was taken. Count the number of words in the passage and compute the miscue deduction for each by dividing the number of words into 100.00. Under the passage, type the retelling outline, leaving blanks for checking off, and the list of questions for each passage, leaving enough space between questions to write in the student's answers and your probes and observations. Code each question by type (MI = main idea, V = vocabulary, etc.). You may include allowable answers in parentheses if you wish.

6. *Make up a summary sheet to record scores and observations.* This form allows you to compare performance across and within levels and to record your judgments and recommendations. Figure 4.6 is an example that can be adapted to include other information. (On Figure 4.6 we have included space for scores on the word recognition inventory, to be discussed in the next section.)

Testing and Evaluating Your IRI. If you are a wise consumer of tests, you would never use a completely untried test and assume its value or accuracy without evidence that it did what it purported to do. So it must be with teacher-made IRIs. You can validate and test out your instrument before you use it to make judgments about students' reading in a number of ways:

FIGURE 4.6. Informal reading inventory record sheet.

Student_____

Age_____ Grade_____

Date tested_____

Tested by_____

GRADE	WORD RECOGNITION INVENTORY FLASHED	UNTIMED	ORAL READING (IN CONTEXT)	COMPREHENSION ORAL	SILENT	LISTENING
PP						
P						
1st						
2nd						
3rd						
4th						
5th						
6th						
7th						
8th						
9th						

READING LEVELS   Strengths:_____

Independent_____   _____

Instructional_____   _____

Frustration_____   Weaknesses:_____

Listening_____   _____

Recommendations:_____

_____

_____

1. Double-check the readability of every passage with a readability formula. If a passage you selected has a higher readability level than you wanted, select another passage. Don't try to make a passage "easier" by rewriting, creating shorter sentences or using different words. This may have little or no effect on the actual difficulty of the material (Hansell, 1976).

2. Have several readers try to answer your comprehension questions *without* reading the passage. Any that can be correctly answered in this way should be thrown out, for they call for general information rather than comprehension of the passage itself.

3. Ask other teachers to read passages and questions without knowing how you classified the questions, and to classify the questions themselves. If there is general disagreement about what types of question some are, change the questions or create new ones so they are more clearly and directly classifiable as one type or another (main idea, sequence, inference, etc).

4. Ask a number of students to read passages and give you immediate oral retellings to see if what is typically remembered from passages is reflected in your retelling outlines and in your questions.

5. After making necessary changes in passages and questions, give your IRI to a number of students whose instructional levels and strengths and weaknesses you know about. Do the results of your IRI bear out what you already knew, or do they contradict? This kind of informal field testing will help you determine if your IRI is fairly accurate in placing students at instructional levels.

6. After you have given your IRI to some students and derived a tentative instructional level, cross-check this with a cloze procedure (see the section at the end of this chapter) made up from different text at the same readability level. If your IRI indicates a fifth-grade instructional level, for example, that reader should be able to adequately complete a cloze text for comparable fifth-grade material if he or she has been shown how to complete a cloze test. (See The Cloze Procedure at the end of this chapter.)

The Informal Word Recognition Inventory

This instrument consists of graded lists of individual words which may often occur in text at a particular grade level. These graded word lists, usually primer level through grade six, are included in commercial IRIs and can be quite easily made up if you are constructing your own IRI or to supplement a commercial one. (Directions for WRI construction follow in the next section.)

The word recognition inventory, or WRI, is used to assess sight vocabulary and some aspects of phonic and structural analysis. Since the words appear in isolation, the WRI is not used to assess comprehension or context.

An informal word recognition inventory is useful in assessing sight vocabulary and word analysis strategies. Individual words are revealed for a very brief exposure.

Some clinicians also use the WRI to help them determine where to begin administering the reading passages of the IRI. For this purpose, the WRI is given first, before the IRI, and the examiner begins having the student read story passages at the grade level where he or she first began to miss some words. We prefer to give the WRI after the IRI, because we prefer to have the student begin reading connected text first, since that is our primary diagnostic purpose. But giving the WRI first is an accepted practice, and we feel it should be a matter of individual preference.

The WRI consists of a graded set of word lists for the student to look at and a corresponding set of examiner's pages for the teacher to mark and score as the instrument is administered. The student's copy contains only the words arranged in lists. The examiner's copy consists of the words followed by blanks for filling in what the reader said when errors in word recognition occurred. The examiner uses two small cards to cover each word and then expose it very briefly (referred to as "flashing" the word). This very brief exposure allows the reader only enough time to recognize the word at sight, but not enough time to decode it. Words recognized after the *flashed presentation* are considered to be in the student's sight vocabulary. When a word is unrecognized or incorrectly identified, the word is uncovered and the reader is given sufficient time to examine the word and attempt to use phonic and structural analysis to decode it. This is referred to as the *untimed presentation.* The student's responses after both presentations are recorded on the examiner's sheets. Two blanks follow each word on the examiner's

FIGURE 4.7. Sample examiner's page for WRI.

SECOND GRADE (LEVEL H)

	FLASHED	UNTIMED
present	_____	_____
grove	_____	_____
legs	_____	_____
dish	_____	_____
strong	_____	_____
tying	_____	_____
voice	_____	_____
draw	_____	_____
ahead	_____	_____
cattle	_____	_____
family	_____	_____
five	_____	_____
clothes	_____	_____
bit	_____	_____
humming	_____	_____
spent	_____	_____
charms	_____	_____
dub	_____	_____
baton	_____	_____
pegs	_____	_____
thumped	_____	_____
crawled	_____	_____
artist	_____	_____
guards	_____	_____
life	_____	_____
accuracy scores:	_____%	_____%

SOURCE: From *Boats, Towers, and Bananas* (Boston: Houghton Mifflin, 1982). Reprinted by permission.

sheets: one for response after the word is flashed and one for response if the word is shown in untimed presentation (see Figure 4.7).

These responses are used both for scoring, or counting the errors and determining the levels at which the student is most comfortable in word recognition, and for analyzing the patterns and skills the student uses consistently and those that appear to need review and practice.

Administering, Scoring, and Interpreting the Word Recognition Inventory

The word recognition inventory (WRI) is easy to give and score and usually takes only a few minutes to administer. Here are the steps in administering this test:

1. Seat the student next to you at a table. If you are right-handed, the student should sit on your left; if you are left-handed, on your right. Place the word list in front of the student, face down, along with two 3-by-5-inch file cards. Place the examiner's copy, and a pencil, on the side away from the student.

2. Explain: "I'm going to show you some single words in between these two cards. You'll only see the word for a very short time, so watch closely. Tell me the word as soon as you see it. If you don't know it, I'll give you more time to look at it again. Ready?"

3. Turn the word list face up. With one file card in each hand, cover the first word with one card and cover the rest of the words with the other. Now, moving only the *top* card, expose the entire word for a very short exposure — less than half a second. (This is the flashed presentation, and it shows whether or not the reader recognizes the word at sight.)

4. If the student incorrectly identifies the word, or does not identify it within about three or four seconds, reexpose the word for as long as needed (thus allowing the student to use word analysis to figure out the word). After about ten seconds, go on to the next word, even if the word is not correctly identified on this untimed exposure.

5. If the student does not identify the word correctly, write down what the student says in the appropriate blank on the examiner's copy. If the error was made when the word was flashed, jot down what was said in the flashed column next to the word while you expose the word for the untimed presentation. If the reader corrects an error in either presentation, use a check mark to show the correction. If the word is correctly identified, there is no need to mark anything.

6. Continue down each column of words, giving the flashed presentation for each word and the untimed presentation for miscalled words or when no response is given. When the student fails to recognize about 60 percent of the flashed words, you should stop the procedure.

Score the flashed and untimed columns separately. Give the student credit for spontaneously corrected errors. Record the percentages on the record sheet.

Necessary criteria for the instructional level in word recognition vary somewhat from one expert to another. Some writers of commercial IRIs require 80 percent accuracy on the untimed presentation (Burns and Roe, 1980; Ekwall, 1979), but most authorities use 70 percent as the lower limit (Johnson and Kress, 1965). The point is really academic, since we are not interested in setting an instructional level with the WRI but rather in observing the student's word recognition strategies. Betts himself advocated using the WRI only for such observation (1957), but the following criteria (used mostly for untimed presentations) can be used to categorize the WRI performance:

Independent level: 90% or higher
Instructional level: 70–88%
Frustration level: less than 70%

If you use a commercial IRI, you will probably find that the authors do not give instructions for flashing the words, but only describe how to have students read down the list of words in an untimed fashion. You will also see that on their WRI examiner's pages each word is followed by only one blank for recording errors. Why, then, are we describing the more elaborate procedure?

We use the WRI this way because if you present the words in untimed fashion, you can't tell much about the student's sight recognition of the words. We believe that by omitting flashing we lose important information. The importance of sight vocabulary and rapid recognition of words, and the effect of fluent word recognition on comprehension, is once again being widely recognized after a lengthy period in which fluency was overlooked in favor of decoding and word analysis (see Chapter Five for a discussion of fluency). Also, it is obviously easier to administer a word recognition inventory if you do not flash the words but simply ask the student to read down the list. Since commercial IRI authors use ease of administration as a selling point, they seek to find the simplest means to give, score, and interpret their tests. But we believe that omitting this step causes us to lose information and weakens the instrument's usefulness. Thus we use the flashed and untimed presentations with the WRI. If you use this method with a commercial test, you will need to add another column of blanks to the examiner's pages, and you may need to retype the student's copy of the word lists to create spaces between the words.

Analyzing Word Recognition in Isolation. The WRI can be helpful in assessing sight vocabulary and the use of phonic and structural analysis, but isolated words lack that most powerful word analysis cue: a meaningful context of other words. When words are read from a list rather than in sentences, there are no syntactic or meaning cues to the word's identity, and the reader can only use phonic and structural analysis to figure out unknown words. Thus the WRI gives us information only about those two aspects of word analysis. We must look at actual oral reading for clues to the use of context as a word identification strategy. Within these limitations the WRI can provide valuable information.

Analyzing sight vocabulary. The student's performance on the flashed portion of the instrument gives us information about the general size and strength of the sight vocabulary. We have already shown that sight recognition of a large number of words is necessary to grasp meaning because the need to analyze numerous words in running text is detrimental to comprehension. As discussed in Chapter Two, a large and stable sight vocabulary forms the very basis of fluent reading, and we can gain valuable insight by looking at the student's performance on the word recognition test.

In basal readers, the first few grade levels generally introduce and focus on the mastery of words that occur frequently in text. In general, the more common a word is, the earlier the grade level in which it will appear. Preprimer, primer, and first-grade word lists are usually comprised of common words like *is, the, was, on, I,* and frequently occurring nouns and verbs.

An important aspect to consider, then, is the individual student's performance on the flashed words through the first-grade level. A reader with a large, well-established sight vocabulary will score between 90 and 100 percent on sight recognition of these common words. A reader with a small sight vocabulary, regardless of age, will generally do less well on these first few levels. Scores below the independent range (less than 90 percent) on the first three levels (preprimer, primer, and first grade) of flashed words is an indication that the student's sight recognition of basic high-frequency words needs development.

Analyzing word analysis strategies. The responses on the *untimed portion* of the instrument give us information about the use of phonic and structural analysis. We can tell whether readers are able to make use of word analysis to figure out new words by looking at the difference in scores between the flashed and untimed presentations. Do they consistently correct some of their errors in identifying words on the flashed presentation? If so, the untimed scores will be consistently higher than the corresponding flashed scores, which indicates that they are able to use some word analysis strategies to correct those initial errors. Thus a quick scan of the scores on the untimed presentations compared with the flashed tells us that they have some word analysis skills and understand how to use them.

Knowing whether a youngster can decode is not enough, however. To provide appropriate word analysis instruction, we also need to know *what* skills have been mastered. To learn this, we must look at the individual responses, correct and incorrect, that were made.

We look for patterns of strengths and weaknesses, not isolated incidents, by comparing the elements of the stimulus word to the elements of the responses. We do this by looking across the columns of the word recognition test and comparing the test word with what the examiner has written in the blanks wherever an error was made. What parts of the test word did the student get right when an error was made? Let's consider some samples:

	FLASHED	UNTIMED
trip	0	trap

In this example Mike got both the initial blend sound and the final consonant sound correct but was wrong in the vowel sound in the middle of the word. If Mike used the same strategy a number of times, it would show that he has a grasp of consonant sounds but has some difficulty with medial (middle-position) vowel sounds.

Jim made the following error:

	FLASHED	UNTIMED
trip	*flap*	*flip*

Jim's two attempts show that he preserved the final consonant sound, and he corrected his vowel error on the second attempt. He was unable to produce the correct initial blend, however. Repeated a number of times, this strategy would show a strength in final sounds and some mastery of vowels but difficulty with initial blend sounds.

Here is Becky's attempt:

	FLASHED	UNTIMED
trip	*0*	*tie*

Becky was able to use only the initial consonant sound of *t* to help her. She was not able to decode the blend sound of *tr* and got both the vowel and final consonant sounds wrong. On a number of attempts, this would show that Becky had few word analysis strategies other than beginning consonant sounds and that she needs instruction in all areas of word analysis including a review of initial sounds.

Constructing a Word Recognition Inventory

Developing graded word lists for your own WRI is a fairly simple procedure. Words are selected on the basis of *sampling*. That is, a set of twenty or twenty-five words is taken from the total set of new words introduced at each basal level, which are referred to as "basal words" and are intended to be learned at each level. Lists of basal words are included in the teacher's manuals of basal readers at each level. Sampling is used because we cannot include in a WRI every word a student is exposed to at each level, but we can get a representative group. If a student recognizes most of the words in our sample fairly easily, we assume that he or she could recognize most of the others with about the same ease or difficulty.

To select the words, you will need a teacher's manual for each level of a current basal series, primer through sixth grade. If you made up your own IRI, use the same series from which the passages were taken. If you use a commercial IRI, you may use your current basal series or another series of similar format and difficulty. Use the same series for all the words. (At grades one, two, and sometimes three, there may be two books, one easier than the other. You may construct two lists for each of these grades (e.g., "early first grade" and "late first grade"), or one list (i.e., only the later book for each grade.)

Find the list of basal words introduced at each level, usually listed in the back of each manual.

Here are the steps to follow in constructing a WRI:

1. For each level, determine the total number of new basal words introduced. If you are going to make lists of twenty-five words each, which is a typical length, divide 25 into the total number of basal words and round off the product to the nearest whole number. For example, in a level in which 345 new basal words are introduced,

$$25 \overline{)345.00} = 13.8 \quad \text{or} \quad \underline{14}$$

2. Using the number from step 1 (in our example, 14), count and check off every *nth* word (here, every fourteenth word) in the basal list. If a checked word is a proper noun or a word from another language, select the next word instead.
3. Count up the check marks to be sure you have twenty-five items. If you have fewer, begin counting again after your last check mark, and continue adding items until you have twenty-five. If you have more, delete the last checked items until you have only twenty-five. Make a list of the twenty-five words selected from each level. Cross-check your lists to be sure no item appears more than once. If a duplication occurs, find the word in the basal list and delete it, selecting the previous or succeeding word in the list. If the words in your lists are in alphabetical order, rearrange their order.
4. Repeat this procedure for each level, creating a list of twenty-five sampled items, not in alphabetical order, for each level.
5. To make up a student's copy, carefully type each list of words on a separate sheet, leaving plenty of space between each word. Type the first two or three lists on a large-print typewriter if you can. You may number the words if you wish. For greater durability, mount or laminate the word lists on tagboard or sturdy pages. Place them, in order, with your student's copy of IRI passages.
6. To make examiner's copies of the WRI, type each list of words on a separate sheet followed by two blank spaces, the first column of blanks

headed *Flashed* and the second column headed *Untimed*. Double or triple space lists to allow space for you to write in responses. Type a blank at the bottom of each column for percentages as in Figure 4.7. Leave space on each sheet for your notes and comments. Type the level and book title for each list at the top of each page.

Supplementing Informal Assessments with Commercial Tests

A number of published assessment devices that may be used to supplement informal measures and explore particular areas of reading in more detail are available. Commercial tests are discussed in detail in Chapter Eight, but the brief discussions here are intended to help you become familiar with some specialized commercial tests.

Word Recognition and Phonics Tests

A number of commercial tests intended to test mastery of phonics skills and decoding are available. Usually they consist of letters and letter groups to identify and sound out, real words and pseudowords (nonsense words like *mif*, *dake*, or *faught*) to sound out using common phonic generalizations, and letters-plus-word-stems (like *p - in* or *s - ate*) to combine, or "blend," into pronounceable words.

Some commercial IRIs such as the Diagnostic Reading Scales (Spache), Ekwall Reading Inventory, Classroom Reading Inventory (Silvaroli), and the Bader Reading and Language Inventory include separate phonics inventories. A few standardized achievement tests, like the Woodcock Reading Mastery Test and the Peabody Individual Achievement Test include phonics and word blending subtests. And another group of tests like the Sipay Word Analysis Test, Botel Reading Inventory, and Brigance Diagnostic Inventory of Basic Skills are intended primarily for assessment of decoding skills and do not include other aspects of reading ability.

Tests like these may be useful for screening purposes, since they are fairly quick to administer and do not require analyzing the student's WRI responses. However, it is just this analysis that helps teachers develop the diagnostic skills and judgment they need to fully explore students' abilities. Commercial word attack tests are adequate for screening purposes but should not be depended on to replace careful study of what a child can do. Please see Chapter Eight for fuller discussions of commercial tests.

The Reading Miscue Inventory

In 1972 Yetta M. Goodman and Carolyn Burke published the Reading Miscue Inventory, an individually administered instrument that provided a highly detailed analysis of oral reading. The student read aloud a single story in its entirety and then gave an oral retelling, with probes from the examiner after the unaided retelling. The oral reading was tape recorded. The passage read was selected by the examiner to represent the reader's instructional level. The miscues that occurred and the retelling were extensively analyzed to reveal patterns of strengths and needs in word recognition and comprehension.

The Reading Miscue Inventory (RMI) is presently under revision by Goodman, Burke, and Dorothy Watson. It will be published in 1986 (tentative) by Richard C. Owen Publishing Company, New York, under the tentative title, *Reading Miscue Analysis: Alternative Procedures.* The original Reading Miscue Inventory will be included as well as several new procedures.

In general terms, the procedures for using the RMI are as follows:

1. *The teacher selects material to be read,* usually a basal story or trade book. A typewritten facsimile of the story is made for the teacher's use.
2. *The student reads the story aloud* and the teacher tape records it for greater accuracy in coding the miscues. After the reading, the student retells the story and the teacher probes for all details of plot, characterization, and description that the student can recall.
3. *The teacher evaluates the retelling,* calculates a retelling (comprehension) score, and analyzes the information recalled to show comprehension strengths and weaknesses.
4. *Each of twenty-five miscues is analyzed* according to the degree of correction or dialect involvement, graphic and phonological features, syntactic function and grammatical acceptability, and the degree to which the author's original meaning was preserved. Nine questions are asked about each miscue, which help to reveal the patterns of graphic, phonological, syntactic, and semantic awareness and use.
5. *The teacher prepares a profile* that shows on a bar graph the patterns of strategies used and the strengths and weaknesses in using letter sounds, syntax, and meaning. These patterns are used to plan appropriate instruction.

The Reading Miscue Inventory is a highly detailed device that takes about as long as an informal reading inventory to administer, score, and interpret. The reading and retelling take twenty to forty-five minutes (somewhat less than the administration time for an IRI). Marking, coding, and scoring of miscues, computation, preparation of reader profiles, and recommendations take considerably longer — at least an hour, even for those experienced in using the instrument.

The authors of the Reading Miscue Inventory are well aware that the RMI is a complex instrument that takes considerable time and effort to administer, score, and interpret, and that a lack of clear implications for teaching based on the RMI results has been considered a weakness of the instrument. In their book *Reading Strategies: Focus on Comprehension* (New York: Holt, Rinehart & Winston, 1980), they describe in detail the rationale for the usefulness and practicality of such highly detailed analysis of oral reading, a series of "reading strategy lessons" based on a reader's strengths and needs as revealed by the RMI, and some useful shortcuts that can be taken in the miscue analysis procedure.

An abbreviated procedure Goodman and Burke recommend can be very helpful. They wrote, "Insight into the most significant aspects of miscue analysis can be gained by asking three questions in an informal miscue procedure:

1. Does the sentence the reader finally produces make sense in the context of the whole story?
2. What is the degree of meaning change caused by the miscues as finally produced by the reader?
3. In word-for-word-substitution miscues, what is the degree of graphic similarity between the word in the text and the word produced? (p. 23)

Goodman and Burke then describe how these three questions may be answered by referring to a number of examples, and how bar graphs are developed that show the degree of meaning acceptability, meaning change, and graphic similarity in a reader's miscue profile. These results are then used to develop and implement strategy lessons intended to support the reader's productive strategies and help him or her change unproductive ones.

It is important to note that in this procedure the number of analyses performed by the examiner on each miscue is reduced from nine to three, which makes the procedure much less cumbersome while the most important factors are preserved: the degree to which the reader's miscues resemble the text words in appearance and meaning and the degree to which meaning is changed by them. This suggested modification of the procedure makes it more likely that teachers can and will use miscue analysis in their evaluations, while supporting miscue analysis as a means of gathering important information about a reader's sense-making and word recognition strategies. The Reading Miscue Inventory in its longer form continues to be a useful tool for clinical evaluation.

Goodman and Burke's reading strategy lessons and ways the insights gained from informal miscue analysis can be used to develop teaching strategies are described in Chapter Five.

The Cloze Procedure

Figure 4.8 shows a portion of a cloze procedure. After the first sentence, you will find blanks in the text. Can you figure out what might make sense in each blank? (Only *one* word has been deleted each time.)

FIGURE 4.8. Portion of a cloze procedure.

"When Emily Johnson came home one evening to her furnished room and found three of her best handkerchiefs missing from the dresser drawer, she was sure who had taken them and what to do. She had lived in _____ furnished room for about _____ weeks and for the _____ two weeks she had _____ missing small things occasionally. _____ had been several handkerchiefs _____ , and an initial pin _____ Emily rarely wore and _____ had come from the _____ -and-ten. And once _____ had missed a small _____ of perfume and one _____ a set of china _____ . Emily had known for _____ time who was taking _____ things, but it was _____ tonight that she had _____ what to do."

SOURCE: Shirley Jackson, "Trial by Combat," in *The Lottery* (New York: Farrar, Straus, 1949), p. 35.

The cloze procedure (Taylor, 1953) has students read material from which words have been systematically deleted; that is, every *nth* word has been left out. Frequently, every *fifth* word after the first complete sentence is replaced with a blank, as in our example. Our aim is to see how accurately students can predict or infer the words that should fill the blanks, thus creating *closure*, or wholeness, in the passage.

A completely accurate prediction of every deleted word is usually impossible unless the material is extremely simple in content and vocabulary, but it is not necessary to fill in each deletion with total accuracy. If an adequate proportion of words to blanks is supplied, readers can usually employ their sense of what is going on in the passage to supply words that will complete the author's text. Can you give a "good guess" for each of the deleted words in Figure 4.8? You probably could fill in more than half of the blanks accurately but not every one. For some of the deletions, there are only one or two words that could possibly fit while for others there are more alternatives. The ninth blank, for example, occurs in the phrase, ". . . had come from the _____ -and-ten." You probably recognized almost immediately the expression "five-and-ten" and would have trouble thinking of a better alternative. On the other hand, what about ". . . a set of china _____ "? You could probably think of several good alternatives for that blank: plates, figurines, animals, and the like. In spite of some uncertainty, the whole passage is not too frustrating or difficult to complete.

The cloze procedure indicates the extent to which readers are able to follow the sense of a reading passage. In fact, studies have shown that the percentages of correct words readers are able to supply in a cloze passage constitute as reliable a measure of general comprehension as much more elaborate devices (Bormuth, 1966; Jones and Pikulski, 1974; Rankin and Culhane, 1969).

Purposes of the Cloze Procedure. There are two common purposes for using a cloze procedure:

1. to determine whether a particular piece of written text represents an individual's independent, instructional, or frustration reading level (placement purposes)
2. to assess the quality of an individual reader's use of context as a strategy for understanding what is read (diagnostic purposes)

Using a Cloze for Placement. A cloze placement test is a fast and accurate device for determining whether an individual, group, or whole class can comfortably read a given book or other material. In classes where everyone must read the same required textbooks, cloze results can help the teacher form groups for differential instruction.

When constructing a cloze passage, omit systematically every fifth word; that is, 20 percent of the words. Leaving 80 percent intact gives sufficient context for the reader to supply the remaining words. Deleting every fifth word in order ensures that words of all grammatical classes and levels of difficulty are sampled, not just all nouns or all long words, for example.

Constructing the cloze for placement. Here are the steps for constructing a cloze passage for placement purposes (Estes and Vaughan, 1978):

1. Select a passage the students have not read before, about 300 words long.
2. Leave the first sentence intact, to get the readers started. Then begin counting words, replacing every fifth word with a blank fifteen spaces long. If any word to be deleted is a proper noun, leave it in and delete the next word. (Proper nouns are harder to predict from context than other words.) Continue counting until you have fifty blanks.
3. Finish the sentence in which the last deletion occurs. Type one more sentence intact.

Administering and scoring the cloze. Administering and scoring a cloze are simple:

1. On the blackboard, show the students how to complete the passage. Give example sentences and discuss how to use context clues. Let students work together on short passages for practice. This step is important because even good readers will do poorly if they are unfamiliar with the demands of the task.
2. Direct the students to use only one word for each blank and to try to use the precise word the author would have used.
3. Explain that no one will get each word correct and that about 50 percent correct is a good score. If the students don't know this in advance, anxiety can affect their performance.
4. Give ample time for completing the passage without rushing. The students should not use their books because we want to see if they can read and understand the material without aid.

In scoring, accept only the *exact replacement*. Studies (Bormuth, 1966; Miller and Coleman, 1967; Ruddell, 1964) have shown this to be the most valid scoring system for placement purposes. When you use this activity instructionally to teach the use of context clues or work on vocabulary, you may choose to accept synonyms or make other changes. The rank order of scores changes little, if at all, if synonyms are accepted, but interpreting the results can be difficult. Also, you may drive yourself crazy deciding what is "close enough."

Determine the percentage of correct responses, adding 2 percent for each correct word. (Don't count incorrect *spellings* as errors on the cloze.) You can judge more accurately by averaging each student's scores on two or more passages from the same text.

A score of 60 percent correct or higher indicates that the material is easy for these students and that the material can be used for *independent* reading. A score between 40 and 60 percent indicates that these students can comfortably read the material and that it is suitable for direct instruction because it represents their *instructional* reading level. A score of below 40 percent correct indicates that the material is too difficult and that it represents the readers' *frustration* level (Bormuth, 1968a, 1968b; Rankin and Culhane, 1969).

The cloze procedure can be very useful in classes where a single text or set of materials is required, as is typical of many secondary level classes and some upper-elementary content area classes. It enables the teacher to determine quickly and accurately which students will find that particular material too difficult (Jones and Pikulski, 1974). It is an effective procedure for gathering information about students' reading ability in the first days of school, before their teachers get to know them, especially when a teacher has more than one class. If the same text or material is used year after year, the initial cloze can be used again and again, or shared by several teachers who use the same textbooks.

Using the Cloze Diagnostically

The cloze procedure can be used diagnostically to find out what students know, to help them focus on context clues, and to read critically.

For diagnostic purposes, it is not necessary to delete words systematically. Instead, *key words* can be deleted, words that convey much of the information. When used *after* a reading assignment, the cloze can show a good deal about the concepts and vocabulary that students have gained from the assignment. Used *before* the assignment, the cloze can show their need for vocabulary and concept development prior to the reading.

A reader's tacit grasp of syntactic structures can be explored by deleting words of a particular grammatical class, such as verbs, prepositions, or adjectives. If used on a regular basis, the cloze can help students focus on grammatical forms, learn concepts of parts of speech, become aware of context clues, and infer the meaning of new words (Hall, Ribovich, and Ramig, 1979; Jongsma, 1971; Spache, 1976). Cloze activities can be made up from students' dictated experience stories and their own written productions. This approach will help reinforce recognition of sight words and can be especially helpful for youngsters having trouble recognizing those troublesome structure words (*the, is, there, at,* and so forth). The *oral cloze,* in which selected words are left out and suggestions solicited while the teacher reads aloud to students, can be very useful in encouraging critical listening and comprehension (Blachowicz, 1977).

Cloze activities are particularly worthwhile for students who have relatively good word recognition but poor comprehension. Because they aid students to focus on the meaning and sense of the material, these activities can be invaluable in helping the word caller improve reading and listening comprehension (Bortnick and Lopardo, 1973, 1976).

The Maze: A Cloze Alternative. An alternative to the cloze technique of leaving out words altogether is the use of multiple-choice alternatives. This technique, called the *maze,* was proposed by Guthrie et al. (1974). The maze is a little easier than the cloze and thus is a good alternative for young students or any readers for whom the blank spaces are intimidating. Easily discouraged students and poor readers usually don't do well on a cloze because there is too much that is unknown and too many words to be filled in. With appropriate changes in the criteria for grouping, the maze can be more helpful for these students.

In a maze, the teacher provides three alternatives instead of leaving blanks. The choices are (a) the correct word; (b) an incorrect word from the same grammatical class (i.e., another noun); and (c) an incorrect word from another grammatical class. The order of the choices should be random so that the correct choice does not always occupy the same position. Figure 4.9 shows a portion of a maze procedure.

Though we have used only the first three sentences from a longer selection here, you can see that a maze is constructed much like a cloze, with the first sentence intact and every fifth word altered. More information is available than in a cloze, however, and correct answers can be circled or underlined. At least twenty items should be used for placement purposes.

Readers with scores of 85 percent or better will find that the material is at their independent level. Scores between 50 and 85 percent indicate the instructional level. For students scoring less than 50 percent correct, the text is too difficult to read (Guthrie et al., 1974).

Case Studies

JERRY

Jerry was the passive, disinterested fifth grader with an instructional level of second grade. Because of his age and social development, Jerry was not retained in fifth grade despite his poor reading. Since his teachers were

FIGURE 4.9. Portion of a maze procedure.

There was a person called Nana who ruled the nursery.

	envelope			about
Sometimes she took no	notice	of the playthings lying		under,
	none			table

	rabbit		
and sometimes, for no	rely	whatever, she went swooping	
	reason		

afraid		and		coming
about	like a great wind	or	hustled them away in	cupboards.
over		ankle		cardboard

	also		it
She called this "tidying	out,"	and the playthings hated	at,
	up		them

especially the tin ones.

SOURCE: Margery Williams, *The Velveteen Rabbit* (New York: Doubleday, 1926), p. 20.

concerned that when he went to middle school the next year he would make even less progress, they prepared a detailed analysis of his strengths and weaknesses to send on to his next teachers.

Jerry's reading teacher wanted to include a detailed IRI with the information that would be sent on to the middle school, so she administered an IRI and computed the following scores (Table 4.4).

These scores demonstrated that Jerry had an instructional reading level of second grade. His flashed word recognition was not very good and his oral reading scores fell somewhat below the 90 percent criterion, but his reading comprehension scores were solidly in the instructional range. In addition, his teacher confirmed that he was working comfortably in a supplementary basal of second-grade difficulty. Third-grade material was clearly too difficult for him, and primer level material appeared to be closest to his independent level. His listening comprehension level was fourth grade. However, Jerry's teachers knew that his passivity tended to depress his scores somewhat, and they agreed that he could understand fifth-grade material auditorally if he were interested in it.

These scores showed that Jerry's major weakness was in word recognition. His sight recognition of isolated words and words in context was lower than his comprehension at each level, but he could decode some words adequately through second-grade level if he had time to study them. Analysis of his WRI showed that he was consistently able to decode consonants

TABLE 4.4. Jerry's scores computed from the IRI.

| | WORD RECOGNITION (%) | | | COMPREHENSION (%) | | |
LEVELS	FLASHED	UNTIMED	ORAL READING	ORAL	SILENT	LISTENING
PP	85	95	—	—	—	—
P	80	90	96	100	100	—
1	65	85	92	85	80	—
2	60	70	88	70	75	—
3	—	45	82	50	40	—
4	—	—	—	—	—	70
5	—	—	—	—	—	60
6	—	—	—	—	—	—

and blends, had difficulty with some digraphs, and often confused vowel sounds. He had particular trouble with polysyllabic words.

Jerry's biggest problem was sight recognition of words. His flashed scores of 85, 80, and 65 percent at preprimer, primer, and first grade showed that he did not have mastery of the high-frequency words at these levels. Consequently he stumbled over common words in everything he tried to read and lost the meaning of the words because it took him so long to identify them.

Jerry's oral reading scores bore this out. Although he could adequately understand second-grade material, his numerous miscues made his oral reading slow and laborious. Miscue analysis of the first- and second-grade passages revealed that he made many miscues that caused him to lose meaning.

His comprehension responses were generally poor and showed no particularly marked pattern. He had equal difficulty answering any type of question, and if he was at all unsure of an answer, he would quickly say "I don't know." Also, his reading was slow and halting, even with first-grade material, in both oral and silent reading. He simply didn't recognize enough words at sight to really get going.

To accompany this analysis, Jerry's teachers developed a set of recommendations to send to his middle school reading teacher:

1. *Develop large sight vocabulary.* Jerry needs intensive work in sight vocabulary development, especially simple high-frequency words like *these*, *those, where, what,* and the like. We have used dictated experience stories and rereading of easy material to help him learn these, and he enjoys word hunts where he searches magazines and books for words that he has in his word bank.
2. *Develop use of context in word recognition.* Jerry depends on phonics to figure out unknown words. (In phonics he has a lot of trouble with

vowel sounds, especially variant vowels like *ei, au, ou,* and working with syllabication.) He usually tries to "sound out" rather than using context. We have used stories with words omitted so that he had to guess what would make sense in the blank, and he enjoyed these. He is beginning to understand that he should try to figure out words in this way as well as by sounding them out.

3. *Improve silent reading rate by repeated reading and other rate-building methods.* Jerry reads very slowly because he recognizes so few words at sight. We have tried repeated reading, where he practiced reading the same story aloud over and over and kept a chart showing his rate. This technique is slowly improving his rate of reading new material and also gives him a feeling of accomplishment.

4. *Develop reading attitudes and interest.* Because he does it so poorly, Jerry is very disinterested in reading, but he is interested in sports, cars, motorcycles, and outdoor life, and these can be used to help get him started. He won't read "just to read." He has to see a concrete outcome from his reading, and he works cooperatively on projects that have a real goal.

5. *Read to him.* Jerry enjoys being read to and will sometimes try to read a book he's been read if it is easy enough. Try this to get him started on a book and read aloud to him very often.

6. *Emphasize silent reading.* We have deemphasized oral reading and worked hard on silent reading for meaning. If Jerry *must* read aloud, we hope you will be tolerant of his miscues and let him rehearse by reading silently before he reads aloud. His oral reading is much better this way.

7. *Use appropriate material at second-grade readability level.* We have continued to work in second-grade level materials appropriate for young teens, as well as magazines, newspapers, and any trade books that Jerry will use. He seems comfortable and challenged at this level of difficulty.

BRIAN

Brian, a nine-year-old who had always showed adequate reading achievement, began exhibiting tension and stress in fourth grade. His test scores and daily work suffered and he was unable to deal with fourth-grade reading.

The reading teacher gave Brian an informal reading inventory and word recognition test. Because she was particularly interested in his performance at fourth-grade level, she began the IRI there. As in class, his oral reading was rapid and highly accurate although monotonous in tone. His silent reading of the fourth-grade passage was also quickly completed, at a rapid rate of about 170 words a minute, but his comprehension of both passages was surprisingly poor. He did somewhat better on the oral than on the silent comprehension and had more trouble with inferential and vocabulary questions than with questions of direct recall. The teacher noted that when he was unsure of an answer, he often said something like "I don't remember that" or "The story didn't tell that." After the fourth-grade level administration, she dropped back to third-grade, then second-grade passages. At all levels, his reading was rapid and fluent but without expression, and he had difficulty with a number of comprehension questions. Only in second-grade material was he truly comfortable in both word recognition and comprehension. Brian's teacher then administered the hearing capacity test at grade five, where his listening comprehension was adequate. Following the IRI, she gave him the informal word recognition inventory, levels three through six. His performance, which was excellent through sixth grade, revealed a very large sight vocabulary and well-developed word analysis (Table 4.5).

These scores and test observations indicated that Brian was a *word caller*, a term used for those who recognize words fluently but have problems understanding what they read. Brian's difficulty lay in making sense of print; his comprehension scores showed that he had to read aloud, to hear himself say the words, in order to make much sense of it. Although his silent reading was fluent, it was lacking in meaning. His word recognition scores showed well-polished skills in recognizing and decoding words in isolation and in context. His sight vocabulary was adequate for reading even sixth-grade material, but, for Brian, *saying* the words had somehow become the goal of reading rather than *understanding* them. Third grade appeared to be his instructional level for oral reading, but with silent reading for meaning he would be better off in material of second-grade difficulty.

When his teacher went over these findings with the reading specialist, many of Brian's behaviors began to make sense to her. Because in fourth grade there is more emphasis on silent reading for meaning, especially in subject area texts, Brian was forced to do more and more of what he did least well. His teacher could now see that many of his careless errors, apparent forgetfulness in discussions, and poor test scores were the inevitable result of his comprehension problems. She realized that when she had assumed he was a "good reader" because of his fluent oral reading, she had overlooked a major aspect of real reading ability. She suspected that Brian's word calling

TABLE 4.5. Brian's scores computed from the IRI.

	WORD RECOGNITION (%)			COMPREHENSION (%)		
LEVELS	FLASHED	UNTIMED	ORAL READING	ORAL	SILENT	LISTENING
2	—	—	100	90	80	—
3	100	—	97	70	60	—
4	90	100	94	65	50	—
5	85	95	—	—	—	70
6	80	95	—	—	—	—

had hidden his basic reading problem for some time, and that his zeal to do well and win approval obscured the fact that he didn't understand what he read.

Brian's comprehension ability was underdeveloped, and when he was exposed to more challenging, complex materials where comprehension was critical, Brian was poorly equipped. As things got harder for him, his anxiety grew. The more tense he became, the harder it was for him to do well, and a failure cycle began. He started to manifest behaviors we associate with stress: shortened attention span, nail biting, talking to himself, and constant seeking of reassurance. Brian was rapidly becoming a nervous wreck.

It was apparent that Brian's achievement and emotional distress were closely related, and the teachers agreed that remedial action must take place on both fronts in order to relieve Brian's anxiety and improve his reading. They drew up a list of problems to be dealt with:

1. Reading comprehension poor compared with word recognition.
2. Weak silent reading for meaning; needs to hear himself read aloud.
3. Problems with inferential thinking and word meanings.
4. Growing tension and fear of failure.

Then they made a list of recommendations to attack the problems:

1. Work on reading for meaning only, deemphasizing word analysis.
2. Do silent reading only, to deemphasize word calling.
3. Use easier materials, third- or even second-grade difficulty.
4. Discuss retention in fourth grade so that he can catch up with peers.
5. Encourage him to stop reading at a certain point in a story and predict what might happen next; deemphasize being right; use open-ended writing activities, for example. Encourage him to take the risk of being wrong.
6. In written work and creative writing, deemphasize neatness and correctness; instead, reward creativeness and originality.
7. Read to him daily, just for enjoyment, from fine quality literature, especially themes of success and failure.
8. Give him extra encouragement and praise, especially when he takes a risk, as in predicting how a story might turn out or other use of divergent thinking.
9. Confer with his parents to discuss ways of taking the pressure off him; suggest a physical examination because of the many physical symptoms of anxiety and stress that may be affecting his learning (poor appetite, insomnia, etc.).

His parents agreed to have their pediatrician examine him and together with the teachers discussed ways they could deemphasize achievement and help Brian relax. At school, his teacher concentrated her efforts on comprehension and silent reading. With much encouragement and some of the academic pressure removed, he was able to concentrate on understanding what he had read and began to enjoy reading more.

Summary

Informal diagnostic procedures make possible *qualitative* analysis of reading behaviors as well as use of *quantitative* scores. They are useful in determining a reader's *independent, instructional* and *frustration reading levels* and reading strengths and needs.

An *informal reading inventory (IRI)* is individually administered for these purposes. IRIs consist of story passages for oral and silent reading at consecutive grade levels from primer through high school, and corresponding comprehension questions. During oral reading *miscues,* or divergences from the text, are recorded, counted to determine the reader's oral reading fluency, and analyzed to reveal word recognition strategies and use of context. Responses to comprehension questions are used to determine reading levels and reveal comprehension skills and strategies. *Retellings* may be used in addition to questions. When the frustration reading level is reached, subsequent passages may be read aloud to the reader to determine his or her *listening comprehension* level, an indicator of potential for reading improvement.

An informal *word recognition inventory (WRI)* consisting of graded lists of individual words may be used to assess sight vocabulary and decoding skills out of context. Sight recognition is assessed by *flashing* individual words for a very brief moment, and phonic and structural analysis skills are assessed by reexamining missed words in an *untimed* exposure.

The *Reading Miscue Inventory* is a commercial device for analyzing reading miscues and comprehension after oral reading. *Supplementary phonics tests* may be used to further study the reader's decoding skills. The *cloze procedure,* a passage in which words are systematically replaced by blanks for the reader to complete, is useful in determining whether particular material represents the reader's independent, instructional or frustration level and in making judgments about his or her use of context. The *maze,* using multiple-choice responses instead of blanks, is an easier alternative to the cloze which has the same purposes.

Extension Activities

1. Choose two consecutive grade levels of a basal reader, first-grade level or above. From each level, select two passages of approximately 250 words each to use for oral and silent reading. Construct a set of ten comprehension questions for each passage according to the guidelines presented in this chapter. If you can arrange it, have three different children read the passages and answer the questions.

2. Get a copy of a commercial informal reading inventory, or see if your basal reading series provides an IRI. Read several passages and their comprehension questions critically. Analyze the questions according to the guidelines on pages 119–121. Mark the questions you think are poor. Why are they poor? How could they be improved? What questions do you think should have been included that were not?

3. Administer one (or more) oral reading passage(s) to a student and record the miscues, using the coding system on page 134. Compute the word recognition deduction and determine the gross accuracy for the passage.

4. Using the same passage as in number 3 above, analyze the miscues according to the degree of meaning change involved. (Review the section Analyzing Oral Reading, pages 132–137.) Considering only the meaning-change miscues, rescore the passage and compute the net accuracy. How are the two estimates different? Does the passage represent the reader's instructional level in either case?

5. Construct several levels of a word recognition inventory, or use the word lists from a commercial IRI. Administer the lists to several students using the flashed and untimed presentations. Analyze their responses as demonstrated in the section Analyzing Word Recognition in Isolation, pages 151–153. What strengths and weaknesses does each student show in phonic/structural analysis?

Suggested Readings

Johns, Jerry, Garton, Sharon, Schoenfelder, Paula, and Skriba, Patricia. **Assessing Reading Behavior: Informal Reading Inventories.** *Newark, Del.: International Reading Association, 1977.* A thorough, nontechnical description of commercial IRIs and their use.

Johnson, Marjorie S., and Kress, Roy A. **Informal Reading Inventories.** *Newark, Del.: International Reading Association, 1965.* Practical description of construction and use of IRIs.

Jongsma, Kathleen S., and Jongsma, Eugene A. **"Test Review: Commercial Informal Reading Inventories."** *Reading Teacher 34, No. 6 (March 1981): 697–705.* Concise critical review of commercially available IRIs.

Goodman, Yetta M., and Burke, Carolyn. **Reading Strategies: Focus on Comprehension.** *New York: Holt, Rinehart & Winston, 1980.* Practical handbook of classroom activities to help students develop reading comprehension.

Goodman, Yetta M., and Burke, Carolyn **Reading Miscue Inventory Manual.** *New York: Macmillan, 1972.* Detailed description of miscue analysis with some general corrective strategies.

Stauffer, Russell G., Abrams, Jules C., and Pikulski, John J. **Diagnosis, Correction and Prevention of Reading Disabilities.** *New York: Harper & Row, 1978.* (Chs. 1–6) Thorough discussion of informal methods of diagnosis.

References

Baker, Linda, and Stein, Nancy. "The Development of Prose Comprehension Skills," in Carol M. Santa and Bernard L. Hayes, eds. *Children's Prose Comprehension: Research and Practice.*

Newark, Del.: International Reading Association, 1981.

Beldin, H. O. "Informal Reading Testing: Historical Review and Review of the Research," in William K. Durr, ed. *Reading Difficulties: Di-*

agnosis, Correction and Remediation. Newark, Del.: International Reading Association, 1970.

Betts, Emmett A. "Reading Problems at the Intermediate Grade Level." *Elementary School Journal* 40 (June 1941): 737–746.

Betts, Emmett A. *Foundations of Reading Instruction.* New York: American Book, 1957.

Blachowicz, Camille. "Cloze Activities for Primary Readers." *The Reading Teacher* 31, No. 3 (December 1977): 300–302.

Bormuth, J. "Readability: A New Approach." *Reading Research Quarterly* 1, No. 3 (1966): 79–132.

Bormuth, John R. "The Cloze Readability Procedure." *Elementary English* 55 (April 1968): 429–436. (a)

Bormuth, John R. "Cloze Test Reliability: Criterion Reference Scores." *Journal of Educational Measurement* 5 (Fall 1968): 189–196. (b)

Bortnick, Robert, and Lopardo, Genevieve S. "An Instructional Application of the Cloze Procedure." *Journal of Reading* 16, No. 4 (January 1973): 296–300.

Bortnick, Robert, and Lopardo, Genevieve. "The Cloze Procedure: A Multi-Purpose Classroom Tool." *Reading Improvement* 13, No. 2 (Summer 1976): 113–117.

Branisel, Rose M. "A Study of Black Kindergarten Children's Auditory Comprehension of Stories Presented in Standard English Versus Black English." Master's Thesis, California State University, Hayward, 1977.

Burns, Paul C., and Roe, Betty D. *Informal Reading Assessment.* Chicago: Rand McNally, 1980.

Cagney, Margaret A. "Children's Ability to Understand Standard English and Black Dialect." *The Reading Teacher* 30, No. 3 (March 1977): 607–610.

Carroll, Lewis, "Jabberwocky," in Helen Gardner, ed. *The New Oxford Book of English Verse.* New York: Oxford University Press, 1972, pp. 730–731.

Cohen, Alice Sheff. "Oral Reading Errors of First Grade Children Taught by a Code Emphasis Approach." *Reading Research Quarterly* X, No. 4 (1974–1975): 616–650.

Ekwall, Eldon E. *Ekwall Reading Inventory.* Boston: Allyn and Bacon, 1979.

Estes, Thomas H., and Vaughan, Joseph L., Jr. *Reading and Learning in the Content Classroom: Diagnostic and Instructional Strategies.* Boston: Allyn and Bacon, 1978.

Goodman, Kenneth S. "Behind the Eye: What Happens in Reading," in Olive S. Niles, ed. *Reading: Process and Program.* Urbana, Ill.: National Council of Teachers of English, 1970, pp. 3–38.

Goodman, Yetta, and Burke, Carolyn. *Reading Miscue Inventory Manual.* New York: Macmillan, 1972.

Goodman, Yetta M., and Burke, Carolyn. *Reading Strategies: Focus on Comprehension.* New York: Holt, Rinehart & Winston, 1980.

Guthrie, John, Seifert, M., Burnham, N. A., and Caplan, R. I. "The Maze Technique to Assess, Monitor Reading Comprehension," *The Reading Teacher* 28, No. 2 (November 1974): 161–168.

Hall, MaryAnne, Ribovich, Jerilyn, and Ramig, Christopher. *Reading and the Elementary School Child,* 2nd ed. New York: Van Nostrand, 1979.

Hansell, T. Stevenson. "Readability, Syntactic Transformations, and Generative Semantics." *Journal of Reading* 19, No. 7 (April 1976): 557–562.

Holdaway, Don. *The Foundations of Literacy.* New York: Ashton Scholastic, 1979: (Distributed by Heinemann Educational Books, Exeter, N.H.).

Jackson, Shirley. "Trial by Combat," in *The Lottery* Fawcett Popular Library, 1949 (renewed 1976), 35–39.

Johns, Jerry L. *Basic Reading Inventory,* 2nd ed. Dubuque, Ia.: Kendall-Hunt, 1981.

Johnson, Marjorie S., and Kress, Roy A. *Informal Reading Inventories.* Newark, Del.: International Reading Associates 1965.

Jones, Margaret, and Pikulski, Edna. "Cloze for the Classroom." *The Reading Teacher* 17, No. 6 (March 1974): 432–438.

Jongsma, Eugene. *The Cloze Procedure as a Teaching Technique.* Newark, Del.: International Reading Assoc. 1971.

Lass, Bonnie. "Improving Reading Skills: The Relationship Between the Oral Language of Black English Speakers and their Reading Achievement." *Urban Education* 14 (January 1980): 437–447.

Miller, G. R., and Coleman, E. G. "A Set of 36 Prose Passages Calibrated for Complexity." *Journal of Verbal Learning and Verbal Behavior* 6 (1967): 851–854.

Pearson, P. David, and Johnson, Dale L. *Teaching*

Reading Comprehension. New York: Holt, Rinehart & Winston, 1978.

Peterson, Joe, Greenlaw, M. Jean, and Tierney, Robert J. "Assessing Instructional Placement with the IRI: The Effectiveness of Comprehension Questions." *Journal of Educational Research* 71 No. 5 (May–June 1978): 247–250.

Pikulski, John J. "A Critical Review: Informal Reading Inventories." *The Reading Teacher* 28, No. 2 (November 1974): 141–151.

Pikulski, John J., and Shanahan, Timothy. "Informal Reading Inventories: A Critical Analysis," in John J. Pikulski and Timothy Shanahan (eds.) *Approaches to the Informal Evaluation of Reading.* Newark, Del.: International Reading Association 1982.

Powell, William R. "Reappraising the Criteria for Interpreting Informal Reading Inventories," in Dorothy DeBoer, ed. *Reading Diagnosis and Evaluation.* Newark, Del.: International Reading Associates, 1970.

Powell, William R. "The Validity of the Instructional Reading Level," in Robert E. Liebert, ed. *Diagnostic Viewpoints in Reading.* Newark, Del.: International Reading Associates, 1971.

Powell, William R., and Dunkeld, Colin G. "Validity of the IRI Reading Levels." *Elementary English* 48, No. 6 (October 1971): 637–642.

Rankin, Earl F., and Culhane, Joseph W. "Comparable Cloze and Multiple Choice Comprehension Test Scores." *Journal of Reading,* 13, No. 3 (December 1969): 193–198.

Ruddell, Robert. "A Study of Cloze Comprehension Technique in Relation to Structurally Controlled Reading Material." *Proceedings of*

the *International Reading Association,* 9 (1964): 298–303.

Schell, Leo M., and Gerald S. Hanna. "Can Informal Reading Inventories Reveal Strengths and Weaknesses in Comprehension Subskills?" *The Reading Teacher* 35, No. 3 (December 1981): 263–268.

Schwartz, Judith J. "Dialect Interference in the Attainment of Literacy." *Journal of Reading* 25, No. 2 (February 1982): 440–446.

Silvaroli, Nicholas J. *Classroom Reading Inventory,* 3rd ed. Dubuque, Ia.: William C. Brown, 1976.

Slosson, Richard L. *Slosson Oral Reading Test.* E. Aurora, N.Y.: Slosson Educational Publications, 1963.

Smith, Frank. *Understanding Reading,* rev. ed. New York: Holt, Rinehart & Winston, 1978.

Spache, George D. *Diagnosing and Correcting Reading Disabilities.* Boston: Allyn and Bacon, 1976.

Stauffer, Russell G., Abrams, Jules C., and Pikulski, John J. *Diagnosis, Correction, and Prevention of Reading Disabilities.* New York: Harper & Row, 1978.

Taylor, Wilson. "Cloze Procedure: A New Tool for Measuring Readability." *Journalism Quarterly,* 30 (Fall 1953): 415–433.

Valmont, William. "Creating Questions for Informal Reading Inventories," *The Reading Teacher* 25, No. 6 (March 1972): 509–512.

Williams, Margery. *The Velveteen Rabbit.* New York: Doubleday, 1926.

Woods, Mary Lynn, and Moe, Alden J. *Analytical Reading Inventory,* 2nd ed. Columbus, Ohio: Charles C. Merrill, 1981.

Chapter Five

Corrective Teaching Strategies

After you have completed your diagnostic assessments, you will know a great deal about the student's reading. Now you are ready to begin the second stage in the diagnostic process: planning and implementing corrective teaching. Finding out what the student's present level of functioning is and what his or her strengths and needs are is not the goal, or the end, of the diagnostic process. This information is of no value if it is not used to develop teaching strategies that will further the student's progress. In this chapter we discuss and demonstrate ways to use your diagnostic findings and judgments to plan instruction, and to help students develop strategies for sight word recognition, word analysis, reading fluency, and reading and listening comprehension.

Planning for Corrective Instruction

Corrective teaching is instruction that is specifically directed toward supporting a reader's strengths while teaching and practicing skills and abilities the student is ready to acquire but has not yet acquired. Its purpose is to help students with reading or reading-related problems to overcome (and in some cases, compensate for) their difficulties and develop more balance in their reading strategies. Corrective teaching does not mean applying some preset prescription, method, or program, nor does it necessarily mean removing the youngster with a reading problem from his or her classroom, reading group or book, or "sending the student out" for special instruction. Instead it means planning and goal setting for a particular reader within the context of ongoing instruction, taking into account his or her specific strengths and needs.

How does this differ from ordinary, everyday good teaching? In most ways, it doesn't, when everyday good teaching includes ongoing evaluation, utilizing students' strengths, needs, and interests routinely, and providing an appropriate balance of activities. But what we call everyday teaching has two general underlying aspects that are somewhat different from corrective teaching. One is that most instruction is planned for group progress, and our everyday teaching is generally oriented toward the strengths, needs, and interests of groups rather than individuals. The other is that fairly well-balanced skills, and fairly typical developmental progress are assumed. Because corrective teaching is directed toward those who have experienced difficulties in reading and who generally have not "kept up" with others their age in all aspects of reading, corrective teaching must be oriented toward the specific strengths and needs of these individuals. Successful corrective teaching is built around identifying pupils' strengths and needs and careful instructional planning, our next topics.

Identifying Strengths and Needs

We start planning for corrective teaching where the student is, not where the book, program, curriculum guide, or scope-and-sequence charts

Small groups are ideal for closely observing students' reading strengths and needs and correcting problems. Here, a teacher helps a student locate important information by selectively rereading.

say that student "should" be. Where is the child now? What is our best estimate of his or her instructional level? What has been mastered? What can be done consistently and comfortably? We begin by making a simple chart of this information. Let's return to the case of Jerry, the boy entering sixth grade whom we discussed in Chapter Four. Table 5.1 shows a chart of Jerry's strengths and needs.

From our chart we can see that although Jerry is indeed a problem reader and is in considerable academic trouble, he has a number of strengths. It is very important to search for and list the things a student can do and enjoys doing, no matter how numerous the needs may be. Without rigorous attention to strengths and interests, we risk omitting the things the child does successfully, and we risk becoming discouraged about attempting to help him or her.

We proceed now to creating goals for instruction. What are Jerry's most critical needs for reading improvement? We select the factors that we feel will help him improve his reading most dramatically, as well as those strengths that we must not overlook in teaching, and create a list of goals, in order of their importance for this particular student. From these, our activities will be developed.

TABLE 5.1. Jerry's strengths and needs chart.

Jerry _____, age twelve, entering sixth grade

Functional reading levels:
 Independent: primer
 Instructional: second
 Frustration: third
 Hearing capacity: fourth, possibly fifth

Strengths:
 Comprehension solid at his instructional level
 Working comfortably in low-vocabulary, high-interest material of second-grade
  readability
 Enjoys being read to
 Works cooperatively when he understands what the goal or outcome will be
 Hearing capacity at least two grades above instructional level (i.e., shows potential
  for improvement)
 Has *some* sight vocabulary (although very small)
 Can use decoding, and context to some extent, to figure out words
 Has mastered most consonant and blend sounds
 Tries to make sense of what he reads
 Is interested in sports, cars, motorcycles, and outdoor life

Needs:
 Small sight vocabulary, particularly beyond primer
 Overusing phonics and underusing context in word recognition
 Miscues usually resulted in meaning change
 In phonics, has trouble with variant vowel sounds especially in medial position,
  and most polysyllabic words
 Reading rate slow and halting due to small sight vocabulary
 Very unsure of his ability to understand; says "I don't know" quickly
 Hesitant to risk a guess or prediction
 Avoids reading whenever he can and does no self-initiated reading
 Gives appearance of passivity and boredom, his response to failure and frustration

Goals for Jerry's instruction

1. Develop larger sight vocabulary
2. Develop more effective word analysis skills, especially judicious use of
   context
3. Improve reading fluency and rate
4. Encourage active comprehension, making predictions, and risking a
   guess
5. Increase time spent reading
6. Develop listening comprehension and story sense
7. Encourage greater self-esteem and more positive attitudes toward
   reading

Now we have clarified what Jerry can presently do, what he needs, and
where we must place the most emphasis in our planning. We are ready to

select and devise activities that will fit our listed priorities, and to develop some general plans for Jerry's instructional time.

Below we have listed generic types of activities to fit different purposes. In the sections that follow, these activities are discussed and described in detail. We will select from them as we develop a lesson plan for Jerry and others whose reading is like his.

> *To develop sight vocabulary:*
>   dictated stories
>   repeated reading
>   echo and choral reading
>   labels and signs
>   sight word bank (or notebook)
> *To develop fluency:*
>   repeated reading
>   choral reading with a group
>   practice reading in order to read to others
>   readers theater
> *To develop word attack skills:*
>   word sorting and categorizing
>   word families and letter substitution
>   confirmation exercises (in context)
>   cloze and maze procedures
> *To develop reading comprehension:*
>   using predicting (directed reading-thinking activities)
>   developing awareness of prior information: prereading predicting, previewing, webbing
>   scanning and locating information
>   developing awareness of story and text structures
>   summarizing and restating
>   interpreting what was read through movement, drama, art, and music
> *To develop listening comprehension:*
>   being read to
>   interpreting stories and text listened to through drama, art, and movement
>   retelling stories and text listened to
>   summarizing and paraphrasing material listened to
>   storytelling

Planning Time and Achieving Balance

When we developed our list of priorities, we selected those areas we felt needed particular attention and emphasis. Our list of priorities helps us include what Jerry needs most right now: work on sight words, word attack, fluency, active comprehension, listening, and time spent actually reading.

We will balance our instructional program by making sure that every day Jerry spends time working on the areas of greatest need and filling in around them the other things he will benefit from and enjoy.

Let's say that Jerry will have a fifty-minute period each day for reading. We might plan to divide that time period into the following segments:

sight vocabulary, fluency	20 minutes
word study (i.e., decoding, context, vocabulary development)	15 minutes
comprehension	15 minutes

This totals fifty minutes, but there is much we wanted to do that is left out. Fifteen minutes is about the shortest amount of time for a middle grader to work productively on most tasks. That means that we will have to decide what we must do every day and what we can do on alternate days to accomplish all we need and want to do. Since sight recognition is Jerry's foremost need, we should work on that daily. And since comprehension (which includes listening) is the goal of all reading, we must work on it every day too. We will have to plan our remaining time, and utilize a variety of activities, to achieve balance. We will also have to use our time flexibly, so that over a week we will have allotted enough time to each area.

Let's try mapping out a week's time, filling in activities as we go. Table 5.2 shows how each day's and each week's instructional time might be divided up so that Jerry would participate in a number of kinds of activities based on our priorities for him. This schedule would result in the following division of time weekly:

*	sight vocabulary and fluency	85 minutes/week
○	reading and listening comprehension	95 minutes/week
△	word study	50 minutes/week
□	self-esteem and confidence	25 minutes/week

Jerry's time spent in pleasure reading and free writing could be extended by having him spend some time each day, say fifteen or twenty minutes, doing these activities at home. He and a parent could keep a simple time sheet for this purpose.

The times we have listed are both arbitrary and approximate. Conforming rigorously to a schedule like this would certainly mean dragging some activities out and truncating others and would serve no good purpose. We have listed times only to illustrate that it is important to plan in general how much time will be allotted to particular areas, so that the most time is spent on the most critical areas. Each week, different activities should be used, and some should be phased out as needs change and abilities develop. As Jerry's

TABLE 5.2. Sample week's lesson plan.

Key:	* sight vocabulary and fluency	△ word analysis and vocabulary development
	○ comprehension	□ confidence and self-esteem

MONDAY

*	Group or individual dictated story (transcribing, choral reading)	20 minutes
*	Repeated readings — practice and timing	5 minutes
○	Silent reading and summarizing	15 minutes
△	Sort words by phonic pattern	10 minutes

TUESDAY

*	Choral reading dictated story, identify sight words	10 minutes
□	Pleasure reading and/or free writing	10 minutes
○	Group Directed Reading-Thinking Activity (DRTA)	20 minutes
△	Confirmation exercise	10 minutes

WEDNESDAY

*	Choral and individual reading of dictated story, identify sight words	10 minutes
*	Repeated readings — practice and timing	5 minutes
○	Silent reading and summarizing	20 minutes
△	Cloze procedure from DRTA	15 minutes

THURSDAY

*	Review new sight words, put in word bank	10 minutes
□	Pleasure reading and/or free writing	15 minutes
*	Practice story to read to younger students	5 minutes
○	Group Directed Listening-Thinking Activity (DLTA)	20 minutes
△	Confirmation exercise	5 minutes

FRIDAY

*	Repeated readings — practice and timing	5 minutes
*	Practice and read story to younger students	15 minutes
○	Silent reading and interpretation (drama, art, etc.)	20 minutes
△	Sort words by meaning relations	10 minutes

sight vocabulary grows, for example, dictated stories should be phased out and replaced with more directed reading and rereading of appropriate books, more directed writing and word study.

Balance is achieved when available time is appropriately divided among activities requiring reading, speaking, listening, writing, and areas like drama and art. All areas should be included each week, and most every day. If you make a list of the activities you have planned in a week for a group, and label each activity by what process it primarily requires, you can see if you are including all aspects regularly. (No activity requires one process exclusively, since reading, speaking, listening, and writing are interrelated. Look for what an activity requires most.)

Developing Sight Vocabulary

Individual words become *sight words* (recognized immediately without analysis) when they are seen repeatedly in meaningful context. Many youngsters acquire some sight words before school entry, and without direct teaching or drill, by looking at the same favorite storybooks many times over. First they learn what words are on the page as they hear the same story read to them again and again. Soon they can recite the words along with the reader; soon after that they can recite independently, role-playing reading as they turn the pages.

If at this point the reader casually points to the words as they are read, the child begins to associate the word spoken with its printed counterpart. As we have discussed in Chapters Two and Three, this "speech-to-print matching" is an important foundation for learning to recognize words in print.

It is essential for readers to have a large sight vocabulary, so that they can move through print quickly and efficiently. As we have already seen, youngsters like Jerry who have only a small store of sight words are forced to read very slowly with frequent stops to figure out words, stops that interrupt their comprehension and interfere with their getting meaning. Many youngsters read poorly for this reason. Increasing their sight vocabularies is mandatory for their reading improvement. There are a number of means by which this can be accomplished.

Dictated Stories and Language Experience

Dictated stories are a part of the language experience approach to beginning reading (Allen, 1976; Hall, 1981; Stauffer, 1980). An individual or a small group dictates an account to someone who writes down the account verbatim. The account is reread chorally until the students can recite it accurately and point to the individual words while reciting. Then parts, or the entire account, are read individually, and words that can be immediately recognized first in context, then in isolation, are identified. These new sight words go into the students' *word banks*, collections of sight words on cards or in a notebook.

It was long held that the value of dictated stories lay in the preservation of children's natural language, which may differ considerably from "book language." This is important, but the real usefulness of dictated stories for developing sight vocabulary lies in the repeated rereading of the material. Students may reread dictated stories more willingly than other material because the stories concern experiences the students have had themselves. Rereading the stories chorally and independently, regardless of the topic or syntax used, reinforces the recognition of the words in other contexts.

As the students' sight vocabularies grow, and their word banks come to contain about 100 or more words, dictated stories can be phased out and selective rereading of other material, from books and their own writings, continued or expanded. Dictation works best as an initial means of establishing and fostering sight vocabulary.

When dictated stories are mentioned, some teachers of older poor readers associate the practice with very young children. They may immediately presume that older poor readers will be put off by what they assume is a juvenile practice. Although language experience is common in primary classrooms, it need not be reserved for little children. In fact, with many older and adult poor readers what they dictate may be about the only print they can read successfully.

With young children, you need a concrete "stimulus," or experience, to talk about: an object, picture, storybook or immediate event. With older students, past or future experiences, hopes, fears, reminiscences, content area subjects, and abstract concepts can serve as topics. Older students can usually move through the steps (see Table 5.3) more quickly than younger ones, and can usually skip the voice-pointing step entirely. Older students often work best with this procedure individually or in pairs or threes rather than larger groups. A word notebook may replace the word bank card collection. And if the teacher presents the activity with a businesslike air and explains why it is being done, the experience need not feel like a juvenile one.

Table 5.3 lists the steps in using dictated stories with younger and older students, in groups or individually.

TABLE 5.3. Steps in using dictated stories.

WITH YOUNGER PUPILS:
1. Present a concrete stimulus — an object or event — to discuss.
2. Encourage describing and narrating, so the students will have plenty to say about it.
3. Tell students you will help them write the story using a chart tablet, transparency, or the board.
4. Ask for volunteers to contribute sentences for the story.

TABLE 5.3.   *(Continued)*

5. Print the account verbatim, allowing students to make changes or additions. Read aloud what you have written, including amended portions.
6. Read the completed account to the group.
7. Lead the group in choral recitation, pointing quickly to the words as you read. Repeat until the whole account can be recited fluently.
8. Ask for volunteers to read one or more sentences alone, pointing to the words as in step 7.
9. Ask for volunteers to point to and identify words they know. Keep a list of these for review.
10. Provide individual copies of the story for rereading and sight word identification.
11. Any words a child can identify out of the story context can go into the child's word bank, to be used for sorting and other word analysis activities.

WITH OLDER PUPILS:
1. Work with groups of three or fewer.
2. Suggest, or allow students to suggest, a topic.
3. Lead discussion of the topic, encouraging as rich language use as possible.
4. Take the dictation as above, making minor word changes or additions as necessary to keep the story fluent. Cursive writing may be used instead of printing. Use a regular size sheet of paper if you wish.
5. Lead the choral rereading as above. Students may prefer to do more individual than group reading.
6. Provide an individual copy for each student, typed if possible, for practice rereading and word identification. Encourage rereading to a partner or someone else.
7. As individuals read to you and identify newly acquired sight words, have them enter the words in a sight word notebook. Older students may prefer a notebook to a traditional word bank.

Support Reading

Support reading means helping readers get through text that is too difficult for them to read independently. Although students should never have to read material at their frustration levels without support, sometimes it is necessary for them to get through some difficult material. This is most often the case with older poor readers who are expected to get information from a content area textbook that is beyond their instructional level. If appropriate material at their instructional level is not available, you can help them through difficult text using support reading methods.

Echo reading and *choral reading* are both support measures. In echo reading the teacher reads a sentence or two aloud and the student immediately repeats what the teacher read while looking at, and, if necessary, pointing to, the words. Only one or two sentences, or even one long phrase, are read at a time to allow students to use short-term memory as they "echo." Older students may use specially prepared tapes, with pauses for repetition, to practice echo reading independently. Echo reading is an intensive support measure that is best used with short selections and material that is quite difficult or unfamiliar. Sometimes it may be sufficient to echo read only the beginning of a longer passage to get students started. One important characteristic of echo reading is that it allows the teacher to model fluent oral reading and the students to practice it.

Choral reading means reading aloud in unison. It is somewhat harder to choral read than to echo, so this procedure is best for material that is somewhat easier, or for text that has been silently previewed or echo read first. Choral reading, with the teacher's voice leading and providing the model, is an excellent way of practicing oral reading without the anxiety of a solo performance. Complicated or unfamiliar text should be read aloud to the students first and may be echo read initially as well. Again, tapes can be used effectively for independent practice.

Pattern Books

Many trade books have a rhyming or repetitious structure that makes them easy to read, even for students with small sight vocabularies, once they have heard the book read aloud. This is because the pattern of repeated words or phrases or the rhyme scheme helps the students predict what is coming next. Many of the most popular books for young children are appealing principally because of this patterned element, which makes it easy for even a prereader to memorize the words and then read along. Even if the children cannot recognize all of the words in such a book independently, they can use the pattern and illustrations to help them read the book successfully. Bill Martin, Jr., a pattern book author, explained why such books are so valuable in these words:

> The first and most basic reading skill is the belief, "I can read a book." . . .
> An emerging reader needs a battery of books that he can zoom through with joyous familiarity. . . .
> Dramatic cumulative repetitions of language help children anticipate (and thereby decode) the printed page. . . .
> Dependable schemes of rhyme and rhythm help children read words they didn't know they knew. . . .
> Remedial reading should begin with every child role-playing himself as a successful reader of books. . . . (Martin & Brogan, 1972, pp. 4–5)

Pattern books can serve as independent and pleasure reading material for even the least fluent readers, providing an important success and a powerful motivation for them.

How do pattern books work? *Where's Spot?* (Hill, Eric; New York, G. P.

Putnam's Sons, 1980) is an example of a very easy, highly structured pattern book appropriate for young beginning and emergent readers. *Where's Spot?* tells the story of a mother dog's search for her missing puppy. Bold illustrations clearly show what the words on each page represent, making it easy to predict what the words say. After the first page, which shows Spot's untouched food bowl and poses the question "Where can Spot be?", each successive page bears a similar phrase:

> Is he behind the door? No.
> Is he inside the clock? No.
> Is he in the piano? No.

and so on. On each page, only the preposition (in, under, inside) and the object (clock, stairs, bed, rug) change, and the illustrations cue the identification of those words. After hearing the book read once, or even just the first two or three pages, almost every child can successfully read the book independently. Rereading with practice pointing to the words and identifying the new words on each page helps the reader quickly acquire the words used as sight words.

Where's Spot? is a very simple, easy-to-read pattern book because of its highly structured pattern. *Bill Martin's Instant Readers* (New York: Holt, Rinehart and Winston, 1971) are sets of similar books, each featuring the same kind of high-predictability pattern. There are hundreds of other such pattern books, some with highly structured patterns and others with somewhat less structure. A selected bibliography of pattern books is included at the end of this section.

Every teacher working with unfluent readers should have a collection of pattern books available for pleasure reading, practice rereading, and as "springboards" for children's own writing. To introduce a new pattern book, read it to the group and then choral read it together until the pattern is familiar. Then display the book in a prominent, accessible place for several days, inviting students to read it themselves during free minutes. After several days, put it in the classroom library in a specially marked place for pattern books so it and others like it can be easily located.

Being able to successfully "zoom through" pattern books is as important for older poor readers, who often avoid reading as much as possible, as for young beginners. But, finding patterned material attractive to older poor readers is a special challenge. However with some searching many can be found, and are included in the list that completes this section. *The Bumper Sticker Book* (Merrill, Jean; Chicago: A. Whitman, 1973) is an example. It contains a series of vehicles and the sayings on their bumper stickers in a repeating format. *A Spooky Story, I Paint the Joy of a Flower* and *I Went to the Market* (all from *Bill Martin's Instant Readers*) are other examples using sophisticated illustrations and topics that are not juvenile.

A useful alternative, especially for older students, is to help students create their own pattern books. Older students can change the topics and illustrations of a more juvenile pattern book to create their own innovations. All students, regardless of age, will benefit from the experience of authorship, using a familiar pattern book as a starting point. Also, a small collection of published pattern books can be greatly expanded when students produce their own books to add to it.

To help students write their own pattern books, begin with a pattern they already know or can quickly pick up. Then write the basic pattern, with blanks for the words or phrases that will change, on the board or a transparency. Help the group to choose a new topic, then ask for volunteers to offer a new verse or phrase using the established pattern. After the students have become familiar with the process, let them work in small groups, pairs, or alone to come up with more verses and accompanying illustrations. After revising and proofreading, their contributions can be bound together between simple covers. (See Chapter Seven for discussion of revising, editing, and bookbinding.) In this way a relatively juvenile pattern book may be used with older pupils to illustrate a pattern while their own productions may be more adultlike and tailored to their interests and experiences.

Both commercial and student-written pattern books are extremely useful for independent reading and as springboards for creative writing. They help students acquire and reinforce sight words while they provide successful reading practice for even the least fluent reader. Here are some pattern books you might use:

A Selected Bibliography of Pattern Books

Abisch, Roy. *Around the House that Jack Built.* New York: Parents Magazine Press, 1972.
Barry, Katherine. *A Bug to Hug.* New York: Young Scott, 1964.
Bodecker, N. M. *Let's Marry Said the Cherry:* And Other Nonsense Poems. New York: Atheneum, 1974.
Bodecker, N. M. *It's Raining, Said John Twaining.* New York: Atheneum, 1973.
*Brown, Margaret Wise. *The Important Book.* New York: Harper & Row, 1949.
*Charlip, Remy. *Fortunately.* New York: Parents Magazine Press, 1964.
de Regniers, Beatrice. *May I Bring a Friend?* New York: Atheneum, 1964.
Domanska, Janina. *If All the Seas Were One Sea.* New York: Macmillan, 1971.
Einsel, Walter. *Did You Ever See?* New York: Scholastic Books, 1972.
*Emberley, Ed. *Drummer Hoff.* Englewood Cliffs, N.J.: Prentice-Hall, 1967.
Frasconi, Antonio. *The House that Jack Built.* New York: Harcourt, 1958.
*Joslin, Sesyle. *What Do You Say, Dear?* Reading, Mass.: Addison-Wesley, 1958.

SOURCE: Temple, Charles, and Gillet, Jean Wallace. *Language Arts: Learning Processes & Teaching Practices* (Boston: Little, Brown, 1984).
*These titles may be useful with older readers.

*Joslin, Sesyle. *What Do You Do, Dear?* Reading, Mass.: Addison-Wesley, 1961.

Keats, Ezra Jack. *Over the Meadow.* New York: Four Winds, 1971.

Krauss, Ruth. *What a Fine Day.* New York: Parents Magazine Press, 1967.

Langstaff, John. *Soldier, Soldier, Won't You Marry Me?* New York: Doubleday, 1972.

Martin, Bill, Jr. *Brown Bear, Brown Bear, What Do You See?* New York: Holt, Rinehart & Winston, 1970.

Martin, Bill, Jr. and Brogan, Peggy. *Bill Martin's Instant Readers.* New York: Holt, Rinehart & Winston, 1971.

*Mayer, Mercer. *What Do You Do with a Kangaroo?* New York: Scholastic Books, 1973.

*McGinn, Maureen. *I Used to Be an Artichoke.* St. Louis: Concordia, 1973.

Nolan, Dennis. *Big Pig.* Englewood Cliffs, N.J.: Prentice-Hall, 1976.

Pomerantz, Charlotte. *The Piggy in the Puddle.* New York: Macmillan, 1974.

Quackenbush, Robert. *She'll Be Comin' Round the Mountain.* New York: Lippincott, 1973.

Schultz, Charles. *Happiness Is; Security Is; Love Is.* New York: Determined Productions, undated.

Sendak, Maurice. *Chicken Soup with Rice.* New York: Scholastic Books, 1962.

Shulevitz, Uri. *One Monday Morning.* New York: Charles Scribner's, 1967.

*Supraner, Robyn. *Would You Rather Be a Tiger?* Boston: Houghton Mifflin, 1976.

*Sutton, Eve. *My Cat Likes to Hide in Boxes.* New York: Parents Magazine Press, 1973.

Zemach, Harve. *The Judge.* New York: Farrar, Straus, 1969.

Zolotow, Charlotte. *Someday.* New York: Harper & Row, 1965.

Developing Reading Fluency

Poor word recognition and slow, word-by-word reading reduce comprehension. According to Allington (1983), lack of fluency is commonly noted as a characteristic of poor reading and can be taught, but is often overlooked in corrective teaching. Allington proposed several hypotheses explaining why some fail to become fluent readers:

Some children are not exposed to fluent adult reading models, or to pre-reading experience reciting memorized books.

Good readers are more likely to be encouraged to "read with expression," while poor readers get more instruction on individual words and word parts.

Fast learners are given more opportunities for reading, and hence more practice actually reading.

Successful readers more often read text that is easy for them, while poorer readers more often are faced with frustration-level material.

Successful readers do more silent reading, which provides practice and experience.

Children's ideas differ about what good reading is, with poorer readers often viewing reading not as meaning getting but as "an accuracy competition." (p. 559)

Since reading fluency is an aspect of good reading that many students need to develop, methods that help students develop this skill are both useful and necessary. With greater fluency, readers can concentrate on comprehending what they read, develop greater self-confidence, and enjoy reading more.

Repeated Reading

As its name suggests, repeated reading means reading the same material more than once. Because sight words are acquired by seeing the same words repeatedly in meaningful contexts, reading the same material more than once is an aid to sight word acquisition.

We have seen that young children reread spontaneously and enjoyably, reading and listening to their favorite stories over and over. Yet in school many children resist this practice, because somehow in school we convey the notion that "doing it over" is a sign that it wasn't done properly the first time! Students infer that rereading is to be avoided, and they resist our suggestions that they do so. Also, our curriculum guides (and sometimes our supervisors) continually urge us to move ahead as quickly as possible and not spend "unnecessary" time repeating a story. How unfortunate! All students would probably benefit, at least in sight vocabulary growth, by reading fewer basal stories and spending more time reading each one.

Repeated reading can be informally practiced by having students read material silently for discussion and comprehension activities, then again in part or in its entirety (depending on length) aloud for fluency practice. Poor readers should certainly reread some of their material in this way regularly. The benefits of rereading dictated stories can thus be extended to basal and other text material.

Repeated reading also refers to a systematic practice of using timed oral rereadings to develop reading fluency. Described by Samuels (1979), the method involves helping the student select an instructional level passage and a reading rate goal, timing the first unrehearsed oral reading of the passage and successive readings after practice, and keeping a simple chart of the student's rate after successive timings. When the student is able to read the passage at or above the goal rate, a new passage of equal (but not greater) difficulty is begun.

This method of repeated reading is not intended to directly aid com-

TABLE 5.4. Steps in using repeated reading.

1. Choose, or help each student choose, a fairly comfortable, interesting selection to practice reading. It should be too long to memorize: 100 or so words for younger children, 200 or more words for older ones. Trade books and previously read basal stories are good.
2. Make up a duplicated chart for each pupil (see Figure 5.1). Omit the accuracy axis if you want to simplify the task.
3. Time each reader's first, *unrehearsed* oral reading of the passage. Mark the chart for Timed Reading 1.
4. Instruct the readers to practice the passage aloud as many times as possible for the next day or two. Let them practice in pairs, independently, and at home.
5. Time the reading again and mark the chart for Timed Reading 2, and show the students how to mark their own charts.
6. Continue timing at intervals of several days. As the rate increases for the first passage, help each child set a new rate goal.
7. When the reader reaches the goal set, begin a new passage of equal (*not* greater) difficulty. Successive portions of a long story are perfect. Repeat steps 3 through 6.

prehension, but rather to help students acquire sight words and practice reading fluently and confidently. As they practice rereading their passages for timing, their reading rate for that passage climbs dramatically, and keeping a chart that shows these increases is highly motivating, especially for older poor readers.

Of course we are not surprised that their rates climb as they practice reading the same passage. What is surprising, and is the real benefit of this practice, is that their reading rates also increase on each successive *unrehearsed* oral reading. The reason that this happens is that all that rereading has helped them acquire more sight words and helped them learn to read aloud fluently and confidently.

Table 5.4 shows the steps in using the timed repeated reading method, and Figure 5.1 shows a partially completed chart.

Modeling Fluent Reading

Teacher modeling is very important to developing fluency. We must show students, by modeling, what fluent reading is.

Poor readers are most often grouped with those of similar ability and so usually hear only other unfluent ones reading aloud. This does not provide a good model for fluent reading. It is important, then, for the teacher to read aloud so students can have a model to emulate. Smith (1979) suggested that simply reading aloud the first hundred words or so of each story to the group has a positive effect on pupils' reading, with no disruption of the usual

FIGURE 5.1. Sample repeated reading chart.

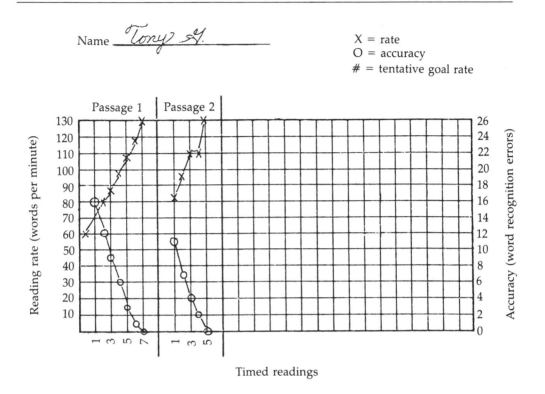

Name _Tony S._

X = rate
O = accuracy
# = tentative goal rate

Timed readings

SOURCE: From Charles Temple and Jean Wallace Gillet, *Language Arts: Learning Processes and Teaching Practices,* Figure 5.1. Copyright © 1984 by Charles Temple and Jean Wallace Gillet. Reprinted by permission of Little, Brown and Company.

routine. This is a simple suggestion; yet how many times in group oral reading does the teacher either read aloud to start the story, or take a turn at reading aloud with the students?

Echo reading and group choral reading also provide important opportunities for teacher modeling of fluent reading. It is the modeling that really makes echo reading work. Reading to students from trade literature and nonfiction, not just basal stories, is important in every grade, particularly with corrective and remedial readers. No poor reader is "too big to be read to" in the classroom. Besides modeling fluent reading, it also brings students to text they could not otherwise read and helps them associate pleasure and success (through listening) with print.

Readers Theater

Readers theater is a form of dramatics in which scripts are always read, not recited, and "acting" is kept minimal while readers use their voices and gestures to interpret literature. As a dramatic form it is relatively unusual, and as a method of helping readers develop fluency it is almost unknown, but it can be both effective and very enjoyable.

In readers theater a play script may be used, or may be rewritten by students from a narrative story or article, and is read and reread both silently and orally for presentation. In preparation readers work on developing fluency and on conveying their emotions, motives, and the like through expression in their voices, known as oral interpretation. This is the same process a storyteller uses to tell a story effectively. Usually none of the trapping of dramatics — props, costumes and sets — are used, and characters do not enter or leave the scene. Instead they may rise, or turn to face the audience or other characters, when speaking and sit or turn away when they are not "on." Scripts are always read aloud, never memorized.

Readers theater is an ideal activity for corrective readers because it allows them to participate fully in drama activities, relieves them of the burden of learning lines and "acting," and requires them to reread material and practice fluent, expressive reading. It also requires students to understand and ponder the events, actions, and characters in a story so that their feelings, beliefs, and actions can be conveyed to others through their dialogue. It can be one of the best reading and dramatics activities available for poorer readers.

Developing Word Analysis Strategies

Immediate, accurate recognition of about 90 percent or more of the words in running text is necessary for effective instructional-level reading. As students read more widely and sample various kinds of text, they will necessarily encounter words they do not recognize at sight. The role of teaching word analysis is to help students acquire efficient strategies for figuring out unrecognized words.

As we discussed in Chapter One, readers may use a variety of *cues*, or signals, in the unrecognized word and in the surrounding text to figure it out. Cues available from the context include *semantic* (meaning-related) cues and *syntactic* (grammar-related) cues. Using them to help figure out an unknown word is called *contextual analysis*. Cues available within the word itself include the letters and the speech sounds they may represent, called *graphemic* (letter-related) and *phonological* (sound-related) cues, and word parts like base words, affixes, syllables, and the like. Using graphemic and phonological cues (primarily the latter) is called *phonic analysis*. Using word parts is called *structural analysis*. Good readers use contextual, phonic, and structural analysis to figure out unrecognized words, using all three appropriately and usually in conjunction with each other, without depending entirely on one strategy.

Contextual Analysis

Using the context to help figure out unfamiliar words is the word analysis strategy good readers seem to use most often. Many poor readers do not know how to use context efficiently and need direct instruction to develop this skill and use it consistently.

Context is important because the meaning of a phrase or sentence is derived not from the meaning of each individual word, but from these meanings combined with word order and the meaning contributed by previous and successive word groups. Each word has a number of *possible* meanings or referents, but precisely *which* meaning is dictated by the context. In the case of connected text, "the whole is more than the sum of the parts." Goodman and Burke (1980) illustrated this point clearly when they wrote:

> A reading *context* is never as ambiguous as are isolated units of language. Only in context is the reader able to make use of syntax and semantics in order to decide on the most appropriate of the possible meanings of a linguistic unit, and therefore approach the meaning of an author. . . . For example, you may be able to assign meaning to some of the following words: *if, myself, for, me, will, I, am, who, be, not,* but not until these words have a syntactic and semantic context — *If I am not for myself, who will be for me?* — can you begin to gain some understanding. (1980, p. 31)

Almost every reading program emphasizes word analysis, sometimes called *word attack,* but few place much emphasis on using context. Instead, it is common practice to teach youngsters to immediately try to sound out, or use phonic analysis, to decode unfamiliar words as they occur. Because they have often had frequent heavy doses of such instruction, many poor readers seem to automatically disregard context and turn to such decoding attempts whenever they encounter an unknown word. This is a poor practice for several reasons.

First, it interrupts the flow of ideas and slows the process of comprehension. It is impossible to simultaneously keep the meaning of what has already been read in mind while switching strategies and trying to decode. The ideas so far acquired must stay in short-term memory during the sounding-out, and, as we have already seen, the capacity of short-term memory is limited to a few seconds. That is why it is not uncommon to find that after several stops, or a lengthy one, to decode a word, the reader has forgotten what occurred before the stop, or forgotten the beginning of the sentence by the time the end is reached.

Second, as we have already seen, it is difficult, and may be impossible, to identify *and comprehend* a word and the meaning it contributes to a sentence when it is considered in isolation. Almost every word you can think of has a number of possible meanings depending on the use of the word in its context. This is particularly true of the 200 to 300 words that occur most frequently and account for some 40 percent or more of all written English (Holdaway, 1979, p. 98). For example, *run* is one such word. Only a few seconds of thought will yield these (and probably other) possible meanings:

- □ gait faster than walking: Don't run in the halls.
- □ a jogger's exercise routine: How was your run?
- □ a tear in a stocking: You have a run in your stocking.
- □ a small creek: We live near Boyle's Run.
- □ a sequence of events: He had a run of bad luck.
- □ a computer operation: The last run aborted.

Identifying *run* without using context will not result in the understanding of the word and identifying words in text without understanding is a meaningless, nonsensical exercise. Unfortunately many poor readers assume that this is expected and normal. Teaching the use of context can dramatically improve their reading, and a number of strategies may be used.

Context Strategy Lessons. Goodman and Burke (1980) recommended that readers' miscue patterns be studied to determine what kinds of words readers often misidentify, and that specific lessons they call *reading strategy lessons* be devised to focus directly on the cues students may be ignoring. Reading strategy lessons involve an overall sequence in which students read some text for a specific purpose, discuss in a group what they have read and what strategies were used, apply the strategy focused on in another reading selection, and practice it in self-selected reading, writing, or some other extension activity.

For example, a reading strategy lesson on pronouns is intended for a group of readers who frequently miscue on pronouns, substituting words like *he* for *we* or *her* for *him*, which results in misunderstanding "who said or did what" in reading. Students begin by reading a list of physical characteristics of people in a family. The list is made up of phrases that are related but unconnected. Next students work alone or in small groups to write a description of each person using all the facts. (Dictation to a "scribe" or onto recording tape could be used for those who write with great difficulty.) Students' written descriptions are read aloud to the group, and their use of referential pronouns is pointed out. Discussion follows with students explaining why *he, she, they,* or the appropriate pronoun was used and to what or whom each pronoun refers. In this way students are encouraged to explain and clarify what they know, since putting what one knows into language for others is an important step in learning. Next a cloze activity is introduced, in which students must supply all the referential pronouns in a short but unified piece of text. (This may be done orally in a group before students attempt the cloze in writing.) Again discussion follows in which students share their choices, explain or justify them and constructively comment on each other's strategies. Follow-up activities include reading self-selected material and noting the author's use of pronouns and explaining their use to the group, keeping track of how animals, vehicles, and the like are referred to in other materials, and interviewing others to find out why they think some objects (e.g., hurricanes, ships, and animals) are often referred to as "he" or "she."

Reading strategy lessons are ideal for corrective teaching because:

a. They are derived from students' demonstrated needs.
b. They focus directly on one topic or process at a time.
c. They emphasize comprehension, with word recognition as a means, not an end in itself.
d. They feature reading of whole text, not single sentences or words, for real reading purposes.
e. They utilize prediction, hypothesis-testing, and open-ended discussion.
f. They move students from directed reading of selected material to applying the skill in self-selected reading and writing.

Cloze Procedures. The cloze and maze procedures were described in Chapter Four as means of identifying students' functional reading levels in relation to particular materials. Both procedures are equally effective as teaching tools for helping students use context to form hypotheses about unknown words. To complete a cloze passage the reader inserts words that make sense and support the author's message. In order to do so, the reader must "think along with the author," using prior information, the meaning suggested by the entire passage, and the semantic and syntactic clues provided by the words surrounding the blanks. Systematic practice with this helps readers to become more sensitive to context cues and better able to use them efficiently when they read.

For instructional purposes, the guidelines for cloze preparation may be changed. It is not necessary to delete every fifth word except for placement purposes. It may be much more effective to delete fewer words, leaving more of the text intact, and to delete particular kinds of words as they occur rather than every *nth* one regardless of its function. For example, in the pronouns strategy lesson described in the previous section a cloze passage was used in which only pronouns were deleted. In another passage the meaning and function of connectives or relational words such as *and, but, although,* and *so* may be emphasized by deleting them.

Also, the rule of "exact replacements only" is not as important when using the cloze for instruction. It is most effective to allow students to insert their "best guesses" and then discuss their choices, guiding them to consider how several alternatives may make sense in one place but only one possible choice would complete another blank, and how different choices can lead to subtle but important changes in meaning.

Sharing and discussion should always accompany such an activity. Its effectiveness is reduced, perhaps even removed, if students complete such an activity as a worksheet, turn it in for correction or grading, and get it back later with little or no exchange. It is important for students to share their hunches and compare their choices to those of others in order to really see how context and individuals' prior information interact, as in the following demonstration.

Ms. Anderson is conducting a cloze activity with fifth graders. She projects a transparency of a paragraph with words deleted:

> When morning came a heavy fog _____ everything. Every branch and leaf _____ with water. The grass looked like a silver _____ . In the garden a spider's web _____ with tiny _____ .

Ms. Anderson explains that for each blank several alternatives exist that will make sense, complete the tone of the paragraph and work well grammatically. She asks for volunteers to read sentences aloud and suggest possible words to complete the blanks. As students do this she prints their suggestions on the transparency with a grease pencil:

> fog _____ everything: *covered, blanketed, hid*
> every branch and leaf _____ : *dripped, ran, was covered*

(Ms. Anderson reminds the group that they should seek single words to complete the cloze.)

> like a silver _____ : *carpet, cloud, field*
> a spider's web _____ : *sparkled, sagged, hung*
> with tiny _____ : *drops, beads, raindrops*

As alternatives are offered the teacher accepts them without evaluation, but asks questions like "Why does that seem like a good possibility?" or "How does that idea work with the rest of the sentence or passage?" She encourages the students to direct questions to each other and offer their reasons for their choices. Throughout the activity emphasis is placed not on guessing a correct answer, but rather on developing alternatives that support the meaning of the passage and sensing nuances of meaning from context.

In this example the teacher helped each student see that in most cases several alternatives are possible and that uncertainty need not stop them in their tracks. Group efforts and thoughtful discussion like this help prepare students for individual efforts and point out the usefulness of this process in word identification during independent reading.

It is important for students to be taught directly, preferably by modeling as well as explanation, how to complete a cloze activity. By working through examples on the board or a transparency, asking for volunteers to suggest words to fill some blanks, completing some yourself while explaining your thinking and your reasons for choosing a particular word, and encouraging students to offer alternatives, you can most effectively prepare them to do this activity independently. Lack of sufficient preparation frequently results in students feeling intimidated and frustrated, in lack of willingness to risk a mistake, and in their finding the activity unpleasant and unproductive.

Because there is considerable ambiguity in the process and because it is so open-ended, material for cloze practice should be either independent-level or easy instructional-level text. Until students become practiced and confident with the procedure, it may be well to prepare exercises that students have already read intact. Previously read basal and other fairly easy text material is good, as well as students' own compositions (with appropriate standard spellings and mechanics inserted if necessary). Beginning readers who are using dictated stories can use cloze procedures made up from these as well, as long as they are not required to use the same word they originally used in dictating. This would make the exercise one in memorizing, not in thoughtfully constructing meaning.

The maze procedure, in which multiple-choice items replace blanks, is considerably easier than the cloze but has limited instructional value. In selecting from predetermined items, readers are less engaged in actively constructing meaning than when they produce words that make sense. Very young readers or those very intimidated by the cloze's blanks may find the maze helpful initially, but they should be slowly and supportively weaned away from the maze procedure after its initial use.

Predicting and Confirming from Context. Holdaway (1979) described a procedure he called "confirming," which helps students use context to make a prediction about what word or words might make sense in a sentence, and then use letters and sounds to confirm or disprove their prediction. This method helps teach students to use both context and phonics to identify unfamiliar words, an almost ideal combination of strategies.

This is an excellent group activity, for students will benefit from hearing others' predictions and justifying their own. The teacher uses a story or other text that is reproduced on a transparency and a "progressive exposure mask," which consists of strips of paper attached to one side of the transparency that cover the lines of text and can be lifted or slid aside to expose portions of each line (see Figure 5.2). The group reads up to (and sometimes a bit beyond) a word that is covered, predicts what the word might be, based on the context, and then the mask is moved to expose the first letter or letter group of the word. If the letters revealed help confirm their prediction, the students read on, sometimes with a comment comparing the word to a similar one. If the letters revealed are not what they expected, their hypotheses are revised to fit the new information. The activity is kept fairly fast-paced and informal, so that the students' curiosity is rewarded and they don't get bogged down. The following excerpt shows how such a lesson might proceed using a story entitled *Red Fox and His Canoe* by Nathaniel Benchley (New York: Harper and Row, 1964). The group has read the first portion of the story when this excerpt begins. On the left side of the page is listed what is shown on the transparency, and at the right the children's and teacher's comments. (Holdaway uses "rerun" to mean going back to the beginning of a sentence and reading it again.)

FIGURE 5.2. A progressive exposure mask.

SOURCE: From Don Holdaway, *The Foundations of Literacy* (Gosford, N.S.W.: Ashton Scholastic, 1979). Reprinted by permission of Ashton Scholastic.

Finally his father cut down a
tree and made a f- - - in it.
"This is too big for you.
But *never mind*.

You'- - gr- - ," he said.

Except for the opening, *Finally*, the children read. Good picture clue.

Seen that before — Magic Fish — the
identify strategy

Read on to *grow*. Then re-run — 'You
will grow . . . you'll grow!' We say,
'And there's the double *l* that we would
expect.'

Red Fox who was helping scr- - -

We look at the *scr. Scratch? Scrape?*
'Yes, could be,' we say.
'If it's *scrape*, what letter should we expect
to see? Yes, a *p* and (as we slide the mask)
there it is.' Re-run.

burned w- - - out of the tree,
said,

Impulsively, *wood!* 'Then what
letter would we expect to see at the end?
Yes *d*.' We expose the *ood* and someone
says, 'It's like *good*- - the contrast strategy.'

"No canoe is too big for me.
The big- - - - - - - - - - - -
I say."

After a moment at *big*- someone says ex-
citedly, 'The bigger the better.' 'O.K. what
letters will we expect to see at the end of
bigger and *better*? Listen again.' And as we
slide the mask, 'we were right.' 'And *better*
starts with *b*,' says someone.

When all the burned wood was
scr- - - out, his father said,
"All r- - - - , here's your canoe.

'What ending?' *ed!* We check.

Impulsively from several, 'All right!'
'What letter will we see at the end?' 'O.K.
- - but hullo! (as we slide the mask) what's
that *gh* doing there?' Someone volunteers,
'It's like night,' and we write this on the
board. (A positive learning from letter-
confirmation.)

Can you l- - - it?

Picture clue — Red Fox struggling. '*Lift*,
and it'll end in *f*.' 'No,' says someone, 'in
t!' We look. 'Well, in a way both of you are
right. Let's listen, *lift*. Which sound do we
hear first, the /t/ or the /f/. That's right, we
hear the sound of the *f* before the sound
of the *t*.' (At this stage we can abbrevi-
ate from 'the sound that *f* stands for' without causing confusion.) We compare
left.

"Sure," said Red Fox.	'What's this?' (at *Sure*). An argument breaks out. 'He can't lift it.' 'Yes he can.' 'No he can't- - it's too heavy. Look at him.' We discuss the problem. Does he think he can lift it? What sort of thing is he *likely* to say, whether he can lift it or not? Someone says, 'He'll say, *A course I can lift it!'*
	'Yeah,' says someone else, 'He'll say, "F'shor I can!"' 'That's it!' shouts someone else, *'sure'* It's got a *s!* 'Alright, let's go on and see if we're right!'
"Eas- - -"	'Easily!' comes the chorus.
"Sure," said Red Fox.	We re-run for clarity and to savour the special effect. 'There's *ly*,' says some bright spark.
So they put it in the - - - - -	Before any letter of the word is unmasked, 'River.' 'Water.' 'Could it be anything else?' 'Stream.' 'Pond.' 'Let's peek.' (showing just the *w*)
w- - - - .	'Water!' they all shout. Re-run from *So.*
and Red Fox p- - - - - - off.	Read-on to *off* keeping *-addled* covered. 'Pushed off.' 'Paddled off.' Picture favours *paddled.* What letter would we expect to see in the middle? We check. 'Two of them,' says someone.
"Oh b- - -! he said	'Boy!'
"Now watch me catch a m- - - - - - fish!"	Read-on to *fish*, covering the *-illion.* 'A million fish!' 'What letter should we see in the middle of *million?*
	Let's listen?' 'That's like my name,' says William. 'It's got two els.' And we note this double letter phenomenon in *little*, *Middle Muddle*, and recall *paddled.*

SOURCE: From Don Holdaway, *The Foundations of Literacy* (Gosford, N.S.W.: Ashton Scholastic, 1979). Reprinted by permission of Ashton Scholastic.

   Excerpt from Nathanael Benchley, *Red Fox and His Canoe* reprinted by permission of Harper & Row, Publishers, Inc.

   Holdaway commented that although teachers reading this description might think it "a terrible thing to do to a good story" (p. 123), in his experience students enjoy the problem-solving aspect of decoding when it is presented in the context of a good story, when they are allowed the support of others working at the same task, and when the pace is kept lively. He cautioned teachers using this procedure to pay attention to the students' degree of curiosity and participation and to drop the prediction and "speed the story on its way" (p. 123) before students lose interest or become confused.

Phonic Analysis

Phonics has long been a controversial topic. The issues involved include:

- whether phonics skills are essential in reading
- when students should be introduced to phonics
- whether a particular sequence of skills should be taught
- whether phonics is "better" than sight recognition
- which of several instructional methods is "best"
- whether phonics produces "word callers" unconcerned with meaning
- whether fluent readers ever use phonics

These issues seem to produce strong feelings and categorical statements on the part of many authorities. A whole spectrum of opinion exists; at one extreme are those who believe that readers should be able to "sound out" any word they see and that more phonics instruction will solve all reading problems, while at the other extreme are those who believe that because fluent readers appear to use phonics rarely, it is simply an extra burden we place on young readers, and that words should never be studied in isolation. Most educators and instructional programs fall somewhere between these polarities.

The phonics-versus-sight word controversy is an artificial dichotomy. Experience and good sense tell us that no "either-or" answer is likely to suit the needs of all learners. No single strategy is sufficient; rather, both a large and stable sight vocabulary and facility with a number of word analysis strategies, including (but not limited to) phonics, are necessary for good reading.

Most readers use phonic analysis as they develop their reading abilities, but tend not to use it after they become fluent readers. This has been used as evidence that developing readers really don't need phonics, but it can be misleading to infer from the performance of experts what beginners need to do. As we discussed in Chapter Two, it appears that readers pass through several stages on their way to reading mastery, in which both use of context and use of word analysis temporarily gain ascendance and are relied upon and practiced, before readers learn to use these skills in conjunction and reach a stage of fluent reading. Neither strategy is necessarily "best," but both have their place in reading development. Students need a variety of word recognition strategies that they can use flexibly and efficiently. Because many poor readers may lack facility with decoding, phonics instruction may be necessary. However, there are several points to consider before embarking on a phonics program.

As we have seen from the predicting and confirming activity just described, being able to use letters and sounds in conjunction with context is very useful in reducing the number of possible alternatives an unfamiliar word may have, and in making the decoding process rapid and accurate. Phonics activities are most often conducted at the "word level," (e.g., by studying and comparing individual words) but in practice we want students to be able to use phonics in context while keeping in mind the other words they have just read.

Another important point to remember is that because phonics is based on the sounds that letters may represent, phonics activities should be primarily *oral*, so that sounds are readily identifiable. Too often phonics activities are paper-and-pencil tasks, which makes them very abstract. They can also be confusing, because it is often difficult to tell what sounds may occur in a word by looking at its letters. Yet very often we see entire programs of phonics activities that consist almost entirely of one worksheet or workbook page after another. Phonics activities should be conducted aloud until students are very adept at discriminating among sounds in words and producing words that contain a particular sound feature, before moving on to written phonics work. Finally, when students are working on paper-and-pencil tasks they should be allowed to "sound out" their hypotheses aloud as they work. We once saw a group of remedial readers who had been given phonics worksheets for independent work and the instruction to work without talking. When they tried to work out sounds aloud, they were reprimanded for not working silently. Their frustration with this nearly impossible task became quickly apparent as many began to make numerous errors and some gave up the task entirely. Phonics is only a silent, internal activity for those who can already do it easily, not for those who are still learning it.

Auditory Discrimination. Learning phonics begins with being able to discriminate between sounds in spoken words. Emergent and beginning readers need plenty of auditory discrimination practice to help them focus on the sounds in words. Corrective readers who are beyond the beginning stages of reading but are having difficulty using phonic analysis may need some review of auditory discrimination, but probably not a lot of instruction. In any case a review and informal assessment of whether a student can adequately discriminate among similar sounds in words is a good practice.

Auditory discrimination means being able to perceive small differences in sounds when comparing two or more similar words. Auditory discrimination tests usually require students to listen to similar words and identify similarities and differences. A good place to start reviewing or teaching this skill is to present (orally) two words and ask students to tell whether they have the same sound feature, like a shared sound or rhyme. For example:

"I'll say two words. Do they have the same *beginning* sound?"

   pat   *pencil*

"Yes, *pat* and *pencil* have the same beginning sound. We hear /p/ at the beginning of each. Who can think of another word that begins like *pat* and *pencil?*"

In this example the teacher has avoided writing the words down, for the time being concentrating on helping the children hear the salient sound. She has also avoided the temptation to teach or identify a letter that represents a particular sound. This comes second, after plenty of auditory practice.

After practice in which students respond by saying whether or not pairs have the same feature, the task may be made a bit more complex by offering three words, only two of which contain the same sound. Students then tell which two have the shared feature and which does not, as in this set:

"Which words begin with the same sound? Which does not?"

milk   *salt*   *money*

As they work on discriminating between and among examples you give, they should also practice producing words to fit a particular pattern. As they do this, it is very important for you to avoid confusing *sounds* with the *letters* used to represent them. Because there is no one-to-one correspondence between the forty-four sounds in English and the twenty-six letters we use to represent them, there is often more than one way to spell a particular sound. So, if you asked students to offer new words that began like *fox* and *fill*, for example, you should accept *phone* as well as *football*. When you move to the stage of writing down the words as well as pronouncing them, you can avoid any conflict between sound and spelling with a direction like: "Who can think of another word that begins with the sound we hear at the beginning of *fox* and starts with an *f?*

Then, if *phone* were offered, you would say, "Yes, *phone* has the same beginning sound as *fox* but is spelled differently. We'll write *phone* over here." As students begin to concentrate on both sound and letter identification, their attention can be drawn to the two different spellings of the same sound, guiding them to realize that there are other letter patterns that may be sounded out the same way.

Auditory discrimination may be put in a gamelike format by naming an object or animal and having students find words that have the same feature, like the same beginning sound, to go with it. For example, a *purple pig* might eat *pancakes, peppers* and *pinto* beans, wear *pullovers, pedal-pushers* and *plaid pajamas,* and enjoy *painting, paddling* a canoe, and *pole-vaulting.* (Again, it is best not to be too strict about spelling, unless you have specified that a sound must be spelled in a particular way.) Students may enjoy illustrating these collections and making their own books or bulletin board displays. Good books to share with students to model this activity include Dahlov Ipcar's *I Love My Anteater with an A* (New York: Knopf, 1964), Robert Tallon's *Zoophabets* (New York: Bobbs-Merrill, 1971), and Eric Carle's *All About Arthur* (New York: Franklin Watts, 1974).

Matching Sounds and Letters. After plenty of oral practice, students should begin to associate the sounds they hear in words with the letters that may represent those sounds. As we have seen, there may be more than one way to spell a particular sound. These are not "irregularities" of spelling and should not be presented as such; with forty-four speech sounds and twenty-six letters, it is apparent that the same letters may have to represent more than one sound and that the same sound may be spelled more than one way because of different origins of words.

Substituting sounds in real words helps students to recognize and decode many words. This is known as working with *word families.* For example, a number of one-syllable words belong to "the *-at* family," and substituting initial sounds can generate *bat, cat, fat, hat, mat, sat, rat, pat,* and so forth. Students may list as many as they can think of, then identify which they think are real words and which may be nonsense words that fit the pattern, as in *bat, cat, dat, fat, gat.* A dictionary may be useful here, since what seem to be nonwords may be real but unfamiliar. Similarly, ending and medial sounds may be substituted: *had — hack — ham — has — hat,* or *bit — bet — bat — but.* Work with word families helps students develop skill in comparing word features.

Sequencing Phonics Skills. Much has been made of the sequence in which letter-sounds should be taught. Most phonics programs base at least some of their claims of effectiveness on their particular sequence of skills. Developers of such programs clearly have a vested interest in convincing teachers that a "best sequence" exists. However, no conclusive evidence exists that a particular sequence is best. What we need to know is, what phonics skills do these students, or this individual, already know? Which skills need to be reviewed and practiced? The answers to these questions lie in our careful observation of the students' decoding attempts during everyday reading and the results of our analysis of their oral reading and word recognition inventories.

Most readers learn initial sounds first, then final sounds, and medial (middle) sounds last. Decoding of an unknown word usually proceeds in the same way: initial, then final, then medial sounds (Ehri, Barron & Feldman, 1978). This occurs for a number of reasons.

One has to do with how we perceive written words. In order to figure out what an unknown entity might be, we need to figure out what its *boundaries* are; that is, where does it start and end? In our discussion of developing word concepts in Chapter Two, we discussed how emergent readers develop awareness of word boundaries in print, indicated in print by spaces that are not usually present in speech. That is, in print each word consists of a *bound configuration* with spaces on each side, while in speech words sound like they are run together continuously, with spaces or pauses used for emphasis. Perceiving the boundaries of printed words leads to awareness of initial and final letters and, somewhat later, to medial letters.

Another factor is the way spelling has evolved to represent sounds with letters. Most words in English begin with consonants, and most consonants represent fewer sound variations than vowels. Some consonants (*j, k, l, m, n, p, b, h, r, v,* and *w*) represent only one sound consistently (Heilman, 1981). (Phoneticians will argue that even these sounds differ depending on their position within a word, such as the slight difference in the sounds of the two *p*'s in *popcorn.* However, these minimal differences are unimportant to developing readers.) Certain other consonants represent two sounds, such as the *c* in *cake* and *ceiling* or the *g* in *gold* and *giraffe,* but their usage is still rule-bound and regular.

Because most words begin with consonants which are consistent and limited in the sounds they represent, using beginning sounds is an important phonic skill. Indeed, it may be all that is needed to provide a sufficient cue so that, combined with "What would make sense here?" the word can be identified.

To demonstrate the usefulness of combining initial sounds with context, suppose the blank represents an unrecognized word in each of these arrays:

1. _____

2. l_____

3. The cat l_____ onto the counter.

(adapted from Heilman, 1981, p. 25)

In line 1 the blank could represent any of the some 600,000 words in English. In line 2 the presence of the letter *l* reduces the possibilities to about 30,000 or so words. And in line 3, even those remaining possibilities are reduced by the context.

Ideally, every reader would be able to look at the *l,* use the context and say *leaped.* But what about the one who says *lawn,* or *love,* or some other word or nonword? Attention must then be directed to the final syllable, *-ed,* to the final sound in the base word *leap,* and again to the context to help identify the word. By doing so the alternatives will be further reduced. Thus beginning sounds, final sounds, and context combine to help the reader arrive at the intended word.

It may be tempting to teach phonic rules as mnemonic devices to help students remember the patterns. Rules can be of some value when the number of words encountered is small, but the problem with rules is that each has numerous exceptions, and the frequency of such exceptions increases with the complexity of text. For example, the rule "when a vowel pair occurs together in the middle of a word, the first vowel will be long and the second silent" (the old "when two vowels go walking" rule) has so many exceptions that it may be more confusing than helpful. Consider, for example, these common exceptions:

oa	*ai*	*ee*	*ea*	*ou*
board	said	been	bread	could
broad	again		break	enough
	aisle		heart	touch

ue	*ie*	*au*
guess	field	caught
guard	friend	laugh
usual	view	
build	piece	

Relatively quickly such rules must be abandoned, or so many exceptions added that the original value of the rule is lost.

This is not to say that there are no regularities, or that all rules are useless. But there are two ways to help students become aware of and use regularities while preparing for exceptions. First, we can present regular patterns as *generalizations* rather than rules. The difference is subtle but important. Students expect rules to be consistent and often find the inevitable exceptions frustrating and confusing. Generalizations, in contrast, are tentative hypotheses; like predictions, they are often borne out, but may be contradicted in some instances without affecting their basic usefulness.

Second, instead of presenting generalizations directly, we can help students to form and verbalize their *own* generalizations about how words work. This involves students actively in studying words, comparing and contrasting their features, and developing hypotheses about regularities. It requires more active thinking and understanding than receiving information someone else has formulated and applying it. *Word sorting* is a powerful way of helping students consider a variety of word features by comparing and classifying words.

Word Sorting

Imagine a teacher working with a group of young beginning readers who have small collections of words printed on cards, words they recognize at sight that have been gleaned from dictated stories, familiar trade books and basal stories, signs, and labels. Such a collection of sight words is called a *word bank,* and today when the children come to the reading circle they bring their word banks along and sit on the floor.

The teacher tells the children to go through their word banks and group some of the words together on the floor in front of them. The words all have to go together in some way, and each child will have to tell *how* they go together. The teacher watches carefully as the students go through their words and sort them.

The first word in Tammy's word bank is *but*. After studying it for a moment, she shuffles through her cards and pulls out several more, arranges them in a line, and sits back with a satisfied smile. The words are:

but		ball		boy		brown		bananas

Chris studies his words intently after spreading them all out before him. With a good deal of muttering to himself he makes this group:

butterfly		tomorrow		potatoes		Christopher

Alicia also spreads her cards out and makes several false starts as she tentatively puts words together, then changes her mind. Finally she appears to be satisfied with this grouping:

puppy		grass		Mother		flower		hamster

Each child in the group has made a unique sort, because each child has somewhat different words in his or her word bank and because each has looked for a different sorting criterion. When told to "put together words that go together in some way," each has looked for certain *word features*.

What feature has Tammy used to categorize *but, ball, boy, brown,* and *bananas?* Obviously, they share the same beginning letter *b*. Tammy has also grouped her words by the same beginning sound feature, which she hears when she reads each word card aloud to the teacher. Tammy has attended to both letter and sound features in this sort.

Chris's words *(butterfly, tomorrow, potatoes, Christopher)* do not share the same letter or sound features. They do not start alike or have a similar vowel sound; two have a double consonant, but not all four. What feature do they share? They are all three-syllable words; Chris checked himself on this feature by pronouncing each word aloud. He attended to features of word parts, in this case the number of syllables in each word.

Alicia has apparently not used the same features as Chris or Tammy, for *puppy, grass, hamster, flower,* and *Mother* do not share the same number of syllables or a common affix, nor do they have a sound or letter feature in common. On what basis, then, has Alicia grouped them? She calls them all "living things," and we can see that she has used word meaning as the shared feature.

There are other word features the children might have used, such as grammatical features — the ways words function in sentences — what we know as parts of speech: for example, *car, mouse, tacos,* and *sea* are all nouns; *run, table, shoe,* and *light* can all be either nouns or verbs depending on how they are used; *happy, run-down,* and *fat* are all descriptive words. There are also spelling pattern features. *Mail, boat, shoes,* and *hear* all share the spelling feature of double vowels (precisely, vowel digraphs) as do *feet, sheep,* and *beer.*

The Importance of Classifying. In our example, the children were *word sorting.* To do this, they must study and compare words and determine the features several words have in common. The word sorting activity is based on principles of induction and discovery learning. The act of classifying stimuli into classes according to their common properties is one of the most basic and powerful operations of human thinking and is responsible for much of a child's natural learning ability, particularly the acquisition of linguistic concepts (Anglin, 1977).

This process can be used productively in school to help children develop strategies for recognizing words in print and analyzing unrecognized words. We often forget that children come to school with five or six years of solid experience in looking for similarities in things, categorizing them, and drawing generalizations about how they work, but they have to be shown how to apply these thinking operations to the study of words in print (Gillet, 1980; Morris, 1982).

Words for Sorting. Since word sorts are done with words on cards, students need a collection of word cards with which to work. Their word banks are particularly good for this purpose because they contain words they recognize at sight. This growing collection of known words is perfect for use in word sorts, because the words must be quickly recognized before their components can successfully be analyzed.

A very quick way of helping children begin a word bank without using dictation is to give them a short story or passage that they can read fairly easily, have them underline each new word they can immediately recognize, and tell them to copy each word onto a small card. Then, working in pairs, they can run through each other's cards to weed out any words that are not quickly recognized. In this way they can develop collections of words they recognize and also accomplish the task of making the cards themselves, which is a time-consuming and tedious task for the teacher.

Using Word Sorts Diagnostically. There are two basic kinds of word sorts: those that call on *convergent* thinking and those that call on *divergent* thinking. In a *closed sort,* the feature that all words in a group must share is stated in advance. For example, the students are directed to search for words beginning like *stop,* having the same vowel sounds as *bake* and *sheep,* the same number of syllables as *feather,* or words that might be associated with a party. Students then search for words that fit the pattern. A closed sort helps them use convergent thinking.

In an *open sort,* which encourages divergent thinking, no sorting criteria are stated in advance. Instead, word cards are examined and categories formed as relationships suggest themselves spontaneously. In closed sorts, students search for instances of particular shared features; in open sorts they consider a number of features simultaneously, searching for those shared by other words. In both types of sorts, children are guided toward *discovering* similarities in words rather than being *told* or *shown* how they are alike (in contrast to some of the more traditional word study activities).

As instructional procedures, both open and closed word sorts are very useful in helping youngsters form generalizations about how known words work, which they can fruitfully apply when they encounter a new word. Word sorts are also a powerful diagnostic tool through which we can learn a good deal about what features of words children can perceive and how they go about learning new word analysis strategies.

Closed sorts. When teachers want to determine if children in the group can recognize certain features of words, they can use the closed sort, in which they specify what the children are to look for and illustrate the salient feature with word or picture cards as examples. The children then search their word banks and word card collections for one or more words with the same feature. Each child then holds up or lays down the cards simultaneously. A quick look around the circle at each child's offering will show the teacher which children have recognized that feature.

Let's say, for example, that a teacher of beginning readers wants to find out quickly what each child in a reading group knows about certain initial consonant sounds, but the teacher doesn't want to give the group a test. Using a diagnostic sort, the teacher uses the regular reading-circle time to determine this information. The children come to the circle with their *word* cards while the teacher brings a set of *picture* cards, commercial or home-made from magazine pictures. The teacher shows them one or more pictures of objects that illustrate the initial sound they will explore — for example, pictures of a *fox* and a *fire* to get at the initial consonant sound of *f,* or one picture for each of several sounds, like a *box,* a *mouse,* a *cake,* and a *hat,* to work on recognition of all four of those initial sounds. The teacher tells the children to find one or more words from their word banks that start with the same sound as these objects. The child names each pictured object, and the teacher observes the words given as a match. (It is easier if the children sit on the floor so they can place their cards on the floor in front of them.) In this activity, pictures, not printed words, are used as exemplars so that the children must rely on an internalization of the sound feature rather than just matching initial letters visually (Gillet and Kita, 1979). The teacher can provide immediate feedback to each child, and time is used efficiently because all the children are involved simultaneously in the task rather than one child performing and the rest watching or waiting their turns. Any letter-sound feature can be assessed as well as any other feature of words. Number of syllables, meaning relationships, parts of speech, and structural elements like affixes are examples of categories that could be formed.

Open sorts. A related assessment activity, a little more open-ended, is the open word sort. A convenient format for this is a game in which students must "read each other's minds" by deducing the criterion another has used to form a group. In this game, each student begins with the same number of word cards; a dozen is an adequate number. Working individually, each child forms at least one category of words. Others must try to "read minds" by either stating the shared feature or, more abstractly, by finding words of their own to add to the category. During each phase of the activity, the teacher discovers what students know about words and what they still need to learn by observing the word groups formed and their attempts to "break" another's category.

Individual sorts. Word sorts can also be used with one child individually, to see how well he or she is able to generalize from known words to similar unknown words. The student's word bank can be used or the teacher can make up a set of word cards.

Any closed or open sort format can be used. The teacher and student can also play the "read my mind" open sort game, in which the teacher forms a group and the student must find another word to fit it, then they reverse roles. This game demonstrates recognition of the shared feature.

The student's ability to generalize can be assessed in this way: the teacher groups several highly similar, easily recognized words like *my*, *by*, and *fly*; then the student is shown a similar but unknown word, perhaps *shy* or *cry* in this example. If the student can use the shared feature of the example words to figure out the new word, *the ability to generalize from the known to the unknown* is demonstrated. This generalizing is the fundamental aspect of all word analysis and decoding, an ability that appears only after children have begun to develop a stable store of sight words and have a clear concept of what a written word is.

The ability to group words by shared features is an important one to assess in beginning readers because if it is not yet developed, instruction in word analysis strategies will be largely misunderstood and confusing for the child. Decoding instruction should be put off until the youngster can do this kind of thinking.

Developing Reading Comprehension

In recent years reading comprehension has become a topic of enormous research interest, and new insights have been proposed that challenge much of the accepted wisdom about comprehension. Such challenges have sparked new controversies and in some cases have led to the development of new approaches in teaching comprehension.

A central issue in current comprehension research is the manner in which readers receive and process new information from print and the degree to which they must relate what is new to what is already known. That we learn by relating and associating new and old, or prior, information is not a new insight, but it is one that has increasingly been studied. Piaget (1969) and many others have proposed that cognitive growth occurs when the learner establishes mental categories, or *schemata*, comprised of concepts about objects and events sharing some general or specific features. As new, unfamiliar things are experienced, they are compared to members of existing categories, and either lumped with prior experiences or placed in a newly established schema. In this way established schemata become more complex while new ones are established, providing more and more ways for the learner to deal with new experiences. Only recently, however, has this process been directly applied to the acquisition of information during reading. *Schema theory* refers to a model of reading comprehension that takes into account what readers may already know and how they go about developing and adding to schemata as they read. In this model prior information becomes critical to understanding and acquiring new information and meaning.

A second important issue is the presence of predictable organizational schemes in text and the reader's ability to perceive and use them. Recent study has shown that all text we call "stories" are organized in similar, predictable ways, different of course in elaboration and detail but structured in basically similar ways. Studies by Stein (1978) and others have shown that understanding and memory of stories are enhanced when readers have a set of expectations about how stories are structured and when what they read conforms to their expectations. Similarly there are characteristic organizational schemes present in well-written nonfiction text, structures that can aid readers in understanding and remembering information from the text if readers are aware of and use them.

A third issue concerns the nature of comprehension skills and the common practice of teaching them as separate entities. As we have discussed in Chapter Two, recent thinking and research challenge this practice. Instructional programs have long been developed from the assumption that comprehension results from the mastery of a number of discrete skills, each of which can be taught and learned separately from the others. There has long been disagreement on just how many such separate skills exist, but most educators have at least agreed on the existence of such skills as getting the main idea, locating supporting details, differentiating between directly and indirectly stated information (usually called facts and inferences), drawing conclusions, recalling sequences, and understanding cause-and-effect relationships.

Traditional practice in both teaching and testing has been to present comprehension skills as separable entities, each of which may be learned and assessed in relative isolation from the others and mastery of which results in overall reading comprehension. The skills controversy centers around the question of whether such skills are actually separable and whether operations of comprehension are really different from one another, as well as around the question of whether meaning exists only in the text or in the reader's mind as well.

Current trends and findings in the study of comprehension have led away from the isolation of specific skills and toward the teaching of comprehension as an integrated process built around the reader's prior knowledge and schemata. In the sections which follow we will describe activities derived from this approach to comprehension.

Developing Prior Information

Prior information is what we already know or have experienced, directly or vicariously, that we bring to the act of reading. When what we read can be related in some way to our prior information, we understand and remember more clearly. When we lack prior information to relate to what we read, chances are that we will become confused, misunderstand, and forget what we read. In this situation we may also become disinterested in what we are reading, calling it boring or dull. And if our need is great to remember it, as in preparation for a test, we may resort to inefficient strategies like memorizing. Helping students develop, organize, and become aware of their prior information is critical to improving their reading comprehension.

But there are two problems associated with prior information. One is that students may lack sufficient prior information about a topic, not having heard or read of it before. A second problem is that much of our prior information about a given topic may not be readily accessible; it has been buried, so to speak, under other information and we can't summon it up and think about it readily. Because we can't bring it to mind immediately, we think we've forgotten it or never had it. Activities that develop prior information center around helping students establish some basis for new information and helping them remember and organize prior information that is not readily accessible.

Webbing. A simple way to help students begin to recall prior information and form relationships is to use *webbing*, in which the teacher writes a topic or term on the board, students offer terms or phrases that may be related, and lines are drawn connecting those that are associated with each other. In the following reading, terms and relationships are noted and the "web" may be revised to reflect new information acquired. The webbing exercise serves to help students remember old information related to the reading and to form expectations about what they will be reading.

For example, let's say that Ms. Brown, a fourth-grade teacher, plans to have her students read a nonfiction basal selection about how museums are organized and the jobs museum workers perform. She suspects that some of her students have never visited a museum and that the topic is relatively unfamiliar to many of them. She begins, then, with a web to explore with them what they already know.

First she writes *museum* on the board and begins a *brainstorming whip*, in which every student in turn offers a word or phrase related in some way to *museum*. Because some students look apprehensive, she suggests some questions to help get them started:

> What is a museum for?
> What are the names of some museums?
> What might be in them?
> What work do people do in museums?

As each student responds, Ms. Brown writes the response on the board around the key word. Because this is brainstorming, all responses are accepted without comment or evaluation. She notes that the first few responses appear to remind the others of things they may have forgotten and that many appear excited as their turn nears. After everyone has responded once, volunteers may offer other suggestions until their information begins to wane. Then she reads over all the suggestions from the board.

The next step is to help students organize this seemingly random collection of terms into categories. One way Ms. Brown could do this is to use different colors of chalk to draw connecting lines, but because there are a lot of items on the board, this may not help to clarify. So she selects one term, writes it below the web and says, "What other words go with this one?" Items are checked off and listed in categories, with students explaining why these items go together. These categories resulted:

paintings
mummies
statues
suits of armor
rockets
airplanes
old cars
Indian stuff
animals and birds
furniture
old cars
dinosaur bones

scientists
guards
guides

set up exhibits
clean up
take tickets
tours

Smithsonian
Museum of Natural History

Students then suggested names for these categories: things in museums, museum workers, jobs in museums, and names of museums. Ms. Brown then said, "We're going to read an article about how museums are organized and what kinds of work must be done. As you read, watch for mention of the names of famous museums, their collections, and museum workers' jobs. Let's see which of the things we mentioned are in the article."

After the reading was completed, Ms. Brown led her students in reinspecting the web, adding to the appropriate categories items from the article they had not mentioned, and marking those not appearing in the article to look up in another source.

A webbing activity like this is effective for several reasons. One is that it encourages all students to draw on whatever prior information they have, no matter how extensive or limited, and apply it to the reading task. Another is that hearing others' ideas often triggers a forgotten bit of information in another's mind, so that all benefit from sharing of information. A third is that seemingly unrelated information is directly organized so that relationships are sought and explored. A fourth is that prereading participation fosters curiosity and gives readers something to watch for as they read, and a purpose for reading. And a fifth is that the exercise helps the teacher realize what prior information, if any, students have on the topic before they begin reading.

Previewing. Another way to help students organize their prior information and develop expectations about what they are going to read is to let them quickly preview a reading selection and predict what kinds of information they may find in it.

When students preview a reading selection, they do not begin to read it, but rather they scan each page, looking at illustrations and text features such as boldface print and headings. The time allowed for this is very short so that they can get an overall general idea of the content, just enough to begin to predict about specifics. Depending on the length of the selection, two minutes or less are usually sufficient. Previewing is effective with both fiction and nonfiction, as we will see in these examples.

Mr. Talbott works with a group of fifth graders reading at a third-grade instructional level. He has selected a basal story for them to read and discuss that deals with events surrounding the celebration of the Chinese New Year. Because this holiday and Chinese-American customs in general are unfamiliar to his students, he uses previewing to help them form a basis for their reading. He tells the group to find the first and last pages of the story, and then to look at the title and the pictures but not to begin reading yet. He gives them thirty seconds to do so, telling the group when to begin and stop. Then he asks them to close their books and tell him what they saw in the pictures. He lists all the responses on the board:

Chinese people
a parade

fireworks
people in costumes
people wearing masks
some kind of big snake or dragon
people inside a dragon suit
some children looking scared
people eating
a building with a funny roof

Then he asks, "What do you think is going on in this story? What could be happening?" Again he lists responses:

party
celebration
parade
holiday

Then he introduces some terms from the story and encourages predictions about what they might mean and how they may be related to the story: *festival, calendar, temple, parade,* and *feast.* The students' predictions begin to form around the idea that a Chinese holiday celebration is occurring in which people prepare special foods, observe religious customs, wear ceremonial clothing, and participate in a street procession with costumes and fireworks. From this basis of information, Mr. Talbott guides his students to reexamine the illustrations and predict what might happen in the story: for example, who might the children be who are pictured several times? Why might they be frightened in this picture? What might happen at the end?

At this point, the students have developed a good basis of information and expectation and are ready to begin reading. Their previewing has helped them develop a context for the story's events, introduced some of the story's key vocabulary, and helped them to set purposes for their reading.

Ms. Niles works with older poor readers from several grades. Five of her students must read an earth science selection on glacier formation, but prereading discussion reveals that both prior information and interest in the topic are lacking. She uses previewing to help overcome both problems.

First she asks the group to tell what they already know about glaciers. Other than that they are made of ice, her question is met with shrugs and blank looks. "All right," she says, "you have exactly two minutes to look over these pages and find out as much as you can, and we'll see who is able to gather the most information. Sally and Becky, you look at headings and boldface print. Maurice and John, you look at maps. Sam and Daniel, you look for topic sentences at the beginning of each major section. Jessica, you look at photographs and their captions. All set? Begin!"

Ms. Niles has adapted the previewing task to fit the special informational demands of this selection, and has given each student a specific task. She has also used a team approach and introduced an element of competition to arouse the students' interest in the task. After two minutes of silent study, she asks each student or pair to report on their specified area, and begins listing terms, topics, and descriptions on the board under general headings. She compliments each responder on the amount of information gathered, without designating any "winner." After a quick review of the lists on the board, the students begin to read the selection, armed with an array of facts, terms and concepts they had not possessed before, as well as with some confidence that they could read the chapter successfully.

Previewing is an effective means of helping students acquire some prereading information about topics of which they know little beforehand and set some expectations about the text that they can compare to what the selection conveys. The previewing time should be kept short and the discussion period should be conducted in an accepting, encouraging manner. Reading should begin when interest is aroused and some basis for reading has been established.

Developing Prediction

Closely related to the topic of prior information is the process of prediction, in which students compare what they already know or remember to what they think they are going to read. Prediction requires that students relate their prior information to the reading task at hand and form expectations they will apply to the reading. Thus, prediction forms the connection between prior information and the new information coming in.

The directed reading-thinking activity, or DRTA, is a guided group discussion activity that focuses on the formation and testing of prereading predictions. The DRTA is a teaching method that helps students improve comprehension of and interest in fiction and nonfiction text. In essence, it is a set of procedures for guiding prereading and postreading discussion. In a fiction DRTA, children develop critical reading and thinking by predicting possible story events and outcomes, then reading to confirm or disprove their hypotheses. As described by Stauffer (1975), in a DRTA the student forms a set of purposes for reading, processing ideas, and testing answers by taking part in a predict-read-prove cycle. The teacher *activates thought* by asking "What do you think?"; *agitates thought* by asking "Why do you think so?"; and *requires evidence* by asking "How can you prove it?" (Stauffer, 1975, p. 37). The DRTA format helps students to read more critically and with improved comprehension because it engages them in this process of fluent reading in a structured fashion, slowing down and making concrete the phases of the prediction process.

The DRTA differs from the traditional group reading discussion in two major aspects: the *types* of questions asked and the *timing* of the questions. Table 5.5 shows the fundamental differences between these activities.

In a DRTA, the teacher asks open-ended questions that can be answered

TABLE 5.5. Comparison of guided reading activity and DRTA.

	TRADITIONAL GUIDED READING ACTIVITY	DIRECTED READING-THINKING ACTIVITY
QUESTION TYPES	Generally convergent and closed-ended; often there is one right answer.	Divergent and open-ended; call for predictions; several answers are possible.
QUESTION TIMING	Asked after passage is read, to gather information; few pre-reading questions are generally used; when used they are more often for general "motivation" than to focus expectation on the story.	Asked before passage is read to elicit predictions and after passage is read to confirm or deny predictions; questions in both cases are story-dependent rather than general.

in many ways and that encourage divergent thinking. Most of the questions are asked prior to the reading because they require predictions and hypotheses rather than specific facts, and the reading is done to test the veracity of the predictions. When the students read, they are reading not to determine the answer to somebody else's question, but to find out if they were correct. Thus the students set their own purposes for reading.

There are two "basic" DRTA questions: What do you think will happen? and Why do you think so? These two open-ended questions, or variations of them, usually form the backbone of DRTA questioning, although an occasional closed-ended question is helpful. As long as the majority of the questions are open-ended, it is a good practice for the teacher to ask some convergent or factual questions in order to ensure that students understand important details and to challenge and extend their thinking.

A Directed Reading-Thinking Activity with Fiction. In this example, Ms. Bennett uses a third-grade basal story with a reading group of eight students.

MS. B: Today we're going to read a story called "Amy for Short." Look at the title and picture on page 207. What do you think this story might be about?

SARAH: A girl with a really long name, maybe, and they just call her Amy for short.

TOM: Or a girl who's really short.

(Ms. B. jots "really long name" and "short girl" on the board.)

NICK: She doesn't look short in the picture. Maybe she *wants* to be short.

MS. B: These are all good ideas. Let's read the first page and see if any turn out to be true. (The students read silently. Amy, the main character, is introduced and then her pal Mark. Amy is very tall.)

MS. B: Now what do we know about the title? Were any of our first guesses right?

ANDY: She does have a really long name, it says here, but that's not what the title means.

SARAH: She's not real short, she's real tall. She's as tall as her best friend, that boy.

MS. B: Sarah, please read us the part that told you she was really tall.

SARAH: "But I'm tall. The tallest girl in my class."

MS. B: Good. Now, with this title, and what we've read so far, what do you think might happen in this story?

SUE: Maybe she'll grow up to be *real* tall, like a basketball player! I saw some girl basketball players on TV.

TOM: Yeah, maybe she'll get to be taller than the boy and he'll get jealous.

NICK: Maybe she'll just keep growing and never stop!

MS. B: (jotting these ideas on the board) Any other ideas? Okay, read the next three pages of the story and stop.

(The students go on reading. In this part, Mark and Amy save up to buy a secret code ring, but Amy leaves for camp before they have enough money. Amy is the tallest girl at camp. When she returns, she has grown an inch taller than Mark, and she fears for their friendship.)

MS. B: Were any of our earlier guesses right?

TOM: She's afraid Mark won't be her friend anymore because she's gotten so tall. It didn't say anything about playing basketball.

MS. B: Tom, what sentence told you how she felt about getting taller?

TOM: (after a lengthy search) Here it is. "I was afraid Mark wasn't going to be my best friend anymore, just because I was an inch taller than he was."

MS. B: Good. Do you think they might stop being friends?

MARY: She can't help it that she's so tall. He shouldn't stop being her friend because of that.

DAVY: Maybe he's afraid she'll beat him up!

MS. B: Tracy, what do you think? Do you think she might beat him up?

TRACY: I don't know. I guess not.

MS. B: Why do you think so?

TRACY: She doesn't look mad.

MARY: I think they'll work it out okay. In the picture on the next page it looks like she's going to have a party. Maybe the party is for Mark.

MS. B: (writes "party for Mark?" on the board) Okay, let's look at that picture. What might happen next?

DAVY: Maybe the boy won't go.

SUE: Maybe she won't even ask him!

MS. B: (jotting these ideas down) Okay, read the next two pages and see if any of our predictions turn out to be true.

(The silent reading continues. Amy plans a birthday party and Mark makes a weak excuse for not planning to come. Amy is really worried about their friendship now.)

MS. B: Tracy, what did happen in this part?

TRACY: He's not gonna go to the party. He says he's gonna play baseball.

MS. B: How might the story end up?

SARAH: Maybe she'll go to the baseball game instead of having the party. Then he'll see she really does like him.

MARY: He *knows* she likes him all right. Maybe she'll go play baseball too, and she'll beat him!

TOM: Naw, it's gotta turn out happy. And it's gotta have something to do with the code ring, remember? Maybe she'll get one for her birthday, and she'll give it to him, and they'll be friends again.

MS. B: How many think Mark will go to the party? How many think he won't? (She counts hands after each question.) Let's read the next two pages and see what happens. We're almost at the end of the story now. (The students read: On the day of the party Amy finds a mysterious package at the door, with a coded note on it.)

MARY: It's gotta be from Mark, because it's in code. He's going to come and be friends now.

DAVY: Maybe he's giving her a mitt or something.

ANDY: Maybe it's something to make her short again!

MS. B: Any other, final guesses as to how it will turn out? Okay, read the end of the story. (The story ends with Mark giving Amy the code ring and saying he'd rather go to her party than play ball. All ends well.)

MS. B: Did the ending surprise you?

ANDY: We forgot about the ring. We should have guessed that's what he'd give her.

TOM: I didn't forget it! I knew it all the time.

MS. B: Okay, let's see if we can answer these questions now that we've read the story.

In this example, Ms. Bennett used DRTA questioning with material from fiction. Before the reading, students hypothesized about the story's title and the first illustration. They could have been asked to look at other illustrations or to read the first sentence, paragraph, or page. They were asked to predict what might happen in the story and how it might end up, and at times they were asked to justify their predictions. The predictions were recorded on the board and all were accepted as possible unless they contradicted previous story facts.

Then the students read a portion of the story and were asked to stop reading just prior to some event or some important piece of information. Stopping before, rather than after, an event allowed the students to predict what might happen next. Prior predictions were reviewed, and those no longer probable could be erased with new hypotheses replacing them. At some points students were asked to prove their ideas by finding and reading a sentence aloud. The cycle of predict-read-prove continued throughout the story, and as the students got closer to the end, their predictions became somewhat more convergent and specific since they had now gained more information.

In our example, Ms. Bennett stopped four times within the story to let students predict, but fewer or more stops may be better for a particular story. To complete a DRTA in one sitting, it is better to limit the number of stops to less than five; otherwise it takes a long time to finish the story, and too many enforced stops can fragment the children's thinking and cause them to lose interest in the activity.

The passages between stopping points need not be of equal length. Students might read a single paragraph that contains a lot of new information, stop to predict, then read several pages at one time. The important factor is not the length of the passage but its *content*. You should stop just prior to some crucial event or outcome, whether the passage is short or long. As you move toward the ending, fewer alternative outcomes are possible, so the discussions will be shorter and more specific. If the DRTA is going well, student interest will be growing, so don't keep them out of the story too long.

A Directed Reading-Thinking Activity with Nonfiction. A DRTA with nonfiction material is conducted quite differently from one with fiction. To see the differences, let's observe a nonfiction DRTA.

In his sixth-grade social studies class, Mr. Taylor summons a group of twelve students to a discussion circle and tells them to bring their social studies textbooks.

MR. T: Today we're going to begin reading Chapter Four, which starts on page 116. We won't read the whole chapter today, but we'll read the first part, up to page 125. Open your books to page 116 and I'll give you three minutes to look at all the illustrations and maps on those pages and to read the section headings in dark print. Don't begin reading, just *look over* these pages and get a feel for what it's about.

(The students scan nine pages as the teacher watches.)

MR. T: Okay, now let's try to answer some questions, or make some guesses about what's in the chapter before we read it. First, what's the *topic* here?

JANE: It's about the old West.

BRIAN: It looks like it's about the olden days when there were covered wagons and settlers.

MR. T: Why do you think so?

JANE: Because there are old pictures of cowboys and maps of where the covered wagons went.

RUTH: Also the title was something like "The Westward Expansion."

MR. T: Okay, let's get specific. *When* did the opening of the West take place? Brian, you said "olden days." When were they?

BRIAN: You know, like a hundred years ago.

MR. T: Give me a year.

BRIAN: 1880.

JOY: No, earlier than that; 1800.

ANNE: After the Revolution, after 1776.

(Mr. T writes these dates on the board under "When?")

MR. T: When do you think the expansion was completed? How long did it take?

TIM: Less than 100 years. By about 1850 or so.

ALEX: No, it was still going on during the Civil War.

MR. T: When was that?

ALEX: I think 1860 or so.

BILL: I think it was pretty much settled by the 1900s; I think I read that someplace else.

MR. T: Okay, that gives us a rough time span, sometime between 1800 and 1900, but we're not sure. Now, where did "The West" start?

MIKE: In the movie *Centennial* they talked a lot about St. Louis. I think they left from there.

MR. T: Who did?

MIKE: The wagon trains.

MR. T: What other cities were settled first?

ANNE: Abilene? Isn't that where they had the cattle drives?

KEN: Yeah, they drove them from Texas through Abilene to Chicago, I think. They sold them in Chicago.

(Mr. T. lists "Abilene — cattle drives, Chicago — cattle markets, St. Louis — wagon trains.")

MR. T: What problems did the first settlers encounter?

BONNIE: Indians!

MR. T: What tribes, specifically?

KEN: The Sioux and the Apaches.

BONNIE: Yeah, they were the ones that attacked the wagon trains.

JANE: Also I think the Cherokee, and, uh, another one, Pawnee?

MR. T: Where did these tribes live?

CARTER: All over — Kansas, Wyoming, all the way to Canada.

MR. T: What other problems besides Indians?

ARLENE: Deserts — not enough water.

RUTH: Yeah, they had to cross Death Valley. They were always dying.

JOY: Also mountains; sometimes their carts went right off the cliffs.

TIM: And they got sick too, and had no doctors, and a lot of the women and children died off.

MR. T: (Mr. T. lists "Problems: Indians — Sioux, Apache, Cherokee, Pawnee; deserts; water shortages; mountains.") Now, how long might this journey take? How far do you think a wagon train could go in one day?

ARLENE: Just a few miles. In the movies they're always walking real slow.

KEN: Oh! Sometimes the horses died, too, and they needed mules or something to pull the wagons.

MR. T: Anything else?

CARTER: Poisoned water? There were some places you couldn't drink from, I don't know why.

MR. T: Okay, we've gotten a lot of information. We said the time was between 1800 and 1900. The settlers used wagon trains, leaving from St. Louis. They drove the cattle from Abilene to markets in Chicago. They suffered from illness and lack of water. They crossed mountains and deserts and fought with many Indian tribes, and they traveled very slowly. We tried to answer specifically *when, where, how, what problems, how long.* Now, read pages 116 to 125. Make a little check mark in the margin next to any information that might answer these questions. (As the students read, Mr. T moves among them answering questions and helping with unfamiliar words.)

In this example, Mr. Taylor asked his students to bring forth any information they had, from any source, regarding the topic they were reading about. He asked broad general questions about dates, places, and problems and pressed them for as much specificity as they could provide. He accepted all hypotheses noncommittally and organized them topically on the board for later reference. After the students had provided most of the information they had available, they read the selection with the goal of finding specific information.

Following the reading, original hypotheses were reviewed, and the answers the selection provided for the original questions were discussed. From this point, any desired comprehension exercise, like completing a study guide or writing an outline, could be used.

In this activity the prereading discussion helps the students recall and organize what they believe or already know about a topic. With prior information activated, acquiring new information is easier. Also, the hypothesizing helps awaken students' curiosity and sends them into the reading assignment with increased interest.

Developing Awareness of Story Structure

As you may recall from Chapter Two, recent study (Applebee, 1978, 1980; Stein, 1978; and others) reveals that all texts we call stories contain characteristic elements, called *story structures*, that occur in a particular sequence and serve to relate the story's characters and events in a logical order. These structures include:

1. *setting:* a direct or implied statement that places the story in a physical, historical, or temporal context and introduces the protagonist.
2. *initiating event:* an action, idea, or situation setting the story's plot in motion.
3. *internal response:* protagonist's response to the initiating event, including the setting of some goal and decision to pursue some course of action.
4. *attempt*:* an effort to achieve the goal
5. *outcome*:* a direct result of the action
6. *consequence:* a result of the attempts to reach the goal and their outcomes. This may be an action, a change of behavior, or a state of affairs.
7. *reaction:* protagonist's response to the consequence of the story's events, which may take the form of a change in opinion or belief, a statement of what has been learned, or a "moral."

Studies by Stein (1978) and others have shown that readers' understanding and recall of stories is influenced by their degree of experience reading or listening to stories and by the presence and order of story structures in what they read. Those who have heard or read a variety of stories in the past develop a set of expectations about how new stories will unfold. When what they read is logically organized and well structured, readers appear to compare what they expect to what they read, and mentally reorganize and remember depending on those comparisons. When they have few expectations, or when stories do not conform to their expectations, their understanding and memory of what they read declines.

These findings have important implications for teaching:

1. What students read should be well-written, clearly organized stories. Material made up of unrelated sentences ("Pam has a ham. Nick has a stick. Is the pig in a pan?") or "stories" that go nowhere, with little story line, should be avoided.
2. Students should have their attention drawn to the structures in the stories they read, and be made aware of similarities in story structure.

We cannot leave it to students' intuition alone to develop story sense. Guided discussion of stories read and listened to should include discussion

---

*Sets of attempts, outcomes, and consequences make up *episodes*. A story may have many episodes, or only one.

of how they are structured and what story parts give particular kinds of information. Teaching story structures need not mean learning the names for the structures, although older students can learn to use these terms if they help them. Story structures should not be taught as an end in themselves, for little is learned by remembering terms or definitions outside of their function in stories. Instead, discussion should focus on how different stories are structured and how these structures lend cohesion and predictability to text.

After reading a story and discussing it, using a DRTA or other discussion format, questions can be posed which guide students to reexamine the story and locate where particular structures occurred. The terms *setting, initiating event* and so on may be used if they are familiar to the group, or they may be paraphrased.

For example, here is an account of how a teacher combined a DRTA and a focused discussion of story structures with a fourth-grade basal story.

The story read concerned a young boy and his grandfather, who herded sheep in the arid Southwest. The boy knew little about coyotes, but expressed both fear and hatred of these desert animals, and ignored the grandfather's gentle insistence that the coyote should be respected for its place in nature and was not man's enemy. When one of his sheepdog's pups disappeared, the boy's hatred focused on searching out and killing a coyote he held responsible. Boy and man tracked the pup and found that it had wandered away and been adopted by a coyote. Observing the animal's nurturing and protecting of the pup, the boy realized that the coyote and pup loved each other. He was forced to revise his notion of coyotes and came to a new respect both for the animal and for his grandfather's quiet wisdom.

The teacher prepared in advance for the DRTA by creating these stopping points and general questions:

1. Inspect title and illustration: What might the story be about? Time, place, characters?
2. Read to the end of p. 25: What predictions were borne out? What might be the main problem or conflict in the story?
3. Read to end of p. 27: Who are the characters? What do they do? What might happen next? (If not mentioned, what might the *dog* do?) Turn page, inspect picture: What might happen next?
4. Read to bottom of p. 30: What did happen? What might happen next? (Use illustration if needed for verification.)
5. Read to bottom of p. 31: What might happen next?
6. Read to bottom of p. 34: What did happen? What might happen next? (Use picture if needed.)
7. Read to end of story: What did happen? What did Antonio learn from this experience? On p. 37 Antonio talks of someday understanding what the coyote says with its cries. What might the coyote be saying at the end of this story?

Following this discussion, the teacher asked questions designed to help students locate and attend to the specific structures of this story. Students located and selectively read aloud short portions of the story to support their answers. Previously the students had been introduced to the terms for various structures, so the teacher used the terms in her questions:

1. Where in the story is the element we call *setting?* What information does it include? (campfire, desert, sheep, characters' names and dress; may include response to coyotes howling)
2. What is the *initiating event,* the event that sets the story's action in motion? (pup disappears)
3. What is Antonio's *response* to this event? (determined to find pup and punish coyote)
4. What *attempts* does he make to achieve this goal? What are the *outcomes* of each attempt? (follows tracks, finds cave, steals pup back)
5. What is the *consequence* of these actions? (gets pup back, sees its attachment to coyote)
6. What is his *reaction* to this? (learns that coyote can be loving and nurturing, leaves fear and hatred behind, learns to respect coyote and his wise grandfather)

Discussion focusing on specific story parts and structures should be used routinely, although of course it should not be used every time a story is read. Also, it need not be used with a DRTA, but can be incorporated into any read-and-discuss format. Systematic practice of this kind will help readers use their sense of story to better comprehend all fiction.

Further strategies for improving comprehension of nonfiction text in content areas are discussed in Chapter Six.

Developing Skills in Locating Information, Summarizing, and Interpreting

Locating information, summarizing, and interpreting what has been read are all reading skills that go beyond recall. They are important because they are skills frequently used in everyday, out-of-school reading. They are practical, real-life reading skills.

Locational skills are practiced when students scan, or quickly read over material in order to find a specific piece of evidence for an argument, fact, or event, a phrase defining a vocabulary term, and the like.

Often students need practice in learning to scan. As you may have observed through the use of locational questions on an IRI, students often seem to equate "scan" with "read it again" or "start at the beginning and read every word." But scanning does not mean rereading, or reading carefully until a particular item is found. Scanning means looking over a passage without reading every word, but taking mental note of titles, headings, illustrations, text features like maps and charts, italics and boldface type, and summaries. It takes practice to learn to scan efficiently.

You can help students develop this skill by giving them a specific purpose or something they must look for, and by limiting their search time. We have already seen how scanning may be practiced before reading in conjunction with previewing, in order to develop some expectations about what is covered in a passage. This should be done not only when material is likely to be unfamiliar to students, but also on a regular basis as a skill in itself. It should also be practiced after a careful reading of the passage, not always before reading.

You may begin by giving students a specified amount of time for their search, a time period much shorter than it would take them to read the passage carefully. Begin with fairly short passages, perhaps only two or three pages (less with younger or less fluent readers) and a reasonably short search time. This allows students to get feedback on their efforts quickly. As they become better at scanning short passages, longer ones can be introduced. Likewise, begin with a concrete item to be searched for. Directions like:

> Find the place where
>   the word *hydroplane* is defined . . .
>   Becky's grandfather is first mentioned . . .
> or
>   the graph on page 226 is discussed . . .

are explicit and concrete. When students have developed facility in following directions like these, you can move toward scanning for more abstract purposes, such as:

> Find the place (or *a* place) where
>   you first suspected that Al was not what he seemed . . .
>   the author revealed his opinion of the candidate . . .
> or
>   the most important information about X was given.

After plenty of practice in scanning for information you select, students should be introduced to setting their own purposes for scanning. You might begin by group brainstorming everyday situations in which scanning is used. Both in-school and out-of-school reading tasks should be considered. If students are unable to come up with many examples of their own, you might suggest some of these to get them started:

- □ finding a name in a phone book
- □ finding a word in the dictionary
- □ completing questions on a study guide
- □ looking for a category of ads in the classified section of the newspaper
- □ checking ingredients needed for a recipe

□ looking for a particular item in a sale advertisement
□ looking for a quotation to use in a paper
□ finding a fact to back up an argument

Students might also keep track of how often they use scanning and location-al skills in a week's time. These activities can help reinforce the practical usefulness of this practice.

They can also practice setting their own purposes for scanning if you give them directions like:

Look over this material and tell us
   what one main topic is . . .
   one fact you didn't already know . . .
   something you found interesting . . .
or
   why someone else might want to read it.

Directions like these help students begin to apply the skill they are develop-ing to their own reading purposes and make it part of their everyday reading habits.

Summarizing and restating are also lifetime skills. They demand not only understanding of what was read, but also the ability to put that understand-ing into one's own words. By explaining what we know to others, we truly come to know it. For this reason, summarizing and restating should be a routine part of every day's activities.

Summarizing should be modeled and practiced *orally* many times before students are required to compose written summaries. Plenty of oral practice is needed before they will be able to combine in writing the processes of synthesizing information, discriminating between more important and less important information, and condensing longer passages into concise forms. Students can practice summarizing orally after discussions and demonstra-tions, after viewing a film or hearing a speaker, after reading, and the like. Book sharing, in which a student briefly discusses a book he or she has read in order to interest others in reading it, offers many opportunities for summarizing.

It is important to remember that *we must model for students what we want them to do.* Every day you will have opportunities to summarize for students: stories you have read aloud to them, news events, things to be accomplished in the days to come, material covered in a discussion or demonstration, steps to be followed in a procedure, decisions reached in a class meeting, even predictions offered in a DRTA. Take advantage of these opportunities to model summarizing and point out what you are doing: "I'll summarize for you what we've discussed so far," for example. Remember that students learn best when we *show* them, rather than just *tell* them, what to do.

After plenty of oral practice, students should begin writing summaries and restatements as well. In content areas, keeping a notebook is very helpful. (It is also a good way to develop the habit of keeping notes, papers, and materials together for a subject.) A notebook with dividers is fine. Frequent short assignments to compose a brief summary of a chapter or article read, a class discussion, an experiment or demonstration, results of ongoing observations of weather, plant growth, or the like, a speaker or field trip, a group meeting, or discussion, and steps in solving a problem or completing a sequence are all helpful. Students can date their entries and, if you wish, periodically submit their notebooks for a quick review and your comments. If you do review their notebooks periodically, it is best to limit your comments to the content of their summaries and to resist the temptation to correct mechanical errors (e.g., spelling, punctuation, and usage). If their notebooks are too heavily corrected, students will resist using them, and we want instead to help them develop the habit of keeping them. You will find plenty of opportunity to teach and correct writing mechanics in other activities. (You will read more about this issue in Chapter Seven.)

Interpreting what has been read involves several important higher-level comprehension operations. One is taking what has been learned and applying it to new situations or contexts. Another is translating what has been learned into a very different form. A wide variety of activities can be used to guide students in interpreting what they read. For example:

- select music to accompany a story that adds to and develops the mood of the text; prepare a dramatic oral reading accompanied by the music
- interpret story characters' feelings, actions, and the like through silent movement
- develop and tape record sound effects to accompany a dramatic reading of a selection
- use finger paints, water colors, paper tearing, or other nondrawing art media to create a poster, mural, or illustration for a selection
- compare and contrast two or more accounts of the same event (using newspaper or magazine articles, editorials, campaign speeches, interviews, biographies, letters to the editor, etc.) and locate how the writers used words to reveal their opinions or beliefs
- locate a point in a story where a character had to choose a position or course of action and rewrite the story with a different choice and outcome
- rewrite a story in the form of a character's diary or letters to someone else
- act out a story or event using mime, puppets, or a simple skit
- create a newspaper front page with reports of a real (or imaginary) event from current news or the past; include reporters' accounts, interviews with "eyewitnesses" and public figures, human interest stories, even a weather report
- select one or more quotations from a book, story, or article that represent a character's feelings, attitudes, or personality. Copy them and write a

short essay on how they reveal what kind of a person the character was. Include an illustration of the character or an important story event if desired.

You will probably be able to think of many more ways your students can show what they have learned or read about.

Developing Listening Comprehension

Listening comprehension is related to reading ability in that students who are not yet fluent mature readers can usually listen to and comprehend text that is read to them that they cannot yet read for themselves. The most common example of this is with emergent and beginning readers, who can listen to and understand a wide variety of materials but may not yet be able to read anything for themselves.

As students' reading abilities develop and their instructional levels go up, the gap between the instructional reading level and listening level may begin to close, and by the time one has become a fluent mature reader there may be no difference between what can be listened to and what can be successfully read. But for much of the time before a student has reached this zenith in reading development, there will be a gap between these two levels.

Experience is an important factor in listening comprehension. Even if all other things are equal, a student who has been read to and whose school and home environments are rich in oral language (regardless of dialect or language origins) has an advantage over the student who has not had this experience. In the same way, students who can read fairly effectively have a greater store of information, concepts, and vocabulary than illiterate students or very poor readers, and the first group's listening comprehension levels are likely to be higher.

A student's listening comprehension level is important because it shows us how closely his or her ability to understand written text approaches the demands of the student's grade level, and gives us an indication of how much potential for reading improvement the student has *at this point in time*. We must remember that unlike I.Q. or other intelligence measures, the listening level is not fixed; as the student's reading ability improves and he or she reads more, the listening level also rises. Thus progress today paves the way for more progress tomorrow.

The Interaction of Listening and Reading Comprehension

There are several typical patterns in listening comprehension and reading. One is that a student may have a below-grade level listening level and an instructional reading level that matches it. Take, for example, Sam, a fourth grader whose listening and instructional reading levels are both at second grade. This means that Sam is presently reading about as well as he is able to, and that he lacks the verbal concepts and vocabulary to understand third- or fourth-grade text either by reading or listening. To attempt to raise Sam's reading level without *also* developing his listening comprehension will likely result only in frustration, for he will be asked to do what is beyond his present capability. In Sam's case, listening comprehension must be fostered so that his reading ability can grow.

Another common pattern is exemplified by Elaine, also a fourth grader. Elaine's instructional reading level is also second grade, but her listening comprehension level is fourth grade, and even includes some fifth-grade text when the topic is something she knows about. Elaine is a poor reader in fourth grade, but she already has verbal concepts and vocabulary appropriate to other fourth graders and text typical of that grade. Elaine needs to develop her reading ability so that it more closely approaches her present listening level, which indicates that she has the present potential to improve her reading significantly.

Other patterns that occur less often are equally important. One is exemplified by Sarah, a fifth grader. Sarah's instructional level is only about third grade, but her listening level is at seventh. Sarah is a poor reader in fifth grade, but she has the verbal capacity to understand much more difficult text. In Sarah's case this capacity far outstrips present performance, and she can benefit from intensive remediation. Her problems may lie in motivation, inappropriate instruction, or other factors that must be overcome. But she has the measured potential for *at least* grade-level reading achievement.

Consider, in contrast, the case of James, a ninth grader in a remedial program. James is functionally nearly illiterate, with only a second-grade instructional level. His listening level is fourth grade. James may or may not be classifiable as a slow learner; he is certainly verbally impoverished, and his illiteracy has kept his listening comprehension from developing. Still, because there is a gap between the two levels, he can improve his reading somewhat. And if he does, his listening comprehension is likely to increase also, which in turn will make possible further reading progress, assuming that James is motivated toward such improvement. In his case, both reading remediation and listening comprehension development are needed.

Strategies for Developing Listening Comprehension

The key to developing students' listening comprehension lies in immersion in a rich language environment and stimulation of their language. First and foremost, such students must be read to, regardless of their age. Reading to James in ninth grade is every bit as important to his literacy as reading to a primary grader, for it is by listening that all readers develop their first concepts about stories, a sense of how written language differs from talk, and a store of information to bring to reading. Students whose listening comprehension levels are below grade level should be read to daily, from a wide variety of kinds of materials. Good literature appropriate for their age and written at a level they can understand should be a mainstay and should include nonfiction and poetry as well as fiction. Older students should also be read to from newspapers and magazines, since we want to encourage them to use these sources as well as books. Tapes can be used, but they are not as effective as a live reader because a tape cannot monitor listeners' interest, stop to answer a question, or reread a part for emphasis. Taped readings should never be used as a substitute for live reading, but are useful for additional practice.

A directed listening-thinking activity, or DLTA, is a good alternative to straight reading aloud. A DLTA is similar to the DRTA discussed previously in this chapter, wherein students make predictions about upcoming story events or, in the case of nonfiction, assert what they already know of a topic before reading and compare their predictions and assertions to what the text says. The only difference between a DRTA and a DLTA is that in the latter the material is read aloud *to* students. DLTAs are an effective means of monitoring listening comprehension and fostering interest in listening.

Immersion in a rich language environment also means that students should be actively engaged in oral discussions and conversations. They must be guided to do more than just answer questions, the most common form of classroom talk. They should also describe, summarize, persuade and argue, using as specific, vivid, and precise vocabulary as possible. Many of the typical composition activities suggested in reading and English books, such as making up stories, recounting real events and reminiscences, describing objects, persuading others to some action or belief, arguing for or against some course of action, and composing directions, are just as useful for oral language and listening development. Speaking and listening cannot be separated; they will develop together. Students with underdeveloped listening comprehension need daily experience with both.

Oral reading by students for other students can be useful, too, but must be used with care. All oral reading should be rehearsed and prepared by the reader beforehand. No one is served by listening to someone stumble through text. Material for oral reading should be read silently several times, then read aloud for practice before the final reading. Also, oral reading should be done for some purpose, not as an end in itself. Some material deserves to be read aloud and enjoyment of it is enhanced by being effectively read: poetry, vivid descriptions, and good dialogue are examples. The purpose of oral reading should be to share and enhance such material, not just to practice reading aloud.

And again we return to the point of teacher modeling. The teacher sets the tone and provides the model by which students judge what is useful and important. Without dominating activities, we must show students by our modeling what we want them to be able to do. We should prepare what we read aloud to the class so that our reading will be fluent and expressive. We should share portions of material we find appealing or especially effective with them and work to make our descriptions and summaries colorful and precise. We should exhibit interest in and curiosity about words and expressions, and share with students interesting and unusual language in what we read. We should respond to students' efforts to use language more effectively with sincere interest, attention, and positive reinforcement. We should listen more to *what* they say than to *how* they say it, and respond first to the message they have.

The more direct experience with language students have, the more their language use will expand. The more it grows, the more their listening comprehension will improve. The more listening comprehension develops, the more they will be able to bring to reading and thus their reading will improve. The roots of reading ability are buried deep in oral language, and we cannot overlook this foundation if we wish to help our students read better.

Summary

Corrective teaching is directed toward supporting a student's strengths while teaching and practicing skills and strategies the student needs. From the diagnostic data resulting from various assessments, strengths and needs are identified, and needs are prioritized. Instructional time is then planned to fulfill these priorities and to provide a balance of types of activities.

Sight vocabulary is developed when readers see the same words repeatedly in meaningful context. Dictated experience stories feature rereading of the material until fluency is achieved and individual words can be identified in and out of story context. Dictation can be successfully used with older students with some modifications in the basic procedure. Support reading measures help readers get through difficult text and reinforce word recognition. Support measures include echo reading, or repeating what another reader has read aloud, and choral reading, reading aloud in unison. Pattern books, featuring a predictable rhyme or repeating element, are useful because the same words and patterns appear repeatedly, and help build confidence and motivation. They can also serve as models for children's writing.

Reading fluency contributes to comprehension and is developed when students read material more than once. Repeated reading may be done by timing unrehearsed and rehearsed oral reading of a passage and keeping a chart of increasing fluency. Teacher modeling of fluent oral reading is very helpful. Readers theater, in which scripts are read aloud rather than memorized, is useful because it requires practice and rereading of the script.

Word analysis strategies are needed when students do not recognize a word at sight. Contextual analysis, or using surrounding context to identify a word, may be practiced in strategy lessons that focus on using contextual cues a student may be ignoring. Cloze and maze procedures, in which selected words in text are deleted and blanks or multiple-choice items are substituted, require readers to use context. A confirming strategy may be used in which parts of words or lines are covered, students predict what might come next, and the covered words are revealed to confirm or disprove the predictions. Phonic analysis, using letters and their sounds to decode words, can be developed by practice in auditory discrimination, study of "word families" and substituting sounds in similar words, and combining both sounding out and context clues. Phonics activities should be done orally before moving to paper-and-pencil decoding practice. Teaching phonics rules may be made less confusing and more useful by teaching generalizations, or regularities, and by helping children come up with their own generalizations about regular patterns. Word sorting activities, in which words are categorized by shared features, help students compare words, perceive patterns, form generalizations, and develop word analysis strategies they can apply to new words.

Recent research in comprehension has led to the development of teaching strategies focusing on the use of prior information, text structures, and prediction. We can help students recall and organize their prior information about a topic, and acquire new information prior to reading, by webbing and previewing. Prediction requires students to use prior information and parts of text already read to predict possible story events and outcomes or suggest what information they expect to be revealed. Directed reading-thinking activities engage students in a predict-read-prove cycle that fosters both comprehension and interest in reading.

Story structures are predictable structural elements that appear to be present in all fiction. Awareness of these structures helps readers develop expectations about story information and promotes recall and understanding of stories. Story structure awareness is fostered by hearing and reading well-structured stories and by postreading discussions in which story structures are identified and discussed.

Locational skills can be developed by systematic practice in scanning and locating specific information in text and selective oral rereading to justify choices. Summarizing should be modeled by the teacher and practiced by students first orally, then in writing in all content areas and subjects. Interpreting what is read is developed when students apply what they read to new situations or contexts and can be practiced through music, dramatic oral reading, movement, art, drama, and writing activities.

Listening comprehension is an important adjunct to reading comprehension. In developing readers, the listening level is usually higher than the instructional reading level and is an indicator of potential for reading improvement at the present time. When listening comprehension levels are much below grade level, efforts must be made to improve the students' listening comprehension so that further reading progress can be made.

Reading to students is one of the best ways to develop their listening comprehension, help them develop a sense of how text is structured, help them acquire new vocabulary and information, and foster their interest in reading. Directed listening-thinking activities, in which text is read aloud to students and they predict upcoming story events, are useful in developing listening comprehension. A school environment rich in language, in which students are actively engaged in discussing, describing, telling stories, summarizing, debating, and persuading is also necessary for students with listening comprehension problems. Purposeful oral reading by students and teacher modeling are also effective.

Extension Activities

1. After completing a diagnostic assessment of a student you choose, analyze your findings and develop a set of goals for the student in order of their importance. Then develop a weekly plan for that student's reading instruction time, focusing on developing your priority areas and working in other activities to achieve balance. Code your planned activities by type, as exemplified in Table 5.2. Implement as much of your plan as possible.

2. With a student whose sight vocabulary is small or a group of such readers, plan and try out a week or more of dictation activities including taking dictation, choral rereading, and word identification activities. Adapt as necessary for older readers (see Table 5.3). At the end of your plan, see if new words have become part of students' sight vocabularies.

3. With a group of students whose reading fluency is weak, try a readers theater unit. Select and prepare a story, practice oral interpretations, and plan other activities in spelling, word analysis, comprehension, and the like to accompany that story. Let your students perform with or without an audience, as they choose. Evaluate the effectiveness of readers theater as an aid to developing fluency.

4. Conduct an open-ended cloze activity with a group, focusing on developing alternatives rather than "right" answers.

5. Plan and conduct a group DRTA or DLTA with fiction or nonfiction material. Afterward evaluate the group's use of the prediction process and decide what else you might do to help them further develop this ability. Also evaluate the group's response to the DRTA process.

6. Choose a corrective teaching topic discussed in this chapter that is new to you or about which you feel less than confident. Choose a student or group and plan at least one activity to implement the suggested activities. Afterward evaluate your result and decide how to improve or extend your plan.

Suggested Readings

Applebee, Arthur N. **The Child's Concept of Story: Ages 2 to 17.** *Chicago: University of Chicago Press, 1978.* A fascinating account of how children develop this basic set of ideas of how stories work, liberally illustrated with children's examples.

Goodman, Yetta M., and Burke, Carolyn. **Reading Strategies: Focus on Comprehension.** *New York: Holt, Rinehart & Winston, 1980.* Detailed examples of miscue analysis and how strategy lessons are planned and conducted.

Holdaway, Don. **The Foundations of Literacy.** *Sydney, Australia and New York: Ashton Scholastic, 1979.* A gifted teacher's warm and practical account of day-to-day teaching of young readers.

Stauffer, Russell G. **The Language Experience Approach to the Teaching of Reading, rev. ed.** *New York: Harper & Row, 1980.* The classic description of the use of language experience in beginning reading.

References

Allen, Roach Van. *Language Experiences in Communication.* Boston: Houghton Mifflin, 1976.

Allington, Richard L. "Fluency: The Neglected Reading Goal." *The Reading Teacher* 36, No. 6 (February 1983):556–561.

Anglin, Jeremy M. *Word, Object, and Conceptual Development.* New York: W. W. Norton, 1977.

Applebee, Arthur N. *The Child's Concept of Story: Ages 2 to 17.* Chicago: University of Chicago Press, 1978.

Applebee, Arthur N. "Children's Narratives: New Directions." *The Reading Teacher* 34, No. 2 (November 1980):137–142.

Ehri, Linnea C., Barron, Roderick W., and Feldman, Jeffrey M. *The Recognition of Words.* Newark, Del.: International Reading Association, 1978.

Gillet, Jean Wallace. "Sorting: A Word Study Alternative." *The Journal of Language Experience* 2, No. 2 (1980):17–20.

Gillet, Jean and Kita, M. Jane. "Words, Kids and Categories." *The Reading Teacher* 32, No. 5 (February 1979):538–542.

Goodman, Yetta M., and Burke, Carolyn. *Reading Strategies: Focus on Comprehension.* New York: Holt, Rinehart & Winston, 1980.

Hall, MaryAnne. *Teaching Reading as a Language Experience,* 3rd ed. Columbus, Ohio: Charles C. Merrill, 1981.

Heilman, Arthur W. *Phonics in Proper Perspective,* 4th ed. Columbus, Ohio: Charles C. Merrill, 1981.

Holdaway, Don. *The Foundations of Literacy.* Sydney, Australia and New York: Ashton Scholastic, 1979.

Martin, Bill, Jr., and Brogan, Peggy. *Bill Martin's Instant Readers,* Level 3 Teacher's Guide. New York: Holt, Rinehart & Winston, 1972.

Morris, R. Darrell. "Word Sort: A Categorization Strategy for Improving Word Recognition Ability." *Reading Psychology* 3, No. 1 (September 1982):247–259.

Samuels, S. Jay. "The Method of Repeated Reading." *The Reading Teacher* 32, No. 4 (January 1979):403–408.

Smith, Deborah D. "The Improvement of Children's Oral Reading through the Use of Teacher Modeling." *Journal of Learning Disabilities* 12, No. 3 (March 1979):39–42.

Stauffer, Russell G. *The Language-Experience Approach to the Teaching of Reading,* rev. ed. New York: Harper & Row, 1980.

Stauffer, Russell G. *Directing the Reading-Thinking Process.* New York: Harper & Row, 1975.

Stein, Nancy. *How Children Understand Stories.* Urbana, Ill.: University of Illinois Center for the Study of Reading, Technical Report No. 69, March 1978 (ERIC: ED, 153–205).

White, E. B. *Charlotte's Web.* New York: Harper & Row, 1952.

Chapter Six

The Reading Problems of Older Students

You have a child who makes nearly average progress in acquiring reading skills in the first and second grades. In the third grade she still does nearly average work in her reading group, but is beginning to have difficulty with her science and social studies assignments. By the time she reaches the upper elementary grades, her work in these subjects is suffering, resulting in poor grades, and her difficulties are attributed to a reading problem that manifests itself only in content subjects, not in language arts.

This pattern is common. Children who progress adequately in beginning reading instruction often have difficulty in the upper grades applying their reading abilities in their content subjects. Why? Chall (1979) finds an answer in the differences between the tasks of beginning reading and later reading. In early elementary years, the focus is on *learning to read.* In later years, it is on *reading to learn.*

Schematically, we can depict some of the most basic differences between beginning and later reading as in Table 6.1.

Older students must make a transition from beginning reading to reading as a medium for learning. The strategy of rendering print out loud or practicing sentence-by-sentence comprehension may be fine at the beginning, but it will be inadequate later on. Reading to learn requires the student to (a) do active thinking about the content of the material; (b) be familiar with and responsive to different structures of text; (c) learn new words encountered in books, not only decoding them but also determining their precise meaning in context; and (d) develop certain study skills for locating information and remembering it.

In this chapter we explore each of these requirements and present techniques for their development and instruction.

TABLE 6.1. Some differences between beginning reading and later reading.

	BEGINNING READING (PRIMARY GRADES)	LATER READING (MIDDLE ELEMENTARY GRADES AND UP)
FOCUS	Learning to read	Reading to learn
MATERIAL	Mostly fiction Short passages, changing topics	Mostly nonfiction Long sections, continuous topics
PURPOSES	Short term, explicitly set by teacher ("Read this sentence [perhaps aloud] and tell me what it says")	Long term, generally set by teacher or by student ("Study pages 140–158 for a quiz on Friday")
TEACHER RESPONSE	Immediate and directly related to the act of reading ("You missed three words, Jerome.")	Delayed and indirectly related to reading ("You didn't know the material, Linda.")
EVALUATION	Oral reading, comprehension of short, explicit questions	Silent reading, learning of longer material, the ability to use information

Strategies for Comprehensive Reading Development

In our experience, the children who require help with their reading from the regular classroom teacher are like those we just described, whose indifferent reading skills do not hold up well when reading tasks grow to include learning from text. But there are other children whose problems are even more severe. These are the children who were not ready to learn basic reading in the first two grades along with their class. By fourth grade, these children still have not learned to read meaningfully. Yet the curriculum no longer includes basic reading instruction, and their teachers are hard pressed to give these children the basic help in reading that they need.

Older poor readers often find themselves overwhelmed in their classes as the reading demands and difficulty of materials far outstrip their reading abilities. Often, content area teachers working with these students find themselves spending nearly all their time trying to support students' efforts in the materials they are supposed to read for their classes. But for many poor readers, support measures are not enough. To develop their potential as readers, and to reach the point where support measures are not needed so much, these students need sustained instruction in basic reading, and much practice actually reading real text.

But many poor readers have such low instructional levels, small sight vocabularies and undeveloped comprehension strategies, and so little confidence in their reading ability, that there are few suitable materials available for them to work in. Low-level basal readers, for example, may be comprehensible but are uninteresting and even demeaning for older poor readers. These students may find that about the only text they can comfortably read, understand, and profit from is that which they develop themselves through dictation. The following two sections detail how to use the dictation process and repeated reading to help older poor readers develop word recognition, comprehension, and fluency skills in basic reading.

The Language Experience Approach

The language experience approach is highly recommended for those students whose reading development is severely delayed. The method of dictation can be adapted to help poor readers gain experience reading in their content area subjects following a pattern like this:

1. *A stimulus experience and discussion.* Begin with an activity that generates the students' real interest. Encourage them to talk about the activity, using questions and probes that spur them to use extended sentences and vocabulary related to the topic from which the activity came (some words unknown to the students are introduced into the discussion by the teacher). The discussion serves to allow the students to rehearse their ideas in a freer

spoken form before the dictation, in which they have to choose their words more carefully.

As a stimulus activity for older delayed readers, try:

a. Beginning with an interesting presentation related to some subject under study. Take a field trip or hear a guest speaker or view a film — or have students listen as you read interesting passages from the textbook. Next, discuss the material in detail. Make sure students understand that they are trying to interpret the experience — to recreate it in a way that makes sense to them. Finally, they will dictate sentences to you to create their own written version of the material. This version can be written on a chart to read together, but older students should also have a notebook for their dictations. These dictations can be used for reading exercises. Also, if this exercise can be done weekly with the material from one or more academic subject, the students who are poor readers can gradually collect their own version of the subject area textbook — one that they can read more easily, and expect to discuss and even to be tested on.

Leave room for the students to draw pictures, charts, and maps, or to paste in visuals from other sources to give their books visual interest and to remind them what the surrounding text is about after the dictation has been forgotten.

b. A subject of the student's own choosing. The dictation may be treated essentially as if it were an exercise in a writing workshop. The student may prepare by making a list of topics he or she would like to dictate about and choosing one prior to the dictation session; or a group of students may agree on a common topic they would wish to develop in a written work — be it a story or film script, or a nonfiction work — about sports or nuclear weapons or vocations.

In any case, the students should be told to prepare as carefully for the dictation as they would for a panel discussion or a radio interview. The dictation is important. It should generate valuable material. Students must be ready for it with something to say.

2. *The dictation.* The traditional method involves teaching groups of four to seven students at a time. Each is asked to volunteer a statement, which is written by the teacher on a piece of newsprint, in letters large enough for all to read. With beginning readers, this offers valuable opportunities for the teacher to point out many metalinguistic elements of the text: the units that are referred to by the terms *letter* and *word*, the *beginning* of the text and the *end* of it; the directionality of the writing; and the speech-to-print match. Older delayed readers may have these concepts. If so, the dictation should be transcribed onto notebook-sized pieces of paper. If large sheets of newsprint are used, you will need to transcribe the text onto smaller paper for individual reading after using the large version in a group reading exercise.

There are other ways to approach the dictation. You can record it on audio tape, and edit it later into a coherent piece — leaving out the um's and uh's. Better yet, if you have access to a computer with word processing equipment, you can write down the dictation as it is given. You and the students can read the transcript back on the screen and decide on corrections and clarifications before printing it out.

When you type up or print the work out, remember to

☐ write the students' names beside the passages they contributed (this gives students reference points to help them reading: it steers them to the parts they know best, an advantage in reading the work back).
☐ leave spaces in the individual versions of the text for the students to draw in illustrations or diagrams, or to cut out and paste in magazine pictures to illustrate the text.

3. *Reading back the dictation.* In traditional language experience teaching, the period immediately following the dictation is a time of intense reading practice, highly supported by the student's understanding of and interest in the topic of the dictation. This knowledge and interest enables them to forge associations between spoken words and written ones, which, when the students have the appropriate prereading competencies in place (see Chapter Two) results in their acquiring new sight words. Also, when the teacher models fluent reading of the text and has them practice reading it fluently, they have an experience with reading like having an adult running alongside holding up the bicycle when learning how to ride.

The activity normally proceeds like this: You read the whole page through once or twice pointing at each word as each student reads. Then read the work *chorally.* Next, the students *echo-read* the piece. That is, you read a line, then they read the same line (see Support Reading in Chapter Five). This is followed by individual students being invited to read a line back — easiest if each student reads back the line he or she dictated. Now point to an individual word, and ask a volunteer to read it. Even if the student does not know the word, it is possible to figure it out by using the "voice-pointing procedure," that is, jumping along word by word from an anchor word the student does know (see Chapter Two). As a more difficult word recognition exercise, you can bracket a word (using tagboard cards or your hands) and ask a volunteer to read it without benefit of context.

Following the group reading of the text, make a copy for every student in the group. Work with each student individually. The first step is to see how much of the text the student can read back unaided. If the student is able to read most of it without help ask the student to read individual words and draw a circle around those that the student can recognize quickly and confidently. If the student cannot read the text independently, then back up to the steps of choral reading, echo reading, and asking the student to read a line at a time, before going on to the word recognition step.

Those words that were recognized by the student and circled are now copied onto word cards to form a *word bank* (3-by-5-inch index cards cut twice across the short side will yield three nice-sized word cards apiece). Word banks are made for each student and should be reviewed with him or her every week or so to ensure that they are still current; those that the student cannot recognize are taken out of the bank. Besides forming a tangible record of the student's growing reading vocabulary, word banks are worthy for use in activities to help students develop their ability to recognize words (see Word Recognition, below).

The Method of Repeated Reading

An obvious way to get better at any skill is to practice it over and over again. There is a method of reading based on this idea of "practice makes perfect": the method of *repeated reading* (Samuels, 1979; Cunningham, 1979). Samuels and Cunningham report that having students practice reading short, interesting passages over and over until they can read them flawlessly improves skill in fluent reading and does marvelous things for the motivation of poor readers.

The method works as follows:

First, a student chooses or is assigned a story or a passage of no more than 100 words on a topic of real interest. The passage should be written on the student's *instructional level*. A simple way to determine if the passage is on the instructional level is suggested by Cunningham (1979). Have the student read the passage silently first, then read it aloud to you. If the student makes more than five errors per 100 words, the passage is too difficult and should be replaced by an easier one. The teacher times the student's reading of this passage, and tells the student his or her reading rate. Then the teacher tells the student to practice reading the material silently until he or she reaches a criterion rate of 85 words per minute. This may require several rereadings. However, Samuels' research has demonstrated that as students gain experience using this method, the number of practice readings required to reach the criterion of 85 words per minute diminishes greatly.

Variations on this procedure include giving shorter passages (down to 50 words) or longer ones (200 or more words); or having the students listen to a tape-recorded version (with earphones) in their first several practice readings.

Strategies for Teaching Word Recognition

Two techniques for helping older students recognize words are recommended. The first is to teach a systematic strategy that they should use when they encounter an unfamiliar word. The second is a more involved program of word study using word-bank words.

A Strategy for Word Recognition

"What would make sense there?" is the first question you should ask students when they get stumped on a word in a passage they are reading. It is first question we should ask them, and — when they are reading alone — it is the first question they should ask themselves. Normally if a student can't read a word after this much prompting, tell what the word is — you don't want the student to get so bogged down with word recognition that the thread of the meaning is lost. Sometimes, however, you may want to make more of an exercise of word recognition in context, asking questions about the word in the order shown below — stopping the procedure at any point the child becomes confused and simply telling her or him the word; otherwise going through all of the steps until the student is successful. Note these questions:

1. "What would make sense here?"
2. "Look at the beginning of the word. Can you think of any word that begins this way that would make sense here?"
3. "Put your finger on the word. Now go back to the beginning of the sentence and begin reading again. Can you decide now what would make sense here?"
4. Tell the student the word.

Of course if the student is missing more than one word out of twenty running words, the text is too difficult and should be replaced with something on his or her instructional level (for group work) or independent level (for independent work).

A Modified Cloze Procedure

A structured activity to exercise children's word recognition skill in context uses a modification of the cloze procedure (see Chapter Five). Choose a passage of about 250 words written on the student's independent reading level. Leave the first and last sentences intact, and beginning with the second sentence, use a marking pen to black out all but the beginning consonant or consonant cluster of every fifth word. If the fifth word begins with a vowel, skip it and choose the next word beginning with a consonant or consonant cluster.

Cunningham (1979) recommends that the passage be given to the student to read silently first, along with some follow-up comprehension questions. The student should be encouraged to guess at the blacked-out words and read on. Later, several students can take turns reading the passage orally and comparing answers.

Word Study with Word-Bank Cards

Word-bank cards (see Chapter Five) can be sorted into categories according to their spelling patterns, common stems they contain, or some semantic category to which they can be assigned.

Word sort activities work best when the teacher searches through one or two students' word banks and finds four or five words each that contain the same spelling pattern or common stem (*-ight; -ate; -ab*, etc.; *telegraph, telephone, telephoto, telescope*, etc.). Begin by spreading the cards out in front of the students, then choose one of the words to serve as the keyword for the category. Have the students make a column of like words underneath the keyword. If the draw cards contain members that could be sorted into another category, ask the students if they can find another way to sort them together (it helps if there are a few extra words thrown in that won't obviously fit into either of the other two categories, since that's the way things work in real life).

Following this activity, direct students to write the words that were sorted together into a notebook, one category per page, with the category written at the top of the page in bold letters (e.g., *-AB WORDS*). After they have taken part in several teacher-led word sort activities, they can sort through their own word banks to find categories of words. Older categories might well be subdivided again as they learn to make finer and finer discriminations between spelling patterns. These categories can be written into their notebooks.

Word games to be played by two or three or four students can easily be constructed around word-bank cards. Just about any game structure that operates on the principle of categorization will do; however, the following games seem to be especially interesting to the fourth- to eighth-grade set, and to a few older students.

Open Sorts. Get forty or fifty cards that every student in the group can read. Divide them equally among the members of the group. As soon as the cards are dealt, every player sorts her or his cards into as many logical categories as there seem to be (spelling pattern, common roots, parts of the body, feeling words, etc.); a little discussion of what makes the game interesting will discourage students from using categories such as "words" or "words with letters in them." To play, the players put down all of the cards they can arrange into groups, without voicing aloud the basis on which they grouped them. Then one at a time, beginning with the player to the left of the dealer, the players put down cards on the other players' piles, having guessed the principle of the grouping. If they guess incorrectly, they have to take their card back, plus discard from that player's hand. The first student with no card left is "the winner," although the emphasis should be on interesting sorts and discoveries about words, not on winning.

Concentration. Choose thirty to forty word cards that all the students can read. The words should contain several with the same spelling pattern. Another version has pairs of stems and affixes that can be joined together variously to make words (*tele-, micro-, bio-, sphere, graph, scope,* etc.) Number the cards on the back, one through the highest number, and arrange them on the table, number side up. One by one, the players turn up pairs of cards. If a pair goes together (the members fit the same spelling pattern, or the two parts form a word), that player gets to keep the pair.

Other Games. Word sorts can be adapted to the format of Go Fish or even poker. Or devise a board game comprised of a racetrack marked off into card-sized spaces. At the roll of the dice, players proceed around the track. At first, the players put down groups of cards sorted into categories when they reach a square. Then, as one player's marker lands on a square that another player has already staked out with a sort, that player must put down another card that fits the category, or forfeit a turn. The game continues until all have put down all their cards.

Periodically, students should be asked to record in their notebooks the groups of words they have generated in the course of playing one of these games.

Vocabulary

Vocabulary is an important and troublesome issue in content area reading. By the time they reach third grade, students must be able to read and understand many words they usually do not use in speech (Chall, 1979). When they are successful at gleaning new words, we rightly conclude that reading has made a major contribution to their education. For those who do not succeed, however, vocabulary constitutes a widespread problem in the middle and upper grades, especially in the content subjects.

We will deal with two main aspects of vocabulary: (a) background concepts to which vocabulary words can be related and (b) strategies to derive approximate word meanings from surrounding context.

Vocabulary and Background Concepts

Words are labels for concepts. Concepts are stored mental patterns that are derived from experiences. If, for example, we have enough experience with wildflowers, we may begin to recognize different varieties of them. With the help of a guidebook or other information source, we can learn words to associate with the various wildflowers we have come to recognize.

Relating New Words to Personal Experiences. Words are names for concepts. Concepts are categories of experience. New words are learned when experiences are organized into concepts for the new words to name. When students lack concepts, we must help them organize their experience before teaching the words.

To do this is to ask students to share in a discussion of what they already know about a new vocabulary term, any personal experiences they may have had that relate to the term. Possible confusion about new words' meanings can be straightened out. Moreover, a discussion of this type yields diagnostic insights, because you can find out if the students are able to associate words and ideas with the terms under study. (See The Structured Overview at the end of this chapter.)

If discussion does not uncover many associations, set up an activity to help build associations. In science or social studies this may involve field trips, experiments, demonstrations, or guest speakers. Or it may involve role plays: the students can act out *avaricious, hostile, laconic,* and other such words. Role play will often do as a substitute for real experience, and it has much potential for teaching vocabulary.

Treating Meanings Categorically. Semanticists, specialists in the study of meaning, suggest that it is useful to think of the meaning of one word in relation to the meanings of others. To semanticists, meanings come not by themselves but in family or hierarchical relationships. A duck can be thought of not just as a white or yellow creature with a beak and feathers but as a kind of bird. Moreover, it is useful to know that there are varieties of ducks: mallards, teals, wood ducks, mergansers. Ducks are seen in stages too. A little fuzzy yellow-beaked thing grows up to be a brown-and-green adult duck; ducklings and ducks are varied stages of the same bird.

One semanticist, Albert Upton (1973), has suggested a set of three questions that people should ask when they are striving for exactness in meaning:

1. What is it a kind of/what are the kinds of it?
2. What is it a part of/what are the parts of it?
3. What is it a stage of/what are the stages of it?

To these we have added a fourth:

4. What is it a product or a result of/what are the products or results of it?

These four questions can be adapted to yield much information about any meaning or word under consideration. Depending on whether the item under scrutiny is a *class of things* (i.e., ducks in general) or a *particular thing* (that mallard over there with the twisted beak), one side of the questions or the other will be useful but not always both.

Hence for *duck* in general we can say:

1. It is a kind of bird; the kinds of ducks are mallards, wood ducks, etc.
2. (The first part of the question is not relevant.) Its parts are the wings, legs, body, neck, head, feathers, beak, gizzard, etc.
3. (The first part is not relevant.) Its stages are the egg, the chick, the young duck, and the mature duck.
4. (The first part is not relevant.) Ducks lay eggs that are good to eat, their feathers make soft pillows, the mature birds are thought by some to be tasty eating, good hunting, etc.

Concept Ladders. An exercise called the *concept ladder*, which was developed around these four questions, is good for both instruction and assessment. Since it is a paper-and-pencil exercise, a concept ladder used instructionally may be given out for students to complete individually as they do a reading assignment or it may be given to a small group of students to be completed together.

In creating a concept ladder, set up columns to correspond to Upton's questions and leave blanks above or below the target word, depending on the information that is needed to understand the term. The students fill in the blanks. Concept ladders are somewhat open-ended, since there may be several correct answers for each blank, but you can limit the choices at first by restricting the answers to a set list from which the students must choose. (See Tables 6.2 and 6.3.)

It may have occurred to you that the concept ladder pins down the meanings of some words better than others. Many words seem to have a

TABLE 6.2. Concept ladder for *guitar*.

A. Kind of?	B. Part of?	C. Function of? (How is it made?)
musical instrument	*a band?*	*out of wood, I guess*
GUITAR	GUITAR	GUITAR
electric, classical, folk	*neck, strings*	*makes good music*
Kinds of it? (name 3)	Parts of it? (name 4)	Functions of it? (what does it do?)

TABLE 6.3. Concept ladder for *amphibians*.

What kinds of amphibians are there?	What is an amphibian a stage of?	What is an amphibian a product of?
AMPHIBIAN	AMPHIBIAN	AMPHIBIAN
What are the kinds of an amphibian?	What are the stages of an amphibian?	What are the products or results of an amphibian?

POSSIBLE ANSWERS:

frog legs (some folks eat them)   young amphibians on land
frogs   waste products
eggs in water   mature amphibians on land
salamanders   help control mosquito population
neophytes in water   more amphibians
turtles

literal meaning that can be fixed in relation to other words as the concept ladder allows us to do; other words, however, seem to have strong meanings that are not so easy to categorize. For example, we may say of an acquaintance

Sam is a *doctor*.

We can say that a doctor is a professional and that there are many subspecialties of doctor; that being a doctor is the result of long training, and that a doctor produces health care, and so on. However, we can also say

Sam is a *jerk*.

Now there is strong meaning, but it is not so specific. The thrust of this word is more emotional than scientific. Now we are hearing not so much what Sam is like literally, but how we feel about him. We can invite students to deal with this dimension by appending another question to the concept ladder:

What kinds of feelings does this word give you?

Analogies. Analogies, another form of exercise in categorizing word meanings, are suitable for students in late middle grades or beyond. Analogies compare relationships between sets of things or ideas and thus go a bit deeper than synonyms in tapping vocabulary development. You set up analogies by (1) thinking of how the concept represented by your test word relates to another concept and (2) thinking of a familiar pair of concepts that share the same sort of relationship. For example:

Nests are to birds as _____ are to beavers.
(a) dams, (b) lodges, (c) hives, (d) trees.

It is advisable to provide multiple choices, since choosing from alternatives is easier than guessing from scratch. If all the analogies in a single exercise draw from a single pool of possible responses, the students have an opportunity to check themselves. Here is an example:

Fill in the blanks with the appropriate word:

1. Fresh water is to salt water as the desert is to _____ .
2. Water is to a fish as land is to _____ .
3. Gills are to tadpoles as _____ are to frogs.
4. Ammonia is to fish as _____ is to land animals.
5. Urea is to a grown bird as uric acid is to _____ .
6. Jelly-like coating is to frogs' eggs as _____ is to chickens' eggs.
                         (Asimov and Gallant, 1975, pp. 306–308)

Vocabulary and Surrounding Context

When authors use unfamiliar vocabulary, it is not always possible for the reader to determine the meaning directly from context. Hittleman (1978) suggests that the best strategy in such cases is to formulate a hypothesis as to what the word might mean and then test that hypothesis against the other occurrences of the word in the text. To do so, readers must be aware of structural devices authors use to signal meaning. According to Deighton (1959) and Hittleman (1978), writers generally use five types of signals:

1. *Definition.* They may use sentence forms like "X is (or "is called") Y." These sentences communicate an explicit definition of the word.
   An iconoclast is a person who deliberately breaks other people's traditions.
   A person who deliberately breaks traditions is called an iconoclast.
2. *Example.* When examples are given of an idea named by an unknown word, we may be able to figure out the word if we recognize the example. Sentences so constructed often use words or phrases like *for example, such as, like,* and *especially.*
   Venomous snakes, such as the rattlesnake, the copperhead, or the coral snake, are to be avoided.
3. *Modifiers.* Even when a word is not known, the modifiers used to describe it may give an indication of what it is. Modifiers may be relative clauses as well as adjectives or adverbs.

The minaret that the Moslems built stood tall, slender, and graceful above the other buildings in the town.

4. *Restatement.* Sentences sometimes state the unknown idea a second time using other, more familiar words. One such device is an appositive, a group of words following the word defined and set off by commas or dashes. Restatement is also done by using key words or phrases like *or, that is,* and *in other words.*

   Chauvinism, an aggressive loyalty to one's own group at the expense of others, originally applied to national patriotism only.

   They fired the attendant because of her indolence; in other words, she was lazy.

5. *Inference.* Several grammatical patterns writers employ signal the meaning of unknown words are:

   a. *Parallel sentence structure.* When series are used either in the same sentence or in groups of sentences, we can often get an idea of the nature of an unknown word by recognizing a known word in the series.

      Each office contained some type of medical specialist. In one was a family practitioner; in another, an obstetrician; in another, a radiologist; and in another, a hematologist.

   b. *Repetition of key words.* Sometimes, if an unknown word is of sufficient importance in a passage, the author will repeat it enough times in enough different contexts for its meaning to be figured out.

      It is sometimes said that only primitive people have taboos. That is not necessarily so. Even advanced cultures like ours have them. In America, for example, it is taboo to speak directly about death, or about a grown person's age or weight.

   c. *Familiar connectives.* Some familiar connectives, especially subordinating or coordinating conjunctions, show us the relationship between ideas and thus allow us to associate an unknown idea with a known one.

      John was very excited about the award, but Judith seemed indifferent.

The devices for identifying meanings in context can be taught. If they are clearly introduced, well practiced, and returned to often, they can become a valuable addition to a reader's strategies for dealing with difficult material. Assessing vocabulary in context should include exercises that deliberately test familiarity with and sensitivity to these contextual clues to word meaning.

Schema Theory and Text Structure

In Chapter Two we shared a currently popular explanation of the process by which people understand what they read. The explanation we shared is called *schema theory.* Given a passage about a birthday party, we found that most of its meaning was supplied by the reader, not the writer. Schema theory holds that the author communicates meaning by mentioning items that form part of our *schemata*, or frameworks of remembered information. For our part, we summon up schemata that fit the supplied details and help us to flesh out and make sense of the text. Our schemata have stored in them an array of details that an author may not make explicit, but which help us to understand a text. We could not understand text otherwise.

According to some theorists, all comprehension employs the summoning up of schemata, from the recognition of letters and spelling patterns to the interpretation of nuances and literary allusions. For our purposes in this chapter, it is important that we recognize two general kinds of schemata. The first is the kind that organizes our knowledge and experiences of the world in our memories and that helps us construct the meaning of what we read. We sometimes call this *world knowledge*. The second consists of schemata for kinds of *text structure*. These cause us to respond one way to the information in a story, another way to the information in a political campaign speech. Both types play an important role in reading for meaning.

We have seen already how schemata for world knowledge are used. Under what circumstances are schemata involved in failures of reading comprehension?

First, authors sometimes cause problems. If they are too stingy with details, we will not know which schemata to summon. In the sample passage on page 64, for example, the author might have said, "Johnny was nearly in tears. His classmate was having a party, and he had forgotten to tell his mother." In this case, it would have been less clear what prior knowledge about parties would help us interpret Johnny's distress.

Second, we may lack some necessary schemata in our memories. If we had never attended an American birthday party or experienced one through the media, we would not understand what was wrong with Johnny. Likewise students may not understand what they read if they lack compatible experiences to which they can relate the information in the text. In schema theory, these experiences are the material out of which the author's meaning is made clear. When students lack important background experiences, the teacher must make sure this background is provided, through such means as films, field trips, demonstrations, and class discussions, or else they will not be able to learn from reading and studying a topic.

A third problem may arise. The author may have written clearly, and we may have the appropriate schemata in memory, but we fail to summon up the schemata. Problems of this kind show up in various ways, from a failure to realize that we have misread a word to the discovery that we cannot remember the last six pages we read (see the discussion of "metacognition" in Chapter Two). As important as having the appropriate schemata for reading a text is our using them actively.

Understanding Patterns of Text Organization

The way that information is organized in text makes a difference in the way we understand and use the information. Good readers recognize and correctly respond to different arrangements of text while poor ones often do not (Marshall and Glock, 1978–1979). Consider how some typical patterns of text structure affect the reader's response to the text.

Taxonomy. What pattern of organization do you perceive in this passage?

THE GUITAR

The guitar is one of the most popular stringed instruments. Because it has a fretboard, and strings stretched across a soundbox that are played by plucking, the guitar is considered a member of the lute family.

For centuries the guitar had a rather small wooden body with soft strings fashioned of animal gut. In the present century, however, several distinct classes of guitars have emerged. The traditional version has lived on as the "classical" guitar, but there are now steel-string guitars and electric guitars as well.

The steel-string guitar has a long, narrow neck and an enlarged body. It makes a louder, more piercing sound than the classical guitar. The electric guitar, an offshoot of the steel-string guitar, has its sounds amplified and its tones modified by electronic devices. It can make sounds loud enough to deafen a rock musician. It can also make a variety of tones, many of which do not sound guitarlike at all.

This piece of text is organized by classifying, by listing and defining the different instruments collected together under the label "guitar," and by showing their relationships to one another. Classifying is a fundamental act of the intellect, and text such as the above is usually the result. This passage could also be outlined by means of a tree diagram, as in Figure 6.1. Classification charts like this are called *taxonomies.*

If readers are to understand this passage, they must perceive the taxonomic structure. If you asked them to recall what the passage said, you would expect them to remember the kinds of guitars discussed, what makes them different from one another, and how they are related within the "family." Taxonomic text structures are frequently encountered in science materials, especially in biology.

Chronology. What pattern of organization do you perceive in this passage?

FIGURE 6.1. A taxonomic outline.

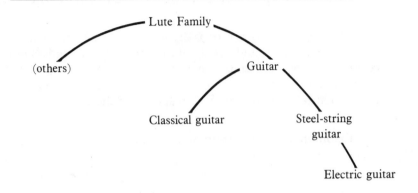

BURTON

The town of Burton, in the Midlands of England, has a history that is typical of trading villages of the region. Nothing of the town existed before the ninth century A.D. The hill overlooking the Avon River where the town now sits was covered with an impenetrable wood.

In about 870 A.D., Northumbrian knights cleared the hillside and erected a rude fortress as an outpost against the South Saxons lurking across the Avon, which then served as the southern frontier of Northumbria. By the time peace was effected some thirty years later, a stone castle had been built, surrounded by about thirty dwellings. Some crops had been grown nearby.

With the peace and political stability of the tenth century, Burton grew in earnest. Pastures were cleared for five miles during the first half of the century, and fine manor houses erected from the wood and the profits of sheep raising. Trails that crisscrossed the settlement grew to well-traveled roads, and by the middle of the eleventh century, Burton served as the chief market center for the surrounding thirty- or forty-mile area. The town grew comparatively wealthy.

But prosperity came to an end when Cromwell and his Roundheads burned the town in the seventeenth century. They marched the residents of Burton off into captivity, and few ever returned.

This account is arranged according to a sequence of events. Its most prominent organizational feature is *chronological*. In order to comprehend the passage successfully, readers have to picture the unfolding of events across the perspective of time. If you asked them to recall this passage you would expect them to remember the events that were described, the time they occurred, and the order in which they occurred. Chronologically organized text can be reduced to a timeline, as shown in Table 6.4. Chronological structures are frequently encountered in historical text.

TABLE 6.4. A chronological outline.

BEFORE 870 A.D.	AFTER 870 A.D.	TENTH CENTURY	ELEVENTH CENTURY	SEVENTEENTH CENTURY
No town; thick woods	Northumbrian fortress built	Pastures cleared; manor houses built	Roads; market center	Town sacked by Cromwell; town abandoned

Cause and Effect. The passage about the town of Burton also used cause and effect for organization. How would you outline the following passage in which this pattern is more pronounced?

BLACK ROBES IN THE DESERT

Scientists sometimes question the wisdom of "folk wisdom." The case of the Tuaregs' robes is a case in point. These nomadic people live in the area of the southern Sahara desert, the hottest terrain on earth. For centuries they have worn the same head-to-toe black wool robes. Since black absorbs more heat from the sun than any other color, scientists wonder why they've kept them through the years. Some people speculated that they had only black sheep as a source of wool, but an inspection of their herds dispelled that notion. Others speculated that black might have been chosen for its protection against the nightly desert cold, but scientific tests showed that black robes held heat no better than white ones.

Finally, through a series of experiments it was discovered that the black robes are actually cooler than white ones. The explanation is that the sun heats the upper part of the robe, which causes air to rise up through the loose-fitting robe and out through the open neck. In this way a constant draft is maintained through the robes. This draft evaporates perspiration, which cools the wearer.

In order to understand this passage, readers must operate on at least two levels: they must recognize the larger cause-and-effect question, Why do the Tuaregs wear black robes in the desert? and recognize its answer, Because their black robes keep them cool. They must also recognize the more specific set of cause-and-effect relations that explain the seemingly contradictory statement that black is cooler in the desert. An outline of this passage that would link causes and effects is shown in Figure 6.2. Cause-effect writing is found in many content subjects, including health, social studies, the sciences, and home economics.

Written Directions. Some written materials give instructions for carrying out a procedure or performing some action. Simpler materials of this sort communicate a series of tasks that must be performed in some order:

FIGURE 6.2. A cause-effect outline.

CAUSE	EFFECT
Black robes keep Tuaregs cool ———→	Tuaregs wear black robes
Sun heats black robes ←————→	Air rises inside robes
Air rises ←————————	Perspiration evaporates
Perspiration evaporates ←———→	Tuaregs are cooled
Tuaregs are comfortable ←————→	Tuaregs prefer black to other colors

HOW TO START YOUR CAR

Making sure the emergency brake is fully engaged, depress the clutch and move the gear shift lever to NEUTRAL. Pull the choke out all the way. Push the throttle to the floor, release it, then push it halfway down. Now, insert the key in the ignition and rotate the key forward to the START position. After the car has started and warmed up, push the choke in fully.

To understand this passage adequately, readers must attend to the steps described and to the order in which they are given. They could show that they understand by getting into the car and trying to follow the steps. Short of that, they could write a list of the steps in the proper order or properly arrange a set of pictures detailing each step.

Some descriptions are more complicated than the one just described in that they set up *contingencies*, or alternative sequences.

WHAT TO DO IN CASE OF FIRE

In the event of a fire in this building, students must immediately and quietly stand beside their desks. The teacher should press his or her hand against the classroom door. If the door feels hot to the touch, the door must *not* be opened. Instead, the teacher is to lower the rope ladder stored in each classroom from the window ledge. The children will then climb down the rope ladder one at a time. As they reach the ground they are to proceed at a walk to the west end of the playground, where they will line up and remain silent.

If the door is not hot to the touch, the teacher may open it and inspect the hall for flames or smoke. If the fire is at the north end of the building, the class will exit by the south stairway. Conversely, if the fire is at the south end of the building, the north stairway will be used. Each class will proceed at a walk to the west end of the playground to line up and remain silent. Each teacher will ascertain whether all the pupils are present at that time.

The understanding of this passage cannot be done by carrying out one sequence of tasks, because no *one* sequence is appropriate for all situations. Readers must recognize not only the tasks and their sequence, but also the

FIGURE 6.3. An outline of written directions containing contingency sequences.

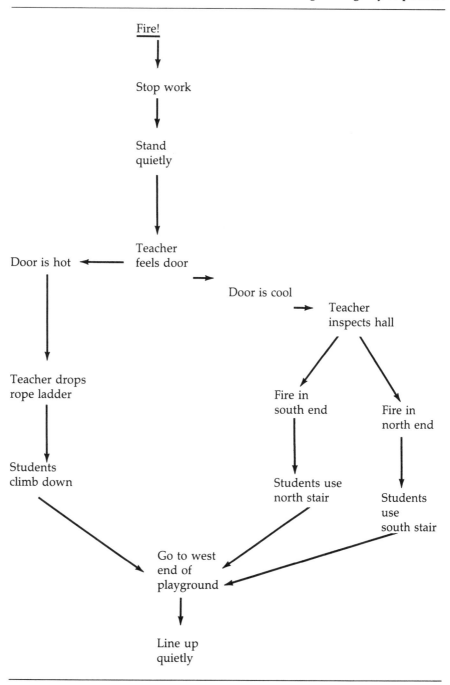

situations in which each alternative sequence should be followed. They should be able to role-play the correct procedure for each situation or answer questions like "What should you do if the fire alarm rings and the teacher tells you the door feels hot?"

The relationship of the ideas in the fire drill passage may be outlined as in Figure 6.3. Material that takes the form of written directions is seen most frequently in math, science, home economics, and vocational education.

Comparison and Contrast. In order to understand what something *is*, it is often helpful to know what it *is not*. Comparison and contrast go beyond simple description by describing two or more things simultaneously and pointing out their likenesses and differences.

WILL THE REAL COWBOY PLEASE STAND UP?

So many people pretend to be cowboys these days that it is getting harder to tell the real cowboys from the dudes. Dudes and cowboys both wear Western hats, wide, tooled leather belts with ornate buckles, jeans, and boots. The jeans of both dudes and cowboys may be worn and faded, in contrast to their boots. Both dudes and cowboys are likely to wear shiny, expensive-looking boots, but the real cowboy's belt is usually sweat-stained around the top edge, and he often tucks his jeans into the tops of his boots. The brim of the cowboy's hat is sometimes tipped at a rakish angle, but so is the experienced dude's. Neither is particularly bowlegged anymore, although this used to be one way to distinguish between the two. Nowadays both dudes and cowboys are apt to drive pickups or jeeps instead of riding horses.

The surest way to tell a real cowboy from a dude is to look at his eyes. The cowboy's eyes are clear and steady, and he holds your gaze. The dude's eyes flicker this way and that, as if to see what impression he is making on others.

TABLE 6.5. A comparison-contrast outline.

	COWBOY	DUDE
LIKENESSES	Faded jeans Expensive boots Western hat Hat probably bent Wide, tooled belt Pickup truck	Faded jeans Expensive boots Western hat Hat probably bent Wide, tooled belt Pickup truck
DIFFERENCES	Sweat stains on belt Pants tucked into boot tops Clear, steady gaze	No sweat stains on belt Pants worn over boots Shifty eyes

When a description is formulated for one of the things being compared but not the other, we must mentally supply its opposite to the things not described. For instance, if one man's belt is sweat-stained, the other's belt must not be so.

The ultimate test of a reader's comprehension of this passage would be to distinguish between a cowboy and a dude. To demonstrate comprehension by means of an outline, the reader might produce something like Table 6.5. Comparison-contrast structures are found in many content subjects, especially social studies and science.

Explanation or Exposition. Much text material in schools is used to describe or explain. Since its organization varies widely, it does not lend itself to a cut-and-dried description. The material may be entirely verbal, as the example below, or it may include numbers and formulas, charts, graphs, and pictures.

THE DEADLY COBRA

The cobra is one of the most deadly snakes in the world. Many wildlife experts consider it *the* deadliest animal. Its venom, its mobility, and its behavior are legendary.

The cobra's venom is more powerful even than that of the rattlesnake. Its large fangs do not inject the venom as do the fangs of other poisonous snakes; instead the fangs are used to pierce deep wounds in the victim's flesh, and the cobra releases venom from sacs in its mouth into these punctures. The deadly venom is carried by the bloodstream and attacks the victim's central nervous system. One African variety spits its venom at its victim's eyes; it can spit up to eight feet with almost pinpoint accuracy, and the highly corrosive venom blinds the victim unless it is immediately washed away.

The cobra's mobility is chilling. In spite of its size, it can move with great speed almost soundlessly. It creeps up on its intended victim undetected and can move on or above the ground with equal efficiency. It glides silently along the branches of trees or building rafters as well as along the ground. Its mottled skin provides a good camouflage since it blends almost perfectly with dead leaves, tree bark, grasses, and dusty earth.

The cobra may be the only snake that seeks out humans. Most snakes and other animals avoid contact with humans at all costs and attack them only when escape is blocked or in defense of their young, but cobras seem to have no such avoidance instinct. Instead, they have been known to seek out and follow humans before attacking them without provocation. Their actions are those of a predator hunting, and the prey is man.

Comprehending expository material usually entails recognizing main ideas and supporting details. Expository material is often captured nicely by the traditional outline format because it explicitly shows the relation among ideas of different levels of importance. Table 6.6 shows an outline of this

TABLE 6.6. Expository outline.

THE DEADLY COBRA

    I. Venom
       A. More deadly than rattlesnake
       B. Puncture wounds made by large fangs
       C. Released from sacs in mouth
       D. Attacks central nervous system
   II. Mobility
       A. Has great speed in spite of size
       B. Moves silently
       C. Moves on or above ground easily
       D. Is camouflaged by coloration
  III. Behavior
       A. Does not avoid human contact
       B. Seeks out, follows humans
       C. Attacks without provocation

---

expository piece. Expository writing is encountered in virtually every subject in the curriculum. Whenever information has to be explained, expository prose is the choice.

Textbooks from elementary school through college employ a wide variety of patterns for organizing information. The mental activity involved in comprehending a passage written in one pattern may be somewhat different from that required to comprehend a passage written a different way (Estes and Shibilski, 1980).

We can demonstrate this point by studying the questions that are asked for each pattern (see Table 6.7).

Strategies for Building Reading Comprehension

As we said in Chapter Two, in order to comprehend text, readers must have background schemata that relate to the material in the text, they must be alert enough to relate the new material in the text to their own schemata, and they must monitor their own comprehension — know when what they construe to be the meaning of a particular passage meshes or fails to mesh with what they expected, based on what they understood so far. Add to that the need to have mental models for the structures of various kinds of text (so that they can read stories, explanations, and persuasive arguments as they should be read), as well as a vocabulary equal to the terms used in the text, and we have a rudimentary but serviceable description of comprehension. How do we teach all of this to the older poor reader? The following sections describe some possible procedures.

TABLE 6.7. Information patterns and questions.

ORGANIZATIONAL PATTERN	TYPES OF QUESTIONS
Taxonomy	What kind of thing is X? What defines it as such? What varieties of X exist?
Chronological	What happened first? What happened next? What did these events lead to?
Cause-effect	What caused X? What were the effects of X?
Comparison-contrast	How are X and Y alike? How are they different? How are X and Y related to Z?
Direction sequences	What do I do first? How do I do it? What do I do next?
Expository-explanatory	What is the main idea? What supports that idea?

We have said before in this book that the language of print is not like everyday speech. Nowhere is this point more pressing than in the plight of the poor reader in a content subject such as social studies or science. Content area textbooks use a sort of language found only in content area textbooks. Students who do not read these books will not know this language. Hence they will have a task much like learning to read in a foreign language as they seek to make up their reading deficits in these textbooks. The task cannot be avoided, but it can be made easier.

The first way to ease the difficulty of reading the language of text is to expose students to it in aural form as much as possible. Textbook assignments can be tape recorded, and the tapes (and, if need be, the recorders) checked out for the students' use. Or parents or other volunteers who are fluent readers can be assigned to read to them. This reading should be paired with other tasks described below, both to introduce the material of the passage before the reading and to give the listener a more active role. The point is that extensive listening to text material helps students become adjusted to it. A few months of this exposure alone can sometimes enable a student to read difficult text material independently.

The Directed Reading Activity

The directed reading activity has three parts:

1. Ask students to state what they know about a reading passage beforehand, in order to clarify what they need to find out from reading the passage. This preliminary questioning phase can take the form of a minilecture on the selection, accompanied by purpose-setting questions. The minilecture can give a bit of a preview in order to arouse curiosity. At the same time it can introduce in a meaningful context a select few terms that may be unfamiliar. Finally the questions can take a form such as: "How do you think a _____ works? Give your best guess, and read to find out how right you are."
2. Ask students to read the passage. More difficult passages should be read in sections of about a page.
3. Ask confirming or recall questions. These do little to help the students comprehend, but they do provide students with feedback and a chance to tell if their comprehension was adequate or not. They may be used to suggest applications of the material, or further reading, and deeper thinking about it. Answering these questions is often (wrongly) taken by most students to be the main purpose for reading the passage. If they do assume this, the questions should be thoughtful ones; they can challenge the students to further thought about the subject and encourage them to trust the validity of their own thoughts about the selection.

Confirming questions should send the students back into the text to find support for their answers. The sequence can proceed from asking students to decide what they need to find out, having them read it, and having them confirm what they found out by first giving an answer and then going back to the text to support their answer.

The DRA that we have described is best used in the format of a group discussion. Then the introductory talk and the questions can be developed in a dialogue with the students rather than imposed rigidly by the teacher. Otherwise, the DRA can be written up as a study sheet: introduction, purpose-setting questions, directions to read a certain amount, more questions, and summary questions at the end.

The Content Area Directed Reading-Thinking Activity

The basic DRTA procedure, which we described in Chapter Five, differs from the directed reading activity in that the purpose-setting questions at the beginning are framed entirely so that the students are asked to decide what they already know about a topic, what they don't yet know, and what they need to know (see pages 212–218).

The content area DRTA is fitted closely to the unique reading demands of nonfiction text. As a preliminary question routine, you might ask the students to look over the whole selection, considering the title, the subheadings, the illustrations, and graphs. Then, ask the students What do you expect this piece to tell you about? and *How do you think the piece is going to tell you?* Will it tell a story? Give a sequence of things that happened. Explain how to do something? Describe something? Explain how something works, or how it came to be? These questions will seem strange at first, but with repeated experience students will begin to think explicitly about text structure.

In the content area DRTA, ask the students to tell us what they already know about the topic, pressing them for exact details. The idea here is to have the students summon up the most relevant schemata for the information in the text and recognize those points where their schemata are incomplete or confused. The goal is to push until they can pinpoint exactly what they need to know, exactly where they are unsure of their information. This preliminary discussion may take longer than the reading in a content area DRTA. But it is time well spent, because it not only summons up what students know about a selection before reading, but it also gives you a valuable opportunity to observe the students' "world knowledge" as it pertains to a topic.

One of the authors was doing a DRTA with a seventh grader, using a passage set in Austria. It was not really surprising that she did not know where Austria was; somewhat surprising that she could not find neighboring Germany; very disturbing that she did not know where Europe was; and downright alarming that she could not find North America or the United States on the globe. Fortunately these places came up in the DRTA and were discussed at length. But who knows what other fundamental information we take for granted that children know — that they cannot possible make accurate sense of a reading selection without knowing? The preliminary questioning in the DRTA lets us explore such things.

Stauffer (1972) suggested that having students commit themselves to a hypothesized answer to a question they have identified before they read pulls the most passive and reluctant students off the sidelines and enlists their curiosity in the reading. Before they read, the students' questions and predictions (including predictions about the nature of the information in the text and the structure of it) should be written on the board or on a chart stand.

Students read designated amounts of text, usually about one-fifth of the whole selection at one time. Go through in advance and choose these stopping places. They are analogous to the places where the commercial breaks come in a television show: first enough information is presented to get the reader clued in and hooked on the show, then there are pauses after a reasonable amount of text has been presented and just before something really significant is about to be revealed.

When they reach a stopping point, ask them to review their predictions and decide which ones were confirmed (they may write a light pencil check in the margin beside the information in the text that confirms a prediction), which predictions were proved wrong (these get a light x beside them), and which points in the text were unanticipated by their predictions (these get a light +). Before reading on, students should determine what they still need to know, make predictions about what they will yet learn, and read on to the next stopping place. Once the students all seem to have worked up a high level of curiosity and purpose for reading the text, it is all right to suspend the stopping points and let them read to the end. When the whole selection has been read, they can go back and point to unfamiliar terms. Use this opportunity to point to the contextual clues that might enable them to approximate the meanings of words without a dictionary (for a summary of these clues, see Vocabulary). If students are interested in the topic still, as many of them might be, this is a good time to suggest further reading on the topic, a writing task, or some other follow-up project.

DRTAs generate excitement. Many teachers find the hardest part is keeping students from reading ahead. However, most find that after the students try it a few times, they discover that the activity is most enjoyable if everyone stops reading where told to. In the meantime, some teachers duplicate copies of the text and hand these out one section at a time so that the students will learn the dynamics of the activity without the option of reading ahead; once they have become used to it, they can read from a textbook. Another issue in DRTAs is the reading level of the participants. DRTAs are more interesting when there are several (say, between four and ten) students participating. The students should be roughly equivalent in reading ability, reading a selection at their instructional level. Otherwise, some students will never quite finish reading before other students are ready to discuss what they have just read. In the real world, this frustration will always be there, but we can sometimes make the activity more interesting for the slowest readers if we do a DRTA as a listening activity — that is, the teacher reads the text aloud but the students make predictions in the normal fashion. It is highly recommended that very delayed readers participate in DRTAs as listening activities often.

Bear and Invernizzi (1984) found that DRTAs work well when pairs of students are given the task of conducting a DRTA lesson for their classmates. After the teacher has conducted DRTAs regularly for a couple of months, he or she has pairs of students prepare a reading lesson for the whole class, giving them what guidance they need in the process.

Categorizing Terms: A Modified DRTA

Suppose you are teaching a lesson on a topic about which students know very little. The normal DRTA exercise will usually show that they know more than they thought, but there are still those topics where the material presented in the text greatly outstrips their predictions. In these cases, Hammond (1985) suggested that you search through the reading passage in advance to find eight to ten specific terms that are integral to the meaning of the passage. Then, write these terms on a transparency and project them before a class (or put them on the board or a chart stand if you are working with a small group). After telling the students the topic of the reading passage, ask them to categorize the terms — that is, explain what they have to do with the topic. The students do the categorizing in pairs, before reading the passage, and they discuss their ideas with the whole group before reading. Then they read, and afterward they compare their findings with their initial guesses.

As an example, suppose you were using this exercise with the Burton passage on page 248. Go through and pick out key terms, for example:

Cromwell	seventeenth century	Northumbrian knights
tenth century	South Saxons	
sheep raising	ninth century	
Midlands of England	Avon River	

Then have the students categorize and explain. Discuss their ideas, read, verify, and discuss.

The ReQuest Procedure and Reciprocal Teaching

Designed by Manzo (1969), the ReQuest procedure gives insights into a child's sense of text structure. The ReQuest is an individual procedure, though it can be adapted for a small group. It proceeds as follows:

1. The teacher and student both read the first sentence of a passage to be studied. They read it silently.
2. After they both have read the passage, the student asks as many questions as he or she can think of. The teacher answers the questions clearly and completely.
3. Then it is the teacher's turn to ask the questions about the same sentence, and the student answers as fully as possible. By forming questions which call upon the student's grasp of text structures, the teacher models good questioning strategies. This helps the student see how good readers ask themselves questions about text as they read.
4. When the student has finished answering, teacher and student read the next sentence and proceed as before.
5. When the teacher feels that a sufficient amount of the text has been read in this way to make comprehension of the remainder of the passage possible, the student is asked to read to the end (Manzo, 1969, p. 125).

The ReQuest procedure can be modified in several ways. First, a group of two to five students can team up against the teacher and take turns asking questions. Second, the reading can be increased to cover a paragraph at a time if proceeding sentence by sentence does not generate many questions. Third, teacher and student can work together on interpretative and predictive questions — the latter especially, before the ReQuest is suspended and they read to the end.

This procedure is indirectly diagnostic. By noting the kinds of questions the students ask for each kind of text structure, you can tell whether or not they are on the right track, as in the DRTA example.

An activity that is a significant step beyond the ReQuest procedure is the activity of *reciprocal teaching*. Developed by Ann Marie Palincsar and Ann Brown, reciprocal teaching has been put forward as an attempt to teach comprehension skills systematically. The authors note that while word recognition skills are already taught in a carefully sequenced and managed fashion, comprehension instruction in many classrooms seems designed mainly to practice skills that have not really been taught (Brown, Palincsar, and Armbruster, 1984; Pearson, 1985). Reciprocal teaching was developed to take students through the steps of reading-with-comprehension, so that after repeated practice, the students come to use, on their own, reading strategies that pay off in high rates of comprehension.

To carry out reciprocal teaching, meet with a group of five to fifteen students, each of whom has a copy of the same content area reading material. Begin by modeling four tasks related to a segment of the material.

1. Summarize the segment in a sentence.
2. Ask the students one or two good questions about the segment.
3. Clarify the difficult parts.
4. Predict what the next segment will be about.

The students' responsibilities are to judge whether or not the summary is accurate; to decide whether or not the questions tap what is important about the passage and to answer them; and to help clarify the difficult parts.

After you have modeled the teacher's role five or six times, ask a student to be the teacher. The student then carries out the same steps the teacher did, while you

1. conduct the activity as often as your turn comes up
2. join the others in judging the accuracy of the summaries and the importance of the questions
3. support the "teacher" with frequent but appropriate praise
4. keep the students on task
5. challenge the "teacher" to perform slightly above his or her immediately past level of performance (give a more comprehensive summary, ask a "main idea" question following several factual ones, make a more logical prediction of what will follow).

Finally, at the end of each half hour's reciprocal teaching, give the students a passage they have not read before and ask them to make a summary of it or answer a few substantial questions about it (Pearson, 1985).

After performing the outward activity of reciprocal teaching over several weeks, students internalize the strategies of summarizing, questioning, and predicting and use them when reading independently. Palincsar, Brown, and their colleagues have evidence of dramatic gains after reciprocal teaching with junior high school students who were fair in word recognition but poor in comprehension of content area material (Palincsar, Brown, and Armbruster, 1984).

Study Guides

Something like the effect of a guided reading exercise can be put down on a handout sheet for students to use *as they read* a selection (not just after they read it). Such sheets, called study guides, direct students into a more active reading of an independent textbook assignment than they might do otherwise. Study guides can carefully draw out the students' thinking from literal comprehension of the text to a deeper understanding. They have the potential disadvantages of creating a dependency, having students read only those parts of the text indicated in the guides, or limiting the students' interpretation of the text to those that the teacher anticipated. For these reasons, you should not use them more than occasionally.

The Three-Level Study Guide. The three-level study guide is a sort of miniature exercise in Bloom's taxonomy. It starts with questions at a factual level, questions that ask for literal recall of the text. It proceeds to the level that Bloom called "comprehension," being an interpretation or a categorization of the meaning, or a set of inferences drawn from the literal information asked about first. It culminates at the "application" level: students are asked to do something with the information: solve a problem, project a trend into the future, write a parallel account, and so forth. Estes and Vaughan (1978) summarized the three kinds of questions as follows:

- □ What did the author say? (literal level)
- □ What did the author mean? (interpretative level)
- □ What can we do with the meaning? (applicative level)

In constructing a three-level study guide, it is necessary to go through the reading selection and take careful notes of the main points, which a teacher would presumably do in any case. Then it is best to proceed from the last category of questions toward the first. Decide first to what use the information in the text should be put. What should a person be able to do, mentally or physically, who has understood it? Write questions that develop these points. Next, decide what major concepts and premises in the selection make the application of it possible. For example, what would a student have to have learned in order to use the information to its fullest? Finally, look for the literal information — the actual sentences — a student would have to have read and understood in order to derive the concepts and comprehend the central premises of the work. In giving students their first experiences with study guides, it is helpful to indicate the pages on which they will find the answers to the literal questions (if you are reluctant to do that, at least indicate a narrow range of pages where the information may be found). This gives you your three levels.

Three-level study guides can be introduced with a paragraph-length discussion of the topic of the text, including necessary vocabulary used clearly in context so that the students can understand it. The effort required to create study guides can be reduced by these considerations: first, it is not necessary that all reading assignments be accompanied by study guides; second, the guides once written can be used over and over as many years as you teach from the book; third, if more than one teacher in a building or even a district teaches from the same book, it is certainly possible to divide up the task of writing study guides for the book; fourth, many textbooks come with study guides.

The Pattern Guide. Another kind of study guide is the pattern guide, which is useful in texts where the organization is clear enough to aid the students' access to the information.

Pattern guides take as many forms as there are structures of text. What they have in common is that they all direct the students to construct or fill in some sort of outline that is consistent with the pattern of the text. In order to construct a pattern guide, then, you must (a) decide what pattern of text structure organizes the reading assignment and (b) create an exercise that requires students to manipulate information according to the structure.

It is best to introduce and discuss the procedure of using pattern guides before assigning one. Then, after the students have completed their guides, it is important to discuss what they did and why, to make sure they see the relationship between the exercise and the pattern of the text; students are often so inundated with worksheets they are not in the habit of looking for much significance in them. During the follow-up discussion of the pattern guide, be sure to listen for how aware they became of the pattern of the text and how much they were able to use this pattern to make predictions about and gain information from the passage.

After the students have had experience working with some of your pattern guides, assign some of them the task of constructing pattern guides of their own. This is an excellent way to call their attention to text structure, though it is not an exercise that every student will find easy to do.

Examples of pattern guides are found in Figures 6.4 and 6.5.

FIGURE 6.4. A chronological pattern guide for "Burton."

A. Fill in the blanks with an event or events that happened in Burton in each time
period:

BEFORE 800 A.D.	AFTER 870 A.D.	TENTH CENTURY	ELEVENTH CENTURY	SEVEN- TEENTH CENTURY
_____ .	_____ .	_____ .	_____ .	_____ .
_____ .	_____ .	_____ .	_____ .	_____ .
_____ .	_____ .	_____ .	_____ .	_____ .

B. Fill in the blanks with a brief description of what the town of Burton might have
looked like in each period:

BEFORE 800 A.D.	AFTER 870 A.D.	TENTH CENTURY	ELEVENTH CENTURY	SEVEN- TEENTH CENTURY	PRESENT
_____ .	_____ .	_____ .	_____ .	_____ .	_____ .
_____ .	_____ .	_____ .	_____ .	_____ .	_____ .
_____ .	_____ .	_____ .	_____ .	_____ .	_____ .

The Structured Overview

The structured overview is an illustrated discussion led by a teacher for a
group of students before they read an assignment. The teacher raises the
major concepts dealt with in the assignment. Using the blackboard or
overhead, the teacher elicits and writes down the students' own terms for
the concepts. Then, in diagram form, he or she illustrates (or asks the
students to suggest ways to illustrate) the relationships among the concepts.

The following example is taken from a discussion conducted by a fourth-
grade teacher prior to making a reading assignment in a health book.

MS. LEE: This chapter is about *stress*. When you feel stress how do you
think you feel?

PETER: Kind of scared.

ANDREA: Worried.

LIVONA: I feel like somebody's hassling me.

JAMES: It's like you do your homework but you forget it, and you
remember on the bus that you forgot it, and you feel like jumping off
the bus but you can't.

CINDY: Yeah, like you don't want to do this but you have to — that's
stress.

(Ms. Lee writes: *Stress* — scared; worried; hassled)

FIGURE 6.5. A taxonomic pattern guide for "The Guitar."

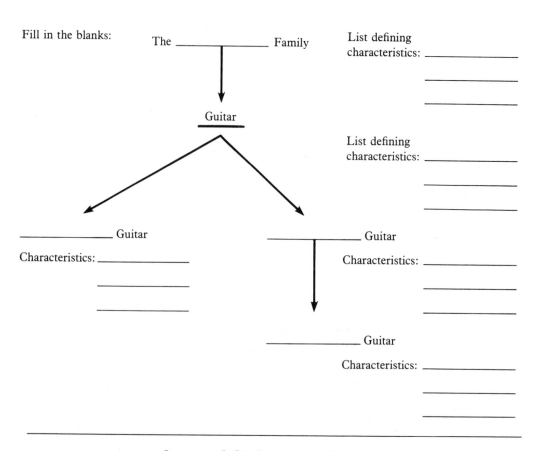

MS. LEE: James and Cindy are describing times you feel stress. Can anyone think of some more?

PETER: Like when you have to fight someone after school and you don't want to.

JAMES: Yeah, but you know you have to or people will say you're chicken.

CINDY: Or when you broke a bowl or something and you know your parents will be mad.

ANDREA: . . . and you hear them drive up in the driveway!

(Ms. Lee writes: *Times we feel stress* — forgot homework; having to do things you don't want to; about to have a fight; broke something — waiting for parents)

MS. LEE: Now think. At times like those when you felt stress, how did you deal with it? What happened to make your stress go away?

FIGURE 6.6. Diagram of a structured overview.

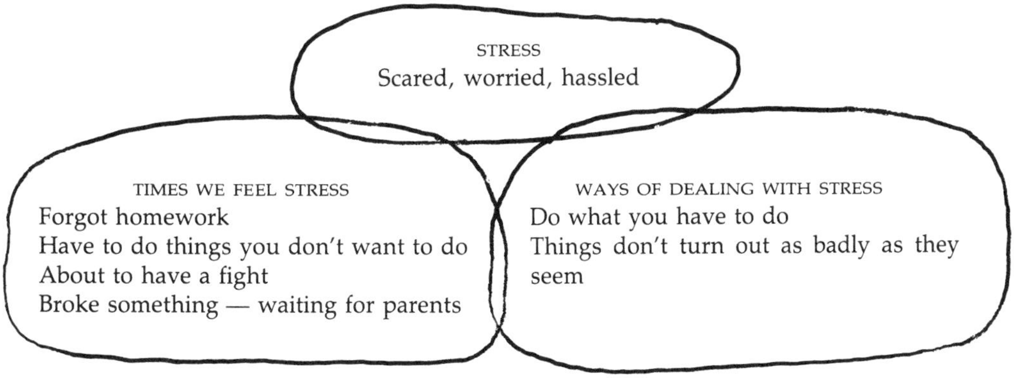

STRESS
Scared, worried, hassled

TIMES WE FEEL STRESS
Forgot homework
Have to do things you don't want to do
About to have a fight
Broke something — waiting for parents

WAYS OF DEALING WITH STRESS
Do what you have to do
Things don't turn out as badly as they
seem

JAMES: Well, when I lost my homework once and I wanted to jump off the bus, I just made up my mind, I was going to go to school and tell the teacher I forgot the homework and see what happened. She was kind of mad, but it wasn't too bad.

PETER: Once this boy told me to meet him after school and we'd fight and I was kind of scared and I didn't want to go but I went. And then he came and he said I better never call him names again or he'd beat me up. Then he just got on his bike and rode off.

MS. LEE: How did you feel?

PETER: Well, kind of better, I guess, but I really thought we were going to have a fight. It was like it wasn't so bad once I went. I don't know. . . .

(Ms. Lee writes: *Ways of dealing with stress* — do what you have to do; things don't turn out as badly as they seem)

When she finished, her diagram on the blackboard looked like Figure 6.6.

Then she explained that stress, kinds of stress, causes of stress, and ways of dealing with stress were going to be the subject of their reading. She asked them to look in their reading for the points they had already made as well as things they hadn't thought of.

When a structured overview is used diagnostically, its function is to determine how well students can relate personal experiences or world knowledge to a topic they are about to read. It does not yield generalizable data about their levels of comprehension. Rather, it reveals, *for a particular assignment,* to what extent they can relate experiences and the terms they normally use to think about the topic.

As an instructional device, the structured overview makes students think about relevant experiences before reading and helps them match book terms with words in their own vocabulary. They often read with better comprehension after building a structured overview than they do without this activity.

Assessing Study Skills

The term "study skills" is usually used to refer to students' use of textbooks, book parts, and visual aids during independent reading and study. These skills are not usually taught in elementary grades, although specific skills such as using a table of contents or an index may be introduced in language arts in the later elementary years. By the time they reach fifth or sixth grade, many students need these skills but may have had little sustained instruction and practice in using them. Study skills seem to be more easily picked up and are sometimes figured out independent of instruction by those who are good readers; average and struggling readers may have few, if any, real study skills. This lack creates a handicap in addition to their reading difficulties, for they fail to use the aids and features textbooks have, struggle along trying to read everything carefully in its entirety, and do not use efficiently what reading time they have.

Teachers in content areas may find it useful to be able to assess what study skills their students have and how effectively they can use the textbook and its maps, charts, headings, summaries, and the like, so that they can tell which students will need further instruction and practice to get the most from their texts and study time. Teachers working with poorer readers, in reading or in content area classes, will find that determining what textbook skills, if any, these students have will help them plan appropriate instruction in these areas and help them provide the support these readers will need as they work in any subject area, regardless of the difficulty level of the materials. Thus, study skills assessment can be very useful to teachers working with remedial students as well as to regular content area teachers.

A group instructional inventory (Rakes, 1975) is an informal teacher-made study skills test that can be used with a whole class, a group, or an individual student. This instrument, sometimes called a GII, is a paper-and-pencil test made up from the content and book features of whatever textbook is used in a particular class. It has two main purposes: to help you determine whether students can effectively comprehend and use a particular text and to show which study skills students can use and which they need help with.

A group instructional inventory can be constructed as follows:

1. Select a two- or three-page passage from within the second fifty pages of a textbook. The passage should pertain to a unified topic and should completely develop one or more ideas.

2. Count the total number of words in the excerpt.
3. After studying the selection, construct ten general reading questions covering its content. Questions that tap (a) facts, (b) inferences, (c) main points or applications, and (d) vocabulary are generally recommended (see the directions for writing questions for the informal reading inventory in Chapter Four).
4. Construct ten to fifteen questions that require reference, location, or other special study skills. These questions should reflect the skills that you think are important in a particular course. They might include questions that demonstrate ability to use the table of contents, the index, chapter headings, previews and summaries, and the glossary. You may decide to add map reading or table and graph interpretation. The more concrete the question, the better. It is preferable to ask "What does *parabola* mean?" rather than "What is the glossary for?" as a test of the student's ability to use the glossary.
5. Prepare a response sheet on which students can write their answers.
6. Prepare an answer key for yourself. Write a detailed answer to each question and the pages on which the answers may be found (this will come in handy if other teachers use the inventory or if you use it again in future years). On your answer key, code each question by type (e.g. vocabulary, map reading, table of contents).
7. Develop a summary chart on which you can enter the performance of each student for each type of question. You can use this chart as a guide in assembling small groups for later instruction on specific skills. The group instructional inventory may be given to large groups of students at one time. It usually takes a whole class period. Here are the steps:

   1. Hand out the student response forms.
   2. Explain the purpose of the activity. Alert the students that each question will be read two times.
   3. Explain that they will be asked to read silently.
   4. Ask them to place their texts on their desks.

   Begin with the questions related to locational/study skills.

   5. Ask the students to open their texts to the designated section of the book.
   6. Introduce the material to be read.
   7. Explain that as soon as they finish reading the assignment, they should write down the exact time on their paper. Be sure to make a note of when they begin. Later you can compute their reading rate by dividing the total number of words in the passage by the number of minutes they required to read it.
   8. After the students have read the passage, tell them to put their

FIGURE 6.7. Group instructional inventory: An example.

PART I. TEXT USAGE SECTION

Use your textbook to find the answers to these questions.

1. According to the chart on page 96, what is the body temperature of a goat? (interpreting charts)
2. Write out the definition of the term *half-life*. (using the glossary)
3. According to the figure on page 314, what do *carbohydrates* and *fats* turn into? (interpreting figures)
4. According to the figure on page 315, what do *proteins* turn into? (interpreting figures)
5. On what page do you find a discussion of mammoths? (using the index)
6. On what pages is *lead* discussed? (using the index)
7. On what pages is the *table of contents* found? (locating the table of contents)
8. What is the subject of the *appendix*? (using the appendix)
9. Locate the *pronunciation key* on page 407. How would you use these symbols to write the word *bacon*? (using the pronunciation key)

PART II. COMPREHENSION SECTION

Read the section, "Life Begins in Water," pages 306–308. Start reading at the signal and record your time when you finish. Then close your book and write out the answers to the questions written below.

1. How long ago do scientists believe evolution began? (fact)
2. In what parts of the earth did living things first develop? (fact)
3. What two main groups of organisms developed first? (main idea)
4. What things did these first living organisms need to stay alive? (fact)
5. What does *freshwater* mean? (vocabulary)
6. What disadvantages would freshwater organisms face? (main idea)
7. From the information presented in this section, are you more likely to catch fish in a big lake or in the ocean? Why? (inference)
8. Explain what the term *selection* means in this sentence: "By this process of selection, scientists think that a whole new world of life came to occupy . . . freshwater. . . ." (vocabulary)
9. Could the offspring of a freshwater fish live in saltwater? Why or why not? (inference)
10. What are some things that would have to exist on the moon for living things to survive? (inference)

SOURCE: Based on a selection from Isaac Asimov and Roy A. Gallant, *Ginn Science Program: Intermediate Level C*, Ginn and Company, Lexington, Mass., 1975.

books away. Now read aloud each of the comprehension questions twice and direct them to write down their answers after each question is read.

9. Collect the papers. Later you may wish to redistribute the papers so the students can mark their own answers and calculate their reading rates (Rakes, 1975, 596–597).

Students who answer 85 percent or more of all the questions correctly should have no trouble carrying out assignments. Those who score in the range from 60 to 85 percent will require assistance. This assistance may include not only general instruction in locational or study skills but also careful development of reading purposes and vocabulary. Figure 6.7 shows a sample group instructional inventory.

Helping Non-English-Speaking Students

Working with non-English-speaking children used to be the preserve of teachers along the border between the United States and Mexico, in southern Florida, in Alaska and Canada, Hawaii, and in the largest North American cities. However, in recent years large groups of political refugees from Southeast Asia, Haiti, Cuba, and Central America have come into the United States and Canada, and with the help of sponsoring church and civic groups, are being resettled in communities that have rarely hosted non-English speakers. In the 1980s, children who do not speak English are walking through the doors of schools all over North America. These children need thoughtful help both in coping with schoolwork in a language that is strange to them and in learning that language.

Coping with Academics

Students whose native language is not English will have the most difficulty in "conceptual" subjects (e.g., science and social studies). Experience shows that mathematics presents less of a problem for older non-English students who have studied the subject before if the teacher takes care in presenting instructions, because this subject relies least heavily on language skills. Language arts and reading will have to be individualized for the non-English speaker, but here at least, we are not concerned about covering content other than the use of the language itself, which is what the student needs to help him or her in other subjects.

The non-English-speaking student will have the most difficulty in the content subjects. The student will need to be well along in English before she or he will learn steadily in these subjects. Still, for those students who have studied the subject before in their native language, there is a predictability to the structure of class lectures and demonstrations that makes the language considerably easier to follow than conversation in the schoolyard. It's best to give the students all the chances you can to follow along, not only to minimize their lags in the content subjects, but also to make use of a valuable opportunity for language learning.

Note that non-English speaking students will need someone to act as a translator. Perhaps this role can be played by other bilingual students in the school, students in a foreign language class, or by a speaker of the child's first language from outside of school (hiring someone from the community could be made a project for a PTA or church group).

Here are some suggestions for helping students follow along in the content subjects:

☐ Write up an overview of the material to be presented in the subject either by unit or by week, whichever is shorter. Tailor the overview to the age and skill of the student, keeping it as brief as possible. Have it translated for the student, give it to her before the lessons begin, and ask her to study it carefully. Remind her that this material will be covered in class that week and challenge her to listen carefully and see how much she can understand.

☐ Make a list of concepts and terms that will be covered in the subject each week. The list should be as long as the student's capacity permits. Have the list translated and given to the student, along with the explanation that the terms will be discussed in class that week. As the week proceeds, the student should listen for the terms and take as many notes as she can about each, in her own language at first, but increasingly in English. Check in with the student frequently to ask what she's finding out about the terms.

☐ Ask the student to keep a notebook in which she writes down everything she understands from class every day. The entries should include, at a minimum, a statement of what the class was about and, preferably, both the key terms that she understood and any that she did not understand. The entries should be made in English.

☐ Be sensitive to important management directions that are used in class, such as

☐ "Open your books to page . . ."

☐ "Close your books."

☐ "Take out a sheet of paper."

Have these translated for the student, and check periodically to see if you can add to the list of familiar phrases she understands. You should also prepare a list of basic requests the student needs (e.g., requests for permission to go to the bathroom). She should learn these in English, but you should learn them in her language too.

Language Partners to Help the Non-English Speaker Learn English

Youngsters can learn language from each other. One of the most effective things you can do to help a student learn English is to match that student up with a language partner, a native English-speaking student who can devote herself to working with the non-English speaking student for an extended period of weeks and months. The language partner should agree to accompany the non-English speaking student outside of school for at least an hour a day, to take him around the community and prod him to talk about the things they encounter. Language partners take their charges to the drugstore and have them buy candy, to the clothing store to price clothing, or to the library to discuss checking out books. The partner's role is to get the student to express himself in English as much as possible, and, as necessary, to tell him how to say things.

If the language partner is chosen well, little supervision should be necessary — just a conversation every several days to find out what is happening and to underscore for both students that you care about the progress they make. Language partners may be recruited from the future teachers' club at the high school or another service club, or from a foreign language class or club (in this case, the language partners might switch roles, so that the English speaker could practice the other language).

Summary

Some children experience reading problems in content subjects in later elementary and secondary grades even though they made fair progress in early reading instruction. These problems usually arise because there is a difference between learning to read in early years and reading to learn in later years. Reading to learn requires familiarity with and responsiveness to different types of text structures, broad vocabulary skills, and a variety of comprehension and study skills.

For students who are seriously delayed readers in the middle elementary grades and up, a teaching strategy based on the language experience approach and also the method of *repeated reading* are recommended.

Very often, poor readers need to add to their ability to recognize words. We outlined several approaches to teaching *word recognition* in this chapter, including word identification strategies, a modified cloze procedure, and a variety of word sorting activities.

Schema theory helps us to see how readers understand and learn from text material. *Schemata*, or cognitive frameworks, contain information we have about the world. When ideas are expressed in print, they are related by the reader to other ideas and information, which are organized in mental schemata. Two schema types are especially important: those containing our world knowledge and those concerning different text structures.

Perceiving the organizational structure of text helps readers to understand and remember what they read. Some common text structures are: *taxonomic,* classifying information in superordinate and subordinate categories; *chronological,* organizing facts sequentially across time; *cause and effect,* linking events with their causes and outcomes; *written direction,* sequencing the steps to be followed, sometimes with alternate contingency sequences; *comparison and contrast,* describing by pointing up similarities and differences among things; and *expository or explanatory,* featuring hierarchies of main ideas and supporting details. To adequately comprehend different types of text structures, the reader must tacitly ask different types of questions.

The use of schemata can be assessed informally to determine (a) what information readers already have about the topic and (b) how they relate new information to already acquired information. Activities such as the *directed reading-thinking activity* for nonfiction material, the *ReQuest procedure* for reciprocal questioning, *pattern guides* to perceive text organization, and the *structured overview* are useful aids in making assessments.

Vocabulary activities help students develop labels for existing schemata, remember new information, relate new words to personal experiences, learn and construct categories of meaning for new words, and derive meanings from the context in which new words appear. Concept ladders, analogies, categorizing activities, and context activities are worthwhile vehicles for vocabulary study.

The Rakes *Group Instructional Inventory* is a two-part written test that assesses skills in locating book parts and visual matter as well as comprehension of text passages.

Finally, suggestions were given for helping foreign students as they try to cope with the burdens of following academic studies in English-speaking classrooms.

Extension Activities

1. Interview a random group of five students in any grade between the fourth and twelfth. It is better if all five are in the same grade (and, if you are teaching, that they not be your students). Find out:
   a. in what subjects they have reading assignments for homework or in-class reading
   b. approximately how many pages they are assigned per day in each subject
   c. what portion of the assignments they actually read
   d. whether they find the reading of these assignments easy or hard, interesting or boring

   Take your findings to class and discuss them. What generalizations can you draw about the use of assigned reading in content classes?

2. Select three different textbooks on the same subject from your curriculum laboratory or school bookroom. Randomly select three pages of running text from each book and analyze all three passages.
   a. What text structures are prominent in the three? Is there a consensus?
   b. How would you construct a pattern guide for the structures you find?
   c. Compare your findings with those of classmates who selected books from different disciplines. Is there a preferred text structure for each discipline?
3. Select a content area textbook and decide what features students should know how to use: glossary, charts, chapter overviews, etc. Construct the text usage portion of a group instructional inventory for that text.
4. Construct a concept ladder for the term *reading*. Exchange your views with another student in your class.
5. Devise a set of analogies involving each of the following terms (you will have to think up other terms to give shape to the analogies):

frustration level	purposes for reading
vocabulary	concept
content areas	tape recording (as a verb or noun)

Suggested Readings

Estes, Thomas, and Shibilski, Wayne. **"Comprehension: Of What the Reader Sees Of What the Author Says."** *In Michael L. Kamil and Alden J. Moe, eds. Perspectives on Reading Research and Instruction. National Reading Conference, 1980, 99–104.* An early report from a research project investigating the demands different forms of text structure placed on reading strategies.

Upton, Albert. **Design for Thinking: A First Book On Semantics.** *Palo Alto: Pacific Press, 1973.* A concise treatment of issues of definition, word usage, and meaning.

Vacca, Richard T. **Content Area Reading.** *Boston: Little, Brown, 1981.* Covers many aspects of assessing and teaching reading in the content areas.

References

Asimov, Isaac, and Gallant, Roy A. "From Land to Water: How Organisms Adapted," in *Ginn Science Program: Intermediate Level C.* Lexington, Mass.: Ginn, 1975.

Barron, Richard C. "The Use of Vocabulary as an Advance Organizer," in Harold Herber and P. L. Sanders, eds. *Research in Reading in the Content Areas: First Year Report.* Syracuse, N.Y.: Syracuse University Reading and Language Arts Center, 1969.

Bartlett, F. C. *Remembering.* Cambridge, England: Cambridge University Press, 1932.

Bear, Donald, and Invernizzi, Marcia, "Student Directed Reading Groups." *Journal of Reading.* 28, No. 3 (December, 1984) pp. 248–252.

Brown, Ann L., Palincsar, Annmarie S., and Armbruster, Bonnie. "Instructing Comprehension-Fostering Activities in Interactive Learning Situations," in Heinz Mandl, ed., *Learning and Comprehension of Text.* Hillsdale, N.J.: Lawrence Erlbaum Associates, 1984

Chall, Jeanne. "The Great Debate: Ten Years Later, With a Modest Proposal for Reading Stages," in Lauren Resnick and Phyllis Weaver, eds. *Theory and Practice of Early Reading*, Vol. I. Hillsdale, N.J.: Erlbaum, 1979.

Cunningham, James. "An Automatic Pilot for Decoding." *The Reading Teacher*. 32, No. 4 (January, 1979), pp. 420–424.

Deighton, Lee. C. *Vocabulary Development in the Classroom*. New York: Teachers College, Columbia University, 1959.

Estes, Thomas H., and Shebilski, Wayne. "Comprehension: Of What the Reader Sees of What the Author Says," in Michael L. Kamil and Alden J. Moe, eds. *Perspectives on Reading Research and Instruction, The 29th Yearbook of the National Reading Conference*. Washington D.C.: National Reading Conference, 1980.

Estes, Thomas H., and Vaughan, Joseph. *Reading and Learning in the Content Classroom*. Boston: Allyn and Bacon, 1978.

Hittleman, Daniel R. *Developmental Reading: A Psycholinguistic Perspective*. Chicago: Rand McNally, 1978.

Manzo, Anthony V. "ReQuest Procedure." *Journal of Reading* 13 (1969): 123–126.

Marshall, Nancy, and Glock, Marvin D. "Comprehension of Connected Discourse: A Study into the Relationships Between the Structure of Text and Information Recalled." *Reading Research Quarterly* 14, No. 1 (1978–79): 10–56.

Minsky, Marvin. "A Framework for Representing Knowledge." In P. H. Winston, ed. *The Theory of Computer Vision*, New York: McGraw-Hill, 1975.

Pearson, P. David. "Changing the Face of Reading Comprehension Instruction." *The Reading Teacher*. 38, No. 8 (April 1985), pp. 724–738.

Rakes, Thomas A. "A Group Instructional Inventory." *Journal of Reading*. 18, No. 5, (May 1975): 595–598.

Samuels, Jay. "The Method of Repeated Readings." *The Reading Teacher*. 32, No. 4 (January 1979), pp. 403–408.

Stauffer, Russell. *Directing the Reading-Thinking Process*. New York: Harper & Row, 1975.

Tierney, Robert J., Readence, John E., and Dishner, Ernest K. *Reading Strategies and Practices: A Guide for Improving Instruction*. Boston: Allyn and Bacon, 1980.

Upton, Albert. *Design for Thinking: A First Book On Semantics*. Palo Alto: Pacific Press, 1973.

Chapter Seven

Spelling and Reading

Even in a book about reading, the topic of spelling has two valid claims to our concern. First, students who are poor readers are almost always poor spellers, too; and, as students grow beyond the primary grades, poor spelling becomes the more public and hence the more embarrassing disability. Second, and less obviously, children's spellings can be read as signs of their word knowledge. As we said in Chapter Three, spelling errors can be interpreted as sensitive measures of the concepts that underlie the ability to recognize words, especially in beginning readers. In this chapter, we will examine spelling in these two ways: as a source of insight into children's word knowledge, an important component of reading ability; and as a skill that should be developed in its own right.

If spelling were not a special kind of developmental learning, we would not have a whole chapter's worth to say about it. If (as many still believe) learning to spell were simply a matter of memorizing the letter sequences that make up each of the hundreds or thousands of words we have to spell, we would simply be talking about rote memorization. But learning to spell is much more like learning to talk than like memorizing telephone numbers.

When children learn to talk, as we hope we made clear in Chapter Two, they go for patterns and structures, for unspoken rules that lie below the surface of the language they hear and that give it predictability. Children become talkers by venturing their own versions of the rules, and their versions are elaborated over months and years until the child's conceptions of the rules of language are pretty much like an adult's. Thus the adult question "Where are you going?" comes out at age two as

"Where going?", then
"Where you going?", then
"Where you are going?", and finally, by age three,
"Where are you going?"

Just as the learning talker looks for rules or patterns that relate a certain ordering of words to the intention of asking a question, so does the emergent speller seek patterns that relate orderings of letters to spoken words. As the developing talker ventures her own versions of questions, versions that reveal underlying conceptions of grammar that are growing step by step, month by month, so the emerging speller ventures his own versions of the spellings of words, versions that belie his own developing conceptions of the ways spoken and printed words are related to each other. Thus the word *train* is spelled by one child at age five years, six months (5;6) as

HN; but at age 5;9 as
HAN; then at 5;11 as
CHRAN. At 6;3 the spelling is
TRANE; and finally at age 6;9 the correct form,
TRAIN, is produced.

In this chapter, we will present the stages through which children's concepts of spelling structure pass. Much of this material is based on very recent research, so we will assume little background and explain things in detail. Second, we will share a device that can tell us in which stage of spelling development a student falls. Third, we will set out procedures for teaching students who fall in each stage of spelling development. Finally, we will summarize the ways in which students' spelling behavior can inform us about their development of reading-related concepts.

The Stages of Spelling Development

It is not well known that most children, given encouragement, can write before they can read. It is not well known because most teachers and most parents do not ask young children to write. One researcher who did, however, was very surprised at the results she got. Carol Chomsky (1971) asked the four-year-old who drew the picture in Figure 7.1 to write a caption for it. After a moment's hesitation, she did. A brief glance at her writing will show that it is a deliberate attempt to write English. In the following sections, the letters that do not seem to make sense will be explained. For now, we should note that we asked a hundred other children to write before they could read and we discovered these three things they had in common:

1. The spellings were almost all systematic, resulting more from deliberate choices of letters to represent sounds than from guessing what a half-remembered spelling might have looked like.
2. From child to child, the spellings were quite similar, even though they looked very little like the adult spellings for the same words.
3. There were developmental stages through which the children's spellings passed, ranging from highly primitive productions to those that looked much like standard spellings.

Table 7.1 shows some sample spellings from children in kindergarten, first grade, and second grade when they were asked to spell a list of words in a study by Gentry (1978). Note how the spelling of each word changed at different levels of development.

Studies have indicated that children pass through the following stages

TABLE 7.1. Examples of developmental spelling.

BRIAN KINDERGARTEN	ANGELA KINDERGARTEN	CHRIS 1ST GRADE	JOYCE 2ND GRADE	LORRAINE 2ND GRADE
MPRMRHM	J	GAGIN	DRAGUN	DRAGON
BDRNMPH	P	PRD	PURD	PURRED
Prephonemic	Early phonemic	Letter-name	Transitional	Correct

SOURCE: J. Richard Gentry, "Learning to Spell Developmentally," *The Reading Teacher*, 34 (January 1981). Reprinted by permission.

FIGURE 7.1. "Once a lady went fishing and she caught Flipper."

SOURCE: From Carol Chomsky, "Invented Spelling in the Open Classroom," *Word*, 27 (April–December 1971), pp. 499–518. Reprinted by permission of the author and the International Linguistic Association.

in their invented spelling: *prephonemic spelling, early phonemic spelling, letter-name spelling, transitional spelling*. Let us look at each of these in turn.

Prephonemic Spelling

Figure 7.2 shows eight spellings done by a six-year-old. He was asked to try to write eight words (*fish, bend, jumped, yell, learned, shove, witch, piece*) that he did not know. Figure 7.3 shows the attempts by another youngster to spell the same eight words.

FIGURE 7.2. Kenny's spelling: Prephonemic.

1	SRY	fish
2	LVh	bend
3	yeB	jumped
4	RB	yell
5	SB	learned
6	LS	shove
7	Be	witch
8	yVL	piece

Although the second youngster wrote more letters for most words, the spellings share a basic attribute: *there is no discernible relation between the sounds of the word spelled and the letters put down to spell those sounds*. No one looking at these inventions could guess what words the children were attempting, and even the children themselves could not remember a few minutes later which word was which. The productions are made up entirely of alphabet letters,

FIGURE 7.3. Rob's spelling: Prephonemic.

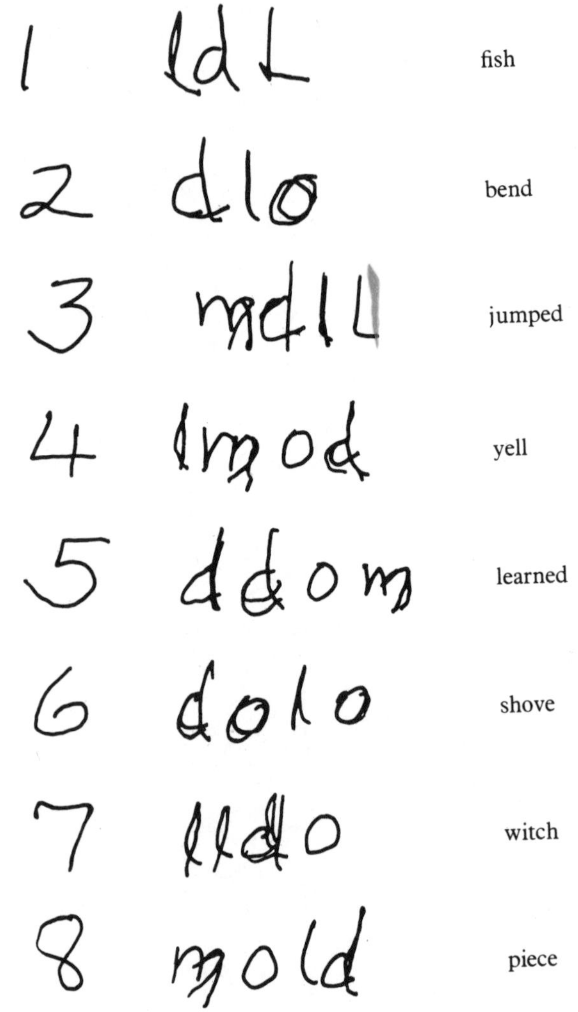

1	ldL	fish
2	dlo	bend
3	mdll	jumped
4	lmod	yell
5	ddom	learned
6	dolo	shove
7	lldo	witch
8	mold	piece

however, so they are not completely random markings. There are no numerals, stars, or "squiggles" even though many preschoolers include them when they pretend to write. The children who produced Figures 7.2 and 7.3 do know that words are made up of letters and they know how to produce at least some letters fairly accurately.

Prephonemic spelling is not spelling in the usual sense. It is the written production of children who know what writing is supposed to look like but who have not yet discovered the phonetic relation between letters and parts of words, upon which our spelling system is based. We classify spelling as prephonemic when we cannot discern any relationship between the sounds in the words and the letters that are written. Prephonemic spelling looks like random strings of letters.

Early Phonemic Spelling

At the next developmental stage, children discover that spelling honors a relationship between speech sounds (phonemes) and letters. In this stage of early phonemic spelling, a child's representation of phonemes in words is severely limited.

Figure 7.4 shows early phonemic spellings by Jerome, a six-year-old

FIGURE 7.4. Jerome's spelling: Early phonemic.

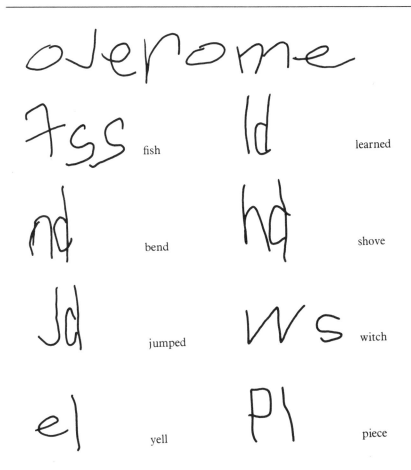

prereader. Here it can be seen that he represented at least one of the phonemes in each word he wrote. When he wrote FSS for *fish*, he represented the initial sound and attempted the final sound, which does sound something like *ss;* ND for *bend* represents the sounds we represent with the letters *en* as well as the final sound. Likewise each of the rest of Jerome's attempts show at least one of the sounds in the word (HD for *shove* may confuse you, but we'll consider this use of H in the next section).

Unlike prephonemic spelling, in the early phonemic stage, there is a clear link between the letters a child writes and some speech sounds in the words being spelled. However, the spelling is incomplete. Only one or two phonemes are spelled for each word. Some of these are the first phonemes in the word, some the last. What defines early phonemic spelling is that *the letters represent phonemes but only an incomplete number of phonemes for each word.*

Why don't children represent more phonemes per word? Because they cannot. The difficulty lies not in the number of letters they know, nor so much in their notions of which letters should represent which phonemes. It is rather that they are unable beyond a very limited extent to break a word down into its phonemes, a task psychologists call *phonemic segmentation.* Their inability to segment phonemes is related in turn to another factor: children at this stage lack a stable concept of word in print (Henderson, 1980; Morris, 1980).

When children try to spell a word, they must perform several tasks in close harmony. They must first say the word over to themselves; they may do this out loud, as many children do, or silently in the "mind's ear." Next, they must mentally break off the first sound. To spell *tooth,* for example, they must rehearse the word, then mentally break off the /t/ sound. Now they must think of a letter to match with the sound of /t/. Assuming they think of the letter *t,* they must next remember how to write it, decide where it should go on the page, and carry through the motor activity of forming the letter with their pencils. That done, they must remember what word it was they were trying to spell! If they still can, they must rehearse it mentally, then remember which sound they had already broken off, mentally separate it from the rest of the word and decide which sound should be spelled next. If they get this far, they must decide what letter represents *that* sound, recall how to write it, and decide where it should be written. Does it go above or below, to the right or to the left of the *t?* Once they decide, they must write that letter down, recall the word again, and so on.

If all of this were not complex enough, there is also the fact that phonemes are not so easy to separate from one another as this scenario may have suggested (Liberman et al., 1974). In fact, when we say the word *tooth,* we do not pronounce the /t/ and the /u/ distinctly from each other. We pronounce them practically at the same time. To separate them from each other is really an abstraction that we impose on the sounds of the word *tooth,* much like what we do when we separate a wave from the surface of the

The development of writing ability is a creative, thoughtful process. Young writers learning to spell need many opportunities to invent their own spellings and reflect on their approximations of adult spellings.

ocean, though in fact no objective dividing line is present in nature between the two. As adults it is easy to separate /t/ from /u/, but this is because we can already read, and we are used to seeing the separate phonemes depicted in writing. For beginning readers, this act is much more difficult.

Children in the early phonemic stage will fall by the wayside in the middle of the steps we described above. Part of the reason will be the difficulty of phonemic segmentation, but it is also believed that children must be able to reflect on words and segment phonemes before they can make real strides in beginning reading (Ehri, 1980). Since they are able to produce early phonemic spelling before they have begun to read, their reaching this stage may be taken as a predictor of reading development to come and a sign that an important prerequisite for that development has been met.

Letter-Name Spelling

As children move closer to the point when they begin to read and acquire more experience looking at printed words, their invented spelling strategies undergo many changes. From being able to represent only one or two sounds in a word, their spelling productions reflect most or all the sounds they hear. Their productions may look somewhat bizarre at first, but when considered carefully, these productions do make sense. As they try to represent more and more sounds in words, they begin to use what has been called the *letter-name strategy* (Beers and Henderson, 1977); that is, they analyze the words they want to spell into their component sounds and then find a *letter name* to represent each sound. *To spell each sound, they choose the letter name that most closely resembles the sound they want to represent.*

In many languages, the relationship between speech sounds and letter names is very close. Finnish is one such language, having an alphabet with the same number of characters as there are speech sounds in the language. Children find Finnish quite easy to spell; the letter-name strategy results in correct spellings in most cases (Temple and Salminen, 1981). In English, however, there is quite a bit of variance between letter names and speech sounds. The twenty-six letters (three of which, *j, y,* and *x* are redundant — they stand for sounds that are already represented by other letters) must represent forty-four speech sounds. Some sounds, such as the long vowels, have corresponding alphabet letters that sound like them. Others, like the short vowels, have letters that regularly represent them, but don't sound like them. A number of consonant sounds in English need two letters to represent them (these are the digraphs *ch, th,* and *sh*). Too, there are many occasions in English spelling where letters have no sound, but rather serve to indicate the sound other letters have (such as the *e* in *gate*). Still other letters appear to have no function at all (such as the *ugh* in *though*). It has been said that modern English spelling most closely represents the way English words were pronounced five hundred years ago, before many substantial changes in pronunciation took place. One writer thus has called English spelling "historically phonetic" (Vallins, 1954). Because of these factors, there is not a very close relation between letters and sounds in English. Our spelling system is learnable, to be sure, but it is complex and not very directly phonetic.

Beginning spellers seem to expect a close relationship to exist between letters and sounds. Thus their spelling is very different from standard spelling. When they choose letters to represent sounds, they don't use silent letters. They represent many sounds with letters that adults would not choose, both out of ignorance of the way standard spelling works and because they perceive similarities among sounds that years of experience with print have conditioned adults to ignore.

Let's observe this process in action by looking again at Figure 7.1. Consider the spelling YUTS A LADE YET FEHEG AD HE KOT FLEPR for "Once a lady went fishing and she caught Flipper." This work was generated by using the letter-name strategy. Can you decide *why* the child used the letters she did to spell each sound in those words?

The letter-name strategy yields some spellings that appear immediately reasonable and others that seem very peculiar. We can understand this better if we consider how a letter-name speller handles several aspects of words.

Long Vowels. Long vowels are usually spelled with the letter name that sounds like them. Although standard spelling requires that a marker letter be present in most cases to indicate when a vowel letter is to have a long pronunciation, such markers are usually absent in letter-name spelling. For instance, the word *name* has a silent *e* marker that indicates that the *a* is long. But in letter-name spelling, the same word would be spelled NAM. Figure 7.5 shows other examples of long vowels spelled by letter-name spelling: *hates, likes,* and *playing.*

FIGURE 7.5. Frank's spelling: Letter-name.

DONALD HATS ME DONALD LIKS
PLAG SOKR DONALD
OLWES bREGS A SNAK

FIGURE 7.6. Billy's spelling: Letter-name.

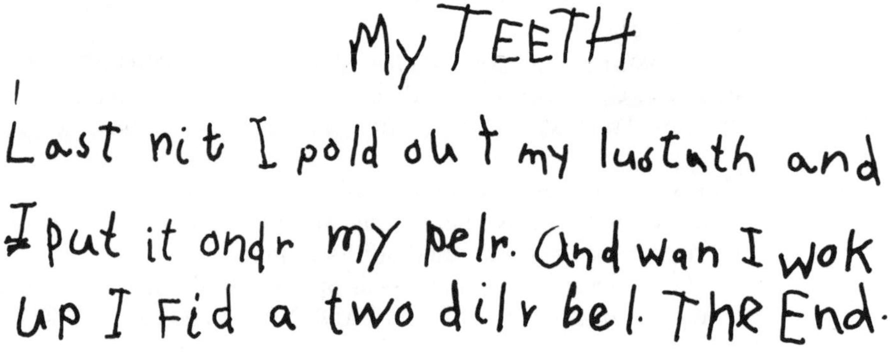

My TEETH

Last nit I pold oht my lustath and
I put it ondr my pelr. And wan I wok
up I Fid a two dilr bel. The End.

Short Vowels. How the short vowel sounds in English should be spelled is not so easy to guess. By simply saying the names of the vowel letters, *a, e, i, o,* and *u,* we cannot find a letter name with the sound of the vowels in *bet, bat, bit, but,* or *bottle.* The solution that letter-name spellers most often find for this problem is to choose the nearest fit — to choose a letter whose name sounds the most like the short vowel sounds they want to spell, which leads to some interesting pairings of sound and letter. In reality the long and short vowels that are paired in standard English spelling do not sound much alike. Consider /ā/ and /ă/; /ē/ and /ĕ/; /ī/ and /ĭ/; /ō/ and /ŏ/; /ū/ and /ŭ/. These pairings are not the ones children who use letter-name spelling produce (see Figure 7.6).

In "My Teeth" the writer has used *o* to represent the vowel sound in *pulled* (POLD), *put* (POT), and *under* (ONDR). He has used *i* to represent the short vowel sound in *dollar* (DILR). He has used *e* to represent the short vowel sound in *pillow* (PELR) and *bill* (BEL). These are common substitutions because letter-name spellers often substitute short vowel sounds:

> A for ĕ: BAT for *bet*
> E for ĭ: BET for *bit*
> I for ŏ: HIT for *hot*
> O for ŭ: BOT for *but*
> (Read, 1971, 1975)

Though at first these pairings seem strange, on reflection they are not if we consider how vowel sounds are made in the mouth. Vowels are formed when vibrated air is passed out through the mouth without being interrupted. The difference between vowel sounds is determined by the position of the tongue in the mouth. The tongue can move to an infinite number of positions as vowels are formed, but it is customary to refer to its positions in terms of the dimensions of front to back and high, middle, and low. Take, for example, the sound $\bar{e}$, which is formed with the tongue high and in front of the mouth, while ah is formed with it low and back. If you pronounce $\bar{e}$-ah, $\bar{e}$-ah, $\bar{e}$-ah many times in quick succession, paying attention to where your tongue goes, you will get a feel for its positions in the formation of vowels. Now as it turns out, there is another important factor in the formation of vowels, and that is whether or not the tongue is tense or relaxed as the vowel is made. A tense high front vowel is $\bar{e}$, for example. A vowel made in the same position but with the tongue relaxed is $\breve{\imath}$. Similarly, a vowel made in the front of the mouth midway between high and low is $\bar{a}$ if the tongue is tense, but if the tongue is relaxed, the vowel is $\breve{e}$ (Langacker, 1973).

The tense-relaxed dimension can be demonstrated in the following manner: Hold your thumb and forefinger against the flesh beneath your jaw. Alternate saying the vowels $\bar{e}$ and $\breve{\imath}$. You should be able to feel the muscle in the bottom of your mouth literally tense up for the sound $\bar{e}$ and relax for the sound $\breve{\imath}$. The same tensing and relaxing can be felt with $\bar{a}$ and $\breve{e}$.

The vowel pairings that letter-name spellers make are exactly these tense-relaxed pairings. The vowels that they consider similar for the purpose of spelling are made in the same positions in the mouth and differ only according to whether or not the tongue is tense or relaxed in forming them. Again, they are *paired* in the sense that the letter name containing the name of the tense vowel is used to spell the corresponding relaxed vowel phoneme.

N's and M's before Consonants. In Figure 7.7, look at how Daniel has spelled *monster, bumpy,* and *lunch.* He consistently omitted the nasal letters n and m when either occurred before another consonant. In *stamp* he included the m and omitted the p. He can certainly perceive the nasal sound, for he has represented it in the beginning of *monster* and in *bottom.* Letter-name spellers usually omit n's and m's when they fall before consonants, though they usually include them when they occur in other positions within words. Why do they omit these letters?

The reason is that in deciding which consonants a word contains, children apparently concentrate on what their mouths do when they say it. When they pronounce a word with the phoneme /t/, they can clearly feel the tip of their tongue touching the fleshy ridge behind their upper front teeth and then releasing a little blast of air. Letter-name spellers know that this movement in the mouth indicates the necessity of writing a letter t. Similarly, when their two lips close, followed by a puff of air, they know that there must be a letter p in their written version of the word.

FIGURE 7.7. Daniel's spelling: Letter-name.

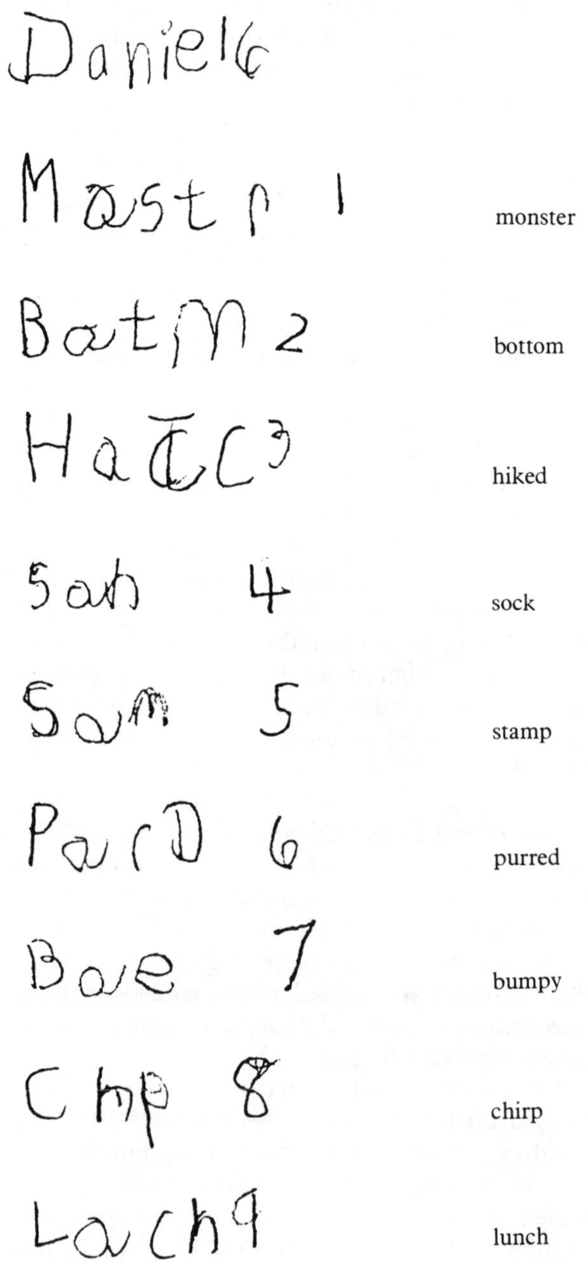

Daniel 6

Mostp 1	monster
Botm 2	bottom
HaTC 3	hiked
Sab 4	sock
Sam 5	stamp
PaD 6	purred
Bae 7	bumpy
Chp 8	chirp
Lach 9	lunch

When, however, they say a word that has the phoneme *n* coming just before the phoneme *t*, a strange thing happens. There is nothing in the motion of the tongue against the back of the teeth to indicate that the sound of *n* is present with the *t*. If you say *can't* and *cat* in alternation several times, and pay attention to the motion of your tongue, you will find that there is virtually no difference in the formation of the two words in the mouth.

How is the difference made between the two words? In saying the word *can't*, we direct the flow of air out through the nose when we pronounce the second part of the word. You can feel this if you hold your nose while saying *cat—can't, cat—can't* several times. You will feel a vibration in the nose as you pronounce *can't* but not *cat*.

Because they are produced with air going through the nose, *n* and *m* are called *nasal consonants: n* is produced by touching the tongue behind the front teeth while directing air out through the nose; *m* is produced by closing the lips while directing air out through the nose. When *n* occurs before another consonant made with the tongue behind the front teeth, we still can recognize its presence independently of the other consonant because of the vibration of air through the nose (consonant sounds that can be made in this position are /t/, /d/, /ch/, /s/, /z/, and /j/). Children, however, attend only to the motion in the mouth when they are spelling — they ignore the passing of air out through the nose (Read, 1975). Thus when n occurs before the sounds of /t/, /d/, /ch/, /s/, /z/, or /j/ (regardless of how these sounds may be spelled), youngsters are likely to leave out the *n*. The very same thing happens with *m* before /p/ or /b/ as in *bumpy* or *mumble.*

Syllables without Vowels. Another strategy of letter-name spellers is to let a consonant sound or a consonant letter's name represent a whole syllable in which the vowel sound is reduced. In Figure 7.8, Joey used *l* for the last syllable in *little,* which he spelled LETL. Look again at Figure 7.7, in which Daniel wrote MASTR for *monster* and BATM for *bottom.* Here Daniel used *r* and *m* to represent whole syllables in which an adult would have included a vowel. As we saw in Figure 7.6, the child who wrote "My Teeth" used *r* to represent the final syllable in *under* (ONDR), *pillow* (probably pronounced *piller*) (PELR), and *dollar* (DILR).

What LETL, MASTR, BATM, ONDR, PELR, and DILR have in common is the absence of a vowel in the final unstressed syllable. In English, when words end in unstressed syllables containing the consonant *r, l, m,* or *n,* it is difficult to tell what vowel they are spelled with. Note the sound of the second vowel in *castle, common, letter,* and *bottom.* It is not very distinct; in fact it is hard to discern a vowel sound at all that is separate from the sound of the consonant itself. Only a few English words allow these syllables to be spelled without a vowel: for example, *prism* and *chasm.* Children usually spell these syllables without a vowel at all (Gentry, 1977, 1978).

Tr and Dr. In normal speech, our pronunciation of the consonant blend at the beginning of *truck* sounds like *ch,* and our pronunciation of the blend

FIGURE 7.8. Joey's spelling: Letter-name.

Bozo the dog is goep to the
store with me.
I sol a mas.

a big rat,

a big mas.

I sol a rat.

a letl mas.

a letl rat

I can see the letlm
mas.

I can see the letl
rat.

at the beginning of *dragon* sounds like *gr* or *jr*. Few of us say *t-ruck* or *d-ragon* unless we're calling out words in a spelling test! Because beginners spell what they hear, they are likely to write JRAGN or GAGN for *dragon* and CHRUK or even HRUK for *truck*. The latter spelling needs further explanation because *ch* represents a sound that children could not possibly guess on their own. There is only one sound, but two letters; that is, *ch* is a *digraph*, and the relation between the digraph and the sound it represents is not discoverable by logic.

Letter-name spellers use the strategy of finding a match between a speech sound and the name of a letter of the alphabet. In our alphabet, the only letter name that contains the sound *ch* is the name of the letter *h:* "aitch." Thus *truck* might be spelled HRUK: *h* for the sound /ch/ which is the sound actually heard at the beginning of truck (Gentry, 1977, 1978). And look again at Figure 7.4, where Jerome wrote HD for *shove*. The presence of

FIGURE 7.9. Fergus's spelling: Letter-name.

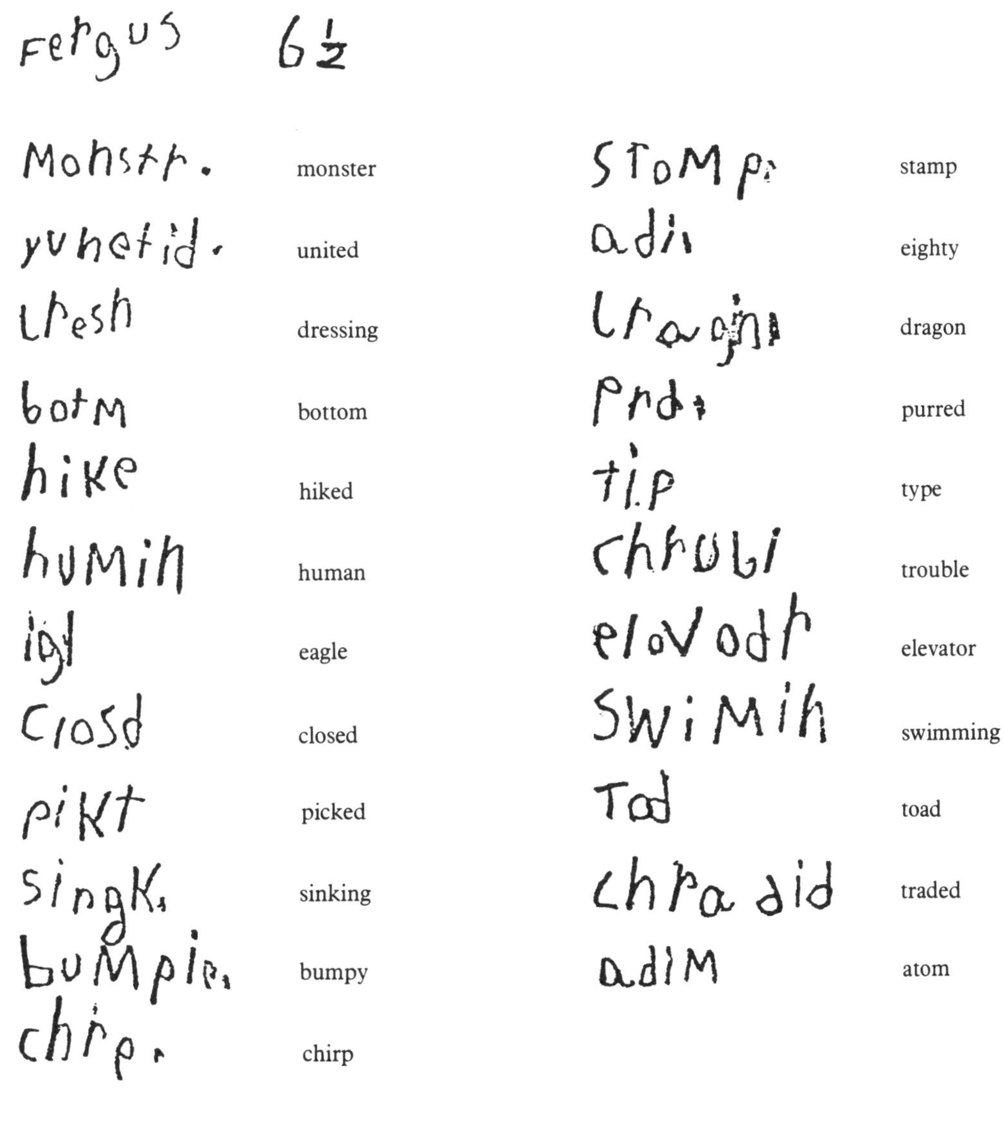

Fergus   6½

Mohstr.	monster	STOMP:	stamp
yuhetid.	united	adh	eighty
Lresh	dressing	Lraqn	dragon
botm	bottom	Prd:	purred
hike	hiked	tip	type
humih	human	chrubi	trouble
igl	eagle	elovodr	elevator
Closd	closed	SwiMih	swimming
pikt	picked	Tod	toad
singk.	sinking	chra did	traded
buMpi.	bumpy	adiM	atom
chrp.	chirp		

the letter *d* is random, which often happens in early phonemic spellings, but the *h* is used there because of the similarity between the letter name "ait*ch*" and the /sh/ sound. The letter name "aitch" is as close as one can come to the sound of /sh/.

In Figure 7.9, Fergus used JR and CHR to represent the initial sounds

FIGURE 7.10. Carla's spelling: Letter-name.

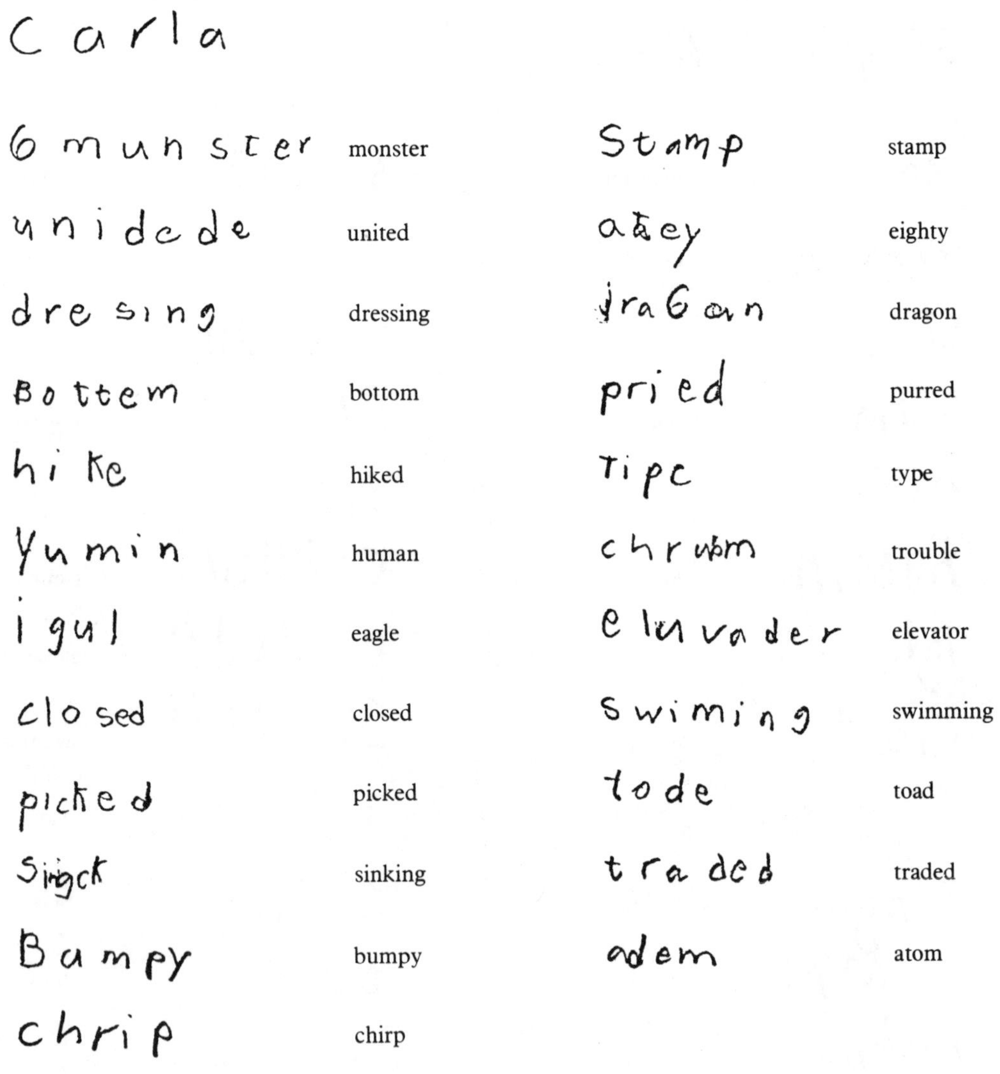

Carla

6 m u n s t e r	monster	S t a m p	stamp
u n i d c d e	united	a t e y	eighty
d r e s i n g	dressing	d r a 6 a n	dragon
B o t t e m	bottom	p r i e d	purred
h i k e	hiked	T i p c	type
Y u m i n	human	c h r u b m	trouble
i g u l	eagle	e l u v a d e r	elevator
c l o s e d	closed	S w i m i n g	swimming
p i c h e d	picked	t o d e	toad
S i n g c h	sinking	t r a d e d	traded
B u m p y	bumpy	a d e m	atom
c h r i p	chirp		

in *dragon, trouble,* and *traded.* In Figure 7.10, Carla used CHR to begin *trouble* but TR to begin *traded.* Like Fergus, Carla used JR for the initial sounds in *dragon.*

Letter-name spelling has a number of characteristic features, which are summarized in Figure 7.11.

FIGURE 7.11. Some prominent features of letter-name spelling.

Long vowels

Closely matched letter names are used for long vowels, but without silent letters as markers:

> BAT *(bait),* STAN *(stain),* JRIV *(drive),* BOT *(boat)*

Short vowels

Short vowels are represented by pairing the desired short vowel sound with the long vowel sound that is similarly produced in the mouth and then spelling by means of a letter-name match:

> BAT *(bet),* PAT *(pet),* BET *(bit),* STAP *(step),* BITL *(bottle)*

N's and M's before consonants

When *n*'s and *m*'s come before "hard" consonants, such as *d, t, ch,* or *p,* they are omitted:

> STAP *(stamp),* BOPE *(bumpy),* TET *(tent),* PEH *(pinch)*

Unstressed final syllables

With words that end in unstressed syllables, the vowels in those syllables are usually omitted:

> LATR *(letter),* LEDL *(little),* PECHR *(pincher),* BIDM *(bottom)*

Tr and Dr

Words that begin with *tr* or *dr* are often pronounced as if the letters were *chr* and *jr,* respectively. *H* is often given for the digraph /ch/, and *g* or *j* for the sound, /j/. These sounds are spelled as they are heard:

HRUK *(truck),* GRIV *(drive),* CHRUBL *(trouble),* JEK *(drink)*

Transitional Spelling

When children produce spellings like Eric's in Figure 7.12, the spellings look a lot more "wordlike" than Daniel's, Fergus's, or Carla's. More word features are present in Eric's spellings of CETER *(setter)*, SHUVE *(shove)*, SAILER *(sailor)*, SPASHAL *(special)*, and FECHER *(feature)*.

Unlike the highly original forms produced by the letter-name strategy, transitional spellings take on many of the features of standard spellings. They employ short vowels appropriately, if not correctly: HAV *(have)*, GURL *(girl)*, LITL *(little)*. They use silent letters for markers: WEPE *(weep)*, REDE *(read)*, BIEK *(bike)*, and ROAP *(rope)*. Sometimes they use long vowel markers for short vowels and vice versa: GETE *(get)*, GOTE *(got)*, RALL *(rail)*, and STELL *(steal)*. Transitional spellers often forget to double the consonants when syllables are added to one-syllable words with short vowels: GETING *(getting)*, BEDER *(better)*, LITLE *(little)* (Gentry, 1981).

They also spell the grammatical ending *ed* the way it sounds. In some

FIGURE 7.12. Eric's spelling: Transitional.

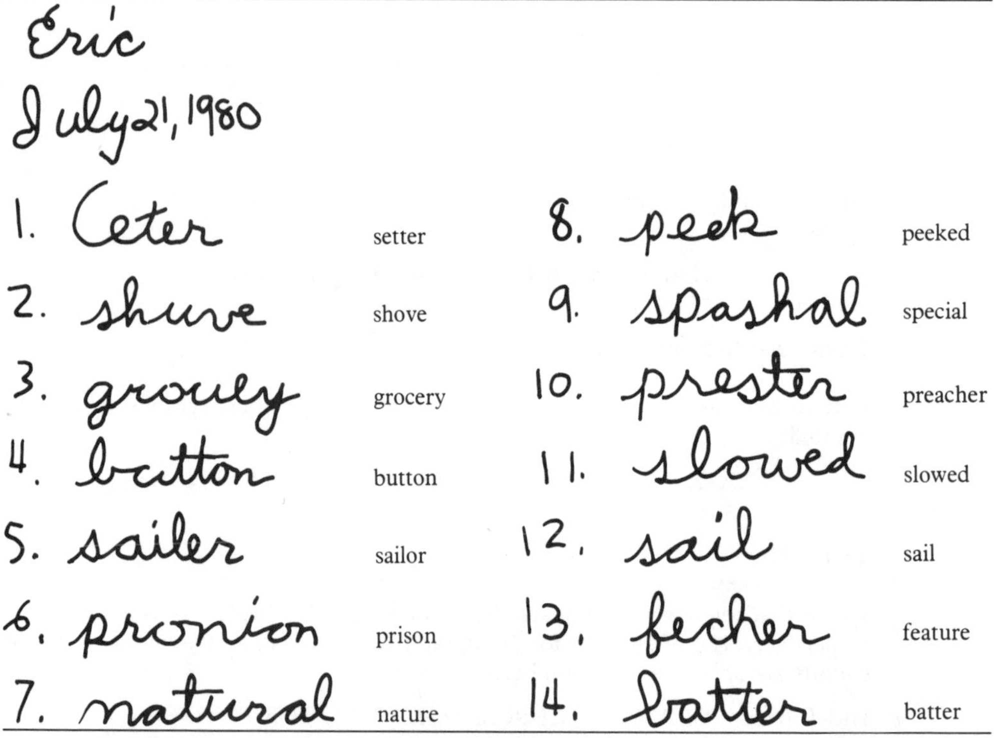

Eric
July 21, 1980

1. Ceter — setter
2. shuve — shove
3. grouey — grocery
4. batton — button
5. sailer — sailor
6. pronion — prison
7. natural — nature
8. peek — peeked
9. spashal — special
10. prester — preacher
11. slowed — slowed
12. sail — sail
13. fecher — feature
14. batter — batter

words *ed* sounds like *t* and is spelled that way by both letter-name and transitional spellers: PEEKT *(peeked)*, TRAPT *(trapped)*, BUNCHT *(bunched)*. In other words it sounds like *id:* WONTID *(wanted)*, CARRID *(carried)*, TASTID *(tasted)*, and sometimes *ed* sounds like *d:* SLODE *(slowed)*, USDE *(used)*, STADE *(stayed)*.

Transitional spelling takes in a wide range of spelling behaviors that can be observed from first or second grade through high school. Those that affect older students are discussed in the following sections.

Errors from Pronunciation Changes. Some characteristic posttransitional spellings for words with /ch/ and /sh/ sounds are:

VACASHUN *(vacation)* SPESHLE *(special)*
FORCHUN *(fortune)* GROSHRY *(grocery)*
NACHER *(nature)* FUCHURE *(future)*

Words from Latin origin with /ch/ or /sh/ sounds in them are troublesome for many children because they seem illogical: How does one ever get from *future* to its pronunciation, which sounds like *fewcher*? What has occurred here is a very common pronunciation change. It happens that whenever /t/ and /y/ come together, we tend to pronounce them as /ch/. Note how *got you* becomes *gotcha* and how *bet you* becomes *betcha*. An early pronunciation of *future* was *fyute-yure;* in fact BBC announcers still favor this pronunciation. In ordinary speech, however, the /t/ and /y/ have come together as /ch/, as in *nature, suture,* and similar words.

When /t/ and /i/ or /y/ come together, they are also often pronounced as /sh/. The same is true of /s/ and /i/ or /y/. Thus *I want to kiss you* comes out *I wanna kisha; this year* is often *thishyear*. *Initial, vacation,* and *nation,* had they ever been pronounced precisely as they are spelled, would have changed either to their actual pronunciation — or to *inichle, vacachun,* and *nachun,* respectively.

Errors from Vowel Reduction. /ə/ is the symbol for a speech sound called *schwa*. Schwa is the most frequently heard vowel in the English language (Bollinger, 1975). It is the sound you hear for the underlined letters in the following words:

symbol syllables
frequently about
vowel enough
language initial
bottom liberate

Schwa can be spelled by any vowel letter if it occurs in a syllable that is unstressed. Since the schwa sound can be spelled by any vowel letter, it is often very difficult to tell which letter should be used to spell it. Thus we see spellings such as:

LITTUL *(little)*   INUFF *(enough)*
BOTTUM *(bottom)*   NASHUN *(nation)*
UBOUT *(about)*   BUSHLE *(bushel)*

Linguists say that schwa occurs in reduced vowels, vowels that are unstressed to the point that their identity is indeterminate. But there is a useful key to their identity: a word that has schwa for a certain unstressed vowel will often have a related form in which that vowel is stressed and made identifiable (e.g., *symbol→symbolic; syllable→syllabic*).

Likewise, words that have the /ch/ or /sh/ pronunciation for *ti* or *ty* can have related forms that make the identity of the letters in question easier. *Vacation* can be related to *vacate; national* can be related to *innate* and *native*. *Special* can be related to *specific*.

Errors Stemming from Scribal Traditions. Spellings like LUV, ABUV, SHUV, SUME, CUM, DUN, and WUNTS are reasonable guesses for some seemingly unreasonable words, but the correct spellings turn out to have a common and interesting source. If the source is learned and remembered, the errors can be reduced, if not completely eliminated.

Before the printing press was invented and all reading material had to be copied by hand, the professional copiers of the Middle Ages, the scribes, proudly cultivated a beautiful handwriting called *Gothic script*. Unfortunately, this script sacrificed legibility for beauty. This fact, as well as some holdovers from Latin traditions of spelling, led to some curious spellings (Scragg, 1974; Vallins, 1954).

Written Latin made no distinction between the letters *u* and *v*, and this ambiguity was adopted into English writing, where it remained into the beginning of the eighteenth century. One was as likely to be used as the other when either the /u/ sound or the /v/ sound was intended. In Middle and early modern English writing, the *love*, for example, could be written *loue*; and *very* could be written *uery*, or they could be written the other way around. Apparently it didn't make much difference, except to the scribes. While they failed in trying to separate the use of the two letters, they did establish the following rule: whenever a word ended in the sound of *v*, the consonant would be followed by the letter *e*. Thus *love*, which had originally been spelled *luv*, became *luve* (or *luue*) and *abuv* became *abuve* (or *abuue*). That rule has stayed with us, and to this day you won't find an English word that ends in the letter *v*.

Why then did the *u*'s turn into *o*'s? That change was deliberately made to distinguish the vowel from the consonant in words where *u* and *v* came together, as in *love, above, shove,* and *move* (all of these were originally spelled with *u* vowels). To make reading these words easier, the scribes changed the *u*'s to *o*'s when they came before *v*'s. While they were at it, they extended this practice to *u*'s that fell before *m*'s and *n*'s: the repetition of short vertical lines in such words made it easier to read the vowels if the *u*'s were closed and made into *o*'s.

Although these changes did not affect many words, those that were affected were of such high frequency that today we see many spelling errors committed by writers who are not sensitive to patterns that have come down to us from medieval times.

Consonant Doubling Errors. The necessity of doubling the consonants in the middle of two-syllable words results in many errors like:

LITLE *(little)*	BUTER *(butter)*
BATER *(batter)*	BOTLE *(bottle)*
MITEN *(mitten)*	SETLE *(settle)*

The principle behind consonant doubling goes back to the system of vowel markings (Venezky, 1970). As we all know, single vowel letters that come before single consonant letters are given a short pronunciation: *bat, but, bit,* and *bet.* The vowel would be pronounced long if another vowel came after the consonant: *Bates, bite, Pete, NATO, data, veto,* and *credo.* (Note that whether or not the following vowel is silent does not affect its function as a marker for the preceding vowel). If we add another syllable directly onto a single vowel word like *bat,* it has the effect of making the vowel long, and we get *bāter.* The remedy, of course, is to double the consonant at the boundary between the original word and the new syllable: *bătter.* This solution is very common, and most two-syllable words are spelled by this pattern. To children who are learning to spell, however, the consonant doubling rule adds considerable complexity to the task. Those who are just learning that endings can be added to root words, may be so taken with this discovery that they have little attention left over for the idea that vowels in the root word must be insulated from the lengthening effect of any vowel in the ending. It is natural at first to write *bat* and simply append *-er* to it; it calls for a higher level of circumspection to notice that the *e* in *-er* has an effect on the preceding vowel. With practice, and also having their attention called to these matters, most children learn to master these complexities.

Transitional spelling has a number of characteristics, which we have summarized in Figure 7.13.

Using a Features List to Assess Spelling Development

It is possible to evaluate samples of writing to determine the stage of spelling development that children have reached. For this evaluation to work properly, we must work with their errors, because correct spellings might have been copied or memorized. To make an accurate assessment, it is important

FIGURE 7.13. Some characteristics of transitional spelling.

Long and short vowels

The letters used are correct, but there are problems with the ways these vowel sounds are marked:

METT *(meet)*, PIKE *(pick)*, BOT *(bought)*, SPRINGE *(spring)*

Plural and past tense markers

The *ed*, *s*, and *es* markers, which are pronounced several ways, are spelled as they are pronounced:

PICKT *(picked)*, SLODE *(slowed)*, CRIZE *(cries)*, HUGZ *(hugs)*

Pronunciation-change errors

Here words are spelled as they sound rather than by the predictable rules adults use:

VACASHUN *(vacation)*, SPESHLE *(special)*, GROSHRY *(grocery)*, NACHER *(nature)*

Vowel-reduction errors

Vowels in unstressed syllables, which are reduced to schwas, are confused with other short vowels:

BUSHLE *(bushel)*, FORCHUN *(fortune)*, INDIUN *(Indian)*, LITTUL or LITTEL *(little)*

Scribal tradition errors

The rules made to make the writing of Latin easier to read are treated phonetically:

LUV *(love)*, SUM *(some)*, BRUTHER *(brother)*, DROAV *(drove)*

Consonant-doubling errors

The rules for marking short and long vowels in syllables before consonants are frequently confused:

BETER *(better)*, GETING *(getting)*, SCRAPPING *(scraping)*, FINNISH *(finish)*

---

to study the words they have generated by using their own rules or concepts about spelling.

There are two ways to elicit spelling errors for analysis. One is to have the children write free compositions. The trouble with this method, however, is that many youngsters are inhibited about their writing. They often believe they *cannot* write, since they equate writing with correct spelling, neat handwriting, and correct punctuation. A better approach is to dictate a word list. If the teacher provides enough reassurance, the task of spelling individual words is normally not as intimidating as free composition may be.

The *features list* is a list of words selected to test spellings of certain word features that invoke characteristic invented spelling strategies. The features are such things as long and short vowels, *n*'s and *m*'s before other consonants, unstressed final syllables with *l, r, m,* or *n,* and others. We have set up two levels so that we can test the particular strategies of both younger and older students. The beginners' list (Table 7.2) is designed for children in kindergarten through second grade (though it may be used with older children who are poor spellers). The advanced list (Table 7.3) is for grades three and up (though it may be used with advanced youngsters in lower grades).

When the features list is administered, several conditions should be observed. Assure the children that you do not expect them to know how to spell all, or even *any,* of the words correctly but that you simply want to know how they *think* the words are spelled. You should encourage them to do their best, however, and if they don't know how to spell a whole word, they should try to spell as much of it as they can.

Read the word clearly, illustrate it with a sentence so they understand the meaning, and then repeat the word, but don't *exaggerate* the parts of the words and distort their pronunciation. We once heard a teacher giving a

TABLE 7.2. Beginners' features list (for grades K–2).

1.	late	Kathy was late to school again today.
2.	wind	The wind was loud last night.
3.	shed	The wind blew down our shed.
4.	geese	The geese fly over Texas every fall.
5.	jumped	The frog jumped into the river.
6.	yell	We can yell all we want on the playground.
7.	chirped	The bird chirped when she saw a worm.
8.	once	Jim rode his bike into a creek once.
9.	learned	I learned to count in school.
10.	shove	Don't shove your neighbor when you line up.
11.	trained	I trained my dog to lie down and roll over.
12.	year	Next year you'll have a new teacher.
13.	shock	Electricity can shock you if you aren't careful.
14.	stained	The ice cream spilled and stained my shirt.
15.	chick	The egg cracked open and a baby chick climbed out.
16.	drive	Jim's sister is learning how to drive.

NOTE: With younger children, this list should be administered over two or three sessions. Do not give more than six to eight words in one sitting.

TABLE 7.3. Advanced features list (for grades 3 and up).

1.	setter	My dog is an Irish setter.
2.	shove	Don't shove your neighbor in the lunch line.
3.	grocery	I'm going to the grocery store.
4.	button	A button popped off his jacket.
5.	sailor	A person who sails the seas is a sailor.
6.	prison	If you break the law, you may go to prison.
7.	nature	The park just put in a nature trail.
8.	peeked	The spy peeked out from his hiding place.
9.	special	The store had a special sale on blue jeans.
10.	preacher	The preacher talked for an hour.
11.	slowed	The truck slowed down for the curve.
12.	sail	The boat had a torn sail.
13.	feature	The drive-in showed a double feature.
14.	batter	The first batter struck out.

spelling test say, "Banana, bay-nay-nay." This sort of well-intentioned help is hopelessly confusing to children.

Scoring for the Features List

Scoring on the features list is done holistically; that is, for each word, the teacher makes an overall determination as to whether the spelling is prephonemic, early phonemic, letter-name, transitional, or correct.

To make this determination easier, the categories of spelling errors are summarized below:

1. *Prephonemic spelling.* None of the letters written for a particular word has any apparent relation to any sound in the word. Example: LDLL for *wind*. Give each word spelled prephonetically 1.

2. *Early phonemic spelling.* Sounds *are* represented by letters, according to the letter-name strategy, but *fewer than half of the sounds* are represented, and the missing letters are those that the more advanced letter-name speller would have included. Example: YN, YE, WN, or YBBAR for *wind*. (The *y* can represent the sound /w/ in letter-name spelling; the *w* represents the same sound by conventional spelling.) Each early phonemic spelling is given 2.

3. *Letter-name spelling.* Half (or more) of the sounds in the word are represented by letters. The relation between the letters and sounds rests on the similarity between the sound of the name of the letter and the sound to be represented. Examples: YUTS for *once*, FEHEG for *fishing*. Each letter-name spelling is given 3.

4. *Transitional spelling.* More than half of the sounds in the word are represented, but here *the relation between the letters and the sounds is not based on letter names but on conventions.* Short vowels, consonants, and

digraphs are spelled correctly. Marker letters appear, but they may be used incorrectly. Examples: GETT or GETE for *get;* THAY or THAE for *they.* Each word classified as transitional is given 4.

5. *Correct spelling.* The entire word must be spelled correctly to qualify. If only a minor part of it is incorrect, the spelling is coded as transitional. Correct spellings are given 5.

To score a particular child's paper, the teacher must first classify each spelling into one of these categories. The category in which a majority of the spellings fall represents the strategy or stage of spelling that best describes that child (see Table 7.4).

The child who wrote the words in Table 7.4 was a second grader who had a preprimer instructional reading level. Though some features of stan-

TABLE 7.4. Analysis of beginner's features list: Second grader.

	RESPONSE	TEST WORD	SCORING
1.	LAT	late	3
2.	WND	wind	3
3.	SEAD	shed	4
4.	GEES	geese	4
5.	GOMT	jumped	3
6.	UL	yell	3
7.	CUTP	chirped	3
8.	UOS	once	3
9.	LUD	learned	3
10.	SUF	shove	3
11.	TRAD	trained	3
12.	YER	year	3
13.	SOCK	shock	4
14.	SAD	stained	3
15.	CEK	chick	3
16.	DRIF	drive	3

STAGE	NO. OF EXAMPLES
Prephonemic	0
Early phonemic	0
Letter-name	13
Transitional	3
Correct	0

KEY: 1 = prephonemic, 2 = early phonemic, 3 = letter-name, 4 = transitional, 5 = correct.
NOTE: This eight-year-old second grader is clearly in the letter-name stage of spelling.

TABLE 7.5. Analysis of advanced features list: Fourth grader.

	RESPONSE	TEST WORD	SCORING	STAGE	NO. OF EXAMPLES
1.	SETTER	setter	5	Prephonemic	0
2.	SHUVE	shove	4	Early phonemic	0
3.	GROSHERY	grocery	4	Letter-name	0
4.	BUTTON	button	5	Transitional	9
5.	SAILER	sailor	4	Correct	5
6.	PRIZIN	prison	4		
7.	NATCHER	nature	4		
8.	PEKED	peeked	4		
9.	SPEICLE	special	4		
10.	PRECHER	preacher	4		
11.	SLOWED	slowed	5		
12.	SAIL	sail	5		
13.	FETCHER	feature	4		
14.	BATTER	batter	5		

KEY: 1 = prephonemic, 2 = early phonemic, 3 = letter-name, 4 = transitional, 5 = correct.
NOTE: This ten-year-old fourth grader is predominantly in the transitional stage of spelling.

dard spelling show up in her words (the two *e*'s in GEES, the *ck* in SOCK, she has been remarkably little influenced by her year and a half in school.

In addition to determining a child's predominant spelling strategy, the features list can also be used to identify features of spelling that are causing problems. Note the fourth grader's spelling in Table 7.5. This boy's spelling is transitional, but we can go further and note some specific difficulties. He must learn to preserve long vowels in two-syllable words, as we can see in NATCHER, PRECHER, and FETCHER. He has to become aware of the phonological spellings of *tu* in words like *nature* and *feature*. Also he must learn how the short *u* sound is spelled before *v* (SHUVE).

Must the features list always be scored? No. Scoring it should lead you to scrutinize a child's spelling more carefully than you otherwise would — that is its main advantage. But scores can take on lives of their own. Remember that the judgment is the main thing, not the numbers.

What Spelling Shows Us about Children's Word Knowledge

All of us know at least one well-read adult whose spelling is embarrassingly unorthodox. Because fluent reading is not a letter-by-letter process, it is possible for a person to read words fluently without paying much attention to their spellings. Possibly this explains why some highly literate people are terrible spellers. This is not the norm, however. Children who, early on, possess the word knowledge that enables them to become good spellers tend to become more fluent readers than those who lack this word knowledge. Thus while it is more profitable to look at other measures when investigating older readers' performance, the spelling behavior of younger students can provide valuable insight into their knowledge of written language, knowledge that is of crucial importance for beginning reading.

Prephonemic Spellers

Prephonemic spellers, those who write down letters at random with no thought of the sounds they should represent, are not yet readers. They have not yet discovered the *alphabetic principle* that governs writing: words are divisible into phonemes and letters correspond to the phonemes. Before they make that discovery, direct reading instruction aimed at helping develop sight vocabulary will be fruitless. Instead, use activities aimed at a general orientation to literacy, including reading to these children from books that they enjoy, exercises that call attention to words as units of language (e.g., pointing to words as you read them, framing words with cards — see Don Holdaway's approach to this in Chapter Two), and opportunities to try invented spellings (further teaching suggestions for children in each spelling stage are given in the next section of this chapter).

Early Phonemic Spellers

Early phonemic spellers are those that write one or two letters per word and give up. Other sounds in the words they write should be represented, but aren't. These children are not yet readers, but they are within weeks or months of arriving at the point at which they will begin to pick up sight words rapidly (Morris, 1980). They have discovered the alphabetic principle, but they are not yet adept at phonemic segmentation, dividing words into phonemes. Nor do they yet have a stable concept of a word: they cannot hold a word in their minds long enough to subject it to the sort of rigorous examination that spelling it requires.

Most early phonemic spellers, *if* they are given plentiful opportunities to write, will make progress both in firming up the concept of word and in filling out their spellings, representing more of the sounds in the words they write. However, some children may settle into a strategy of representing only a few sounds per word without really exerting their growing ability to identify sounds in words and match them with letters. These children need careful encouragement to do all they can do in their spelling. It is likely that more attention to spelling the sounds in words will pay off in greater ability at word analysis when the task is word recognition.

Letter-Name Spellers

Letter-name spellers are those who are able to represent most of the sounds they hear in words, with letters chosen for the similarity between the name of the letter and the sound in question. They are in the process of making the bridge into active reading. They have developed a stable concept of word and are adept at segmenting words into phonemes. They are certainly already reading individual words in familiar contexts (e.g., names of chain restaurants), and they may already be reading material with a limited vocabulary, or material for which their reading is heavily supported by background meaning (e.g., dictated experience stories). They have not yet developed a systematic sense of the structure of words in standard English spelling. They are just facing the task of building up a set of generalizations that will help them move from the spelling to the pronunciation of words. That they have not yet formed such generalizations is evident in the highly unorthodox way they have of spelling features of words that are seen very frequently, such as short vowels, *th* and *ch* digraphs, and other features of spelling.

The period of letter-name spelling overlaps the time when most children make their first breakthrough into reading. For a brief, curious period, beginning readers will read words spelled one way and spell them another: a child who can read the word *rain* might spell it RAN, and then later read her or his own spelling as *ran*. Most children's spelling will rapidly fall under the influence of the spelling patterns they see in print, however, and we will see whole words spelled correctly, as well as conventional spelling patterns used incorrectly, showing up in their spelling. As this occurs, the children are, of course, moving into the transitional stage of spelling.

Transitional Spellers

Transitional spellers, those who use conventional spellings for digraphs and long and short vowels and who use some letters silently for markers, have begun to read. In fact, some may have been reading for years (some may be adults!). The spelling patterns they see in their reading have provided them with more or less conventional strategies for rendering English words in print. These renderings make sense: the results are easily readable, though we note that the particular word has been spelled incorrectly, as in "IE THOT YUDE LIEK WHUT IE ROTE."

Armed with the conventions that relate English sounds to spelling, transitional spellers are able to read many words they have not learned before because they can use familiar patterns along with grammatical and semantic cues within the text to translate the graphic symbols into spoken words they know.

Most children remain in the transitional stage of spelling through second and third grade. After that, it is a relative thing: good spellers will spell most of their writing vocabulary correctly, but will use what appear to be transitional spellings for many words at the periphery of their vocabularies. For many students, transitional spelling is difficult to move beyond. To do so seems to require a combination of rote memory and a sensitivity to spelling patterns that go beyond the relation of letters to sounds (Nelson, 1980), especially those patterns that relate spelling to the origins of words (Templeton, 1979).

When children reach the transitional spelling stage, reading and spelling diverge; that is, they may continue to make progress as readers at the same time that they continue to make many spelling errors. As their strategies develop, many students concentrate more on meaning contexts and grammatical structures to recognize words, which reduces the necessity of attending closely to spelling structures of words in order to read them (Gilooley, 1973; Gray, 1956). Thus reading may appear to leave spelling behind, like a childhood friend one has outgrown. Once the transitional stage is reached, it is not particularly productive to analyze spelling to learn about children's reading although it is still useful for its own sake. Spelling errors tend to come in patterns in these students and slowly yield to instruction that stresses spelling patterns in the richer context of grammar, meaning, and word origin (see next section).

Relating Spelling Development and Instruction

Children entering the different stages of early spelling development think differently about written language, and our goals for them differ accordingly. In general, we want to take them from where they are and coax them up through the higher stages, but the strategies for doing so are different for different children.

Teaching Prephonemic Spellers

Prephonemic spellers are usually found in preschool, kindergarten, and early first grade, although occasionally an older child will be a prephonemic speller.

Children in the prephonemic stage are really not spellers at all because they have not advanced very far toward a working grasp of written language. With a four-year-old, this is not surprising or alarming, but with a six-year-old, perhaps a child from a home where no one reads, it is a signal that a rich saturation in written language must begin immediately.

Prephonemic spellers have to be shown that books and magazines carry messages and that the messages are interesting and pleasurable. The best way to do this is by reading to them. Half an hour a day is certainly not too much, even if it preempts so-called skills instruction. At this stage, it is far more important.

It is also important to find out what books they like best, read the same book to them several times, and then leave it in the reading area so they can look through it on their own. If children do not have favorite books at home, find some way to provide them. The *Reading Is Fundamental* program (RIF, The Smithsonian Institution, Washington, D.C. 20560) is one possible source; the local parent-teacher group may be another. Try to get the children and their parents interested in the local public library's programs for young people. Talk to the children's librarian there, so she can pass on word of these offerings to parents.

Prephonemic spellers have to learn that the print in a book conveys a message. As Marie Clay (1979) has pointed out, many youngsters believe the pictures tell the story. Such children have to be taught that print corresponds to words and that it is arranged in lines running left-to-right, top-to-bottom on the page. To get this information across, read familiar books to them and run your finger along the print as you do so. Another valuable procedure is to take dictation from them, perhaps with a group of other children. It will not make readers out of them right away, but it will help them begin to see that there is a relation between language and print.

Prephonemic spellers should be induced to write, even if only in play. When they draw a picture, encourage them to write a caption underneath. Assure them that if they put down whatever they think looks most like what they want to say, they will eventually get the hang of it and learn to write the way writers do. The purpose behind this approach is to put the issue of "making print" squarely before them. They can begin to learn to write by comparing their own graphic productions with the print they see around them.

Teaching Early Phonemic Spellers

Early phonemic spellers know that "print talks" and that letters correspond to phonemes, but they are lacking in three areas:

1. They have only a fragile facility at breaking a spoken word down into phonemes; thus it is difficult for them to match the phonemes with letters.
2. They lack a stable concept of a word in print; it is difficult for them to perform much of a mental operation on a word because words won't hold still for them in their minds.
3. They have not fully worked out which letters should represent which phonemes; in fact, they may not be able to form more than a dozen different letters in print.

The third deficit, not knowing very many letters with which to spell phonemes, will work itself out in the next stage, letter-name spelling. The first two problems are the ones that instruction should deal with at the beginning.

Everything we have recommended for prephonetic spellers is advisable for the early phonemic spellers as well. They still have to be read to, not so much to initiate an interest in written language, but to deepen and broaden such interest. They also need supported encounters with print. Read to them and point to the words as you read. Read a line of print and see if they can read it back to you, pointing to the words as they go. Then point to the first word in the line and see if they can read it; then the last; then one in the middle. This exercise is very important because it leads the children to practice thinking of words as units of print that correspond to units of language that they can speak (see the discussion of voice pointing in Chapters Two and Three).

Early phonemic spellers must have allowances made for their inexperience in writing letters. For example, provide preformed letters for them to use in composing words, such as Milton Bradley's Link Letters. Every kindergarten and first grade should have several boxes of Link Letters readily available because they are excellent for helping children to form words. Plastic letters are more durable, although more expensive.

Encourage them to spell words part by part, spelling what they can and drawing a line for the parts they don't know how to spell (Stauffer, 1980). Thus an early phonemic speller might write M____KT S S____K for "My cat is sick." The important thing is that their uncertainty over some parts need not prevent them from writing something.

Finally, encourage them to write. They should be induced to take risks, to write things as best they can even when they know they cannot be correct. Two specific steps can be taken to encourage risk taking. One is to talk to them about what they are achieving. If they write KT for *cat*, you can congratulate them on hearing the first and last sound in the word. You can also applaud them for putting the last letter to the right of the second, showing a grasp of left-to-right order in writing. Early phonemic spellers know many things about our writing system. Our job is to tune into some of these things, talk about them, and prod the children to make further efforts.

The second specific strategy is to convey your teaching strategies to the parents and to any other teachers who work with these children. Your efforts to get them to write the way they think words are spelled can be seriously undermined by well-meaning parents or teachers who point out that their spelling is wrong. This is likely to happen unless you assure them that a little freedom from mechanics now is very likely to pay off in enthusiasm for and fluency in writing later on.

Teaching Letter-Name Spellers

Letter-name spellers have a stabilizing concept of a word in print, and their phonemic segmentation ability is well developed. At this stage there is a period of exuberant spelling, where invention has reached its highest point and the examples of the correctly spelled words around them are rarely reflected in their own approach to spelling.

The inventions of letter-name spellers look so little like the other words in their environment that it is apparent they are not studying the features of the words they encounter in any detail. Hence it is still too early to teach them very much directly about the spelling patterns of words. It is more productive to wait until the next stage. For now, it is enough to encourage them to write copiously and to help them learn the spellings of interesting words as wholes. We can do this by keeping a variety of stimulating writing tasks before them at all times — not just "Once upon a time" stories, but instructions to friends on how to carry out some activity; suggestions in a suggestion box; secret messages to the teacher; notes on a science experiment; reports on a field trip; letters home; and so forth.

Studying words as wholes can be done in various ways. Word-bank cards are an excellent vehicle (Stauffer, 1980). Cut from 3-by-5-inch index cards, the word-bank cards constitute a tangible record of the words a child can read at sight. Since the words are spelled correctly on the cards, they will enjoy spreading them out and choosing words to use in creative writing. At this stage they will frequently ask someone else how to spell words. When they ask you, tell them, so they can go on creating. If some children seek such help too frequently, encourage them to take a guess. Tell them to write down at least one letter and leave a line for the rest.

Another approach is to write and post word lists on newsprint or on the blackboard after they have had an experience they are eager to write about. Labeling objects around the room is a good idea, as is hanging pictures of favorite objects with captions: motorcycle, starship, skateboard, minibike, etc. Picture dictionaries are also useful.

Teaching Transitional Spellers

Transitional spellers are concerned with the patterns of standard spelling, which is evident from their inclusion of long and short vowel markers and other features that could not arise from invention. Their need is to sort out these conventions and use them correctly. Transitional spellers are found from late first grade on up, including many youngsters in third or fourth grade.

A most productive activity for this group is the word sorting activity described in Chapter Five. Word sorts have two features to recommend them:

1. They employ words the children are very familiar with and thus enable them to see relations between spelling and meaning and grammar, not just spelling and pronunciation.
2. They proceed inductively; that is, children study patterns of words they already know to form generalizations to test against words they do not

know. Thus they have to contend only with generalizations they are able to see in concrete form.

Helping Older Students to Develop Word Knowledge

Older poor spellers often have one thing in common: they try to spell all words the way they sound, and it is no wonder. With all the emphasis given phonics instruction in the early grades and even greater emphasis in many remedial reading programs, it is natural to conclude that spelling is a simple matter of relating letters to sounds. But in order to spell correctly, we have to go well beyond phonics and look very carefully at words. We have to consider what words mean, what other words they are related to, and how they function syntactically. We also have to be open and curious about our written language, learn something of its history, and be sufficiently reflective to apply our learning to spelling.

There is more involved than memorizing hundreds of spellings, although that in itself does provide patterns that can be extended to the spelling of unknown words. We have to do more than memorize dozens of phonics rules and all their exceptions. We should be curious about language, explore it, and play with it to see how it works.

Many approaches to word study can be useful. Word games of all sorts, whether they play on meaning or structure, are recommended: Perquackey, Boggle, Spill 'n Spell, Hangman, Password, and other commercially available games. Frequent trips to the dictionary can also be beneficial. Raise regularly challenging questions that can be resolved by the dictionary, for example:

"What do *nature* and *national* have to do with each other?"
"Why are the *u*'s in *united* and *uninterested* pronounced differently?"
"Where does the word *boycott* come from?"

At least one dictionary in the classroom should have etymologies. There are also many fascinating books that tell stories about the origin of words. The linguist Mario Pei has written fact-filled books on words, language, and the English language in particular for a general audience (1952, 1962). Wilfred Funk's *Word Origins and Their Romantic Stories* (1950) and Charles Funk's *Thereby Hangs a Tale: Hundreds of Stories of Curious Word Origins* (1972) are amusing, engaging introductions to etymology. *Word People* (Sorel, 1970) is similar. A more difficult, but perhaps even more informative, book on the background of our language and its relation to other languages is Lancelot Hogben's *The Mother Tongue* (1964). Geared to a high school audience, it is a fascinating excursion into, among other sources, the Latin, Greek, and Old English roots of our language.

Etymological dictionaries provide information on word origins, original meanings of words, and the relationships among words. Some paperback versions are available at moderate cost. Perhaps the best of these is the Dover reprint of Ernest Weekley's *Etymological Dictionary of Modern English* (1967).

Summary

Mature reading, utilizing as it does syntactic structures, information structures, and words recognized as wholes, is not a letter-by-letter operation, but beginning reading makes fairly heavy use of spelling patterns. More specifically, it demands some working familiarity with the alphabet, the ability to think about and mentally manipulate words (the concept of word), and the ability to mentally isolate component sounds in words (phonemic segmentation). All three of these abilities are demonstrated in *invented spelling*. Since children can begin invented spelling before they begin to read, it serves as an early indicator of the development of some centrally important prereading competencies.

Spelling growth advances developmentally, and progress is related to the emergence of prereading competencies as well as the child's reading and writing experience. Spelling ability advances through recognizable stages. These stages, and the reading advancement related to each one, are as follows:

1. *Prephonemic spelling*. At this stage children have a notion of what written language ought to look like, but they have not discovered the phonetic principle, the link between letters and speech sounds. These youngsters may be a year or more away from beginning to read.

2. *Early phonemic spelling*. At this point children have discovered the phonetic principle and try to spell words by matching phonemes (speech sounds) with letters of the alphabet. The matching of letters is incomplete, however, because of an unstable concept of word or undeveloped ability to segment phonemes in words. Early phonemic spellers are approaching beginning reading and are often within a few months of the period when rapid sight word acquisition begins.

3. *Letter-name spelling*. At this stage children give full renditions of the sounds in words by matching them with letters of the alphabet according to the similarity between the speech sound and the letter name. Letter-name spellers are just at the threshold of beginning reading; they may begin to read while still using the letter-name strategy to write.

4. *Transitional spelling*. Children in this group have begun to read and are aware of the spelling patterns on which standard English writing is based. These standard patterns begin to show up in short vowel spellings, silent letters, and consonant digraphs, but the patterns are not used with full accuracy and the words are often still misspelled. Transitional spelling is not very informative in reading assessment, although children in third grade or above who are still transitional spellers may lack exposure to written materials and an awareness of the patterns of written language.

5. *Correct spelling*. These children have memorized the spellings of some

words and learned to employ those patterns to spell other words. Correct spelling varies, of course, with the level of difficulty of the word. Faced with too difficult a word, normally correct spellers may revert to phonetic strategies or give up altogether.

The various levels of development can be determined by using a *features list*, which is designed to elicit spelling errors. These errors can be analyzed according to the strategy that seems to have produced them, and the teacher can make an approximate judgment as to a child's level of development. Features lists for young children (kindergarten to grade two) and older children (grade three and up) were included in this chapter.

Instructional strategies should be based on the stages of development. At first, the strategies should build competencies that are important both to reading and writing, such as an orientation to written language, the concept of word, and the ability to segment phonemes in words. Later, the instruction should work on sensitizing children to letter-sound patterns in words and eventually to grammatical considerations and spelling concerns related to scribal traditions, etymologies, and pronunciation habits.

Extension Activities

1. The following spellings were written by an eight-year-old boy in response to the beginner's features list (see Beginner's Features List).
   a. Using the categories and scoring system described in the chapter (see pages 297–302), decide which stage of spelling this child is in.
   b. Where would you say he might be in his reading development?
   c. What learning activities would you recommend for him?
2. The following responses were given for the advanced features list by an eleven-year-old girl (see Advanced Features List).
   a. Where is she in her spelling development?
   b. What features of spelling does she need to learn?
   c. What learning activities would you recommend?
3. Study the teachers' manuals of the first two or three levels of a locally used commercial spelling program. How do those teaching instructions and activities compare with the stage theory of development described here? How would you predict young children would spell some of the required words if they hadn't memorized them? On the basis of your prediction, how would you advise a teacher using these materials?
4. Go back and review the word sorting procedure in Chapter Five. Using words that children in an age group of your choice are likely to know, write up sets of about twenty cards each that could be used in word sorts to study:
   a. *o*'s around *v*'s, and so forth (page 296–297)
   b. phonological spelling changes (page 295)
   c. consonant doubling (page 297)
   d. vowel reduction (page 295–296)

BEGINNER'S FEATURES LIST

	TEST WORD	RESPONSE	STAGE	NO. OF EXAMPLES
1.	late	LAT	Prephonemic	
2.	wind	WNED	Early phonemic	
3.	shed	SHUED	Letter-name	
4.	geese	GAEESE	Transitional	
5.	jumped	JUNPT	Correct	
6.	yell	HALL		
7.	chirped	HRED		
8.	once	ONES		
9.	learned	LRNED		
10.	shove	SHUV		
11.	trained	TRANED		
12.	year	YERE		
13.	shock	SHIK		
14.	stained	STANED		
15.	chick	CHEK		
16.	drive	DRIVE		

ADVANCED FEATURES LIST

	TEST WORD	RESPONSE	STAGE	NO. OF EXAMPLES
1.	setter	SETTER	Prephonemic	
2.	shove	SHUV	Early phonemic	
3.	grocery	GROSRY	Letter-name	
4.	button	BUTTER	Transitional	
5.	sailor	SALER	Correct	
6.	prison	PRESEN		
7.	nature	NACHER		
8.	peeked	PECKED		
9.	special	SPESHEL		
10.	preacher	PRECHER		
11.	slowed	SLOWED		
12.	sail	SALE		
13.	feature	FECHER		
14.	batter	BATTER		

Suggested Readings

Bissex, Glenda. **GNYS AT WRK: A Child Learns to Write and Read.** *Cambridge, Mass.: Harvard University Press, 1980.* A teacher-mother's account of her son's journey to literacy.

Chomsky, Carol. **"Approaching Reading Through Invented Spelling."** *In Lauren Resnick and Phyllis Weaver, eds. Theory and Practice of Beginning Reading, Vol. 2. Hillsdale, N.J.: Lawrence Erlbaum Associates, 1979.* Advocates encouraging children to explore writing as a means of developing prereading competencies.

Henderson, Edmund and Beers, James, eds. **Developmental and Cognitive Aspects of Learning to Spell.** *Newark, Del.: International Reading Association, 1980.* These papers discuss children's spelling and word knowledge as well as teaching strategies.

Read, Charles and Hodges, Richard. **"Spelling."** *The Encyclopedia of Educational Research (1982, in press).* A recent definitive compilation of research findings on spelling and how it is learned.

Temple, Charles, Nathan, Ruth, and Burris, Nancy. **The Beginnings of Writing.** *Boston: Allyn and Bacon, 1982.* Four chapters provide a detailed coverage of invented spelling, and teaching word study.

References

Beers, James, and Henderson, E. H. "A Study of Developing Orthographic Concepts Among First Graders." *Research in the Teaching of English* 11 (Fall 1977): 133–148.

Bollinger, Dwight. *Aspects of Language,* 2nd ed. Cambridge, Mass.: Harvard University Press, 1975.

Chall, Jeanne. "The Great Debate: Ten Years Later, with a Modest Proposal for Reading Stages," in Lauren Resnick and Phyllis Weaver, eds. *Theory and Practice of Early Reading,* Vol. 1. Hillsdale, N.J.: Erlbaum, 1979.

Chomsky, Carol. "Invented Spelling in the Open Classroom." *Word* 27, Nos. 1–3 (April–Dec. 1971): 499–518.

Chomsky, Carol. "Approaching Reading Through Invented Spelling," in Lauren Resnick and Phyllis Weaver, eds. *Theory and Practice of Early Reading,* Vol. 2. Hillsdale, N.J.: Erlbaum, 1979.

Chomsky, Noam. "Phonology and Reading," in Harry Levin, ed. *Basic Studies on Reading.* New York: Holt, Rinehart & Winston, 1970.

Chomsky, Noam, and Halle, Morris. *The Sound Pattern of English.* New York: Harper & Row, 1968.

Clay, Marie. *Reading: The Patterning of Complex Behavior,* 2nd ed. Exeter, N.H.: Heinemann Educational Books, 1979.

Doehring, Donald G., and Aulls, Mark W. "The Interactive Nature of Reading Acquisition." *Journal of Reading Behavior* 11, No. 1 (Spring 1979): 27–40.

Ehri, Linnea. "The Development of Orthographic Images," in Uta Frith, ed. *Cognitive Processes in Spelling.* N.Y.: Academic Press, 1980.

Frith, Uta, and Frith, Christopher. "Relationships Between Reading and Spelling," in James Kavanaugh and Richard Venezky, eds. *Orthography, Reading and Dyslexia.* Baltimore: University Park Press, 1980.

Funk, Charles E. *Thereby Hangs a Tale: Hundreds of Stories of Curious Word Origins.* New York: Warner Paperback Library, 1972.

Funk, Wilfred. *Word Origins and their Romantic Stories.* New·York: Bell, 1950.

Gentry, J. Richard. "A Study of the Orthographic Strategies of Beginning Readers." (doctoral dissertation, University of Virginia, 1977). *Dissertation Abstracts International* 39 (1979): 4017-A. (University Microfilms order no. 7901152).

Gentry, J. Richard. "Early Spelling Strategies." *Elementary School Journal* 79, No. 2 (November 1978): 88–92.

Gentry, J. Richard. "Learning to Spell Developmentally." *The Reading Teacher* 34, No. 4 (January 1981): 378–381.

Gilooley, William. "The Influence of Writing System Characteristics on Learning to Read." *Reading Research Quarterly* 8, No. 2 (Winter 1973): 167–199.

Gray, William S. *The Teacher of Reading and Writing.* Chicago: Scott Foresman (for UNESCO), 1956.

Henderson, Edmund H. "Developmental Concepts of Word," in E. H. Henderson and J. W. Beers, eds. *Developmental and Cognitive Aspects of Learning to Spell.* Newark, Del.: International Reading Association, 1980.

Henderson, Edmund H., and Beers, James W., eds. *Developmental and Cognitive Aspects of Learning to Spell.* Newark, Del.: International Reading Association, 1980.

Hogben, Lancelot. *The Mother Tongue.* New York: Norton, 1964.

Langacker, Ronald W. *Language and Its Structure: Some Fundamental Linguistic Concepts,* 2nd ed. New York: Harcourt, 1973.

Liberman, Isabelle, Liberman, Alvin, Mattingly, Ignatius, and Shankweiler, Donald. "Orthography and the Beginning Reader," in James Cavanaugh and Richard Venezky, eds. *Orthography, Reading and Dyslexia.* Baltimore: University Park Press, 1980.

Liberman, Isabelle Y., Shankweiler, Donald, Fischer, F. W., and Carter, B. "Explicit Syllable and Phoneme Segmentation in the Young Child." *Journal of Experimental Child Psychology* 18 (1974): 201–212.

Morris, R. Darrell. "Beginning Readers' Concept of Word," in E. H. Henderson and J. W. Beers, eds. *Cognitive and Developmental Aspects of Learning to Spell.* Newark, Del.: International Reading Association, 1980.

Nelson, Hazel E. "Analysis of Spelling Errors in Normal and Dyslexic Children," in Uta Frith, ed. *Cognitive Processes in Spelling.* New York: Academic Press, 1980.

Pei, Mario. *The Story of English.* Philadelphia: Lippincott, 1952.

Pei, Mario. *The Families of Words.* New York: St. Martin's, 1962.

Read, Charles. "Preschool Children's Knowledge of English Phonology." *Harvard Educational Review* 41 (1971): 1–34.

Read, Charles. *Children's Categorization of Speech Sounds in English.* National Council of Teachers of English Research Report No. 17. Urbana, Ill.: National Council of Teachers of English, 1975.

Scragg, D. G. *A History of English Spelling.* New York: Manchester University Press, 1974.

Sorel, Nancy. *Word People.* New York: American Heritage Press, 1970.

Stauffer, Russell G. *The Language-Experience Approach to Beginning Reading,* revised ed. New York: Harper & Row, 1980.

Temple, Charles, Nathan, Ruth, and Burris, Nancy. *The Beginnings of Writing.* Boston: Allyn & Bacon, 1982.

Temple, Charles, and Salminen, Jaakko. "Invented Spelling in Finnish First, Second and Third Graders." Unpublished manuscript. Victoria, Texas: University of Houston-Victoria, 1981.

Templeton, Shane. "Spelling First, Sound Later: The Relationship Between Orthography and Higher Order Phonological Knowledge in Older Students." *Research in the Teaching of English* 13, No. 3 (1979): 255–264.

Vallins, G. H. *Spelling.* Philadelphia: Richard West, 1954.

Venezky, Richard. *The Structure of English Orthography.* The Hague: Mouton, 1970.

Weekley, Ernest. *An Etymological Dictionary of Modern English.* New York: Dover, 1967.

Chapter Eight

Formal Measures of Reading Ability

The purpose of Chapter Eight is to help answer these questions:

☐ What are the major types of reading-related standardized tests?
☐ How do I interpret these tests to derive the information I need?
☐ How can I use these scores to improve the reading ability of my students?

Standardized tests of various kinds are widely administered in all subject areas, but it is often difficult to make some sense out of the many kinds of tests and the many ways in which they yield results.

This chapter covers two basic kinds of measurement devices: *norm-referenced tests* and *criterion-referenced tests*. Within those generic categories we discuss different kinds of tests given for different purposes, some basic concepts of measurement such as the reliability and validity of tests, how scores are distributed, and how to interpret various forms of test scores.

All teachers, regardless of grade or subject, must know how to evaluate tests and interpret their results. This chapter is aimed toward developing a critical awareness of the characteristics, strengths, and limitations of formal reading tests.

Basic Test Concepts

There are over two thousand educational tests available. A measurement expert has estimated that at least 200 million standardized achievement tests are given yearly, as well as hundreds of thousands of standardized diagnostic, survey, aptitude, and other types of tests (Gronlund, 1976). Every teacher must understand basic test concepts in order to interpret different kinds of numerical results of standardized tests.

There are two qualities that every reading (or other) test should possess: *reliability*, the degree of consistency of test scores, and *validity*, the degree to which a test measures what it is supposed to measure.

Reliability

Reliability is a measure of how stable test scores are. It refers to the results obtained from a test, not to the test itself. There are several aspects of reliability to be considered. One is *stability*, or the consistency of test scores across time, from one administration to another with the same group of subjects. Another is *internal consistency*, or the consistency of items within a test. A third is *equivalence*, or consistency across different forms of the same test.

Stability. If a group of students took Test 1 several times, each individual's score would be somewhat different each time. If the scores are consistent, or reliable, their *rank order* would remain very similar from one testing to another. Therefore, the student with the highest score the first time would have the highest, or nearly the highest, score the second time; the student with the lowest score would retain very low standing, and the order of students between highest and lowest would remain nearly unchanged (Thorndike and Hagen, 1977). If stability is lacking, a score attained once is unrelated to the score attained another time. Obviously, such scores would have little meaning or usefulness, because they would be heavily affected by random chance.

Stability can be built into a test in several ways. One way is through standardized administration procedures: administering the tests at the same time of day under the same or highly similar physical conditions and utilizing identical directions, examples, and time limits.

Another, more important, way of building in stability involves the nature of the test itself. It must be developed so that students will rank about the same each time the test is given to them. Test length is a critical factor.

Generally speaking, the longer a test is, the more reliable the scores from it will be (Sax, 1980). Since any test represents only a sampling of what students know and can do, a longer test yields a more accurate estimate of their capabilities. On a longer test with many items, random effects tend to cancel out. Therefore, random chance has less effect on the total score of a long test vis-à-vis a short one.

Of course, there are limits to *how* long it should be. A test with 50 items will yield more reliable scores than one with only 5 items, but a test with 500 items will only exhaust those trying to take it. There is no particular rule of thumb for length, but standardized test developers try out different lengths and add or delete items to arrive at an optimum length.

Stability is estimated using the *test-retest method*. The same test is given twice to the same group of subjects, and the rank order of their scores on each one is compared. If the interval between administrations is fairly short, students will remember a number of items and will be familiar with the format. This method will tend to raise everyone's scores, but the rank order of the scores will remain much the same. The rank order of the scores, not the numerical value of the scores themselves, is what is important here. If the interval between administrations is very long, maturation and the acquiring of new information will affect performance.

Internal Consistency. Internal consistency refers to the degree to which items within a test are related. We can determine internal consistency by comparing a student's performance on an entire test to his or her performance on two halves of the same test administered separately, but since the more difficult items often come toward the end, it would not be a good practice to split a test at the middle. Instead, alternate items should be selected: one-half with all the odd-numbered items, the other half with all the even-numbered items. If the scores on each half are closely related, a measure of good internal consistency has been provided. If performance on the two halves is not closely related, the total test score will not be reliable, and its value is questionable.

Sometimes internal consistency is estimated by the *split-half method* in which students take the two halves of a test as separate tests. The scores on each half are correlated, and an arithmetic formula is applied to relate the correlation to the entire test. Other ways of estimating internal consistency involve giving the whole test once and applying one of several arithmetic formulas to the total score. These computations are beyond the scope of this discussion, but you will find detailed information in almost any text on tests and measurement methods.

Equivalence. When alternate forms of a test are being used, equivalence is important. Many standardized reading tests feature alternative forms that are used for pre- and posttesting, but they must be highly equivalent for the scores to have any usefulness.

The *equivalent forms method* is used to estimate this aspect of reliability. It requires the construction of two different tests, each one an equally good sampling of the content being tested. Each form must also be equivalent in difficulty and length. The two forms are administered to the same students in close succession, and the scores on the two forms are correlated. This method usually yields the most conservative estimate of reliability.

Every standardized reading test being considered for use should have reported reliability estimates, and it should indicate what methods were used to determine such estimates. Reliability can be expressed in numerical terms by a *reliability coefficient*. This coefficient, a decimal number between zero and one, shows how consistent the scores were after using the test-retest, split-halves, or equivalent forms assessments. The closer to 1.0 the reliability coefficient is, the more reliable the scores. Some experts recommend that for evaluation of a single student, a test should have an overall reliability coefficient of at least .90; somewhat lower figures would be acceptable if the test is to evaluate groups of students rather than individuals. In the case of groups, the overall reliability estimate should not be less than about .70. If it is, you should look for another test.

Overall reliability can be profoundly affected, for good or bad, by the consistency of individual subtests. Survey reading tests, generally used for screening large numbers of students, usually have few subtests, and the expressed reliability coefficients refer to the test as a whole. Quite a few reading achievement tests and most standardized reading diagnostic tests, however, have many separate subtests, and the reliability of subtest scores can vary widely. These tests should have reported subtest reliabilities as well as a coefficient for the entire test, and scores on subtests of questionable reliability must be discounted. If a test under consideration has more than one or two subtests of low reliability, another one should be considered.

A final point about judging reliability concerns the standard error of

Tests are one of the primary means schools use to measure students' progress. But test results should always be supplemented by observation, informal assessments, and ongoing class work.

measurement. This term does not mean there are mistakes in the test; it refers to the fact that no score is absolutely precise. The standard error of measurement (SE) is a number that indicates how much an individual's score might have varied depending on random chance factors. Take, for example, a test with a reported SE of plus or minus three points (± 3) and a student with a raw score of 67. We can be about 70 percent sure that the student's true score lies somewhere between 64 and 70. If we double the SE to ± 6, we can be 90 percent sure that the student's true score lies between 61 and 73 (Bertrand and Cebula, 1980).

The standard error shows numerically how accurate any score is likely to be. A small standard error indicates high reliability, because we can be fairly confident that the student's test score and the true score closely approximate each other.

Validity

High reliability is necessary, but not sufficient, for a test to be a good one. A test can yield consistent scores but still not truly measure what was intended to be measured. This quality of actually measuring what was supposed to be measured is referred to as *test validity*. There are several types of validity that are often referred to in test reviews and manuals, and teachers should understand how validity is developed in test evaluation. While reliability is quantitatively estimated, validity involves qualitative judgments as well.

Content Validity. In assessing content validity, we ask if the test is an adequate sample of the content area or process being tested. Content validity is particularly important in achievement tests, which are designed to show subject mastery (Mehrens and Lehmann, 1978). An elementary spelling achievement test with only very long, difficult, infrequently used words from college texts would lack content validity because it does not represent what elementary children study in spelling. Content validity is established when test makers study both school curricula and tests and submit their tests to the scrutiny of subject area experts. Some authorities claim, however, that many reading achievement tests lack content validity because they measure only a narrow range of real reading behaviors.

Construct Validity. Human traits or qualities that are not directly observable or measurable, but which are widely inferred from behaviors, are called *constructs*. Running speed or hand width are directly observable or measurable entities. Traits like attitudes, intelligence, or aptitudes are not directly measurable and must be inferred from observable behaviors. Thus intelligence, musical or mechanical aptitude, judgment, problem solving, attitudes, and interests are constructs.

If a test has good construct validity, it allows the student to demonstrate behaviors directly related to the construct. In a test of attitudes toward reading, for example, students should be able to show how positively or negatively they would feel about getting a book for a gift, hearing a book discussed, going to the library or bookstore, or seeing someone vandalizing a book. Construct validity is important in all tests, but it is critical in psychological and personality tests and attitude inventories.

Criterion-Related Validity. Another way of establishing a test's validity is to relate it to other validated measures of the same ability or knowledge. The predetermined *criterion* may be other test scores, grades or subject area performance, or other observable behaviors. A test has criterion-related validity if it calls for responses that relate closely to actual performance. Concurrent and predictive validity are criterion-related.

When a new test is found to be highly correlated to an existing test of established validity, it is said to have *concurrent validity*. Coefficients of concurrent validity are frequently reported by test makers. Just because two tests are closely related is no guarantee that either one is valid, only that they measure the same attribute.

When a score is found to be closely related to later performance on some criterion, the test is said to have *predictive validity*. This aspect is critically important in aptitude tests, since they purport to determine whether someone has the potential to become skilled in a particular field at a later time. If students who do well on a test of mechanical aptitude later excel in school courses like "shop" and drafting and then go on to college engineering and technical schools or seek careers as engineers, architects, and machinists, that test is a good predictor of mechanical aptitude. The Scholastic Aptitude

Test (SAT), used to predict the potential of high school students for college studies, is believed to be high in predictive validity because SAT scores and subsequent college grade-point averages are closely related.

Simple Descriptive Statistics

Standardized tests often yield numerical information in statistical terms that must be understood for appropriate interpretation, and although teachers don't usually have to compute statistics, they must understand some of the basic principles.

Distributions. This term refers to the span or array of test scores achieved by any group. From highest to lowest, scores are "distributed" across a range of numbers. The nature of this distribution is an important concept.

If a large number of people were assessed according to some attribute and their scores were rank-ordered, they would form a distribution. Let's say we measured the height of a hundred adult men and women and asked them to stand on a line with the tallest person at one end and the shortest at the other. At each end of the line, the extremes, there would be a few very tall and a few very short people; toward the middle there would be many people of average height all clustered together.

A symmetrical distribution with many scores in the middle and a few

FIGURE 8.1. **Normal distribution.**

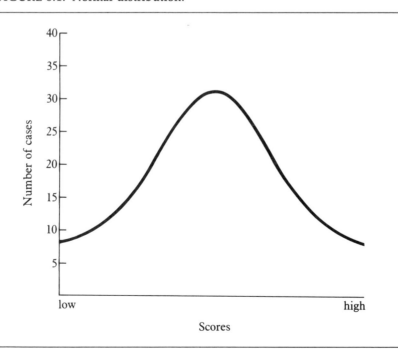

arrayed at the extremes is called a *normal distribution*. It is sometimes called a *bell-shaped curve* because it looks like a bell (see Figure 8.1).

The normal distribution is a hypothetical construct similar to the distribution of scores on most standardized tests and similar to many human characteristics, like height. If large numbers of people are assessed, the scores may approach the normal distribution on many attributes. If a distribution is normal, or is assumed to approach this model, we know that most of the scores will be clustered around the center with progressively fewer and fewer scores arrayed near or at the two extremes. Test makers and publishers use this distribution to report individual scores in a variety of ways, which we will discuss in the next section.

Not all distributions are normal. Instead of most of the scores clustering in the middle, a test may yield a distribution with many very high or very low scores. This is called a *skewed* distribution; it is asymmetrical. (see Figure 8.2.) If most people get high scores, with few average or low scores, the distribution would be skewed toward the high end of the scale. Likewise, a test yielding many low and few average or high scores is skewed toward the low end of the scale. A negatively skewed distribution usually means the test is too difficult for the intended testees; that is, most of them got low scores (Mehrens and Lehmann, 1978).

Indices of Central Tendency. Scores are most often thought of in relation to where they lie on a distribution. Two important indices of central tendency are the mean and median, which are used in computing grade-equivalent scores.

FIGURE 8.2. Skewed distributions.

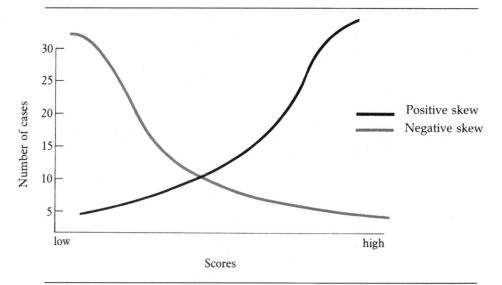

A *mean* is an arithmetic *average* calculated by adding all scores and dividing the sum by the number of scores used.

The *median* is the point in a distribution where there are equal numbers of scores above and below it. If we had scores of 14, 15, 16, and 17 the median would be 15.5, with two scores below that point and two above it. In general, the closer together the mean and median are, the more symmetrical the distribution will be.

Indices of Dispersion. This term refers to ways of numerically indicating how spread out a set of scores are. Two indices of dispersion are the range and the standard deviation.

The *range* indicates the span of scores attained, from highest to lowest. It is calculated by subtracting the lowest from the highest score. The range is less informative than the standard deviation.

The *standard deviation* is an index of how spread out scores are around the mean, regardless of the shape of the distribution. For convenience, we will return to the normal distribution concept to illustrate the standard deviation.

In a normal distribution we said that most of the scores would be grouped near the mean. How many is "most"? How near is "near"? Statisticians have determined that 68 percent of the scores would be arrayed around or at the mean, with smaller percentages near the extremes, as in Figure 8.3.

If a student's score was 1SD below the mean, we would know where the score lay on the distribution; we would know that the student did as well or better than 16 percent of the norm group but that 84 percent did better. The range around the mean, from –1SD to +1SD, is considered the average range. A score of –1SD would be at the bottom of the average range.

The concepts of mean and standard deviation are integral in understanding how most scores such as those described below are reported.

FIGURE 8.3. **Percentages of scores within standard deviation (SD) units.**

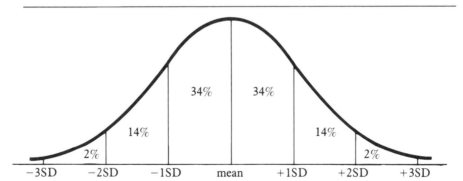

Forms of Test Scores. A *raw score* is the total number of correct items on a test or subtest. Raw scores are usually converted to another form to facilitate comparisons.

Grade-equivalent scores, often called simply *grade scores,* are frequently used in reporting reading test scores. They represent a level of achievement considered average for a particular grade and month of school within that grade. Grade scores are expressed in two-part numbers; the first number indicates the grade level, and the second number indicates the month within that grade. A grade score of 3.1, for example, stands for the first month, September, of third grade.

Grade scores infer that there is some objective, generally accepted standard of achievement for every month of each school grade. In reality, no such agreement exists on what skills or competencies should be attained by all, or most, readers at any given point. Such expectations are too heavily influenced by local standards, curricular goals, scope and sequences of skills within commercial programs, and learner characteristics for there to be any one standard of achievement. Grade scores are often considered, and interpreted to parents, however, as though there *were* such objective standards. Thus, they are often overinterpreted.

Percentiles, another common form of score, are more easily understood than grade scores. Percentiles range from 1 to 99; wherever a score lies within this range indicates relative performance compared with the norm group. A score at the tenth percentile means the student did better than 10 percent but worse than 89 percent of the students in the norm group. A score at the ninety-eighth percentile means that the student did better than 98 percent of the norm group and that only 1 percent attained higher scores. Sometimes percentile scores are misinterpreted by parents who believe the score represents the number of items correctly answered. Such a parent, whose child scored at the fiftieth percentile, would judge that the child had gotten only 50 percent of the items right, instead of correctly viewing the score as average.

Stanines are similar to percentiles; the term is derived from "standard nines," which means that the distribution of possible scores has been divided into nine equal parts. Stanine scores range from one to nine; five is the mean, and scores from just below four to just above six are considered average.

T scores and *z scores* are fairly common standard scores. They indicate how close to the mean of the normal distribution a score lies. T scores range from a low of 20 to a high of 80, with a mean of 50 and a standard deviation of 10. z scores use positive and negative numbers distributed around a mean of zero with a standard deviation of 1; z scores between -1.0 and $+1.0$ are considered average.

Norm-Referenced Tests

Norm-referenced tests are developed by publishers who administer them to large numbers of students in order to develop *norms*. The norms represent average performances of many students in various age, grade, and demographic groups and are used to compare the performance of individuals or special groups to the performance of those in the norm group.

Some test makers go to great lengths to include students from various geographic areas, urban and rural communities, racial and ethnic groups, and economic groups. Many tests feature several different sets of norms for local groups that are unlike "national averages" — for example, center-city schools, rural populations, high-achieving gifted populations, highly affluent areas, and the like.

The information yielded by norm-referenced tests is primarily quantitative, which has relatively little diagnostic value but is useful for comparing achievement patterns. The scores on standardized diagnostic tests must be combined with qualitative information, however, if they are to have real diagnostic usefulness.

Norm-referenced reading tests generally fall into three rough categories: (a) *survey tests*, screening devices that feature a few broad, general subtests and yield a small number of global scores; (b) *diagnostic tests*, given to show skill strengths and needs, with a number of subtests assessing particular skills and yielding a half dozen or more subtest scores; and (c) general *reading achievement tests*, which are given to assess past learning rather than for diagnostic purposes.

Survey Tests

Survey tests are most commonly used to screen large numbers of students for approximate reading levels and identify those with severe problems. Their purpose is to determine general, overall levels of proficiency rather than to pinpoint specific skill strengths and needs.

Because they are intended to be general rather than specific, survey reading tests usually have from one to four subtests, and the subtest scores are combined into a total reading score. Subtests are usually for comprehension and vocabulary, although some include reading speed or study skills.

Survey tests are quite simple to administer to large groups. Because they have few subtests, there are fewer sets of directions, examples, and time limits to monitor. They can easily be given by the regular classroom teacher with no special preparation beyond a careful reading of the test manual, and they can usually be completed in one sitting. They can be scored by hand or by machine. The manuals include tables for conversion of raw scores to standard scores, usually grade scores, percentiles, and stanines.

Some typical group survey tests are the Gates-MacGinitie Reading Tests, Iowa Silent Reading Test, Metropolitan Reading Test, and the reading sections of the Comprehensive Test of Basic Skills and the California Achievement Test.

Advantages. First, they can be administered to large groups. Second, they can usually be completed in a short time, often in one sitting. Third, they are usually easy to administer and score without special preparation. Fourth, they are useful for screening large numbers of students to identify those who are reading very poorly; for example, a survey test might be given to all entering sixth graders in a consolidated middle school. Fifth, test manuals generally allow simple conversion of raw scores to several kinds of common standard scores, which facilitates comparisons of different groups. Many publishers supply norms for special populations as well as national norms.

Disadvantages. First, because of their very general nature they often lack content depth. Scores are yielded in very broad areas like reading comprehension and knowledge of vocabulary, but low scores in these areas do little to indicate specifically what the student knows or has trouble with. When subtest scores are combined into a general reading score, it is difficult to interpret precisely what abilities the score represents. Some experts advocate examining individual items on a survey test to determine a student's specific strengths and weaknesses, but this would be so time-consuming that it would negate the survey's advantage of time economy.

Second, grade scores frequently overestimate reading ability. They are supposed to represent instructional levels, but more often than not they show the student's *frustration* level. If the scores are used to place children at a proper textbook level, a common use, they will often end up overplaced, thus leading to frustration and discouragement. This is a misuse of survey test scores.

A third disadvantage is related to the second. Most survey tests use a multiple-choice format, which allows a student to get some items correct by guessing. Scores are derived by adding the number of correct items, including those answered correctly by chance as well as by true understanding; therefore the scores will be inflated. If items have three alternative multiple-choice responses, students could answer correctly 33 percent of the time even if they guessed at every item. For the typical, four-alternative response, a student's guesses on all items could lead to a 25 percent rate of correct response.

Fourth, because survey reading tests are intended for large general populations, they tend to be better estimates of true ability for students with average performance than for either very good or very poor readers. The scores at either the high or low end of the performance scale are less accurate: superior readers are often underestimated while very poor readers can get scores years above their actual instructional levels. Although survey tests can be useful in identifying very poor readers, a low score indicates only that a reading difficulty exists, but it does not reveal the nature or degree of the difficulty.

Diagnostic Tests

Because survey reading tests offer little in terms of diagnosis, standardized *diagnostic tests* are often given to those students performing poorly on a survey test.

Diagnostic tests differ from survey tests in three major ways (Gronlund, 1976): (a) they have a large number of subtest scores (sometimes called "part scores") and a larger number of items; (b) the items are devised to measure specific skills; and (c) difficulty tends to be lower in order to provide adequate discrimination among students with reading problems.

Diagnostic tests, both the group and individual types, have numerous subtests and yield a profile of scores. Each subtest assesses a particular skill area. Developers of these tests maintain that analysis of a profile of subtest scores will reveal strengths and weaknesses in skill areas and that it is this analysis that makes them more "diagnostic" than survey tests.

Diagnostic tests for group administration frequently include subtests assessing some or most of the following skills: reading comprehension, vocabulary, visual and auditory discrimination, structural analysis, numerous aspects of phonic analysis, sound blending, skimming and scanning, syllabication, sight word recognition, and spelling. Because of the number of separate subtests, they usually have to be administered in several sittings.

A typical group diagnostic test is the Stanford Diagnostic Reading Test. The Stanford, testing grades one through thirteen with four levels and two alternate forms of each level, includes subtests assessing auditory discrimination, word meanings, phonic and structural analysis, and literal and inferential comprehension. Levels for grade four and above include reading speed and skimming and scanning subtests. Scores are reported in grade scores, percentiles, and stanines. The Stanford test takes about two hours to administer.

There are also a number of diagnostic tests for individual use, many of which focus on one or two particular aspects, such as word recognition or phonic analysis skills. Others are like informal reading inventories in that they assess word recognition and comprehension with word lists and story passages. Some attempt a broad-based analysis of skills while others cover a narrower range of skills. When the latter type is used, several different tests must be given in order to derive a more complete picture of a reader's strengths and needs.

Some tests focus on word recognition or oral reading only. The Slosson Oral Reading Test (SORT) is one of the most extreme of these. Its name is misleading because it is not a test of oral reading as most of us would define that term. It is made up entirely of lists of words in isolation. The student pronounces each word in an untimed presentation. No attempt is made to assess knowledge of word meanings since the words are in lists and there is no reading comprehension involved. On the basis of sheer word pronunciation, the SORT purports to furnish an instructional reading level for each student. The instructional level, however, must be based on comprehension ability, and so the reading level this test yields is largely useless.

Several individual tests assess oral reading skill in a slightly broader sense than the SORT. The Gray Oral Reading Test and the Gilmore Oral Reading Test assess recognition of words in context, oral reading fluency, and accuracy. Comprehension questions are usually asked, but in both the Gray and the Gilmore comprehension is not reflected in the score. When comprehension questions are included, these tests take about as long to administer as the oral passages of an IRI, but the results are less helpful because there is no direct assessment of comprehension.

There are a number of "standardized IRIs" that are more comprehensive than the oral reading tests, while saving the teacher the time needed to a make up an IRI. The Durrell Analysis of Reading Difficulty, Diagnostic Reading Scales by Spache, Silvaroli's Classroom Reading Inventory, and the Ekwall Reading Inventory are among the better known. All four of them assess sight vocabulary, word analysis in isolation and in context, and silent and oral reading comprehension, as in a teacher-made IRI. Their components include word lists, graded passages with comprehension questions, occasional supplemental tests, and usually some kind of system for determining independent and instructional levels by counting errors. Although most of these tests have some simple system of coding oral reading errors, there is no qualitative analysis of the errors. The *number* of oral reading errors, not *types*, is what is considered.

In his Diagnostic Reading Scales, Spache uses the terms Independent Level and Instructional Level differently from others. Spache uses the term instructional to mean the level just below the grade where *oral* reading broke down either in word recognition *or* comprehension. He uses the term independent to refer to the highest grade level at which the student can read *silently* with adequate comprehension. Teachers referring to a student's independent or instructional level as indicated by the Diagnostic Reading Scales will mean something very different from those using another IRI, and they should be careful of this difference in terminology. Spache's independent level means silent reading level, and his instructional level means oral reading level.

Some of the standardized IRIs feature phonics or word analysis subtests. The Durrell Analysis of Reading Difficulty contains a number of subtests for students reading at or below a particular level. These include two different "Visual Memory of Words" subtests where the student matches a word flashed on a tachistoscope to a word on the answer sheet as well as several auditory discrimination and auditory analysis subtests called "Hearing Sounds in Words," "Learning to Hear Sounds in Words," and "Sounds of Letters." Subtests on "learning rate," spelling, and handwriting complete the Durrell battery. The Diagnostic Reading Scales contain eight phonics subtests that assess letter sounds, blends, syllables, auditory discrimination, and other aspects of word analysis.

The IRIs by Ekwall and Silvaroli are similar, both featuring word lists and reading passages. The Ekwall IRI has preprimer through ninth-grade passages, word lists, four alternate forms, a phonics survey test, and student pages that are not illustrated. Silvaroli's test has three alternate forms, illustrated passages from preprimer through eighth grade, word lists from preprimer through sixth grade, and a spelling test. (Refer to Chapter Four for other published IRIs.)

The Woodcock Reading Mastery Test is often used in special education. The Woodcock consists of five subtests: letter identification, word identification, word attack, word comprehension, and passage comprehension. Designed for use in all grades from kindergarten through twelfth, it takes about thirty minutes to administer.

The letter identification subtest requires the student to name letters shown in eight styles of type. The word identification subtest consists of 150 words in order of difficulty from preprimer through twelfth grade. They are listed in isolation, and the student pronounces the words in an untimed presentation. The word attack subtest consists of 50 nonsense words to be decoded and pronounced. Items range in difficulty from *bim* to *wubfambif*. The word comprehension subtest contains 70 items presented as verbal analogies: "boy — girl, man — _____." The subject reads the analogy silently and says a word to complete the set. Figure 8.4 shows items from the word comprehension and word attack subtests. The passage comprehension subtest consists of 85 modified cloze items; a word is omitted from a sentence, and the subject reads the item silently, then gives a word to complete it. Early items are single sentences with a picture clue; later items contain two or three sentences and have no picture.

The Woodcock yields grade-equivalent scores and age-equivalent scores for each subtest and for Total Reading, which represents the combined subtest scores. Scores can be converted to percentiles, and there are separate norms available for males and females as well as for different socioeconomic groups.

Like other standardized tests, the Woodcock yields entirely numerical data. A grade-equivalent score, or any other form of numerical score, on subtests like Word Identification or Passage Comprehension does not tell the teacher what the student can or cannot do. The examiner still does not know *what* letters the student can identify or what phonics skills have been

FIGURE 8.4. Sample items from the word comprehension and word attack subtests of the Woodcock Reading Mastery Test.

WORD COMPREHENSION SAMPLE ITEMS —
DO NOT RECORD ON THE RESPONSE FORM

>   Point to the first sample item and say: **Listen carefully and finish what I say** (point to each of the three words and the blank space, in turn, while reading the item).
>   **A dog walks; a bird . . .** (pause). *(flies)* If the subject gives an incorrect response or does not respond, read the item again, completing it with the correct word.
>   Continue with the remaining sample items in the same manner (point to each word as the item is read to the subject):
>
> **One is to two as three is to . . .** (pause). *(four, six)*
> **He is to she as boy is to . . .** (pause). *(girl)*
> **Grass is to green as snow is to . . .** (pause). *(white)*

dog — walks	bird —
one — two	three —
he — she	boy —
grass — green	snow —

mastered without detailed item analysis, which is not discussed in the manual.

Some individual diagnostic tests focus particularly on word analysis skills and not comprehension as such, like the Botel Reading Inventory and Sipay Word Analysis Test.

The Botel does not measure comprehension of sentences or paragraphs but does include comprehension of single words. The Botel is made up of a Word Recognition Test for identification of isolated words, Word Opposites subtests, both reading and listening, for selection of opposites in a multiple-choice format, and a Phonemic Inventory for the usual phonics skills like consonant and vowel sounds, blends, syllabication, and accents. The Botel is sometimes administered along with a commercial or teacher-made IRI to assess reading comprehension.

The Sipay test begins with a survey test that indicates which of the subsequent sixteen subtests should be administered. The survey portion serves as a pretest; adequate performance in any area means that the teacher can delete the corresponding subtest in further testing — a good feature since administering all sixteen subtests would be very time-consuming.

FIGURE 8.4.
(continued)

WORD ATTACK SAMPLE ITEM —
DO NOT RECORD ON RESPONSE FORM

Say: **I want you to pronounce some words that are not real words. I want you to tell me how they sound.** Point to "tat." **How does this word sound?**

Sample: **tat**

If the subject incorrectly responds to "tat," point to "tat" and say it clearly. Do not pronounce any other words during the Word Attack Test.

Proceed to the next page and begin the test. Continue testing until the subject has missed five or more consecutive words, or has responded to Item 50.

How do these words sound? Point to each word if necessary. If the subject fails to respond in a few seconds, encourage a response. If the subject still fails to respond, continue the test by pointing to the next word.

1. **ift**	2. **bim**	3. **ut**	4. **rayed**	5. **kak**
(ift)*	(bim)	(ət)	(rād)	(kak)
6. **aft**	7. **nen**	8. **ab**	9. **tash**	10. **wip's**
(aft)	(nen)	(ab)	(tash)	(wips)

---

*Pronunciation symbols used by permission of the publishers of the Merriam-Webster Dictionaries. See test manual for further explanation.
SOURCE: From Richard W. Woodcock, *Woodcock Reading Mastery Tests* (Circle Pines, Minn.: American Guidance Service, 1973). Reprinted by permission.

Subtests are very specific, ranging from simple Letter Names to such discrete analysis skills as Vowel Combinations, Final Silent-*E* Generalization, Vowel Sounds of *Y*, and Blending. It is hard to imagine a test that would partition word analysis into more molecular units. It does a thorough job of assessing a very narrow range of reading behaviors.

Advantages. First, as with group survey tests, the most obvious advantage is economy of time. With a *group diagnostic test* like the Stanford, a large group can be tested in under two hours. Second, some teachers find the information generated by such a test more specific, and thus more helpful in planning instruction, than the results of a general survey test with its relatively undifferentiated subtests and global scores. Third, group diagnostic tests, like their survey counterparts, are easy to administer without special preparation and are usually easy to score.

An advantage of using a standardized individual diagnostic test lies in the opportunity to closely observe one student's reading. A second advantage is the detailed analysis of discrete skills that many of these tests allow. Also, an advantage of standardized IRIs over similar informal measures is that the teacher does not have to make up or find word lists, comprehension passages, or comprehension questions. As long as the passages and questions are interesting and of high quality, the teacher can save valuable time. Just because an IRI is commercially available, however, does not guarantee the quality of its components.

Disadvantages. First, a disadvantage of using multiple subtests is that they may represent a very limited sample of the desired behavior. They are usually kept very short in order to save time, but subtest length can critically affect reliability. Although there is no general rule of thumb, tests in which individual subtests have few responses should be suspect because they may sacrifice in-depth analysis of specific things for a quick glimpse at many things.

Second, tests can be seriously flawed by poor passages and poor questions. The passages are usually written to conform to readability formulas, which make them sound stilted. Often they are bland, dull, and sometimes very short. A student's comprehension will be radically affected by interest in what is read, and dull passages written poorly do little to promote anyone's reading comprehension. The number of questions following a passage is another important variable. Ten questions of different types will make a fairly good sample, but ten questions all requiring literal recall will not, and asking only four or five questions is usually not enough to really test comprehension.

Third, tests that yield an overall reading level but do not assess comprehension are of dubious value. The heart of reading is comprehension, and a reading level that has not included comprehension, even indirectly, is not very useful. The Gilmore and Gray tests both ask comprehension questions, but the questions play no part in the resultant score. The Slosson Oral Reading Test does not even have the student read sentences, only lists of undefined words. The Word Opposites parts of the Botel test do include word meanings, but again the reader has no opportunity to read connected text. The reading assessed by these tests is actually a group of reading-like behaviors. Their diagnostic usefulness is limited to precisely what they test, which is *not* reading for meaning.

Achievement Tests

Reading achievement tests are somewhat difficult to characterize because they share certain characteristics with both survey and diagnostic tests. The ones most commonly used are actually batteries. A *battery* is a collection of tests in separate subject areas, administered separately but based on the same norm group. The results on various parts of a battery, like tests in math, science, and language arts, are easily comparable since all the parts are based on similar norms. It is misleading to try to compare scores on two completely different tests because each one has been standardized using different groups, and yet this error is made quite often. Achievement test batteries were developed specifically to meet the need for tests in different subject areas that shared the same norm group. Their format makes it easy to compare results of the different parts of the same battery.

The reading or language arts portions of these batteries may be broad and general, yielding global reading and language scores like a reading survey test. Or they may be as detailed and specific as a group diagnostic test. So it is not the type or number of subtests or scores that helps us differentiate an achievement test from other types, but rather the testing purpose.

Achievement tests are designed to show the depth of one's knowledge and mastery of subject area curricula. Because they are designed to assess mastery, or achievement, they are usually administered *after* the appropriate instruction has been given. Tests used for diagnostic purposes are often given *before* a program of instruction, or early on, to reveal strengths and so that instruction can be modified appropriately. Diagnostic and survey tests are usually given "before the fact"; achievement tests "after the fact." Their content is sometimes very similar, but the purpose and timing of the testing differ.

Standardized achievement tests are probably the most common type of formal tests used in schools. Most students take a standardized achievement test of some kind yearly, often a battery covering the major curricular areas. Because subtests are usually given in separate sittings, completion of a battery can take several days or a week. Achievement tests must be given under strictly standard conditions in order for results to be compared across groups, so sometimes a team of school personnel administers all the tests, and sometimes the regular daily schedule is suspended so that all students can be tested simultaneously. They are machine-scored by the publishers and results are sent back to the school.

Almost all achievement tests are group tests and should be used to evaluate groups of students, not individuals. For this reason, they are of very limited diagnostic use. They are useful for evaluating the progress of large groups like whole schools, or all the students from one grade.

Publishers attempt to make the content of their achievement tests represent typical school curricula. A math test, for example, will generally be made up of problems and calculations common to most school math programs for a particular grade. What is "typical" is decided by consulting subject area experts, by studying textbooks and material in wide use, and by

FIGURE 8.5. Reading comprehension items from the reading subtest of the SRA Achievement battery.

Color serves a protective function for many animals. It makes some hard to see against their backgrounds. This helps to protect them from their predators — other animals that kill and eat them. Color also serves to protect some predators. It warns them that some animals they would like to eat can harm them.

5   Many insects are the color of leaves, twigs, or bark. When they rest quietly on a plant or tree, their predators have a hard time spotting them. For example, the underwing, a kind of moth, has gray-and-brown wings that blend with the color of bark.

The color of some animals changes to blend with their backgrounds. The arctic hare, a rabbit, is brown in summer. In winter its fur becomes white to match the snow on the

10   ground. The color of some animals changes more quickly. The mosquito fish, for example, becomes darker or lighter to match its background as it moves around.

Some investigators experimented to see if color really does protect animals from predators. They put mosquito fish in a tank with a white bottom. A few hours later all the fish were light-colored. The investigators then put half the fish in a tank with a black bottom.

15   They immediately freed penguins, seabirds that eat mosquito fish, near the two tanks. After several hours they counted the number of fish in each tank. Most of the fish in the black tank had been eaten. Most of the fish in the white tank were still alive. Thus the investigators found that color does protect mosquito fish. But color is not a foolproof source of protection.

20   Color serves as a warning to some predators. Some animals are poisonous, sting, give off a bad smell, or taste bad. Many of these animals are brightly colored. They are easily seen by predators.

Investigators experimented to see whether predators know instinctively which bright-colored animals to avoid or whether they learn only by experience. In their experiments

25   they used monarch butterflies and blue jays. Monarchs have bright orange-and-black wings and are believed to taste very bad. The investigators put a hungry young blue jay into a cage with the monarchs. The blue jay caught and ate just one. It did not chase any others.

field-testing experimental test forms. Content validity, or how well a test represents the major aspects of the subject area, is of particular importance, but how closely the curriculum of an individual district, school, or classroom coincides with national trends is difficult to say. Achievement tests in any subject area should be carefully evaluated in light of how well their content matches the local programs and materials in use.

Most of the widely used achievement batteries measure reading, language (English), science, math, and social studies. Most have forms for every grade from early elementary through high school, although some school districts do not begin using them until third or fourth grade. Some batteries have reading readiness tests for kindergarten and first grade. Figure 8.5 shows reading subtest items from an achievement battery. Among the typical wide-ranging achievement batteries are the following: the Metropolitan Achievement Test, with reading comprehension, lan-

FIGURE 8.5.
(continued)

---

11. In line 7, *bark* means

A. the sound a dog makes
B. a loud and angry cry
C. the outside of a tree trunk
D. a kind of beetle

12. Where would you be LEAST likely to find animals like the arctic hare that change color in winter and summer?

A. Canada
B. Florida
C. Alaska
D. Colorado

13. In the test with mosquito fish, what did the investigators find when they counted the fish?

A. All the fish in both tanks had been eaten by the penguins.
B. About half the mosquito fish in each tank had been eaten.
C. The penguins had eaten more fish from the black tank than from the white tank.
D. Penguins don't like mosquito fish and so had eaten only a few.

14. What was the investigators' last step in the test with the mosquito fish and penguins?

A. They counted the number of fish in each tank.
B. They freed penguins near the tank.
C. They placed mosquito fish in a white tank.
D. They put half the mosquito fish in the black tank.

15. After they placed the mosquito fish in the white tank, the investigators waited before placing half of them in the black tank. Why did they do this?

A. They wanted to make sure the penguins would be hungry.
B. It took several hours for the mosquito fish to become light-colored.
C. It took several hours for the mosquito fish to become dark-colored.
D. They had to count the fish in the tank.

SOURCE: From R. A. Naslund, L. P. Thorpe, and D. W. Lefever, *SRA Achievement Series, Level F/Form 1, Test Booklet* (Chicago: Science Research Associates, 1978). Reprinted by permission.

guage, social studies, science, and math subtests and a separate readiness test; the Comprehensive Test of Basic Skills, with readiness, reading, language, arithmetic, and study skills; the Stanford Achievement Test, with reading, spelling, language, math, science, social studies, and listening; and the California Achievement Test, with reading, spelling, language, math, and reference skills subtests. All those mentioned, except the Stanford, are designed for kindergarten through grade twelve; the Stanford is for grades one through nine.

There are a few achievement tests for individual administration. Two examples are the Peabody Individual Achievement Test (PIAT) and the Wide Range Achievement Test (WRAT). These instruments are hybrids that have characteristics of both group achievement tests and individual survey tests. They are most often used like individual survey or diagnostic tests.

The PIAT contains reading recognition, reading comprehension, spelling, math, and general information subtests. Because it includes math as well as various reading skills and general information, the PIAT measures mastery of the largest part of typical elementary curricula. The WRAT has reading, spelling, and arithmetic subtests. Like the PIAT, it covers the areas most heavily concentrated on in elementary school. Both tests are often given as diagnostic screening devices to students experiencing difficulty in either reading or math or those with generally poor school achievement. Like other achievement tests, the results they yield are solely quantitative, and they have little, if any, diagnostic value.

The PIAT, for kindergarten through twelfth grade, has two reading sections. Reading Recognition includes letter and single word identification; word recognition is on an untimed basis. Figure 8.6 shows items from this subtest. The comprehension subtest requires reading of one or several sentences and then matching a picture to the text. Pictures are in a multiple-choice format, and written sentences cannot be referred to by the student. At the upper levels, the comprehension sentences are extremely complex and words are highly unusual. The picture selection process is unlike any other reading comprehension test, but is similar to the format of the Peabody Picture Vocabulary Test.

The WRAT, often used in screening students for special education programs, is designed for ages five years old through adulthood. The reading subtest deserves special attention. Like the Slosson Oral Reading Test, the reading portion of the WRAT is made up entirely of lists of single words. Pronunciation within ten seconds is the only criterion. It does not measure comprehension of either text or words, and no reading of connected text is included. Consequently, it does not measure real reading at all. If the test makers do not include comprehension in their view of reading, they should at least acknowledge what the test does *not* do. Far from doing that, the manual states that the test allows for accurate diagnosis of reading disabilities and placement of students in instructional groups, all without reading of words in sentences! We believe that these claims and the content validity of the reading subtest are doubtful.

Advantages. First, like other group tests, group achievement measures offer schools a reliable, uncomplicated way to gather information on large numbers of students.

Second, a maximum of data can be gathered in a minimum of time. If the batteries include a number of subjects, many curricular areas and processes can be assessed at one time.

Third, if properly administered and scored, they yield potentially informative data on the progress of groups of students, such as the total population of a given grade. When patterns of progress or lack of progress

FIGURE 8.6. Items from the Reading Recognition subtest of the PIAT.

(Point to "was" in the stimulus area.) **Find one like this — down here.**
(Point in a sweeping motion to the response area.) **Point to it. (l)**

was

was		mas
SAW		man

For subjects progressing to item 19 and beyond or starting at this level

(Say the following:) **Now we are going to do some reading aloud. This page
has rows of words on it.** (Point, in a sweeping motion across each of the
rows from the subjects's left to right.) **Read each of the words aloud going
across the rows this way.** (Point again across the rows from the subject's left
to right.) **As you finish each row, go on to the next one. Start here** (Point to
the first word to be attempted) **and read them to me.** (If necessary, elicit
responses by pointing to each word in turn, and using such phrases as:
What is this word?) **Give me a pronunciation you would expect to find in
the dictionary.**

are discerned, curricular changes at the school and district levels can take
place.

Fourth, these tests are usually extensively field-tested and standardized
with great precision. Norming and validating achievement batteries is a big
and complex business, and since millions are taken yearly, test manufactur-
ers try to make them as reliable and valid as they can.

Disadvantages. Standardized reading achievement tests are not designed to give diagnostic data, so they cannot be criticized for not doing so,
but if used for their proper purposes, they can be effective measures of prior
learning. There are some cautions, however, that should be kept in mind.

First, administration procedures must be followed to the letter. Students
should take these tests in their regular classrooms rather than in huge
groups in the cafeteria or gym, as sometimes happens.

Second, as with diagnostic reading tests, subtests are sometimes quite
short, and their reliability coefficients may be low because of this and other
factors.

Third, the time and cost involved sometimes contribute to gross overinterpretation of their scores. Retention of students because of scores on a
single achievement battery or public humiliation of school groups and

FIGURE 8.6. (continued)

19. **run** rən	20. **play** plā	21. **jump** jəmp

22. **kit·ten** kitən	23. **wag·on** wagən, waig-	24. **fishing** fishiŋ, -ēŋ, ən, -ēn	25. **brook** brůk, brük

26. **gloves** gləvz	27. **smile** smīl	28. **colt** kōlt	29. **round** raůnd

NOTE: Accept the first scorable response, unless the subject spontaneously corrects it. Ask the subject to repeat a word only if the response is not loud and clear enough to score. If the subject is hesitant about pronouncing the words, encourage responses by such phrases as: Try it. Say it as best you can, etc. (See Part I of the manual for further instructions.)

Items 19 to 29 Plate 16

run	play	jump	
kitten	wagon	fishing	brook
gloves	smile	colt	round

SOURCE: From Lloyd M. Dunn and Frederick C. Markwardt, Jr., *Peabody Individual Reading Achievement Test* (Circle Pines, Minn.: American Guidance Service, 1970). Reprinted by permission.

personnel because of score comparisons are clear abuses of test scores, yet such abuses are not uncommon.

Fourth, achievement tests tend to call upon recall of factual material rather than higher-level thinking skills (Bertrand and Cebula, 1980). Factual learning and recall are among the easiest processes to measure, but they do not represent all learning or achievement. We must not lose sight of the many additional aspects in reading and other subject areas, such as learning rate, interest, or creative thinking, which achievement tests do not measure.

Minimum Competency Tests

The minimum competency testing movement began in the early 1970s and became a focus of attention and controversy quickly. The movement is both praised and criticized, depending on whose opinion is being expressed. This section is intended to provide an overview of the issues involved.

Goals and Components of Minimum Competency Programs. These programs have one overriding goal: to produce pupils with demonstrated mastery of basic skills in reading, composition, and arithmetic calculation. But secondary to this goal, some or all of the following may be attached: to motivate students to better achievement, to make teachers work harder or teach more effectively, to make schools more cost-effective, and/or to create greater accountability in schools (Airasian, Madaus and Pedulla, 1979, p. ix).

Minimum competency programs differ from state to state and from one school district to another. Most commonly, however, they feature:

- ☐ statements of specific skills, often called "performance standards," "basic competencies," or "learning objectives," in reading, writing, and mathematics that schools are responsible for teaching all children and that all students are responsible for mastering
- ☐ tests to determine if students have mastered the required skills
- ☐ requirements that students cannot be promoted to the next grade and/or cannot graduate unless the tests are passed
- ☐ requirements concerning extra courses, placement in special programs, remediation, and the like to correct deficiencies

Minimal competency tests differ widely depending on what the particular state legislature, state board of education and/or local school board and administration has determined are "basic competencies." Most often the tests measure either or both of the following:

1. *School skills,* or skills in the defined areas taught in school (e.g., students may answer questions about a passage read, choose meanings or opposites for vocabulary words, spell words or detect misspellings, locate mechanical errors in writing, write sentences or paragraphs, and do arithmetic problems)
2. *Life skills,* or skills using reading, writing, and arithmetic applied to typical real-life situations (e.g., students may complete applications, read and follow directions, interpret warnings on medicine labels, compute a bank balance or merchandise bill, or write a letter of application or complaint

Options available to students who do not pass the tests are as varied as the skills and tests themselves. Again, state and local attitudes determine what the consequences of such failure will be and what the school's responsibility will be toward such students. According to Mizell (1979), schools may encourge or allow students failing competency tests to drop out of school; refuse to allow students to graduate until tests are passed; refuse to grant regular high school diplomas to failing students; refuse to allow promotion to the next grade until tests are passed; or assign failing students to a less demanding academic program or "track." These options penalize the student and do not assure that minimum competencies will be acquired. Other options that attempt to provide help to these students may include: early identification and remediation of basic skills deficiencies before the student approaches the age or grade to take the tests; individualized instruction for failing students featuring smaller classes, special materials, skill laboratory work, work with an aide or tutor during the school day, and the like; summer school remedial programs; after-school tutoring programs; work with parents to teach them how to help their children learn basic skills at home and how to prevent skill deficiencies in the younger children; or special classes integrating learning and using basic skills with regular course content.

Problems and Issues of Minimum Competency Programs. A number of complex issues are involved in this movement. In general, supporters of minimum competency testing believe that it will

□ help identify and better serve those students with the greatest educational needs
□ motivate students toward greater achievement in school
□ motivate teachers to teach all students more effectively
□ make high school diplomas more meaningful (in states that have "diploma sanctions," or regulations requiring mastery on tests before a diploma may be awarded)
□ place pressure on schools to provide more instruction in basic skills and to become more accountable for student achievement
□ create an objective data base regarding school achievement patterns. (Lazarus, 1981)

But there are a number of unanswered questions and concerns regarding this movement. According to Lazarus (1981) and Mizell (1979), they include the following:

1. Minimum competency testing may exclude more children from schools and stigmatize underachievers. When such programs result in denial of promotion or graduation and even implicitly encourage dropping out of school, such programs may be "punitive and exclusionary" (Mizell, 1979, p. 10).
2. Programs may focus on identifying students with basic skill deficiencies without aggressively pursuing effective remediation. Testing is certainly easier than remediating, and effective long-term remediation is both difficult and expensive.

3. Such programs and the rhetoric associated with them may oversimplify the basic competency issues, seeking or creating pat answers to exceedingly complex issues of adult literacy.

4. Such programs may be viewed as a "quick fix" to the problem of the community's loss of confidence in the schools, or as an attempt to restore such confidence while actually having little effect on the complex underlying causes of illiteracy.

5. Students with special educational needs (e.g., the handicapped, severely learning disabled, emotionally disturbed, and mentally retarded) may be penalized and further shut out from equal educational opportunity by their failure to meet standard objectives or pass the typical group-administered, paper-and-pencil tests of basic skills. Few states so far have rigorously examined the implications of these programs for exceptional learners.

6. The emphasis such programs place within the school and in the larger community on "minimums" may result in a narrowing of curricular goals, with greater emphasis on so-called "basics" and lesser emphasis on, or omission of, a broad range of school topics and educational experiences for all learners.

7. Although the student failing such tests is the one who ultimately pays the penalty, teachers may be forced by community pressure to restrict the range of topics and methods to those most likely to be tested, so that they can more clearly justify the use of student time and effort. This can result in students' passing the required tests but being poorly prepared in the more global reading, writing, and thinking applications.

8. So much emphasis on "minimums" may create a climate in which the minimum becomes the maximum. Many critics already charge that schools in general do not fully challenge the average or talented pupil, but seek only to assure that everyone has a minimum level of achievement. The motivation of average and above average students may suffer as a result.

9. When such programs are mandated by the state, local school divisions may wonder who will absorb the cost. The state may finance the actual testing but not the remedial programs that must be a necessary part of the process if it is to serve the students' needs. Localities may balk at subsidizing the necessarily expensive remedial efforts if they are made to feel that the state has usurped local autonomy.

10. Finally, the question of whether students' competence in applying school literacy skills to life experience can be accurately, fairly and comprehensively tested by means available today must be addressed. According to Lazarus (1981), "the art of testing is not yet sufficiently advanced to meet the demands that minimum competency places on it" (p. 18).

Criterion-Referenced Tests

During the 1960s and 1970s, a new approach to test construction was developed: *criterion-referenced* evaluation. As educators began to give more thought to the need for individualized instruction, criterion-referenced tests gained in popularity. They enabled teachers to compare a student's performance to a predetermined goal or outcome, while norm-referenced tests, on the other hand, aid in comparing one student's performance to someone else's. Since criterion-referenced tests provided a way of determining whether a student had met instructional goals, or *criteria*, they quickly became the major kind of measurement device for many different kinds of individualized programs.

Characteristics

In individualized reading programs, each student works toward mastery of skills that he or she has not yet learned. Pretests are most often used to determine which skills need improvement. In theory, every student in a classroom might be working on mastering a different skill at any given time. In practice, few teachers can effectively manage such a program, and students are temporarily grouped with others who need work on the same skill or process. Even though the instruction usually takes place in groups, these programs are called individualized because each student works on those particular skills in which he or she is thought to be deficient.

This instructional model requires a measurement method that helps the teacher determine not how students compare to one another but how each student's performance compares with the goals of the program. Individual differences among students are less important than whether or not an individual student can meet the stated criterion (Sax, 1980; Thorndike and Hagen, 1977).

When criterion-referenced tests are used, the instructional outcomes to be aimed for are always determined and defined before instruction takes place. Therefore, instruction is deliberately aimed toward "teaching to the test," which is not a criticism in this case. When goals and outcomes are predetermined, instruction must be directed toward achieving those particular goals.

In reading and language arts, where criterion-referenced tests and individualized programs have gained great popularity, the result has been that the skills tested came to define the reading program. Reading instruction in many cases became little more than a cut-and-dried sequence of skills to be mastered, with the major goal that of passing the mastery tests. We believe, with many others, that reading is more than a set of mastered skills and that mastering sequenced skills does not guarantee that the student will read effectively or enthusiastically.

Specially designed programs for the teaching, mastery, and testing of specific skills, often referred to as *skills management systems,* usually rely on criterion-referenced tests for their evaluation component. Developed to make the teaching of reading skills systematic and sequential, these systems have become popular adjuncts to basal reading programs in recent years. They have found a particularly enthusiastic market in compensatory and remedial programs, where it has been thought that students would benefit from "extra doses" of skills instruction. The Wisconsin Design for Reading Skill Development, the Fountain Valley System, and the Read System are typical management systems.

Whether commercial or locally developed, a management system usually features specific skill objectives arranged in some sequence, materials and activities coded to the objectives, criterion-referenced pretests and posttests, record-keeping procedures and materials, and suggestions for teaching and practicing the skills (Cheek and Cheek, 1980). By systematic use of the pre- and posttests and careful record keeping, these programs claim that it is possible for the teacher to determine quickly and precisely what skills have been mastered by any individual student at any given time. The availability of this precise information on each student has done much to satisfy public demands for increased teacher accountability. Some educators, however, remain unconvinced that reading can or should be partitioned in this manner, or that better readers emerge from this type of reading instruction.

For a criterion-referenced test to achieve its purpose, each item must define the task, skill, or process to be demonstrated. These definitions, called *objectives,* must clearly state what is to be demonstrated, under what conditions, and at what level of quality or accuracy. These three characteristics of good objectives are referred to as the *performance, condition,* and *criterion* aspects (Bertrand and Cebula, 1980; Mager, 1962). The performance is the statement of what the student must do; the conditions are the ways in which the student will participate in the learning process and any special conditions under which the task is to be performed; and the criterion is the statement of the level of performance quality required.

As with any other kind of test, criterion-referenced test items should represent essential skills or knowledge. Do they adequately and fairly sample the whole domain of possible items? This is a basic question of content validity, which is a crucial aspect of these tests as well as other types.

Developing an adequate sample of the behavior desired sounds easy enough, but in reading it is very difficult because no agreement exists about what specific skills, attitudes, and/or information are essential. It is easier to develop a multitude of goals than to determine what is important. Like other tests, criterion-referenced tests frequently include tasks that are easily measured but not very closely related to reading. Stauffer, Abrams, and Pikulski (1978) give the example of an objective measuring the student's ability to put stress on the proper syllable in three-syllable words. The test item required the student to choose, from three alternatives, the word *incorrectly* accented. Locating an incorrectly placed accent mark is not much like being able to correctly apply stress when pronouncing a word. Saying the word correctly, or putting in an accent mark correctly, would have been much more productive. Either would have been a better way of assessing mastery of the skill.

Criterion-referenced tests usually have items arranged in some sort of learning sequence or hierarchy. Many reading programs that feature criterion-referenced tests are built on the assumptions that there is a set *number* of required skills and that these skills must be mastered in a particular *order*. Although there is no evidence from research to support either assumption, these tests imply that the assumptions are valid.

What is important is not *which* hierarchy is accepted as absolute truth, but how closely the sequence of reading skills on the test matches what was taught. In commercial programs that supply their own criterion-referenced tests, this consistency is built in, but in some schools, tests are purchased separately from programs, or test packages are bought but instructional goals locally developed. In these cases the tests may set forth a required skills sequence that does not match the way the students were taught. If a commercial test locks students and teachers into a particular sequence of skills, instructional programs must be made to dovetail with it or else students may appear to have learned less than they really have. Of course, tests should be tailored to meet instructional procedures, not the reverse. They are a means to the end: better instruction. They are not an end in themselves.

Gronlund (1978) suggests certain criteria that we have adapted for judging the adequacy of objectives for a commercial criterion-referenced test package:

1. Do these objectives call for learning outcomes that are appropriate to the subject area? What are the most important outcomes to be desired? Are they included?
2. Do these objectives represent a balance of thinking and learning skills? Is factual knowledge overrepresented, with higher cognitive and affective thinking shortchanged?
3. Are these outcomes attainable by our students? What modifications should be made to fit our students' needs and our teaching facilities?
4. Do these objectives fit the philosophy of our school(s) and teachers? Is it reasonable to expect that our teachers and students can achieve these ends?

Advantages. One of the most important assets of criterion-referenced tests is their diagnostic potential. They can indicate with great clarity and precision what a student can or cannot yet do and thus appropriate instructional modifications can be made, which is the major goal of any diagnostic procedure. They have much greater diagnostic power than norm-referenced tests because they yield information related to specific goals rather than information in numerical or quantitative terms.

Second, it is possible for parents and students to see how test scores are related to instructional methods and materials, whereas ordinarily it is difficult for them to see any relationship. This advantage can help to eliminate a misunderstanding between home and school.

Third, criterion-referenced tests make it very clear to the public what goals the school has developed and how these goals are to be attained. There is therefore greater public confidence in the accountability of schools.

Fourth, they can be made to conform to local standards, teaching conditions, and practices and thus reflect the actual abilities and achievement of local students more accurately than standardized norm-referenced tests.

Fifth, they tend to minimize damaging competition among students, since a student's achievement is not measured in terms of someone else's achievement but rather in terms of a preset criterion. Both parents and students can then concentrate on the goals to be attained rather than on invidious comparisons among individuals or groups.

Sixth, they are particularly useful for evaluating the effectiveness of a program innovation or a completely new program. Standardized tests, which measure broad, widely accepted trends within a subject area, rarely show whether or not a new or modified program is effective.

Disadvantages. First, they may be top-heavy with objectives that are easiest to measure, such as factual material. The higher-order learning processes, like evaluation and application of knowledge to novel situations, are naturally harder to assess, and they may be underrepresented in the objectives.

Second, the necessity of being clear and precise may encourage partitioning of reading acts into many molecular units. Excessive partitioning leads to a proliferation of objectives, and reading as an integrated process can get lost. Criterion-referenced tests tend to encourage teachers to think of reading as a conglomerate of hundreds of discrete skills instead of a complex thinking and language process.

Third, since criteria of quality or accuracy are always arbitrary, they should be considered carefully. There is nothing magical about 80, 90, or 100 percent accuracy. If skills are truly hierarchical, as with some math skills, then 100 percent accuracy may be necessary before the student goes on to more difficult skills. If there is no particular sequence of skills in one area, or no generally agreed-upon progression, then all quality criteria are arbitrary and one may be just as good as another. Teachers using any test with criteria for mastery predetermined should decide for themselves if the criteria seem unnecessarily rigid.

Fourth, we must remember that we don't want students to demonstrate mastery only on a one-time basis. We want them to retain what they have learned and be able to apply it to new situations. Important objectives should be tested more than once and mastery should be shown in more than one way.

Perhaps the biggest drawback in criterion-referenced tests is the point made earlier: that objectives to be tested have a way of becoming the reading curriculum itself. Some educators maintain that programs that emphasize testing of discrete skills encourage teaching the skills in the same manner. It is difficult, if not impossible, to isolate skills in actual reading because meaningful reading requires the use of many skills and processes simultaneously, and partitioning overlooks this important factor.

Sources of Test Information

Information on a commercial test or battery can be obtained from a number of sources such as measurement yearbooks, test publishers' catalogs, and technical reports, bulletins, and journals.

Yearbooks and Indexes

These sources are compendia of information and reviews of all current published tests. They can be found in libraries, although many school divisions have a set of their own.

Measurement Yearbooks. The most valuable source, and the first place many teachers turn to with questions about tests, is the series of *Mental Measurement Yearbooks (MMY)* edited by the late Oscar K. Buros. Buros produced the first volume in 1938; the *Eighth Mental Measurement Yearbook* was issued in 1978. They are revised about every six years.

Each *MMY* lists tests that have appeared or been revised since publication of the previous volume. Age and grade levels, time needed for administration, subtests included, publishers, and costs are listed for each test. This information is helpful when initially screening a number of tests, and it makes ordering sample sets easy. Most important, these yearbooks contain extensive reviews of many tests written by qualified experts in the field; synopses of reviews appearing in journals and other sources; lists of pertinent books and monographs; and the names of people and journals that review tests.

Measurement Indexes. The *MMY*s are not cumulative; a test reviewed in a previous *MMY* may not appear in subsequent volumes. To aid in locating reviews and pertinent information without having to go through each *MMY*, Buros developed *Tests in Print I* (1961) and *Tests in Print II* (1974). These volumes are very helpful as indexes to those previously published.

Buros also edited nine monographs, each containing test information and reviews on a single topic: English, foreign languages, math, science, social studies, reading, intelligence, personality, and vocational tests. *Reading Tests and Reviews I* (1968) contains all the reviews of reading tests found in the earlier yearbooks. *Reading Tests and Reviews II* (1975) contains more current reviews.

Additional Sources

There are several other places where you can get critical information about tests, after you have checked the *MMY*s and indexes.

Test Publishers' Catalogs. Publishers of commercial tests usually provide informative catalogs and technical manuals without charge to educators. They can provide a wealth of very current information to add to what Buros's reference books provide. The catalogs usually provide descriptions of the tests, subtests included, time limitations, normative information, types of scores yielded, scoring services, costs, and related specific information. Because catalogs are sales devices, they tend to present the tests in the most positive light, so the publisher's claims should be compared with the critical reviews in the *MMY*s and current journals.

The eighth *MMY* lists names and addresses of all test publishers as of 1978. The Educational Testing Services (ETS) (Rosedale Road, Princeton, N.J. 08540) publishes the *Test Collection Bulletin*, a quarterly publication listing the most current addresses and services of test publishers.

Technical manuals often accompany specimen sets of tests, which usually must be purchased from the publisher. They provide detailed information about the populations used in standardizing the tests, reliability and validity estimates for individual subtests and the entire test, and other statistical data that are very useful for evaluation purposes.

Bulletins. Free or inexpensive bulletins about tests, publishers, and measurement issues are available from a number of sources. ETS publishes the nominally priced *Tests and Measurement Kit*, which includes guides for developing teacher-made tests and selecting commercial ones. ETS also publishes *TM News* and *TM Reports*, bulletins reporting on measurement trends and issues and summarizing papers presented at national meetings of the American Educational Research Association (AERA). *TM Reports* also includes bibliographies on a wide variety of testing topics, which are extremely helpful to those interested in extended readings. In addition to these bulletins, ETS issues *A Directory of Information on Tests*, which will help in locating other information sources.

The National Council on Measurement in Education (NCME) (1230 17th St. N.W., Washington, D.C. 20036) publishes quarterly reports (*Journal of Educational Measurement, Measurement in Education* and *Measurement News*) on a wide variety of topics such as performance contracting, criterion-referenced testing, grading practices, reporting of test scores to parents, and interpreting of national norms.

The Psychological Corporation (757 Third Ave., New York, N.Y. 10017) publishes a number of free or inexpensive bulletins on topics like aptitude testing, test score accuracy, interpretation of reliability coefficients, the costs of tests, and the development of local norms. The Psychological Corporation also provides free single copies of their *Test Service Notebooks,* including reports on such topics as secondary school testing and what parents must know about testing and test selection, as well as their *Focus on Evaluation* monographs, which cover topics like mandated assessment and the political use of test results.

The American Psychological Association, Inc. (APA) (1200 17th St. N.W., Washington, D.C. 20036) publishes a valuable bulletin entitled *Standards for Educational and Psychological Tests* (1974) to guide test developers and test users. It contains information on the proper development and reporting of tests, results and research findings, and the use and interpretation of tests.

Journals. Published several times yearly, professional journals often contain the most current information. Many routinely review new or revised tests in many areas as well as reporting research findings related to testing. In the area of measurement and evaluation are such journals as the *American Psychologist, Journal of Educational Measurement, American Educational Research Journal, Psychological Bulletin,* and *Applied Psychological Measurement.* Reading journals such as *Language Arts, The Reading Teacher, Journal of Reading,* and *Reading Research Quarterly* often include test reviews and critical articles.

Summary

Formal measures of reading ability are of two types: *norm-referenced* and *criterion-referenced.* Norm-referenced tests are used to compare an individual's performance with that of others. They include *survey, diagnostic,* and *achievement tests.* Survey tests are general reading tests with few subtests and are most often used to screen large numbers of students. Diagnostic reading tests have a number of subtests, each stressing a particular skill area, and are usually given to diagnose specific strengths and weaknesses. Achievement tests may be either general or specific; they are intended not to provide diagnostic information but to assess overall effectiveness of instruction in broad curricular areas.

Criterion-referenced tests assess a student's mastery of a predetermined criterion or goal. They do not compare students to one another, but to a stated objective. They provide specific diagnostic information on the mastery of instructional objectives.

The basic test characteristics that teachers should be familiar with are *reliability* and *validity.* Reliability refers to the consistency of scores a test yields. Aspects of reliability are *stability,* or consistency across repeated administrations; *internal consistency,* or consistency among test items; and *equivalence,* or consistency across alternate test forms. Validity refers to how well a test measures what it was intended to measure. *Content validity* is the quality of adequately sampling the subject area or process being assessed. *Construct validity* refers to how well the test measures traits, or constructs, that are not directly observable but must be inferred from observable behavior. Intelligence is an example of a construct. *Criterion-related validity* is made up of *concurrent validity,* or how closely a test is related to another test of established validity, and *predictive validity,* the degree to which test performance is related to some other established criterion, such as grades in college or job success.

Commonly used descriptive statistics include *distributions, indices of central tendency and dispersion,* and forms of *standard scores.* A distribution is an array of scores from highest to lowest. Many standardized tests assume a *normal distribution,* a symmetrical array with most scores falling near the mean and progressively fewer scores at the extreme high and low ends. Asymmetrical distributions are referred to as *skewed.* Indices of central tendency in distributions include the *mean,* an arithmetic average, and the *median,* the point in a distribution at which there are equal numbers of higher and lower scores. Indices of dispersion in a distribution describe how far apart scores are from one another. They include the *range,* or the span from highest to lowest score, and the *standard deviation,* which shows how far from the mean each score is in standard or equal increments.

Standardized reading tests usually yield several forms of test scores. *Grade scores* are two-part numbers that indicate achievement such as we might expect at a given grade level and a number of months within that grade. These scores are meant to represent the performance of an average student in the grade and month indicated. *Percentiles* are standard scores that show what percentage of the norm population scored higher or lower than the individual tested. *Stanines* are scores in which the distribution has been divided into nine parts; a stanine score indicates which ninth a score fell in. *T scores* and *z scores* use the concepts of mean and standard deviation to show where a score lies in relation to the mean of a normal distribution.

Extension Activities

1. Find out the name of a standardized reading test used in your school (or use one mentioned in this chapter). Look up the test in *Reading Tests and Reviews* (look first in Volume II). Read the reviews and the information listed there. Does the test sound like one you would want to use? Why or why not?

2. Find a review or description of a standardized reading test or battery in a recent issue of a professional journal. Do you understand the information given on the test itself and statements of a critical nature? If you are unsure of what some of the information means, what sources could you use to help you make sense of it?

3. Compare a teacher-made and a commercial informal reading inventory. Look critically at the reading passages, comprehension questions, and illustrations, if any. List the strengths and weaknesses in the content of each test.

4. Imagine that your local newspaper published reading achievement scores, showing grade-equivalent averages for the grades tested in each school. Say, for example, the fourth grades in each school attained the following averaged scores:

School A: 4–8
School B: 4–3
School C: 2–9

What data would you need to interpret these scores and the differences among them?

5. If you had access only to norm-referenced test scores for a class but you had to make criterion-referenced interpretations of the scores, what problems would you encounter?

Suggested Readings

Bertrand, Arthur and Cebula, Joseph P. **Tests, Measurement and Evaluation: A Developmental Approach.** *Reading, Mass.: Addison-Wesley, 1980.* One of the most readable texts available on test and measurement concepts and devices.

Farr, Roger. **Reading: What Can Be Measured?** *Newark, Del.: International Reading Association, 1969.* Concise summary of research on measurement of reading abilities and achievement.

Nunnally, Jim C. **Introduction to Statistics for Psychology and Education.** *New York: McGraw-Hill, 1975.* Comprehensive text on measurement concepts, descriptive statistics, and interpretation of test data.

Sanders, Norris M. **Classroom Questions: What Kinds?** *New York: Harper & Row, 1966.* Classic volume on teachers' questioning strategies and how questions affect what is understood and remembered, critical aspects of reading comprehension assessment.

Schreiner, Robert. **Reading Tests and Teachers: A Practical Guide.** *Newark, Del.: International Reading Association, 1979.* Informative description of current reading tests and their use.

References

Airasian, Peter W., Madaus, George F., and Pedulla, Joseph J. *Minimal Competency Testing.* Englewood Cliffs, N.J.: Educational Technology Publications, 1979.

Bertrand, Arthur, and Cebula, Joseph, P. *Tests, Measurement, and Evaluation: A Developmental Approach.* Reading, Mass.: Addison-Wesley, 1980.

Buros, Oscar K., ed. *Eighth Mental Measurement Yearbook.* Highland Park, N.J.: Gryphon Press, 1978. (Previous editions: 1972, 1965, 1959, 1953, 1949, 1940, 1938)

Buros, Oscar K., ed. *Reading Tests and Reviews II.* Highland Park, N.J.: Gryphon Press, 1975. (Previous edition: 1968)

Buros, Oscar K., ed. *Tests in Print II.* Highland Park, N.J.: Gryphon Press, 1974. (Previous edition: 1961)

Cheek, Martha, and Cheek, Earl. *Diagnostic-Prescriptive Reading Instruction.* Dubuque, Ia.: William C. Brown, 1980.

Gronlund, Norman E. *Measurement and Evaluation in Teaching,* 3rd ed. New York: Macmillan, 1976.

Gronlund, Norman E. *Stating Objectives for Classroom Instruction*, 2nd ed. New York: Macmillan, 1978.

Lazarus, Mitchell. *Goodbye to Excellence: A Critical Look at Minimum Competency Testing*. Boulder, Colo.: Westview Press, 1981.

Mager, Robert. *Preparing Instructional Objectives*. Palo Alto, Cal.: Fearon, 1962.

Mehrens, William A. and Lehmann, Irving J. *Measurement and Evaluation in Education and Psychology*, 2nd ed. New York: Holt, Rinehart & Winston, 1978.

Mizell, M. Hayes. "A Citizen's Introduction to Minimal Competency Testing," in Peter W.

Airasian, George F. Madaus, and Joseph J. Pedulla, eds. *Minimal Competency Testing*. Englewood Cliffs, N.J.: Educational Technology Publications, 1979.

Sax, Gilbert. *Principles of Educational and Psychological Measurement and Evaluation*, 2nd ed. Belmont, Cal.: Wadsworth, 1980.

Stauffer, Russell G., Abrams, Jules, and Pikulski, John. *Diagnosis, Correction and Prevention of Reading Disabilities*. New York: Harper & Row, 1978.

Thorndike, Robert L. and Hagen, Elizabeth P. *Measurement and Evaluation in Psychology and Education*, 4th ed. New York: Wiley, 1977.

Chapter Nine

Assessing Reading-Related Factors

In this chapter we discuss intellectual, physical, and emotional factors, topics often thought to be secondary or contributing causes of reading problems.

It is true that these topics are peripheral to reading, but actually it is for this reason that they deserve careful attention. Most classroom teachers are more or less accustomed to testing reading skills within their classrooms. The testing of intelligence, vision and hearing, emotional and personality development, and special learning problems, however, is usually done outside the regular classroom by the school nurse, school psychologist, counselor, and other specialists. As a result, many teachers feel personally uninvolved in the assessment of these factors and often do not know much about how they affect reading.

In the past, children with special intellectual, physical, or emotional needs were largely excluded from the regular curriculum. Now, however, education has changed for children with special needs. New laws and growing public awareness have led to changes in educational policy toward all "special" children (Colley, 1981). By far the most important piece of legislation is Public Law 94–142, enacted in 1975. PL 94–142, the Education for All Handicapped Children Act, affects not only special educators but also every teacher at every level.

Special-Needs Students and PL 94–142

PL 94–142 is often referred to as the "mainstreaming law," but that term refers to only one of its provisions. In reality, it mandates a number of far-reaching changes in the education of students with special needs. Below we have listed the law's major provisions, the immediate implications of each provision for the classroom teacher, and a summary of the basic rights of handicapped students under the law.

Provision: Free public education will be provided for all handicapped persons between the ages of three and twenty-one years of age.

Implications: Schools must serve the needs of students both older and younger than those served in the past. The traditional concept of "school-age children" between five and eighteen has been drastically modified. Since the law provides for grants that create financial incentives for schools to identify handicapped preschoolers and provide special services for them, kindergarten and primary grade teachers are involved in early identification programs.

At the other end of the age scale, teachers in all grades are affected by the mainstreaming of handicapped older students into regular classes (see below). This is particularly important in high schools where pupils up to the age of twenty-one may be included in regular classes. Teachers must be aware of the special needs and interests of handicapped older students and young adults who are placed in classes with younger pupils.

Provision: Handicapped students will be placed in the least restrictive environment whenever and wherever possible. This often means mainstreaming handicapped children into the regular classroom and curriculum.

Implications: The inclusion of handicapped students in regular classrooms for part or all of the school day affects nearly every teacher. All teachers must clearly understand how the handicaps of students affect their learning, how materials and activities must be adapted appropriately, how their performances are to be evaluated, and how to deal positively with their social and interpersonal problems. In addition, regular classroom teachers have to be routinely involved in the assessment of these students' special needs.

Provision: Each handicapped student will be provided with an individualized educational program, called an IEP, which spells out present abilities, short- and long-term goals, and the means by which goals will be achieved. Each student's IEP will be developed jointly by teachers, parents, and the student where possible.

Implications: All teachers working with mainstreamed students have direct responsibility for the planning, implementing, and evaluating of instructional programs. They must expand their understanding of handicapping conditions, management techniques, teaching strategies, and materials in order to develop and use IEPs. In developing IEPs, teachers have to join forces with the parents of handicapped students for greater parental involvement and teacher accountability. In many cases the students can be included in the development of their IEPs, to the extent that they are able to participate.

Provision: All tests and evaluative instruments used will be prepared and administered so as to eliminate racial and cultural discrimination.

Implications: Tests and assessment devices have to be closely scrutinized to eliminate discriminatory aspects. Results of a single test or measure cannot be used to classify students, a practice that has sometimes been followed in the past. In addition, tests must be modified when necessary so that handicapped students can respond to them in ways that are best for them, for example in Braille or in a sign language. They must be administered in the student's native language, or in sign language or cued speech for hearing-impaired students. These modifications entail widespread changes both in test construction and in the ways tests are administered and interpreted.

The provisions of PL 94–142 also establish certain basic rights for handicapped students:

1. the right to due process, which protects the individual from erroneous classification, capricious labeling, and denial of equal education;
2. protection against discriminatory testing in diagnosis, which ensures against possible bias in intelligence tests (and other tests) used with ethnic minority children;

3. placement in an educational setting that is the least restrictive environment, which protects the individual from possible detrimental effects of segregated education for the handicapped;

4. individual program plans, which ensure accountability by those responsible for the education of the handicapped. (MacMillan, 1977, p. 1)

Individual school divisions differ in minor ways in the procedures they follow regarding referral and classification, but a sequence of events such as this is typical:

1. A teacher who suspects that a student needs special services requests special screening for the student by notifying the school principal.

2. The principal obtains parental permission for such screening and arranges for it.

Screening must include educational, psychological, medical, and sociological assessments. Teachers are directly involved in the educational assessments. The law requires that a team approach be used, and most schools have a standing screening committee that is comprised of a special education teacher or assessment specialist, the referring teacher, the school principal or principal's designee, and, in many cases, the child's parent(s). It may also include a school psychologist or psychometrist and a teacher or specialist with training and expertise in the area of the suspected disability, often a reading teacher.

Educational assessment devices vary from place to place, but the use of a combination of standardized and informal tests is common and in some states is required. The Wechsler Intelligence Scale for Children-Revised Form (WISC-R), Peabody Picture Vocabulary Test (PPVT), Peabody Individual Achievement Test (PIAT), Wide Range Achievement Test (WRAT), and Woodcock Reading Mastery Test are commonly used formal tests. Informal assessments may include tests such as an IRI, observations by one or more team members, classwork attempted by the student, and other diagnostic data.

3. The principal or other administrator involved arranges a meeting to discuss the screening results with the parents, the evaluation team, the student's teachers(s), and the special education specialists.

4. At this meeting, all relevant assessment and instructional data are detailed. Teachers may present the results of informal diagnostic procedures, which are very useful in developing a picture of the student's abilities and needs and provide a valuable supplement to the formal tests given by the other members of the evaluation team.

After all data have been discussed, the team members individually indicate whether special education placement is warranted. Parental consent *must* be given for such placement.

5. If placement is agreed upon, an IEP is developed for the student. It must include a statement of the student's present levels of functioning, both

short-term and annual goals, projected dates for initiation and duration of special services, specific criteria and evaluation procedures to be used to determine if goals have been achieved, the names of persons responsible for special services and evaluation, descriptions of special services to be provided, and the extent to which the student will participate in regular education programs. Parental approval must again be given for the IEP to be implemented; if they do not approve it, or do not approve any subsequent changes in it, an impartial due process hearing must be held. Special services cannot be provided until after the IEP is developed and approved.

6. The next step is to place the student in the least restrictive educational environment where special services are provided and implementation of the IEP proceeds. Every educator (or agency) involved is required to make good faith efforts to help the student achieve the goals set forth in the IEP. Parents can request program review and revision if they believe such good faith efforts have not been made, but if in spite of such efforts the student does not achieve the goals of the IEP, no individual is to be held accountable.

The Education for All Handicapped Children Act requires massive changes in attitudes and procedures for dealing with children who have special educational needs. A reading problem may be a symptom of an educational handicap, such as a learning disability, or may result from a handicap such as visual or auditory impairment. Reading teachers must expand their traditional knowledge base about the physical, intellectual, and emotional difficulties involved in order to teach all students effectively. This requirement cannot be overemphasized.

In the following sections we introduce some of the more common terms and their implications, outline the appropriate informal classroom assessment or observation techniques, and discuss the more common intellectual, physical, and emotional factors often involved in reading difficulties.

Intellectual Factors

Intelligence Tests

In diagnosing a reading problem, one of the most frequently used instruments is an intelligence test. Why? Is intelligence so clearly and directly related to reading success or failure, or to the remediation of reading problems, that an I.Q. test will be helpful? What is the relationship between intelligence and reading?

Those questions cannot be answered simply, because the relationship is unclear and poorly understood at best. Broad trends in the research literature show what seem to be contradictory findings: (a) that good readers tend to be smarter than poor readers, at least in terms of I.Q. test performance and (b) that reading problems are not limited to lower-I.Q. students but are found across the whole range of intellectual abilities. How are these findings to be interpreted?

There has long been some general agreement that intelligence and reading achievement are fairly well correlated, particularly in the upper grades. What this means is that better performance on reading tests and intelligence tests tends to occur together; students generally do well on both or poorly on both. It does *not* imply causation; we cannot infer from positive correlations that one factor causes the other, only that they coincide. It may be that above average intelligence encourages above average reading achievement. It may be equally true that good reading helps students do better on intelligence tests. Or it may be that *both* reading tests and I.Q. tests call upon the same kinds of abilities and knowledge. But poor readers may come from all ability levels.

What *do* I.Q. tests tell us? That depends very much on which test is used. Not all measure the same skills, and in order to evaluate results, we have to know something about their characteristics.

Some tests that yield an I.Q., or a kind of "ability quotient," are group tests; many of them require the student to read and mark answers. Some representative group tests are the California Test of Mental Maturity, the Lorge-Thorndike Intelligence Tests, the Kuhlman-Anderson Measure of Academic Potential, and the Short Test of Education Ability (STEA). These are more like reading tests than intelligence tests.

An individually administered I.Q. test that does not require the student to read or write will give a better estimate of real performance, but there are different types of individual I.Q. tests.

Two that can be given by teachers without specialized training are the Slosson Intelligence Test (SIT) and the Peabody Picture Vocabulary Test (PPVT). Both are individually administered and reading is not required.

In the Slosson Intelligence Test (Slosson, 1963), linguistic questions are asked and answered orally. Mathematical problems are done "in the head." The questions, adapted from subtests of the widely known Stanford-Binet Intelligence Scale, call for general information, repetition of digit spans and sentences, arithmetic calculations, verbal similarities and opposites, and definition of vocabulary items. Each question represents an average mental age in years and months. The person being tested is given credit, in months of mental age, for items answered correctly. The I.Q. is calculated from chronological age and mental age. Mental age is calculated by the number of correct answers. Here are some representative questions from the Slosson, with the age for which each is supposed to be typical:

(7–8)   How is a *submarine different* from a *fish?* How are they alike? (p. 7)
(7–10) How many *months* in a year? (p. 7)
(10–8) If a boy had *45 cents,* how many *nickel* or *5 cent* suckers could he buy?
        (p. 8)

(11–4) Say these numbers *forwards* for me: 9 3 5 2 8 6. (p. 8)
(13–6) What is the *difference* between *contraction* and *expansion?* (p. 9)
(17–0) What does *mutilate* mean? (p. 10)
(21–0) A dog is canine. A cat is _____. (p. 11)

(Slosson, 1963)

The Slosson Intelligence Test clearly calls for different kinds of mental operations and information in its questions, but all the items are language-dependent because they must all be solved or responded to through language. The Slosson has no nonverbal component, and the I.Q. thus derived is an estimate of *verbal* intelligence. It is best used only for screening purposes.

The Peabody Picture Vocabulary Test (Dunn, 1959) yields I.Q. and mental age scores, but its content is more limited than that of the Slosson. The Peabody is a test of receptive vocabulary; for each item, the examiner pronounces a single word and the subject chooses one picture representing the stimulus word from a plate of four pictures. The subject responds by pointing; no oral response is necessary. Here are some sample items from Form A:

STIMULUS WORD	PLATE SHOWS
eagle	spider, whale, eagle, giraffe (Plate 43)
stunt	performing seal, deer, horse, penguin (Plate 70)
cascade	mountain, underwater scene, waterfall, garden maze (Plate 104)
ellipse	concentric circles, oval, circle with congruent line, angle (Plate 123)
legume	rose, palm tree, peanut plant, fern (Plate 137)
predatory	ape, sheep, fox eating hen, elephants (Plate 145)

(Dunn, 1959)

Like the SIT, the PPVT tests verbal intelligence only. In fact, it tests only one aspect of verbal intelligence: vocabulary. As a test of vocabulary it is a useful device. As a test of general intelligence, it has clear limitations and is probably better suited for screening purposes.

Some intelligence tests used in reading diagnosis require special training to administer and must be given under strictly standard conditions. The Stanford-Binet Intelligence Scale and the Wechsler Intelligence Scales are usually given by school psychologists or specially trained clinicians.

The Stanford-Binet, last revised in 1972, is descended from the Binet

Scale developed in 1905, the first standardized intelligence measure. Items are arranged according to age level, and at each mental age level the subject is asked several questions of different types. The questions are very similar to those sampled from the SIT, because Slosson adapted questions from the Stanford-Binet subtests for his test. The Stanford-Binet, yielding an overall mental age and I.Q. scores, is not reading-dependent but is heavily influenced by verbal intelligence.

Probably the most widely used individual intelligence tests are the Wechsler Scales. With separate forms for preschoolers, school-age children, and adults, the Wechsler Scales represent an attempt to assess verbal and nonverbal aspects of intelligence separately.

The Wechsler Intelligence Scale for Children-Revised Form (Wechsler, 1974), known as the WISC-R, is widely used in schools and clinics. Items on the WISC-R are arranged by type, in ascending order of difficulty, and there are twelve subtests to measure different skills and operations. Scores from the subtests involving language operations are considered together, as are scores from the nonverbal (performance) subtests. In this way, separate Verbal and Performance Scale I.Q.s are derived, which can be compared to determine if both aspects of the subject's intellect seem to be equally well developed.

When the test is administered, verbal and performance subtests are given alternately, but for descriptive purposes it is simpler to consider all six subtests of each scale together. Tables 9.1 and 9.2 describe the subtests of the verbal and performance scales (Kaufman, 1979).

Raw scores from each subtest are converted to *scaled scores*, standard scores ranging from 1 to 19 with a mean of 10 and a standard deviation of 3. Transforming raw scores into standard units makes it possible to compare results of one subtest to another.

The Digit Span (Verbal Scale) and Mazes (Performance Scale) are optional subtests. When they are given, their resulting scaled scores are not included in the computation of the Verbal, Performance, or Full Scale I.Q.s. Wechsler (1974), however, recommended that Mazes be used instead of Coding when testing children below eight years of age because the Mazes subtest yields more reliable scores than Coding when used with young children.

The Full Scale I.Q. represents the subject's overall intelligence as measured by performance on the ten key subtests. The Verbal, Performance, and Full Scale I.Q.s all have a mean of 100 and a standard deviation of 10. The test uses the following classification scheme for I.Q. scores:

130 and above:	Very superior
120–129:	Superior
110–119:	High average
90–109:	Average

80–89:   Low average
70–79:   Borderline
69 and below: Mentally deficient

Clinicians often look for differences between Verbal and Performance Scale I.Q.s (see Kaufman, 1979) and differences among subtest scores (see Searls, 1975). Although these analyses can sometimes be helpful, we must be wary of overinterpreting any set of scores that represent a sample of behavior taken at one point in time. We can avoid overinterpretation by considering I.Q. scores in terms of the range in which they occurred, rather than as a single, fixed score. The WISC-R has a standard error of measurement of about 5 I.Q. points; a Full Scale I.Q. score could thus be expected to vary by ±5 points because of probable random effects. For this reason it is more informative to speak of a student's I.Q. score as "within the high average range," for example, than to say that the same student has "an I.Q. of 117."

When interpreting scores on the WISC-R or any other intelligence test, it

TABLE 9.1. WISC-R Verbal Scale subtests.

VERBAL SCALE SUBTESTS	ABILITIES ASSESSED	SUBJECT TO INFLUENCE OF	SAMPLE ITEMS
Information	Range of factual information; acquired knowledge; memory (long term)	Life experience; reading; school learning	What does the stomach do? Who was Charles Darwin?
Similarities	Categorical thinking; abstract reasoning; verbal concept formation	Reading; interest; school learning	In what way are a hat and a shirt alike?
Arithmetic	Acquired knowledge; arithmetic reasoning; memory (long term); computational skill	Attention span; anxiety; concentration; time pressure	A workman earning $4.00 per hour was paid $36.00. How long did he work?
Vocabulary	Language development; knowledge; expression	Reading; school learning; environmental and cultural opportunities	What is a *donkey?* What does *gamble* mean?
Comprehension	Practical information; common sense and social judgment	Development of conscience and moral sense; cultural influences	Why are criminals locked up? Why should a promise be kept?
Digit Span (optional subtest)	Short-term memory	Attention span; distractability; anxiety	Strings of 3–9 digits

TABLE 9.2. WISC-R Performance Scale subtests.

PERFORMANCE SCALE SUBTESTS	ABILITIES ASSESSED	SUBJECT TO INFLUENCE OF	SAMPLE ITEM
Picture Completion	Visual alertness; attention to detail; long-term visual memory	Concentration, speed of response	Locate missing item in picture: ladder without rung
Picture Arrangement	Temporal sequence; anticipation of outcomes	Creativity, cultural influences; experience reading comic strips	Arrange 4–5 pictures in story sequence
Block Design	Whole-part analysis; spatial visualization; motor coordination	Time pressure; impulsivity; clumsiness	Reproduce design with blocks:
Object Assembly	Part-whole relationships; flexibility; visual perception and visual-motor coordination	Experience with puzzles; compulsivity; clumsiness; time pressure	Assemble puzzle pieces: face, car
Coding	Short-term visual memory; direction following; motor speed and accuracy	Anxiety, distractibility; lack of experience with writing tasks	Copy symbols corresponding to digits 1–9 in random order
Mazes (optional subtest)	Following visual pattern; anticipation of outcomes	Time pressure; experience with mazes; anxiety	Follow increasingly complex mazes with pencil

is most important to remember that the scores represent only a portion of one's intellectual functioning. Wechsler himself was critically aware of this when he wrote, "I have, however, become increasingly convinced that intelligence is most usefully interpreted as an aspect of the total personality. I look upon intelligence as an effect rather than a cause, that is, as a resultant of interacting abilities — nonintellective included" (Wechsler, 1958, p. vii). Personality, interests, motivation, social and moral values, home and cultural influences all are bound up with intellect and its manifestation on intelligence tests. Kaufman stresses the need for ". . . integration of background information, behavioral observations, and other test scores with the obtained WISC-R scores to properly interpret the intelligence-test data" (Kaufman, 1979, p. 59). Perhaps nowhere in assessment is the consideration of the *whole* individual as critically important as in the interpretation of intelligence tests.

The Role of Experience

When we consider the concept of intelligence in terms of a student's personality, background, interests, and other related aspects as well as in terms of subtest behaviors and I.Q. points, we come smack up against the role of experience. It is difficult to underestimate the importance of experience, both real and vicarious, in shaping intelligence and I.Q. test performance.

Kaufman (1979) and others have described some of the influences affecting performance on the various WISC-R subtests. Many of them are directly related to the degree of experience children have had with objects, events, and people in their home and school environments. It is easy to see how subtests like Information, Similarities, and Vocabulary are influenced by general knowledge and experiences in life. So too are the Performance Scale subtests of Picture Completion, Object Assembly, and Coding as well as nearly all items on the Stanford-Binet, Slosson Intelligence Test, and the Peabody Picture Vocabulary Test. The youngster who has grown up in an environment rich in concrete experiences, extended language use, and intellectual stimulation has an obvious advantage when it comes to taking these tests.

What kind of experience are we talking about? Essentially, we learn about ourselves and our world in two ways: by real, concrete experience with objects and events, and vicariously, by observing and remembering the experiences of others.

Real experiences in the formative years contribute to what most of us think of as an enriched environment. Enrichment has little to do with economics; it has much more to do with having opportunities to manipulate things, experimenting with causes, effects, and consequences, and being consistently encouraged to extend cognitive horizons and try new things. These characteristics of an intellectually enriching environment know no economic, ethnic, social, or linguistic boundaries. They flourish where adults respect and nurture children's attempts to become competent and where those adults give conscious thought to providing opportunities for children to become independent and capable.

Direct, concrete experience with things and events is one critical aspect; experience with language is another. Verbal intelligence flourishes in the home, and later the school, where children are talked to by adults, where adults really listen to their responses and encourage conversation, where events and behaviors are explained and verbal reasoning is demonstrated, where adults model language use by expanding and elaborating on what children say. In environments where children are rarely addressed except in commands, where their spontaneous utterances are rarely listened to or responded to, where their requests for explanations are routinely answered

Reading provides a rich source of vicarious experience that extends and deepens our understanding of ourselves and our world.

by "Because I said so, that's why!" and explanations are rarely given, verbal intelligence is stunted. These children enter the world of language poorly adapted to participate in it fully. Their learning opportunities are restricted by language rather than expanded by it. Whatever their socioeconomic status, they are disadvantaged in school.

The other important aspect of experience is vicarious experience. Fortunately for all of us, we can learn from observing others as well as by experiencing things ourselves. Learning from the experiences of others saves us from having to experience everything personally, and we can derive nearly as much from those experiences as from our own.

Perhaps the greatest benefit of literacy is that through reading we can vicariously experience events, emotions, and ideas completely outside our own environment. We can travel to places we will never go to, including places that exist only in the mind; visit the past and the future with as much ease as the present; meet the most famous people of history and share their innermost thoughts; find the most exciting lovers, battle the most dangerous adversaries, experience joy, rage, grief, amazement, and every other human emotion by reading. All this makes good reading a lifelong joy and sustenance instead of just a useful skill.

Reading and books, however, are more than a source of pleasure. They remain, in spite of the inroads of TV and films, the largest source of information for many people. Schools still use books and other forms of print as the major vehicles for transmitting information.

Yet what happens to the students who cannot read or cannot read well enough to reap all those benefits? They are in large part closed off from those myriad sources of vicarious experience and information. Their literate classmates go on year after year acquiring knowledge and understandings, figuratively laying down layer upon layer of print-conveyed information in their minds. The poor readers or nonreaders don't have this information store, and every year they spend away from the printed word, the less they know in comparison to their age-mates.

The calculation of mental ages and I.Q.s is built on the comparison of people of the same age. The tests of intelligence discussed here call for the kinds of learning an educated person would have acquired in school: facts, word meanings, arithmetic calculations, and the ability to make analogies and get meaning from print and visual arrays. No wonder the illiterate student usually does so poorly even on I.Q. tests that are not reading-dependent. In school, the act of acquiring knowledge is largely reading-dependent!

Do illiterate older students do poorly on I.Q. tests because they are intellectually deficient or because they can't read? The question is like "the chicken or the egg?" The answer hardly matters. If they are ever going to begin to catch up, they must be able to read. Teaching them to read is probably the hardest task in teaching, but it must be attempted because otherwise they face a lifetime of being second class intellectually, and our society just cannot afford it.

Informal Assessment of Capacity

Teachers can use the listening comprehension measure from an IRI to gain informal information about a student's capacity.

Hearing capacity is not the same as I.Q. or mental age. It is a concept specifically related to reading ability. For this reason, it may be more directly useful to the teacher than I.Q. test scores or estimates of mental age.

The listening comprehension measure gives an estimate of students' potential for improvement in reading ability. It does this by allowing a comparison of students' reading levels to the level of material they can understand when hearing it read aloud. By listening to written language read aloud and answering comprehension questions on what they heard, they can use verbal intelligence to deal with information conveyed in print. By comparing the grade level of material the student can read to the grade level of material the student can understand by listening, the teacher can determine approximately how much improvement is possible.

It is not necessary to use this procedure along with an IRI. Even if you use IRI passages and questions, listening comprehension can be estimated at any time without doing any other testing of reading comprehension. If IRI passages are not used, teachers can begin with their regular grade-level reader or other textbook. With questions prepared beforehand (see Chapter Four), a teacher can determine in a few minutes if a student is able to comprehend that text when it is read aloud or discussed in class. If the teacher determines that the text is too difficult for the student to understand on an aural level, an easier book could be attempted, or assessment could end there. One way or the other, the teacher can find out whether the book's concepts and vocabulary are too advanced for the student to deal with even by listening.

This finding is important, because it helps the teacher set reasonable instructional goals. If students can neither read nor listen to the text and make sense of it, there is little reason to believe that they can be taught to read it effectively in the near future. The time-honored remedial practice of having poor readers listen to their textbooks on tapes or others read the books aloud will probably do little immediate good at this point. Materials at a lower level of difficulty must be substituted for the grade-level texts and discussions must be geared to the student's ability to understand.

If, however, teachers find that although students cannot read the text, they can understand it adequately through listening, they have made an important finding. First, they can be confident that the students have the necessary verbal concepts to benefit from discussions, lectures, and other oral activities within their regular grade level. Second, the teachers know that these students have the potential to be able to learn to read at their grade level if they are given sufficient and appropriate corrective instruction. Third, while corrective instruction is going on, the students can gain enough information and vocabulary by listening to tapes to be able to keep up with their peers in classroom oral activities.

Physical Factors

Many physical conditions and processes can be related to reading problems. The factors most commonly considered are visual, auditory, and neurological processes. Each of these areas has been extensively studied in relation to reading difficulties, but the research data and the various conditions and processes themselves are complex and sometimes confusing. In this section we will consider vision, hearing, and some disabilities often attributed to neurological functioning.

Vision

Reading is a visual act (for sighted persons) in that we cannot read in the dark. It is, of course, much more than just a visual act because, as discussed in Chapter One, more goes on behind the reader's eyes than in front of them, but some visual competence is needed to activate the cognitive processes involved in reading. In order to make sense of print, the reader must be able to gain information from print through vision. For this reason, poor readers are often subjected to vision screening in diagnosis. You may find it helpful to review the discussion of eye movements and visual perception in Chapter One.

Common Vision Problems. Teachers are sometimes the first line of defense against vision problems. They are usually in the best position to spot potential problems and refer children for appropriate screening because they, more than parents, observe children in close contact with reading and writing materials. Also, children with vision problems often don't realize that others see differently, and they don't call adult attention to their difficulty. Therefore, it is important for teachers to understand vision problems and their symptoms. Table 9.3 summarizes the nature and symptoms of some common visual difficulties.

These vision problems can be so minor that they have few if any symptoms, and even the reader may be unaware of any problem. Or they can be so severe that normal classroom activities are extremely difficult. Usually the teacher is in a position to detect fairly minor problems which, if treated promptly, are easy to correct. All of the aforementioned vision problems are correctable, most with glasses or contact lenses, some with a combination of corrective lenses and muscle exercises.

Astigmatism, hyperopia, and myopia are by far the most common problems. Astigmatism (blurring of part of the image) can occur in conjunction with either near- or farsightedness, but both conditions are corrected simultaneously with lenses. Hyperopia, blurring of the image at the near point, makes reading and writing uncomfortable and tiring and has long been associated with reading problems. Mild hyperopia is fairly common when children enter school (Spache, 1976; Woodruff, 1972). After more and more close work in the first few years of school, this developmental farsightedness disappears for most children, and many become mildly myopic as they learn to read. Myopia, better acuity (keenness) of vision up close than at a distance, does not interfere with reading; in fact, myopia is common in good readers and students with good school achievement (Ekwall, 1976; Spache, 1976). There is some evidence that myopia may be largely developmental and environmentally produced by the demands of close work with print during the school years (Lanyon and Giddings, 1974). While nearsightedness does not contribute directly to reading problems, it can give children difficulty in doing board work and can be a cause of inattention during such activities.

Although vision problems may be very different, they often have identical symptoms. Teachers can do little more than guess about the precise nature of the problem in many cases, but they should be alert to the continuing presence of the symptoms that Spache claims have been validated by professional eye examiners (see Table 9.4).

TABLE 9.3. Vision problems.

TECHNICAL NAME	COMMON NAME	CONDITION	SYMPTOMS
Myopia	Nearsightedness	Clear vision at near point; blurring of distant images	Squinting at the board; holding print close to face; inattention to board work
Hyperopia	Farsightedness	Clear vision at far point; blurring of close objects	Holding print well away from face; disinterest in close work; eye fatigue during reading
Astigmatism		Distortion and/or blurring of part (or all) of visual field, far and near	Eye fatigue; headache; squinting; tilting or turning head; nausea during reading
Amblyopia	Lazy eye	Suppression of vision in one eye; dimming of vision without structural cause	Tilting or turning head to read; eye fatigue on one side; headache
Strabismus	Crossed eyes	Difficulty converging and focusing both eyes on the same object	Squinting; closing or covering one eye to focus; eyes misaligned
Phoria or fusion problems; binocular coordination		Imbalance of ocular muscles; difficulty converging and focusing both eyes equally	Squinting; closing or covering one eye
Aniseikonia		Differences in size or shape of image in each eye	Blurring; squinting; difficulty focusing or fusing image; closing one eye

As Spache and others have pointed out, many of these symptoms are sometimes demonstrated by poor readers whose vision is unimpaired. When any of these signs are displayed frequently, are not common to the rest of the class, and are evidenced even when performing easy tasks, they should signal a need for referral to an eye specialist.

There are many more elaborate lists of symptoms. Many include behaviors common to most poor readers even with no visual problems. Ekwall (1976), for example, cites a lengthy list of "Observable Clues to Classroom

TABLE 9.4. Symptoms of problems in vision.

APPEARANCE OF EYES	One eye turns in or out at any time
	Eyes or lids sometimes reddened
	Excessive tearing
	Encrusted eyelids or frequent sties (inflammation of sebaceous gland of eyelid)
COMPLAINTS FROM SUSTAINED CLOSE WORK	Headache in forehead, temples or eyes
	Burning or itching eyes
	Nausea or dizziness
	Blurring after reading awhile
POSTURE AND SEATED BEHAVIOR	Squints, closes or covers one eye
	Tilts or turns head constantly to read or write
	Blinks excessively during reading
	Strains forward to see board
	Holds head or book excessively near or far
	Fatigues quickly and avoids near-point tasks

SOURCE: From George D. Spache, *Diagnosing and Correcting Reading Disabilities*, pp. 30–31 (Newton, Mass.: Allyn & Bacon, 1976). Reprinted by permission.

Vision Problems" published by the Optometric Extension Program Foundation, Inc. (1968). Included in this checklist are such ubiquitous reading behaviors as:

□ loses place during reading
□ short attention span in reading or copying
□ omits letters, numbers, or phrases
□ fails to recognize same word in next sentence
□ reverses letters or words in writing
□ confuses same word in same sentence
□ whispers to self while reading silently
□ comprehension reduces as reading continues

Most teachers would agree that "symptoms" like these are extremely common to many kinds of reading problems, including simply having to read at one's frustration level. Many of these behaviors can disappear spontaneously if the reader is given less frustrating material to read. They should not be ignored, but they should not automatically be attributed to visual deficits, either.

Vision Screening Measures. Whenever a teacher suspects that a student has an uncorrected vision problem, the student should be referred to a vision specialist for testing. Referrals should be made through the principal, school nurse, supervisor, or other designated personnel.

In some schools the nurse, reading or resource teacher, or other special-ist will use a vision screening battery prior to referral to an outside expert. A *stereoscopic instrument* is often used for testing vision in each eye and both together. (Stereoscopes are commonly used to test vision for a driver's license; you may have had your vision checked this way.) The following are done with a stereoscope:

- Keystone Visual Survey Telebinocular Test: screens for myopia, hyper-opia, fusion problems, depth perception, and color blindness, using test cards.
- Ortho-Rater: originally developed for adults, recently adapted for use with children, this device screens for acuity problems, depth percep-tion, and binocular (both eyes) coordination.
- Titmus Professional Vision Tester and Titmus Biopter: like the Key-stone, tests for binocular fusion, myopia, hyperopia, astigmatism, depth perception, and color blindness.

Two test batteries can be used together with a stereoscopic instrument and the previously listed tests. They extend the scope of the other tests to include aspects of vision problems sometimes detected only by professional vision experts:

- Walton Modified Telebinocular Technique: Using a Keystone Tele-binocular machine and an additional card, the procedure screens for amblyopia, myopia, hyperopia, and astigmatism and features revised scoring procedures for the muscular imbalance (fusion and phoria) tests. This procedure was found to be as effective in detecting vision problems as much more exhaustive professional exams and is practical for school use (Schubert and Walton, 1980).
- Spache Binocular Reading Test: Tests for suppression of vision in either eye and binocular vision in reading; test cards contain paragraphs to be read aloud at several difficulty levels; cards can be used with most models of stereoscope such as the Keystone Telebinocular or Titmus Biopter.

The Snellen Chart, that familiar wall chart with its rows of letters of decreasing size, deserves a comment. It is a device that measures one's ability to see letters from a distance of twenty feet. It can detect nearsighted-ness (myopia), but myopia rarely has any effect on reading. The chart is useless in detecting visual problems that *can* affect reading such as farsightedness, astigmatism, or binocular fusion problems. The exclusive use of the Snellen Chart is clearly inadequate for effective vision screening.

Hearing

The relationship between auditory problems and reading difficulties has long been established. Hearing and language are as intimately related as language and reading. As teachers observe the oral and written language of their students, they can become aware of possible hearing problems.

When children learn to read, they employ their whole experience with oral language. We know that oral language development and learning to read are closely related and that the ability to process and understand *written* language depends in large part on being able to process and understand *oral* language. Hearing problems can interfere with, delay, or even prevent the development of oral language fluency, and it is in this respect that hearing problems can affect reading.

Another factor is the heavy reliance on oral activities and phonics instruction. Across the entire spectrum of approaches, some features of every beginning reading program are standard: learning letter names and sounds, use of simple phonic analysis strategies to decode words, and frequent oral reading. These activities put a premium on clarity of hearing, and the youngster with auditory problems is at a distinct disadvantage.

Thus hearing problems that occur anytime in the first eight to ten years of life may affect a child's reading by interfering with language development in the preschool years or with the largely oral reading instruction of the primary grades.

Types of Hearing Problems. Testing of auditory acuity (keenness) involves assessment of the ability to hear speech sounds, music, and noises. In reading, it is the speech sounds that are critical.

Speech sounds are measured in terms of *pitch* and *volume*. Pitch refers to the frequency of a sound; speech sounds are high-tone or low-tone depending on their pitch. Pitch is measured in *hertz*, or cycles per second. High-frequency, or high-tone, sounds have a higher number of cycles per second than low tones. Speech sounds of the normal human voice range from 128 to 4000 cycles per second; consonant sounds are higher in pitch than vowel sounds (Bond, Tinker, and Wasson, 1979).

Volume or loudness is measured in units called *decibels*. Normal conversation is usually around sixty decibels, the volume necessary for classroom activities.

Hearing losses can affect the perception of pitch or volume or both. If the child can hear some sound frequencies but not others, it can be devastating in learning to read because it means that the child can hear some speech sounds accurately but not others. Hearing loss involving the high-frequency sounds is more common than loss of low-frequency sounds. Children with high-frequency hearing loss can accurately hear vowel sounds and maybe some consonant sounds but not all of them.

Those with high-tone losses may hear spoken words in a garbled, indistinct fashion, depending on how many consonant sounds are affected. If only vowels can be heard, words are almost totally meaningless because consonant sounds are what make spoken words intelligible. (Read a line of print aloud to someone, pronouncing only the vowel sounds; repeat the line pronouncing only the consonant sounds. Which version could the listener more easily understand?)

Hearing losses are not always as severe as the previous example. Often only a few consonant and blend sounds are affected, but phonics instruction is made very difficult by this loss, and the student may be very poor at word analysis and word recognition. Also, the words that are most often taught in beginning reading frequently vary only in their consonant sounds, as in the "word families" and rhyming word patterns (cat-hat-pat-mat-sat). Learning these words can be very difficult for the child with high-tone hearing loss.

Some hearing problems are caused by volume impairment at most or all frequencies. These cases can be helped by hearing aids, which amplify sound at all levels. Since volume loss affects the perception of all types of sounds, it is probably the most obvious and the easiest to spot in the classroom. Loss of only certain sounds is more difficult to spot because the student will hear many sounds normally and problems may be blamed on inattention or carelessness.

Symptoms of both types of hearing loss are similar. The main difference is that the child with volume loss will have trouble consistently while the child with selective frequency losses will hear many sounds normally. In general, the following physical signs may be apparent:

- □ frequent requests to have statements repeated
- □ frequent confusion of simple oral directions
- □ ringing, buzzing, or pain in ears
- □ turning or tilting head toward speaker
- □ strained posture in listening
- □ cupping of ears toward speaker
- □ unusually loud or monotonous voice

At first glance, some of these signs are similar to those of children with vision problems. Behaviors like inattention, strained posture, scowling, or squinting can be common to children with hearing or vision problems, or to children who are free of physical problems but who are simply frustrated in reading.

Another very important factor in the diagnosis of hearing problems is the *duration* of the problem. While volume losses are usually of a more or less chronic nature, many selective frequency losses are temporary. It is very common for children to experience temporary loss of some sounds during and after a heavy cold or upper respiratory infection. These hearing losses can last from a few days to a few months, and while they exist, they can interfere with normal classroom activities.

Children with colds or other upper respiratory infections and respiratory allergies are subject to middle-ear impairments called *conductive hearing losses* (Dirks, 1978). Two types of conductive problems are particularly common in school-age children. One condition is *otitis media,* a collection of fluid in the middle ear. Fluid in the middle ear distends the eardrum outward, inhibiting its ability to vibrate freely and thus reducing the signal transmitted inward. A second common conductive loss occurs when air pressure on either side of the eardrum is unequal. From the middle ear, a tunnel, the *eustachian tube,* runs to the back of the throat at the level of the nose. This tube's function is to equalize pressure on both sides of the eardrum (Sanders, 1977). When heavy upper respiratory congestion is present, the eustachian tube can collapse or close up. As a result, the eardrum cannot properly conduct sound. Implantation of plastic tubes in the eustachian tube now corrects the problem without surgery.

Children who do not receive the necessary medical treatment for chronic infections may suffer these temporary hearing losses. Those with chronic colds, or those returning to school after a particularly severe upper respiratory infection, should have auditory screening at regular intervals, with particular attention paid to perception of the high-tone sounds.

While middle ear disorders are more common in children, inner ear disorders can also cause hearing impairment. Within the inner ear the *cochlea,* a bony structure looking like a coiled shell, contains the sensory organs of hearing and the components of the body's balance system. Here the sound waves that have been transmitted by vibration to the inner ear are transformed into mechanical, electrical, and chemical signals and transmitted to the brain (Sanders, 1977). The cochlea and its delicate transmission functions can be damaged by excessive noise, certain drugs, and exposure to infections like mumps and rubella (German measles).

Auditory Screening Methods. The most reliable method examines volume in decibels and different frequencies in cycles per second. An instrument called an *audiometer* is used to produce pure tones generally ranging from 125 to 8000 cycles per second in pitch and from about 10 to 110 decibels in volume.

An audiometer can be used for screening groups of students, but the most accurate screening is done individually. The subject is seated so that the audiometer controls are not visible. Headphones are worn so each ear can be tested separately, and a buzzer or other signaling device is used as a means of responding to the test. The examiner uses the audiometer to produce each tone at a full range of volume from soft to loud, and the subject signals when the tone is first audible and also indicates its duration. The examiner can occasionally check to see that the subject is not just signaling randomly by using an interrupter switch to cut off the signal momentarily.

A topic related to auditory acuity is *auditory discrimination,* the ability to distinguish between highly similar sounds and to detect whether two (or more) sounds are alike or different. Being able to detect subtle differences in speech sounds helps students to master phonics; those with poor auditory discrimination may have persistent trouble with phonic analysis and may also have speech impairments (Wilson, 1981).

Auditory discrimination can be assessed formally or informally. The student is required to distinguish between pairs of words or syllables that differ minimally *(rat-rap, ome-ote)*. Teachers frequently make up and give such exercises themselves. Formal auditory discrimination tests are also common, and some standardized readiness tests include such a subtest.

In beginning reading it is common to combine phonics instruction with auditory discrimination practice. Beginning readers or prereaders who at first seem to have difficulty with auditory discrimination often need only to learn what to listen for and how to respond. In other words, they have no auditory disability but have to learn what the task is. Auditory discrimination skill seems to improve sharply as children progress through the primary grades (Ekwall, 1976; Thompson, 1963), which implies that it develops at least partly in response to instruction and experience with the task. It may well be a learned skill as much as an innate perceptual ability.

Learning Disabilities and Dyslexia

Learning disabilities and *dyslexia* are terms used for special learning problems. The issues involved in defining the terms, identifying students with these problems and methods of remediation have aroused considerable controversy for the past twenty or so years. Disagreement over these issues still abounds, but educators appear to be moving toward greater understanding of them. In this section, we will attempt to clarify some of these issues.

What Are Learning Disabilities? A learning disability is a severe problem in learning that qualifies a child for special education services. In 1977 the federal government adopted the following definition of specific learning disability, based on a 1969 definition proposed by the National Advisory Committee on Handicapped Children:

> "Specific learning disability" means a disorder in one or more of the basic psychological processes involved in understanding or in using language, spoken or written, which may manifest itself in an imperfect ability to listen, think, speak, read, write, spell, or to do mathematical calculations. The term includes such conditions as perceptual handicaps, brain injury, minimal brain dysfunction, dyslexia, and developmental aphasia. The term does not include children who have learning problems which are primarily the result of visual, hearing, or motor handicaps, or mental retardation, or of environmental, cultural, or economic disadvantage." *(Federal Register,* December 29, 1977, p. 65083)

This definition does not fully explain what learning disabilities are, for it includes conditions such as "dyslexia" and "minimal brain dysfunction," which are themselves poorly defined and understood. It does, however, serve to narrow the term somewhat by excluding children whose learning problem is primarily caused by conditions like visual or hearing impairment, mental retardation, cerebral palsy, or economic deprivation.

According to Blackhurst and Berdine (1981), while there is widespread disagreement about the specifics of learning disabilities, there is general agreement that learning disabled students show a discrepancy between expected and actual achievement when provided with appropriate instruction, that they have difficulty doing tasks that others their age can do without difficulty, that their problem centers around some form of language use, and that they are not otherwise handicapped by mental retardation, blindness, deafness, or the like.

In 1981 a massive survey of special educators was undertaken to replicate a 1975 survey and determine what consensus or lack thereof existed among special educators on the issues of defining learning disabilities, diagnosis, placement and remediation of learning disabled children and the implications of PL 94–142. The results of this survey and the comparison of 1975 and 1981 responses, which appeared in the *Journal of Learning Disabilities* in January 1983 (Tucker, Stevens, and Ysseldyke, 1983), showed that both surveys revealed fairly consistent agreement on a number of important issues.

In both the 1975 and 1981 surveys, a majority of respondents agreed that learning disabilities is a viable classification for handicapped children, that learning disabilities are clinically identifiable by specific symptoms or a constellation of symptoms, that the percentage of school-age children with identifiable learning disabilities is 5 percent or less, and that such children could be positively identified between the ages of five and seven.

Though the majority of those surveyed agreed on these issues, a wide range of opinions was evident. Those disagreeing tended to find the learning disabled classification overly broad and unspecific, noted problems in accurate identification and revealed a trend away from the early identification procedures of the 1970s.

Tucker, Stevens, and Ysseldyke (1983) noted that although LD experts agree that learning disabilities exist and can be reliably identified, "definitional ambiguities that currently exist" (p. 14) still plague the field. They called for clear description of those individuals to whom LD services are presently being offered as a way of clarifying some of the issues involved.

At the present time it appears that although definitions and descriptions of symptoms of learning disabilities are not clear and distinct, the classification has served to draw attention to a large number of children experiencing learning difficulty and led to providing special services for them. Children identified as learning disabled are a heterogeneous lot with many varied problems, but characteristically are of average or above average intelligence, without other handicapping conditions that are of primary importance, who have been provided instruction from which others of their age and ability benefit, but who are failing to achieve as expected. Reading and reading-related problems (in spelling, writing, and listening) are very common among children identified as learning disabled.

In the long run, this means that LD teachers work with many youngsters who are poor readers and that both regular classroom teachers and reading specialists will find that some of their poor readers may have been identified as learning disabled. Whether or not they have been so identified, poor readers *all* need help in consolidating skills they have mastered, acquiring skills they do not yet have, and closing the gap between their potential as readers and their present performance.

We must all keep firmly in mind that being classified as learning disabled does not mean that a child has a particular set of problems or symptoms that set him or her clearly apart from other poor readers. Nor does it indicate that a particular method of instruction or set of materials is appropriate. Children so classified differ from each other just as much as others do, and no particular method or means have been shown to be more effective than others in remediation. All poor readers, learning disabled or not, require instruction that is tailored to their individual strengths, needs, ages, interests, and prior experiences. All poor readers need to be placed in appropriate materials at their instructional levels, provided instruction that achieves a balance in word identification, comprehension, listening, speaking and writing, and taught at a pace that is appropriately challenging without frustration.

What Is Dyslexia? Dyslexia is a medical term for a profound inability to read or to learn to read. Like learning disability, dyslexia is a condition that everyone seems to agree exists, but about which there is little agreement otherwise. No set of symptoms, means of diagnosis or identification, or method of remediation can be identified. No one even seems to know how many children are affected by this profound disability. In spite of these glaring ambiguities, the term is used frequently and widely, yet it is hard to know whether people discussing the condition mean the same thing. Reporters discussing illiteracy and what they call "the crisis in education" may refer to "illiterates" and "dyslexics" as though they were the same group; educators and parents sometimes refer to "dyslexics" when they mean "poor readers," or even "students reading below grade level." Physicians and other medical personnel may use "dyslexic" to describe learning disabled patients who are poor readers. Perhaps no other term in education has come to mean so many things to so many people. What can be sorted out of this confusion?

First, like "learning disability," different definitions of "dyslexia" abound. The term *specific reading disability* is often used as synonymous with dyslexia. Vellutino (1980) used the terms this way, defined as "severe impairment in word decoding and consequent impairment in all aspects of reading" (p. 251). Staller (1982) defined dyslexia as "a developmental reading disability in children who have otherwise adequate intelligence, personality, and educational opportunities" (p. 115). Orton's (1937) description of dyslexic children as delayed in reading compared to their progress in other areas, who suffered from frequent letter and word reversals and often could read only by holding the print up to a mirror, persists in the minds of many today who still believe reversals are the hallmark of dyslexia. Blackhurst and Berdine (1981) defined dyslexia simply as "A severe disability in learning to read" (p. 583). And in 1969 the National Advisory Committee on Dyslexia and Related Disorders reviewed current definitions and concluded unanimously that "there was no prospect of arriving at a definition of dyslexia which would be accorded general acceptance" (HEW, 1969, p. 9). Thus Singer and Stanovich (1982) concluded, "the first step in *mis*understanding the research on reading disability is to take seriously the terminology" (p. 33).

Second, no general agreement exists on what *causes* dyslexia. Minimal brain damage, gross brain damage, brain lesions, central nervous system dysfunction or disorders, mixed dominance, heredity, and even hormonal factors have been suggested (Adams, 1969; Goldberg, Schiffman, and Bender, 1983; Staller, 1982; Vellutino, 1980; and others). Some authorities beg the question by avoiding any suggestion of causality entirely.

Third, there is no general agreement on the *symptoms* of dyslexia. Different studies proposing discrete sets of symptoms are categorically contradicted by other studies that appear to be just as conclusive. Many still refer to Orton's (1937) description of delayed lateral dominance manifested by reversals in visual perception such as *b* for *d* or *was* for *saw*. Also common are references to poor letter-sound and word decoding skills. Many of the definitions of dyslexia cited previously refer to the inability to *learn* to read, inferring failure to benefit from instruction or progress satisfactorily in beginning reading as a symptom. As with the issue of definitions, some authorities beg the question of symptomatology by stating that "no single etiology" (Goldberg, Schiffman, and Kender, 1983, p. 7) exists. Whatever constellation of symptoms is considered, some of them will appear in poor readers who are not said to be dyslexic, and some even in good readers (see Spache's [1976] review of literature on symptoms). For example, Ekwall (1976) included poor memory for words, unfluent oral reading that is not improved by rehearsal, difficulty concentrating, misspellings such as LIKS for *likes* or HAV for *have*, oral reading omissions and substitutions, stuttering or slow speech, and slow work habits as symptoms of dyslexia. Most or all of these behaviors are common to frustrated or anxious readers of all types as well as to normally developing beginning readers. Staller (1982) listed "difficulties in writing, spelling, cross-modal association, sequencing, visual pattern analysis, spatial activities, and general language skills" (p. 114). Certainly "difficulties in" writing, spelling, sequencing, and general language skills is such a broad generalization that it hardly serves to distinguish dyslexics from other children.

It seems, however, that regardless of the lack of any consensus on what dyslexia is, what causes it and what characterizes it, educators and others have embraced the concept and continue to apply the label, develop procedures that "test" for it, and market programs to cure it.

In the area of remediation of dyslexics, no more consensus exists than upon the previously discussed issues. According to Spache (1976), there are relatively few different treatment methods available, but still there is general disagreement as to the effectiveness of each one. Most treatment methods focus heavily on phonics, visual perception training, language therapy, eye-hand coordination training, and the use of VAKT (visual-auditory-kinesthetic-tactile) patterning to recognize words. Often programs are heavily weighted toward decoding and word recognition skills while they place relatively little emphasis on reading or listening comprehension, developing story sense or awareness of text structures, or acquiring and using prior information. For this reason, such programs may encourage word calling at the expense of comprehension, which does little to further the student's effective reading ability. And sometimes it is only the application of the label *dyslexic* that determines to what type of program the student will be subjected.

The most objective conclusion that may be taken from the foregoing discussion is that the terms *dyslexia* and *dyslexic* are poorly defined and understood, apparently do little to describe the nature of the child's reading problem or success, and probably do more to promote confusion, fear, and discouragement than to aid the child, parent, or teacher. Since the discarding of the terms does not appear imminent, we can all at least refrain from contributing to the problem by developing a healthy skepticism for others' judgments that someone is dyslexic, refraining from automatic acceptance of such labels or of diagnostic or treatment procedures that appear overly pat, narrow, or simplistic, and exercising extreme caution in our own use of the terms.

Reading and Anxiety

Because emotional problems are as varied and individual as the human beings they affect, there are no all-inclusive sets of criteria or symptoms to which we can refer. Our own experience in classrooms and reading clinics has shown us a few characteristic ways in which youngsters react to the anxiety that reading can produce.

Many young children, for example, believe that on the first day of school they will learn to read. They are, by and large, sadly disappointed. Learning to read generally takes a fairly long time, especially if you've been around for only six or seven years. Being able to accept this notion, and have the persistence to stick it out, is related to the early development of *competence* (White and Watts, 1973).

Children who have developed physical and emotional mastery in their early years, by extended experience with things and people, are *confident* and *error-tolerant*. They are secure in their own ability to succeed even if they fail on the first attempts, and they are able to shrug off and learn from mistakes without becoming unduly discouraged by them. Children who develop a sense of their own competence in their early years approach beginning reading with patience and persistence, confidence that they will probably succeed in the end, and knowledge that occasional failure happens to everybody.

Youngsters who lack these notions are often unable to stick to a task long enough to become good at it. They admit defeat after only a few days or weeks of reading instruction. They seem to be overwhelmed by the whole process and often become inordinately discouraged by mistakes or confusion. When they aren't sure of what to do next, they get depressed or panicky. Activities that involve some element of cognitive risk, like predicting what might happen next in a story, are just too threatening. By avoiding risk, these children sometimes appear to be uncooperative or disinterested, but their apparent disinterest is often a cover for fear.

Risk avoiding is a common strategy for children who have not developed the resilience of spirit that we see in a competent child. It is also an aspect of another problem, one related to reading readiness.

Educators, child psychologists, and parents generally agree that children develop at very different rates, each according to an individual timetable. We are rarely seriously concerned if milestones like the first step, first word, or first tooth come earlier or later than those of a sibling or neighbor's child. Likewise we know that children develop the social skills, attention span, self-control, and physical stamina required for school at different ages. Some are able to deal with full half-days of nursery school experience between the ages of three and four whereas some five-year-olds cannot sustain themselves for an entire half day of kindergarten. Kindergarten was instituted to provide a structured environment in which children could develop in areas like socialized interaction, group play, observance of simple rules, attentive listening, following directions, and waiting one's turn. It is certainly a crucial school experience for every child.

Many children who are happy and secure in kindergarten, however, are unready for the greater demands of first grade. First, there are the physical demands: staying at school all day, eating lunch at school, getting on the right bus, staying awake all afternoon. Then there are the social demands: listening, waiting, following directions, lining up, sharing, making friends, keeping your temper. Add the academic demands: remembering your letters, reading all the words, printing neatly, learning the sounds, finishing your seatwork. It can all be too much. For some children learning to read is too difficult right from the start, and their anxiety is soon manifested.

Children who are developmentally unready for first grade instruction may share a number of common behaviors attributed to "overplacement." Physically, they are often chronically fatigued, especially in the afternoon, suffer frequent colds and ear infections, and have much more difficulty than their age-mates in forming letters, following simple directions, and attending to interesting activities. Socially, they often have difficulty making friends and controlling anger, may consistently choose solitary rather than group activities and may prefer to play with much younger children. Emotionally, they may often feel depressed and anxious, cry easily, and avoid school tasks by daydreaming or procrastinating. They may begin or revert to nail-biting, stammering, bedwetting or thumb-sucking. They may hesitate to make a guess or prediction, quickly answer "I don't know" when at all uncertain, exhibit excessive neatness in written work and repeatedly ask for directions to be given again.

Youngsters who chronically exhibit a number of these behaviors are signaling that something is very wrong. Since children cannot be forced or taught how to develop *faster*, the situation must be modified for them. Too often, we expect the *child* to change rather than changing the anxiety-producing environment.

Children are not able to change their school situations because they do not control them; adults do. Children who need more time to grow and develop, to experience and to adapt to school must be given that time, free of stigma. Often, this means an additional year in kindergarten. In some schools, an extra year option has been built into the curriculum. The extra year is a full day of pre-first-grade instruction, often focusing on extended reading readiness, language development, exposure to books, and concrete experiences. It can, in our experience, make all the difference in the world for youngsters not quite ready for a full first-grade experience, because it has no connotations of having failed or not having been promoted. Another year of first-grade instruction is sometimes a good solution. However, the youngster's second trip through first grade should entail different materials and instructional methods, and perhaps a different teacher. It should not mean recycling the child through the same materials and methods that didn't work the first time.

The anxious behaviors being described here are fairly common in young poor readers or prereaders, but they can also be seen in very anxious youngsters who are actually good readers. Fear of failure is no respecter of ability.

Some high-achieving students drive themselves with an intensity that, in an adult, would make friends worry about a heart attack. Such students are often compulsively neat in their written work, scrupulous in attention to detail, and rely on prodigious memory stores. They may take an inordinate amount of time to complete reading or writing assignments because they review and check their work over and over; they may excel at recall of factual information and convergent thinking but have difficulty drawing con-clusions, thinking of alternatives, and predicting; they often get deeply discouraged by a critical remark or a less-than-perfect paper. It is un-fortunate that these signs of anxiety are often overlooked in the classroom if a student's reading ability is at or near grade level.

As children grow older they become more dependent on what their peers think of them and less dependent on teacher or parental feedback. Added to their growing concern for peer approval, though, is their aware-ness that reading is extremely important both in and out of school, and failure to master reading can severely affect their self-esteem. Faced with a situation in which they cannot conform to adults' expectations, they may bend every effort to win approval from other students. They may exhibit hostility, defiance, profanity, aggression, and other behaviors that put teachers in an adversary position. In a review of studies of good and poor readers' personality traits, Spache (1976) listed the following traits as being common in poor readers: aggressiveness, anxiety, withdrawal, negative-ness, depression, and feelings of helplessness in academic and problem-solving situations, while good readers are usually self-confident, persistent, compliant, and have feelings of self-worth, independence, and belonging.

Assessing Interests

Teacher-made interest and attitude inventories are very useful devices for learning how students feel about books, reading, school subjects, and common childhood problems. This information can be used in several ways:

- ☐ to determine if a particular student has very negative attitudes about reading that may affect progress in reading
- ☐ to reveal if a particular student is having serious personal problems that may affect classroom performance and social relationships
- ☐ to discover what specific topics students are interested in reading about as well as what kinds of materials they prefer using

Figures 9.1, 9.2, and 9.3 are sample classroom interest inventories that you may find helpful. Depending on their reading and writing ability, the students can complete them in writing or orally, and you will probably want to add other questions. The incomplete sentences in Figure 9.3 are modeled on those developed by Strang (1969, pp. 262–263). Hall, Ribovich, and Ramig (1979, p. 236) give several excellent examples of reading interest inventories and suggestions for their use, and Figures 9.1 and 9.2 are adapted from these.

FIGURE 9.1. Interest inventory for primary grades.

(The questions are read aloud to students, and their oral responses are written down by the teacher.)

1. If *you* could decide what you would study in school next week, what would you choose? Why? _____

2. If someone asked you to choose a book or story you'd like to have read to you, what would the book be about? _____

3. If you could magically visit any person from now or from the past, who would it be? _____

4. If you woke up one day and found you had superhuman powers, what would you do? _____

5. If someone were giving you a book for your birthday, what would you want the book to be about? _____

6. Do you think a book is a good present? _____
   Why or why not? _____

7. If you could magically turn into any kind of animal or bird, real or make-believe, what would you become? _____

   What would you do in your new form?_____

8. If you could write a TV show or movie, what would it be about?_____

Support and Success

What can we do to help those whose emotional reactions to school, reading, and academic success have become destructively involved with

FIGURE 9.2. Interest inventory for intermediate and upper grades.

(The questions may be given silently or orally, and the student can answer orally or in writing.)

1. If you had a "surprise day off from school," how would you spend the day?
   _____

2. If someone wanted to give you a magazine subscription for a gift, what magazine would you choose? _____

3. If you were hired to write a new TV show, what would it be about? Who would star in it? Would *you* be in it? _____

4. If you won a contest and your grand prize was to meet and get to know any famous person in the world today, whom would you choose? What would you like to talk about? _____

5. If you could transport yourself into any time and place in the past, where would you go? What would you do there? How long would you stay in the past? __
   _____

6. If you could somehow become a superathlete overnight, what would your sport be? What would you do as a superathlete? _____

7. If you could go into a bookstore and get any three books free, what kinds of books would you choose? _____

8. If *you* could choose the books or stories to be used from now on in English (or language arts), what kinds of things would you choose? What would you definitely *not* include? _____
   _____
   _____

their learning to read? We believe it is as important to know what you *cannot* do as what you *can*.

Unless you have special training and expertise in working with disturbed children or in counseling, you will probably not be able to "cure" the severely anxious student singlehandedly. If it consistently takes more than a smile and sincere praise to get a student to try again, if the student is socially

FIGURE 9.3. Attitudes and interests survey.

(The sentences may be completed orally or in writing.)

1. I think reading _____.
2. I wish I could _____.
3. Someday I _____.
4. I wish my teacher _____.
5. My best friend _____.
6. I'd rather read than _____.
7. At home I _____.
8. When I read out loud _____.
9. Science books _____.
10. When I don't know a word _____.
11. I wonder why _____.
12. Reading about the past _____.
13. On test days I _____.
14. Spelling is _____.
15. I really love to _____.
16. Animal stories _____.
17. I don't understand _____.
18. I wish I could _____.
19. Books about famous people _____.
20. When I have to write a paper _____.
21. I felt proud when _____.
22. My mother _____.
23. Sometimes I think I _____.
24. Pictures in books _____.
25. My father _____.

SOURCE: Adapted from Ruth Strang et al., *Improvement of Reading*, 4th ed. (New York: McGraw-Hill, 1967). Reprinted by permission.

isolated, and if you can observe continued signs of frustration and anxiety, seek help from others. The intensity and duration of anxiety are important factors. Everyone has an occasional bout of depression or feelings of worthlessness, but emotionally troubled children cannot shake it off. We all lose our tempers at ourselves or others and let our anger show in words or gestures. Troubled children have difficulty with degrees of emotion, and annoyance may become rage or withdrawal before they can get control of it. If you at all suspect that a student's moods and reactions are beyond average limits, get some professional advice.

In the area of reading, we can always do something to help. Two key concepts are *support* and *success*. The importance of success in every person's life cannot be overstated. Even B. F. Skinner, the acknowledged founder of the behavior modification movement who was often associated with an impersonal, unemotional approach to children, put it this way:

The human organism, fortunately for us all, is reinforced just by being successful. Consequently, if material is designed to facilitate correct responses, the resulting frequent success is enough reinforcement for most persons. Not only will the child's behavior change as he learns to do things he could not do before, but he will become highly motivated, his morale will improve, and his attitude toward teachers will change. (Skinner, 1972, p. 11)

Hewett and Taylor (1980) have written of "the orchestration of success" necessary in dealing with emotionally disturbed children. The concept is generalizable to remedial work with children whose reading difficulties have led to a damaged self-concept.

In describing the orchestration of success, Hewitt and Taylor recount the case of Peter, a subject in a now classic study of operant conditioning to overcome a phobia. Peter, almost three years old, was irrationally afraid of a white rabbit, and his fear had generalized to all furry white things — beards, cotton, fur, etc. In a series of forty-five "desensitization" sessions, Peter's fear was removed by "pairing" the rabbit with Peter's favorite foods. As Peter ate, the rabbit was very gradually moved closer to him in successive sessions. At first, the rabbit's presence in the room caused Peter extreme anxiety. Forty-five sessions later, he let the rabbit nibble at his fingers and spontaneously commented, "I like the rabbit." His fear was gone.

We are not advocating using this type of desensitization, a complex psychological treatment, for unhappy children in the classroom. We use this account to illustrate a point: that by *successive positive experiences* we can help children replace fear and anxiety with confidence.

Hewett and Taylor relate this desensitization process to that of helping children overcome fear and aversion to school tasks. They write:

In place of food we are concerned with giving the child as positive and successful an experience as possible in the classroom. We need to capitalize on the child's interests, ask no more than he or she can comfortably do, and provide meaningful consequences for the child's efforts. Gradually, we may be able to move the aversive "white rabbit of schoolness" with its demands for conformity, rules, competition, and complexity closer and closer until the child is functioning in a normal manner in school. (Hewett and Taylor, 1980, pp. 128–129)

For many children, the white rabbit is reading. By providing support through activities that children can do, appropriate recognition of effort and achievement, no matter how modest, and extended opportunities to practice newly emerging reading abilities, we can gradually move that fearful white rabbit back into their lives. As they become able to do more, self-confidence will begin to reappear. Success begets success.

It will not happen quickly, however. Even with consistent encouragement and support from teachers, family, and peers and consistent, thoughtful instruction, it can still take years to help a child become a functional reader. And many children do not enjoy even the minimal criteria of consistent support and instruction. The problem is further compounded when instruction is haphazard or inappropriate to the student's abilities, which is often the case. Sometimes no one really seems to care whether or not students succeed, and sometimes teachers forget that endless patience is required.

Then there is the matter of finding the right material. The truth is that easy-to-read material doesn't have to mean dull, stilted language written to conform to a readability formula. Any material that is *memorable* and highly *predictable* is easy to read. The most memorable materials are those dictated by the students; after all, they just said it. Dictated accounts are nearly fail-safe because they are memorable, natural sounding (written in the student's own language patterns), and intrinsically interesting (involving the student's own experiences, opinions, and values). Students who can learn to read their individual dictated accounts can move easily into reading group-dictated stories and then into simple text in trade books.

High predictability is found in any written material containing rhythmic or repetitious elements. For young children, books featuring repeated lines, simple rhymes and poems, nursery rhymes, songs, and jingles are good. For older students, song lyrics, commercial slogans, and poetry are all common forms of highly predictable materials. They can be used as a jumping-off place, a source of easy-to-read words and phrases, which, once learned, can be found in other reading materials that may be too difficult to tackle at first. If, at any point in the lessons, the student begins to show the same signs of anxiety and frustration as before, we have to move the white rabbit back; in other words, move to easier, more supportive activities in which the student can succeed.

Echo reading and choral reading are good support techniques (see Chapter Five). In echo reading, the teacher reads a sentence or two of text and the student (one or more) echoes the teacher's words. Choral reading is a bit less supported since it requires the teacher and student(s) to read aloud simultaneously. Students may read fairly difficult material several times by echo reading and then move to choral reading of the same material. Sometimes students read comfortably and successfully in the echo setting, but quickly begin to exhibit tension, fear, and frustration when they move to choral reading. In these cases we must move back and spend more time in the more supportive mode before we move that old rabbit closer again. Patience pays because every time children go through the text their confidence grows, and in time they will be able to choral-read fluently and, finally, without support. Rushing the early stages only delays the development of the confidence that is so necessary. The analogy of Peter and the white rabbit is an excellent model for reading remediation: by moving through gradual stages we can provide sufficient support and continuous success in reading, and by doing so we can modify negative attitudes and repair damaged self-concepts.

Summary

PL 94–142, the Education for All Handicapped Children Act of 1975, has profoundly affected the education profession. The law requires that every handicapped child be provided with special education services appropriate to the individual's abilities and/or disabilities. The major provisions of the law mandate free public education for all handicapped persons between three and twenty-one years of age, placement in the least restrictive learning environment, an individual educational program (IEP) for each handi-capped pupil to be developed jointly by the student's teachers and parents (and the student, when possible), and the elimination of racial, cultural, and other forms of bias in testing and evaluation. Every handicapped student is guaranteed due process, equal educational opportunity, and accountability from teachers and schools in IEP implementation.

The implications of PL 94–142 are numerous and profound. Teachers of reading, and all other educators, must be aware of the effect of intellectual, physical, and emotional factors in reading, how children with special needs are diagnosed and taught most effectively, and how handicapped students are successfully dealt with in regular classrooms.

Intelligence tests are frequently given as a part of a reading diagnostic assessment. Reading achievement and intelligence are correlated, particu-larly in the upper grades, but many poor readers are of average or above average intelligence.

Group intelligence tests nearly always require the student to read and write. *Individual* tests, which are given orally, yield better estimates of intellectual ability. Some individual tests are language-dependent; they estimate only *verbal intelligence,* which is modified and expressed by means of language. The Slosson Intelligence Test, Peabody Picture Vocabulary Test, and Stanford-Binet Intelligence Scales are examples. The Wechsler Scales assess both verbal and *nonverbal intelligence.*

Intelligence test performance is heavily influenced by the amount and kind of experience one has had. Experience is gained concretely, by direct or real experience with people, objects, and events, and vicariously, by observ-ing others' experience and by reading. Much of the learning in school is conveyed by print, and the poor readers who lack such information and experience generally do less well on intelligence tests than their age-mates who do read, even when the test given requires no reading.

An informal alternative to an I.Q. test is the assessment of *listening comprehension,* assessed by reading text material aloud to the student and evaluating the answers to orally administered comprehension questions. Comparison of listening and instructional reading levels allows the diagnostician to estimate the student's present *potential for reading improvement*. Since it is specifically related to reading ability, listening comprehension is more directly useful for instructional planning than I.Q. test scores.

If students can listen to and adequately understand text written at their present grade level and yet cannot adequately read the same text for themselves, they are still judged to have the verbal concepts and vocabulary necessary for learning to read at that level of difficulty. Very poor readers may have listening comprehension levels many grades below their present grade, but this level is *dynamic* rather than fixed, and as reading ability improves, the listening level will probably rise also.

Physical factors in reading include *vision, hearing,* and *special learning problems*.

Common visual problems include *myopia* (nearsightedness), *hyperopia* (farsightedness), *astigmatism, amblyopia* (lazy eye), *strabismus* (crossed eyes), *muscular imbalance* (fusion or phoria), and *aniseikonia*. The first three are the most common. Hyperopia and astigmatism can make reading tiring and uncomfortable, but myopia affects only reading of distant images (blackboard, signs) and is common among good readers. All these problems are correctable. Different vision problems can share similar symptoms, but if any are persistent, *vision screening* should be sought. Vision screening is usually done with a *stereoscopic* instrument and test battery that test each eye separately and both together. *Ophthalmologists* use more technical measures.

Problems of hearing can affect the child's production and use of oral language and interfere with primarily oral early reading instruction, including phonics instruction. Hearing is assessed by measuring perception of speech sounds in terms of *pitch* and *volume*. Pitch, the *frequency* at which sounds are produced, is measured in *hertz* or cycles per second. Consonant sounds are produced at a higher pitch or frequency than vowel sounds. Volume or loudness is measured in *decibels*. Hearing aids are used to amplify sounds and are used to correct volume losses.

Many children suffer temporary but recurrent hearing losses involving the high-frequency sounds, which severely affect phonics instruction and may make speech reception difficult. These losses, called *conductive hearing losses*, are commonly caused by conditions arising from upper respiratory infections, allergies, and childhood diseases. A collection of fluid in the middle ear can result from such infections and can inhibit conduction of sounds to the inner ear. Unequal air pressure behind the eardrum, caused by blocking or collapse of the eustachian tube, can inhibit conduction by distending the eardrum. Conductive hearing losses may recur chronically during the school years, when children often suffer many colds and upper respiratory infections.

In addition, mumps, rubella, certain drugs and exposure to excessive noise can damage structures of the inner ear. Both middle- and inner-ear structures are involved in the transmission of sound signals to the brain.

Auditory screening is done with an *audiometer,* an instrument that tests perception of sounds at a wide range of frequencies and volumes. Children who exhibit persistent symptoms of hearing problems, as well as those returning to school after mumps, ear infections or other upper respiratory illnesses, should be screened routinely.

Dyslexia and *learning disabilities* are terms that are the subject of much controversy and disagreement. *Dyslexia* is often used to mean a specific learning disability that severely affects the ability to read or to learn to read. There is no general agreement on its causes, symptoms, or treatment. The wide use of the term has been criticized because of its lack of specificity. Similarly, there is little consensus on the specific meaning of the term *learning disability.* It is often used to describe the difficulty of a child of at least average intelligence who appears to be free of physical, emotional, and intellectual handicaps. Minimal neurological damage or dysfunction is often presumed from behavioral, rather than neurological, evidence.

The same student with a reading problem may be considered "reading disabled" by a reading specialist and "learning disabled" by a learning disabilities specialist. A child's reading behaviors are frequently interpreted in very different ways by the two practitioners. Remedial methods also differ widely between the two specialties.

Students experiencing difficulty with reading often suffer *emotional* difficulties as a result of damaged self-concepts, loss of confidence, and aversion to school and reading. Those having problems learning to read often show particular *anxiety behaviors.* If preschoolers consider themselves *competent,* they will approach learning with confidence and tolerance for their own mistakes. Children who do not feel competent may not be persistent, may become easily discouraged, and may attempt to avoid risk by acting withdrawn, uncooperative, or disinterested. Some young children also lack the *maturity* to succeed in the early grades; they lack the physical stamina, emotional resiliency, or academic skills necessary to learn to read in first grade. They too exhibit characteristic physical, social, emotional, and academic reactions to the stress they suffer. Additional time for development must be provided for them. Older poor readers may also be withdrawn or disinterested, and their desire for peer admiration may result in episodes of aggressive physical or verbal behavior.

Anxiety is not limited to poor readers; some high achievers gain success at great physical and emotional cost, driving themselves for perfection. Their anxious behaviors are just as damaging but may be overlooked if their reading is at or near grade level.

Students experiencing difficulty can be helped by providing supportive measures, by using materials that can be read easily, by keeping tasks reasonable in terms of what they can accomplish, and by providing enough support for a long enough period of time for their confidence to rebuild.

Extension Activities

1. Choose one of the group intelligence tests and one of the individual tests listed in this chapter. Find the description and reviews of each test n the appropriate *Mental Measurement Yearbook* or *Intelligence Tests in Print*. What are the apparent strengths and weaknesses of each test? For what specific purposes would each test be more appropriate?
2. Interview a psychometrist or school psychologist about the uses of the WISC-R in reading diagnosis. In his or her opinion, what types of subtest score patterns are most characteristic of poor readers? What subtests seem most profoundly affected by poor reading? Are there any particular score patterns or responses the examiner might look for that could explain why the student has reading problems? In his or her opinion, of what use is an intelligence test in reading diagnosis?
3. Select a student and administer a hearing capacity assessment, using any IRI or your own selection of text passages and questions. *After* determining the student's hearing capacity level, find out what intelligence test or similar ability data exist for that pupil. Do your informal findings correspond to the other test scores? If not, why do you think the discrepancy exists?
4. Interview a preschool or kindergarten teacher about the role of experience in developing young children's intelligence. What experiences does he or she consider critical for school success? Which are necessary before school entrance? Which can be provided within the school curriculum? Are they being provided?
5. Find out who is responsible for doing visual and/or auditory screening in your school or division. What tests are used? What machines? How are students referred? If they have positive screening results, what follow-up is done to see if they receive treatment? Find out how the screening procedures work by learning how to use the equipment or see how it is operated. Have your own hearing/vision checked by someone else.
6. Select a "panel" consisting of as many of these people as you can: a reading specialist, a special education teacher and/or an LD specialist, several regular classroom teachers from both elementary and secondary levels, several parents, a doctor or nurse, and a university educator. Ask them to define *dyslexia* and describe its causes, symptoms, and treatment as fully as they can. Keep a record of what each one tells you and compare the responses. Are there agreements? Contradictions? Misinformation? What is the general state of understanding of this term?
7. Ask a reading teacher and an LD teacher to describe the tests each would use to diagnose the reading problem of a child you describe, the same child in each case. How would their assessments differ? Why do they differ? What information might each teacher have that the other could benefit from sharing?

Suggested Readings

Blackhurst, A. Edward, and Berdine, William H. **An Introduction to Special Education.** *Boston: Little, Brown, 1981.* A comprehensive text with particularly informative chapters on special education legislation, language disorders, visual and auditory impairments, learning disabilities, and special intellectual needs.

Heward, William L., and Orlansky, Michael D. **Exceptional Children.** *Columbus: Charles C. Merrill, 1980.* Basic special education text, interestingly written and practical.

Kirk, Samuel A., Kliebhan, Sr. Joanne Marie, and Lerner, Janet W. **Teaching Reading to Slow and Disabled Learners.** *Boston: Houghton Mifflin, 1978.* Reading instruction methods for special education students in a balanced and thoughtful presentation.

Landau, Elliott D., Epstein, Sherry L., and Stone, Ann P. **The Exceptional Child Through Literature.** *Engelwood Cliffs, N.J.: Prentice-Hall, 1978.* Uses of literature to help teachers and students become aware of their feelings and attitudes about handicapped children.

Orlansky, Michael D. **Mainstreaming the Visually Impaired Child.** *Hingham, Mass.: Teaching Resources, 1977.* Handbook for teachers with visually impaired students in regular classrooms.

Sagan, Carl. **The Dragons of Eden.** *New York: Random House, 1977.* Spellbinding discussions of brain and sensory activity, the nature of intelligence, language, and human cultures written for the lay reader.

References

Adams, Richard B. "Dyslexia: A Discussion of Its Definition." *Journal of Learning Disabilities* 2, No. 12 (December 1969): 616–623.

Blackhurst, A. Edward, and Berdine, William H. *An Introduction to Special Education.* Boston: Little, Brown, 1981.

Bond, Guy L., Tinker, Miles A., and Wasson, Barbara B. *Reading Difficulties: Their Diagnosis & Correction,* 4th ed. Englewood Cliffs, N.J.: Prentice-Hall, 1979.

Colley, Relan. "The Education for All Handicapped Children Act (EHA): A Statutory and Legal Analysis." *Journal of Law and Education* 10, No. 2 (April 1981): 137–161.

Dirks, Donald D. "Effects of Hearing Impairment on the Auditory System," in Edward Carterette and Morton Friedman, eds. *Handbook of Perception, Volume IV: Hearing.* New York: Academic Press, 1978.

Dunn, Lloyd M. *Peabody Picture Vocabulary Test.* Circle Pines, Minn.: American Guidance Service, 1959.

Ekwall, Eldon E. *Diagnosis and Remediation of the Disabled Reader.* Boston: Allyn and Bacon, 1976.

Goldberg, Herman K., Schiffman, Gilbert B., and Bender, Michael. *Dyslexia: Interdisciplinary Approaches to Reading Disabilities.* New York: Grune & Stratton, 1983.

Hall, MaryAnne, Ribovich, Jerilyn K., and Ramig, Christopher. *Reading and the Elementary School Child,* 2nd ed. New York: Van Nostrand, 1979.

Health, Education and Welfare (HEW). *Reading Disorders in the United States: On Dyslexia and Related Reading Disorders.* Reprinted by Developmental Learning Materials, Chicago, 1969.

Hewett, Frank M., and Taylor, Frank M. *The Emotionally Disturbed Child in the Classroom: The Orchestration of Success,* 2nd ed. Boston: Allyn and Bacon, 1980.

Kaufman, Alan S. *Intelligent Testing with the WISC-R.* New York: Wiley, 1979.

Lanyon, Richard I., and Giddings, John W. "Psychological Approaches to Myopia: A Review." *American Journal of Optometry and Physiological Optics* 51 (April 1974): 271–281.

MacMillan, D. L. *Mental Retardation in School and Society.* Boston: Little, Brown, 1977.

Optometric Extension Program Foundation, Inc. *Educator's Guide to Classroom Vision Problems and Educator's Checklist.* Duncan, Okla.: Optometric Extension Program Foundation, 1968.

Orton, Samuel. *Reading, Writing, and Speech Problems in Children.* New York: Norton, 1937.

Sanders, Derek A. *Auditory Perception of Speech.* Englewood Cliffs, N.J.: Prentice-Hall, 1977.

Schubert, Delwyn G., and Walton, Howard N. "Visual Screening: A New Breakthrough." *The Reading Teacher,* 34, No. 2 (November 1980): 175–177.

Searls, Evelyn F. *How to Use WISC Scores in Reading Diagnosis.* Newark, Del.: International Reading Association, 1975.

Singer, Martin H., and Stanovich, Keith E. "Reading Disability: Introduction," in Martin H. Singer, ed. *Competent Reader, Disabled Reader: Research and Application,* Hillsdale, N.J.: Lawrence Erlbaum Associates, 1982.

Skinner, B. F. "Teaching: The Arrangement of Contingencies Under Which Something Is Taught," in N. G. Haring and A. H. Hayden, eds. *Improvement of Instruction.* Seattle: Special Child Publications, 1972.

Slosson, Richard L. *Slosson Intelligence Test.* E. Aurora, New York: Slosson Educational Publications, 1963.

Spache, George D. *Investigating the Issues of Reading Difficulties.* Boston: Allyn and Bacon, 1976.

Staller, Joshua. "Neurological Correlates of Reading Failure," in Martin H. Singer, ed. *Competent Reader, Disabled Reader: Research and Application.* Hillsdale, N.J.: Lawrence Erlbaum Associates, 1982.

Strang, Ruth. *Diagnostic Teaching of Reading,* 2nd ed. New York: McGraw-Hill, 1969.

Thompson, Bertha B. "A Longitudinal Study of Auditory Discrimination." *Journal of Educational Research* 56 (March 1963): 376–378.

Tucker, James, Stevens, Linda J., and Ysseldyke, James E. "Learning Disabilities: The Experts Speak Out." *Journal of Learning Disabilities* 16, No. 1 (January 1983): 6–14.

Vellutino, Frank. "Dyslexia: Perceptual Deficiency or Perceptual Inefficiency," in James K. Kavanaugh and Richard L. Venezky, eds. *Orthography, Reading, and Dyslexia,* Baltimore: University Park Press, 1980.

Wallace, Gerald, and Larsen, Stephen C. *Educational Assessment of Learning Problems: Testing for Teaching.* Boston: Allyn and Bacon, 1978.

Wechsler, David. *The Measurement and Appraisal of Adult Intelligence,* 4th ed. Baltimore: Williams & Wilkins, 1958.

Wechsler, David. *Manual for the Wechsler Intelligence Scale for Children—Revised.* New York: Psychological Corporation, 1974.

White, Burton L., and Watts, Jean Carew. *Experience and Environment: Major Influences on the Development of the Young Child.* Vol. I. Englewood Cliffs, N.J.: Prentice-Hall, 1973.

Wilson, Robert M. *Diagnostic and Remedial Reading for Classroom and Clinic,* 5th ed. Columbus: Charles C. Merrill, 1981.

Woodruff, M. Emerson. "Observations on the Visual Acuity of Children During the First Five Years of Life." *American Journal of Optometry and Archives of American Academy of Optometry,* 49 (March 1972): 205–214.

Chapter Ten

Assessing the Reading Environment

Assessment of reading problems sometimes takes place in university reading clinics and private remedial centers, outside the school setting. While the expertise of such sources varies widely, in most cases the examination is thorough and perceptive. A good clinical diagnosis will include tests of reading, writing, and spelling as well as an individually administered intelligence test, investigation of personality development and attitudes toward reading, screening of vision and hearing, detailed medical and school histories, and interviews with the student and parents.

In this way clinicians develop a detailed, generally accurate picture of the student's reading, but there is always a piece of the picture missing: What is the classroom setting like in which the student must operate? What kinds of teaching go on? What are the demands of the school reading program? If any of this information is available, it is often secondhand.

Morris wrote, ". . . learning or not learning to read is a product of the interaction between an individual child and his or her instructional environment. A child does not learn to read in a vacuum, and ultimately our understanding of the reading acquisition process must include an analysis of the environmental factors which facilitate or impede that progress" (Morris, 1979, p. 497). Diagnosis that takes place out of the school setting may ignore this interaction.

And after the assessment, what happens? Are the clinical recommendations carried out? Diagnosticians working in a clinic rather than in a school may never learn what happens after the students return to their classrooms.

When testing is done within the school, it is hoped that this kind of closure can be achieved — that diagnosis takes the *classroom* and *program* as well as the *student* into consideration and that the diagnosis is done in order to make instructional change possible.

Any reading assessment that does not result in classroom action is of little use. Even the most detailed discussion of the learning activities children need to overcome a reading problem or to meet their potential must be put in the context of teaching many children at once. Teachers have to teach children in groups, in classroom settings. When they work with an individual child, they still have to maintain responsibility for all the other children at the same time.

Some classrooms are better environments for learning to read than others and in this chapter we describe a set of factors that may explain why.

Setting Instructional Goals

Are classroom instructional goals set by teachers or dictated by commercial reading or language arts programs? There are really two important assumptions in this question: that the teachers who implement a reading program should have a solid understanding of how children learn to read and that they should be given *real* responsibility for making day-to-day decisions regarding instruction in their own classrooms.

We can illustrate this point with an example. A few years ago we were asked by a county public school division to conduct a study of reading achievement and instruction throughout all the county schools. There was widespread dissatisfaction with reading achievement, and we were asked to report the problems and recommend solutions.

As part of the study we selected students with low reading achievement in grades one through twelve and tested each one individually by using the measures and procedures described in this book. After our assessment was completed, we formed independent judgments of what each student needed. Then we observed them in their regular classes, talked with their teachers, looked at materials, and finally determined whether their instruction matched their needs as we perceived them.

One day in the fall we tested Kevin, a third-grade nonreader. The son of a pulpwood cutter, Kevin had been given few material advantages in his life and had known little intellectual enrichment. We quickly realized that he did not express himself orally with much fluency, had few ideas about what writing or print were for, and had little exposure to books or story structures. In reading he could recognize only a few words at sight; he knew an assortment of letter sounds but not enough to be able to decode very much; and he spelled almost at random. In short, we could see that he was still emerging as a reader and that he would need to be supported by rich oral language practice and prereading experience with books. He should have been read to often and had his interest in books aroused in all of the dozens of ways that good kindergarten and primary grade teachers have practiced for decades. Because Kevin's background had poorly prepared him for the demands of literacy, we hoped that his school environment would be especially rich in oral and written language experiences.

When we returned with Kevin to his classroom, we were unprepared for what we saw. Kevin walked over to his work folder and pulled out a duplicator sheet. After asking another student what to do with it, he went to his desk and began to color it. We looked over his shoulder and saw that he was coloring all the geometric shapes that looked the same. This, the instructions told us, was preparation for learning to discriminate letter shapes. We noticed that all of the twenty-odd children in the class were working on filling in different duplicator sheets. Later we queried the teacher about what Kevin had been doing. We asked why he had been assigned *that* duplicator sheet. Because it was prescribed by the management system that accompanied the basal reading series, she replied. Every child had been tested at the beginning of the year and placed in a sequence of skills to be mastered. Kevin, and a few others in the class, were at the bottom of the sequence. (The sequence, we later found, ran something like this: discriminating shapes, learning letter forms, discriminating sounds, learning letter sounds for word attack, reading single words, reading sentences, and so on.) Kevin was working on readiness skills at his prescribed level, and in the few weeks since school started he had worked through a number of similar skill activities.

We naively asked the teacher why she was using the management system. She rolled her eyes and said that it "came with the job." She was an older teacher who had taught in the primary grades for many years. We asked, "If you were free to teach Kevin in any way you wanted, how would you go about it?" "Well," she said, "before the management system was instituted, I used to read to the children and they would learn their favorite stories, and they would put on plays about them." She smiled as she recalled the puppet shows and storytelling they did. "But," she said regretfully, "now there isn't time." For a large portion of their reading period, the children went to different teachers for a period of forty minutes to work on skills. Kevin had come from someone else's class, and he would go back shortly, so this teacher wouldn't see him the rest of the day.

We were saddened by what we saw happening with Kevin. He was being treated humanely, but he just wasn't being taught. As we talked with administrators and other teachers, we heard over and over that the basal-and-management-system approach had allowed the district to "individual-ize instruction for every child." School personnel told us proudly that all the students in language arts were now working on their level, regardless of grade placement, and that reading achievement groups within the classroom had been replaced by a rotating system whereby each teacher taught children of similar ability. Nobody seemed to realize that in spite of their attempts to streamline instruction and "individualize" by the use of programming, children like Kevin were slipping through the cracks.

This is a sad story, but not an uncommon one. There are many teachers whose programs dictate the way they teach reading. Sometimes they are required to follow them explicitly, as in the case of Kevin's teacher. More often they understandably assume that the reading series is "right," or (sometimes from experience) that they will be reprimanded by a supervisor if they deviate from the teacher's manual. In truth, however, the reading series or method that will teach *every* child to read has not been written, and it probably never will be. Teachers will always have to make numerous modifications in the called-for procedures in the basal readers for one or several children. This is just as true for the individualized systems as for those that are more traditionally organized. The program Kevin was in had an elaborate system of skill lists, placement and checkup tests, and in-dividual lessons, all for the purpose of "individualizing instruction." We believe, however, that most of the activities Kevin really needed to become literate were not included in the program. Since programs will have to be modified if they are to be right for all children, teachers must be more than just free to do such modifying — they must be actively *encouraged* and *helped* to do so.

Our position, that informed teachers should run the program and not vice versa, has another position embedded in it. Teachers must know *how* children learn to read. They should also know how to, and be willing to, use a variety of techniques for reading instruction. The contents of this or any textbook are not enough, but they do give us a starting point.

Think critically about reading in your classroom. Who (or what) dictates what individual children need to do, what they actually do, and how they are evaluated?

Time Spent Reading

It is self-evident that students should spend their time on the "right" tasks in order to learn to read, but this guideline is so regularly and routinely violated that it demands examination. Two crucial aspects here are the *quantity* of time spent on various activities and the *quality* of those activities. Both are essential and yet there are times when neither criterion is met.

What would an uninformed observer see in an elementary school class? Seymour Sarason (1971), a community psychologist, has noted that people who work in complex institutions like schools day in and day out sometimes overlook facts and conditions that would be obvious to another person who had never seen a school. To illustrate the point, he asks us to pretend that a Martian is hovering in a spacecraft right over a school. The Martian has X-ray vision and can see into all parts of the school. Being a careful observer, the Martian is skilled at finding patterns in the activity below but does not know Earth languages and therefore cannot understand what people *say* they are doing. The Martian can only watch what they *do* and draw independent conclusions.

Morris (1979) applied the Martian's observation technique to a third-grade reading class to find out what it is that children actually *do* during reading time in a self-contained classroom. It appeared that they frequently move around from place to place; they spend much time marking in blanks or putting circles around items on printed sheets; and they spend a little time sitting in a circle with an adult. They also did something else: they pointed their eyes at the squiggles of print in books. How much of the time did they do this "pointing"? The Martian concluded that this activity usually accounted for a total of less than five minutes. The Martian in this classroom was Morris himself, who informally but carefully recorded the time each of two third-grade poor readers spent reading connected text (sentences or paragraphs, as in a story or article, rather than individual sentences or even smaller units) in a typical language arts period. Morris found that those poor readers averaged about two minutes of real reading per day during language arts.

We have replicated these depressing findings in a number of classroom observations involving different schools and grades. In each situation, the poorest readers spent the least time even *looking* at text, often five minutes or less per language arts period. The better readers, conversely, generally spent extended amounts of time reading basal stories, library books, and magazines. Even with all other considerations aside, it is not surprising that the poorer readers make such slow progress, if indeed they make any progress at all.

The amount of time students spend actually reading is a critical variable in their success. As we discussed in Chapter Five in the section on developing reading fluency, Richard Allington (1983) noted that successful readers often do more silent reading than poorer readers, are given more time for reading, are encouraged to develop greater fluency and expression during oral reading, and are often given material that is easier for them to read than their less fluent classmates. Research findings also indicate that the amount of time spent reading significantly affected student gains in reading achievement, at both the elementary (Kean, Summers, Raivetz & Farber, 1979) and secondary (Stallings, 1980) levels.

In addition to reading extended text themselves, let us consider what other things children in reading classes do. One activity that would strike any observer is *testing*. A surprising amount of time is taken up with tests of various kinds. A number of basal reading series have adopted a cyclical format for the teaching of skills, and a cycle of pretest-teach-retest-reteach-posttest is common. If teachers carefully follow this format and utilize the activities provided for each step (as many teachers are now *required* to do), as much as 40 percent of their instructional time may be taken up just by the reading series tests. This percentage does not include, of course, the time given to other tests: achievement tests in reading, state-mandated tests of basic skills or minimum competencies, teacher-made tests, and group diagnostic tests of various kinds. As testing proliferates, more and more instructional time is being sacrificed. After all, the time must come from somewhere; the school day has not been significantly lengthened, nor are there fewer subjects being taught now than a few years ago. Is it any wonder that many children spend so little time reading?

We must determine how much time is spent on real reading tasks, but it is also important to see to it that the instructional tasks themselves are really worthwhile. In many current individualized reading instruction programs, a lot of the prescribed activities are of dubious instructional value. Most duplicator work sheets, for example, do not involve real reading (of connected text, for meaning), yet in many programs children work on duplicator sheets more than half of the time.

Even the students come to believe that this is what reading instruction is. In a study of reading interests, students were asked if there should be more time in school for free reading. One child's answer was typical: "Yes, but it wouldn't work because then we wouldn't have enough time to do our work sheets." (Estes and Johnstone, 1977, p. 893). When asked to list the daily schedule of activities in her second-grade class, a daughter of one of the authors recited, "Homeroom, spelling, dittos, reading group . . ."

Rather than list all the questionable instruction activities that might be encountered, however, let us list some activities that should be abundant in every reading class.

Reading to Children

One of the most positive activities is reading to the students. This is true at all grade levels, but it is imperative in the primary grades. Young children must be read to at least once every day, and for those who have not been read to at home, even once a day is not enough.

Why read to children? Aren't there more important readiness and beginning reading skills that they should be working on? In a word, no. Ronald Cramer, a reading and early childhood educator, put it this way:

> Teachers can't teach children to love books, but by reading to them every day they can create an atmosphere that will help children appreciate the gift of literature. The enjoyment of books can be shared. Reading to children helps them learn to read . . . provides models for writing . . . sparks the imagination and provides images and ideas for children to write about . . . enriches their language . . . develops their concepts, knowledge and thinking ability . . . illustrates specific concepts . . . is the surest way to develop a love and appreciation for books . . . establishes a mutual bond among listeners. (Cramer, 1975, pp. 460–461)

In the "old days," perhaps when Kevin's teacher received her training, teachers were often taught to read to their young students for twenty minutes a day. Although twenty minutes a day is more than many students receive, even that much time allows for only a couple of hundred books, short ones at that, to be read in a year. If you read long continuing books like *Charlotte's Web*, you may not even finish a hundred. It helps, but it is not enough. Consider youngsters who, blessed with book-loving families, enter first grade having heard a storybook read aloud every day for most of their lives. They have a background of a *thousand* or more books in their experience (Huck, 1976), which they can apply to make the task of learning to read easier.

Another big plus for children is storytelling. Helen Huus described this aspect of the "good old days," one that many of us never knew. In ". . . the 1920s, schools that followed the platoon system usually had a children's library and a separate period when pupils went to their literature teacher. She was a specialist, just as others were specialists in arithmetic, reading, social studies, or sciences" (Huus, 1973, p. 795). The teaching of literature as a subject included many of the elements in today's language arts, but an important activity in earlier days was storytelling. In fact, in the last century students at the "normal schools" nearly always were required to take a course in storytelling, or oral interpretation, as well as courses in oral reading, elocution, and other skills then thought necessary for all teachers. Today, storytelling is almost a lost art, and the loss is great because, like reading to children, it provides them with a rich store of characters, scenes, and plots. It feeds their desire to read that particular story for themselves. (After you read or tell a story, try displaying the book prominently in the classroom. It won't sit there very long.)

Both storytelling and reading to students help to develop critically important background experiences and concepts readers need to build their reading development: sense of story, schemata for stories, well-developed listening comprehension, concepts about the relationship between print and spoken words, and the intuition that reading is useful and pleasurable (Nessel, 1985; Roney, 1984).

Reading to children and storytelling should not end after the primary grades. Older poor readers or nonreaders have as great a need to hear and enjoy stories as little children do, if they are to improve their reading. In the upper grades, where the range of reading abilities in any class widens rapidly, a listen-and-discuss activity such as a directed listening-thinking activity (Chapter Three) keeps a group together and allows students of very different reading abilities to work together in a discussion.

An anecdote shared with us by an in-service teacher illustrates this point. During her first year of teaching, she struggled hard to get her ninth-grade English students to read selected short stories. The fourth period was a daily trial because Jim, a very poor reader, was constantly disruptive. One day in desperation she read a favorite short story aloud to the class. To her surprise, Jim listened and even answered several questions. On his way out, she commented on his perceptive answers and asked if he particularly liked that story. He glowered at her, leaned forward, and muttered, "It was the first time I finished the story at the same time as everybody else!" As if ashamed of his candor, he stalked out. She never forgot the lesson Jim taught her: that listening can draw a poor reader into a literature activity that reading shuts him out of. Storytelling, too, has its place in the upper grades, especially as a stimulus to writing and acting out scripts (see Moffett and Wagner, 1976).

Having Children Read

Encouraging children themselves to read is another important activity. It is often said that we learn to read by reading, by wading in and making sense of print. That does not mean that we always learn without help, but there is no substitute for reading real text for some purpose, no matter what that purpose may be.

Kevin, compliantly coloring his geometric shapes, was unable to cope with the basals and was not being provided with anything he could read or be helped to read, such as experience stories or pattern books. He was not doing *any* reading. The poor readers in Morris's survey were exposed to text

To understand text, we interpret it in terms of our own ideas about the world — stored in the form of schemata — and, in the process, modify our ideas. Talking to others and investigating their views of the world has the effect of making our schemata more like those of other people's, and probably accounts for much of the similarity in different people's reading of the same text.

for less than five minutes a day. Nobody ever learned to ride a bike by avoiding any contact with bikes, and nobody ever learned to swim by looking at water for a few moments a day. There are, of course, many different ways to approach reading instruction, but whatever the approach it is best for children to read whatever they can read as soon as possible, and then spend more time reading.

Stauffer (1980), Allen (1976), and others who advocate using language experience as a first reading method recommend writing down a group-dictated experience story and choral-reading it on the first day of school. The first graders then go home to report proudly, "What did we do today? We wrote a story and we read it too!"

Language experience is not the only approach that allows an immediate start on real reading, even before children have mastered any skills. Several commercial basal series, such as Holt, Rinehart & Winston's *Sounds of Language* series and Scott Foresman's *Reading Unlimited* program begin with repetitions, patterned stories children can read as easily as a dictated story. The first passage in the first preprimer of *Sounds of Language* is the text of the song, "Happy Birthday." Here are the teacher's manual directions:

These sentence sounds already are in most children's heads. Support their immediate belief that they can read this page. Here's a chance to connect oral and printed language. Role-playing the act of reading is a child's first step in becoming a successful reader. (Martin and Brogan, *Sounds I Remember*, 1974, p. 11)

Martin and Brogan have also produced the *Instant Readers*, sets of highly patterned children's books. A book like *Brown Bear, Brown Bear* may be the first whole book a child ever reads straight through. Its highly repetitious text and picture clues make it a completely supportive experience ("Brown bear, brown bear, what do you see? I see a *red bird* looking at me. Red bird, red bird, what do you see? I see a yellow duck . . . blue horse . . . grey mouse," etc.) Here is what Martin and Brogan have written about such books:

> Children in our society inherit the need to read. They also inherit the expectancy that they will read a book on the first day of school. When they don't, they go home disappointed — and the first breach between a child and reading success has been created. How much better to invite those "first-dayers" to hear a highly structured book that they immediately can "read back" cover-to-cover. . . . Over the years teachers, lacking surefire beginning books, have been forced to engage children in all sorts of reading readiness materials that have no connection whatsoever with a book, and sometimes even less with language. Consequently, children have been denied for six or more weeks fulfillment of their strong urge to read a book . . . all too many begin their reading careers by losing the urge to read and even by becoming confused about the act of reading. (Martin and Brogan, 1971, pp. 12–13)

Martin and Brogan, Stauffer, Allen, and others contend that children's *belief* that they can read, belief in themselves as readers, is the most basic factor underlying the acquisition of all other skills. In addition, the careful studies of beginning reading carried out by Marie Clay (1979) and others have shown us that there are many concepts about print and reading that beginners need to acquire, but most of them are usually not taught explicitly. They include concepts like the direction of the print, the concept of a word in print as a bound configuration, the idea that the print and not the picture tells the story, and others. Our experience tells us that the early scanning of dictations or books like the *Instant Readers* provides these basic orienting concepts much better than duplicator sheets or other lessons that fragment real reading.

In the case of children who have already begun to read, the need for real text is even stronger. Reading is not simply a matter of decoding words or sentences. It is an elaborate response to large structures of meaning — structures like paragraphs, episodes, arguments, chronologies, hierarchies, and whatever other structures authors may choose to convey their thoughts. We find all too often that reading materials are short and sterile. Since learning to read requires learning to respond to and make predictions about these larger structural elements, texts that do not have these structural elements do not teach children real reading. Teachers may not even realize that the reading that results is artificial, as long as reading test scores are adequate. But most testing procedures in regular use in our classrooms do not test real reading either: they test children on the same sorts of short, sterile passages with which the children are so often taught to read.

Our task is to get each student reading extended prose. The job may entail other types of activity, to be sure, but having children read rich, connected text should predominate over everything else.

Reading to Satisfy Inquiry

It is not enough to have children "just read." *What* they read and *why* they read it are also important. Real reading, the kind that fluent readers do every day, means reading to satisfy a variety of purposes. Sometimes we want to entertain ourselves, so we pick something that is really entertaining (we reject anything that isn't) and we normally read it quickly. Sometimes we have to learn about a subject. If we are preparing an academic paper, we may read from several books and look for ideas these several sources bring to bear on a single topic. We may read six novels, for example, to find out how a certain Victorian author developed female characters. Sometimes we read to find out how to do something. We may want to try a new procedure for improving comprehension, for example, and elect to read up on the directed reading-thinking activity described in Chapter Five. In this case we would read the relevant passages closely. We might read them several times and take notes. Then, after we had tried to carry out the procedure with students, we very likely would return to the passages and read them again, this time to make sure that what we did conformed to what the passage in the book described. We read for other reasons too, but the three just described give examples of the very different purposes we may have in mind.

If school instruction is to lead directly into fluent reading habits, it too must include real purposes. Moreover, the purposes must vary from time to time, which means that the tasks must not be limited to the reading period but extended right across the curriculum. Children have to read extensively for all subjects, such as science, social studies, health, art, and music and not just "reading." For a start, the book reports that children are required to do can be broadened out into research reports in some subject area field. The reading, and the discussion of it, should be carried out in the other textbooks a child is assigned, not just the basal readers. When teachers read to the children, the material should include interesting nonfiction as well as fiction. Listening can be made into a stimulating inquiry exercise if the techniques of the directed listening-thinking activity (see Chapter Three) are used.

We are not only concerned with varying the subject areas of the reading materials but also in setting realistic and motivating purposes for doing the reading. Ordinarily, adults read something because they *want* to or because they *need* to. Children usually read something because they are *told* to. The difference in motivation is a big one, and the question is: How can we help children set real purposes for reading? The answer is to create a school situation that will call for reading as a natural means to some important ends. Examples of such situations are inquiry units, when open-ended questions are placed before the whole class, and individuals or groups read and investigate the issues. Ultimately the students publish a newspaper, or hold a panel discussion, or make a television show about the questions. Thus reading is done as a natural and important part of the inquiry. Similarly, the teacher can provide equipment for carrying out an experiment or leave open a book passage that describes the steps for carrying it out. Or the class can plan a group play or television production and consult books on television photography, costume and set design, stage directions, and script writing.

Teachers should cultivate the habit of examining every unit they are about to teach and deciding how reading for a purpose can be incorporated in the most interesting way. Whether the subject is health, science, social studies, or something else, teachers should give the unit an activity component in which the children will have to do some creative project on their own rather than just following directions. It is usually the creative projects that give children the latitude to develop their own purposes for reading, to find out what they need to know to achieve some end, and then read to gain that knowledge. The teacher's role is to raise good questions, encourage children to frame the inquiry or set the plans for a project, and then to provide reading material and other resources that they can use.

On the question of how teachers can set up challenging projects that require real reading as a matter of course, John Merritt (1978) came up with the terms "Mickey Mouse" and "gerbil" activities. Merritt, and the British teachers he works with, noted that the closer a project came to some real purposes that real people would have in the real world, the stronger its potential to summon up real communication on the part of the children. With all due respect to the beloved cartoon character, they chose Mickey Mouse to denote activities that were cute and cleverly designed, but unreal. Gerbil activities were those that were essentially unpredictable and messy, yet capable of yielding real and sometimes unanticipated insights. Gerbils mess in their cages, have babies, and sometimes die. Mickey never gets his white gloves dirty.

How can you tell a gerbil activity from a Mickey Mouse one? Here are two examples.

In some areas, local history is studied by reading histories of the area and doing library research. Such activities often culminate in a written or oral report to the class, a meal of local foods, or an art activity. They are usually fun but of a temporary nature, and the results are of little lasting value: Mickey Mouse.

Loban (1979) describes a project in which elderly people come to the school to record an "oral history." It includes reminiscence of important events as well as the interweaving of events from their personal lives and their personal opinions and values. These recordings are transcribed by the students, illustrated with old or recent photos and other artwork, typed, edited, and bound into books that become a treasured part of the school's and community's heritage. We know one rural area in which this was done, and when some of the elderly participants later died, their recorded accounts and the photographs they donated became a living legacy to those they left behind. The children involved came to know the elderly as real people with fascinating lives the children never guessed they had experienced: gerbil.

In a nearby high school, tenth-grade biology students were dissecting frogs. In one class, students carefully studied the structure of the frog's body, its diet, and life cycle. They completed detailed notes and drawings of their dissections at various stages, and prepared large colored drawings of the various parts of a frog's body, each carefully labeled and displayed around the science room. They painted a large mural of the life cycle of a frog and hung it in the hall. Everyone concerned enjoyed the drawings and the mural: Mickey Mouse.

In another class, after the dissection was completed the teacher proposed two problems. The students chose one that they would investigate and present to the class. The problems were:

1. Would you donate an eye or kidney to an organ bank? Would you donate your body to science? Why or why not? What is involved in doing so? How are the organs taken, stored, and used?
2. Would you eat a frog? Have you ever eaten one? If you were lost in the wilderness and starving, what would you eat? What would you refuse to eat? Why? If you were in a war and starving, where would you draw the line on what animals you would eat? In these situations, what have some people really eaten? Would you?

These studies resulted in such far-flung outcomes as visits to a local organ bank, talks by an undertaker and a surgeon, extended reading about famines, concentration camps, and wilderness survivors, a debate on the relative "value" of different forms of life, and a panel discussion by organ donors and recipients. The unit required weeks of work and took many surprising turns along the way. At times the teacher felt he had lost his grip on the curriculum, but he believed he had brought the students' own values into their study of biology: gerbil.

Interactive reading (Gemake, 1984) is "a method to help children respond meaningfully to text by drawing and by writing ideas that extend and complement the story." (p. 462) Interactive reading activities call for readers to respond to stories by describing, illustrating, and/or acting out their reactions to story events and characters, making their reactions and feelings an integral part of their comprehension. According to Gemake, readers' feelings and reactions "extend, personalize and influence textual comprehension." (p. 462)

A teacher prepares an interactive activity by breaking a story into parts, stopping where readers' feelings are likely to be aroused, important characters are introduced, or story action changes course. Teachers are advised to think, as they read the story, Where can students step into this story and interact with it? At these points, instructions are given for ways that students may personalize and respond to the story. Directions may call for students to write some sentences describing their feelings, draw a picture of some proposed action, locate and list story words that describe a character's mood or feeling, create dialogue, or the like. The teacher then composes a summary page where students can write freely about favorite characters or scenes, evaluate characters' actions or beliefs, compose different endings or change story events, or perhaps create a poster or cover for the story. At the end, projects are shared with the class and work may be displayed.

Inquiry units and interactive reading activities are only a few of the many ways teachers can help to personalize and extend readers' comprehension of and real involvement with text. However it is accomplished, such efforts improve the reading program by replacing "Mickey Mouse" activities with the kinds of purposeful reading people do out of school — the reading we want students to do for a lifetime.

Junior Great Books. The Great Books Foundation publishes anthologies of interesting and provocative stories drawn from folktales, fables, myths, and classical and modern fiction. The foundation also offers training for teachers and other volunteers to conduct penetrating discussions of the stories with students ranging from second grade through high school.

The discussion methods used in the Great Books programs are organized around the idea of "shared inquiry." The discussion leaders make up their own questions, and they ask only questions to which they do not know the answers. An example: for the story "Jack and the Beanstalk" (in the second grade anthology) the discussion leader might ask, "Why does the author have Jack's adventure take place up in the sky?" Once a question is posed, discussion leaders use follow-up questions that press the students to clarify their answers, support them with references to the text, and relate them to others' answers.

There is one anthology available for each grade. Because the stories are intended for average or above-average readers, problem readers should use anthologies from lower grades. Each story is to be read twice before it is discussed. With problem readers it is easy for the teacher to read the story aloud the first time, or even to record it for them on tape so they can listen to it once through before reading it on their own. The reader for each grade level has twelve stories, and each of these is meant to be discussed in a single session of under an hour's length. Thus the program is not intended as a basal reader program, though the discussion techniques can fruitfully be applied to basal reader selections.

Many schools have organized Great Books programs using parent volunteers as discussion leaders. Tips for recruiting and supervising volunteers are covered in the excellent two-day training sessions that are offered in local communities by the Great Books Foundation, 40 East Huron Street, Chicago, Illinois 60611.

Integrating the Language Arts

Children can understand complex grammatical forms they hear before they can produce similar constructions (Brown, 1973). They can become sensitive to spoken language structures by listening and be better prepared to respond to similar structures when they encounter them in print. Therefore, listening practice should be developed at the same time that initial reading instruction is going on. Such practice in speaking and listening can help children because it develops their language base. In time they will be able to transform visual symbols into language structures and thus be able to comprehend what they see in print.

What all this means is that children should listen to and discuss material read aloud to them: books, newspaper articles, songs, and poems. They should listen to one another describing things and be encouraged to press for information. They should summarize and restate what has been said and ask questions when things are not clear. Classroom dramatics activities provide good oral language stimulus, since drama and the physical movement it entails is an early-developing and powerful response to language (Moffett and Wagner, 1976).

What about writing? Writing is sometimes thought of as the "active" counterpart to reading, a "passive" process. We are very unhappy with this view because it takes the position that expression is active but reception is passive, which is, of course, nonsense. Goodman (1970) suggested that we construct for ourselves what an author is attempting to communicate as we predict what words and ideas may occur next. This is certainly a cognitively active process. Writing and reading trade on the resources of written language. They clearly help each other. We would not have the structures of written language available to us if we had not read them elsewhere. We would not have as fine a sensitivity to words and how they go together if we did not write.

Writing forces us to concentrate on choosing words that reflect our meaning as precisely as possible and to compare our own output with the words and letters written by others. Do the letters used reflect the sounds heard? Do the letters look like those others have written (Chomsky, 1971)? It is in writing words that we deal with their features in earnest. Writers are often better readers, and one reason is that they deal carefully with word structures. They take more interest in print than people who do little writing. Mature writers have control over grammar, sentence construction, and paragraph organization. They use story structure phrases like "once upon a time," expressions like "therefore," "however," and other structures that reveal the organization of a piece of writing. People who write, children and adults, are more aware of such elements than those who don't write.

Encouraging children's early writing efforts, and indeed the efforts of all writers in every grade, does more than help children learn to spell (although if it only accomplished this it would be a worthwhile goal). Early writing, and frequent writing in every grade, encourages the development of oral language, reading and listening comprehension (Hipple, 1985), greater understanding of how stories and nonfiction text are constructed, heightened appreciation for well-written literature, and pride in one's growing competence as a reader and writer (Calkins, 1983; Elbow, 1981; Graves, 1979, 1983).

To summarize, one of the characteristics we look for in a productive reading classroom is a wise combination of the language arts: a careful development of spoken language and listening and writing as well as reading. These subjects need not all be pursued at the same time, but teachers should make it their responsibility to see that every child spends part of each day working in each of the four areas of the language arts.

Displaying Reading Materials

It is useful to compare the way schools sell literacy with the way American supermarkets sell their products. The stores advertise with catchy slogans and tunes, wrap their items in colorful packages, give away free samples, feature well-known people giving testimonials, and lay out the stores so you are stopped by artful displays at every turn. In order to enter you must often make your way through a maze of baked goods, soft drinks, potato chips, and beer. Look at the cereal aisle; all the sugary cereals are located at a child's eye level. The checkout aisles are bottlenecks jammed with displays of candy bars, gum, cigarettes, flashlight batteries, small toys, and magazines. *Try* to leave without one of these!

What does your classroom or school library do to sell its contents? Is it possible to get in and out again without being seized with an irresistible desire to pick up something to read?

As part of the countywide reading study referred to earlier, the authors of this book were requested to do a survey of a school district's libraries. These were our findings. Does this sound like your library?

If there is a serious effort in this county to promote literacy, the action has bypassed most of the school libraries. Too many libraries are stuffy, bland,

and uninteresting. If they were grocery stores, nobody would buy anything in them. We looked in vain for eye-stopping displays of reading matter, interesting library activities in progress, or comfortable places to plop down with a book. What we saw again and again were tall shelves looming around the walls with volume after volume of tired old books bearing oppressive titles. We saw children in hard wooden seats at long, bare tables. We saw librarians performing clerical and police functions only. Little use of students' work in any form was seen anywhere. We observed no reading aloud, no book talks, little unrequested aid in book selection, and little encouragement in talking about books.

Our report was harsh but accurate. Particularly ironic was the fact that the school officials talked freely and often about their commitment to reading. Yet the libraries were set up to handle only highly motivated readers, those who knew just what they wanted and weren't put off by unfriendly treatment or faded books tucked cover-to-cover into high shelves. The trouble was that none of the schools seemed to have any such readers. And the libraries weren't circulating many books either.

How can a school library sell reading successfully? Like a supermarket, it has to be full of lots of wonderful things, displayed in such appealing ways that children can't help but pick them up and read them. Books there must be, of course, of every kind, everywhere. As many as possible should be displayed on tabletops and low shelves, standing up with front cover foremost. They must be at a height that invites picking them up. Using the topmost shelves, over the librarian's head, for display of books defeats the purpose. There should be numerous magazines and paperbacks conveniently displayed and located near comfortable chairs or floor pillows to invite readers to begin their reading right there. Traditionally libraries have been furnished as places to study, but to appeal to large numbers of students, they should be furnished as places to read for pleasure. Hence the floor pillows and soft furniture alongside the regular chairs and tables. The library should be gay and appealing with children's art, crafts, and writing everywhere. Mobiles, posters, paper book jackets, poems and stories, jokes and riddles, shoebox dioramas — all can be produced in the classroom and displayed in the library. Students will feel that the library is *theirs* if their work is incorporated in it.

Classroom libraries are another necessary ingredient for a successful reading program. Barbe (1961) suggested a minimum of 100 books at any one time. The school librarian can probably arrange for you to keep a collection of books in your room for several weeks or a month at a time. Building classroom libraries is a good project for PTA groups, and students too can donate books they have purchased through the paperback book club. A great idea is to have stickers that read "Donated through the generosity of _____" to put in these books. Classroom libraries, like school libraries, should be comfortable, inviting places where you can curl up with a book. A

Classrooms that really promote reading and writing feature functional, everyday reading tasks. Here, a classroom grocery store of empty packages is a continuing source of words, directions to follow, and dialogues to make up.

few low shelves and a bit of carpet may be enough, with lots of books arranged with their covers facing out to attract browsers (Fader, 1976; Veatch, 1968).

Classroom libraries have a couple of advantages over school libraries. First, the children have greater access to them. There are many times during the day — before school, at lunch, or between activities — when they have time to browse through the classroom library. Also, students in the class are likely to have read some of the books, and by talking about them they may arouse the interests of others. The teacher can help this process along by inviting children to talk informally about good books they have read recently from the classroom library or elsewhere.

After you read a book to the class, it is a good idea to place it in the classroom library. Usually at least one child will want to read the book after hearing it. Whenever a new book comes in, or if a topic comes up that is covered in a book in the classroom library, call it to the children's attention by talking briefly about it and displaying it prominently.

A special source of books for the classroom library is what the children write themselves. Classroom publishing can be a highly motivating activity for students, and the books that result are usually the most popular in the school. Most teachers use book publishing as an occasion to point out the need for editing and writing a final draft. Once students have written the text for a published book, they can create a hard-cover binding so it can be circulated. Allen (1976) described very fully several classroom centers developed for the purpose of publishing children's writing. He goes into much detail because he believes that publishing their own work is the "peak experience" in early reading and writing. He organized committees to work on the editing, typing or printing, duplicating, illustrating, and binding of books.

Binding sturdy classroom books is easy:

1. Cut two pieces of cardboard for the front and back covers of the book. Make sure they are the same size. Lay the pieces side by side. Leave a space the width of a pencil between the two pieces of cardboard.
2. Place the cardboard on top of the cover material which has been cut 1 inch larger than the cardboard on all sides. Use any attractive paper, wallpaper, fabric or contact paper for covers. Bond the cover material to the cardboard with glue, or photographic drymount paper and a warm iron.
3. Fold down the corners of the cover material over the cardboard. Then fold over the edges and glue the corners and edges to the cardboard.
4. While the glue dries, cut sheets of paper for pages. Cut each sheet slightly smaller than the entire opened cover. Don't cut down the middle of the sheet! Instead, fold here and sew the sheets down the fold using white thread. Place stiches about ¼ inch apart.
5. Place the sewn pages between covers with stitching against the space between the cardboards. Glue the first page to the inside front cover, covering up the raw edges of the material. Repeat with the last page and back cover. This forms end papers and holds the entire book together.

For step-by-step illustration, see Figure 10.1.

Classroom Atmosphere

A classroom atmosphere that promotes active reading has two main features. First, functional reading tasks are made an integral part of classroom life. Second, the psychological climate of the classroom induces curiosity, security, and respect for people and property.

In classrooms that actively promote literacy, important and interesting messages displayed at students' eye level should be very much in evidence. Written instructions for animal care could be taped up next to a gerbil cage, along with pertinent facts about them: their names, when they were born, what they eat, and where they came from. Pictures of class members could be displayed with biographical information about each student written underneath. For activities in which things are weighed, compared, classified, taken apart, and put together, writing projects would be a worthwhile

FIGURE 10.1. How to bind a book.

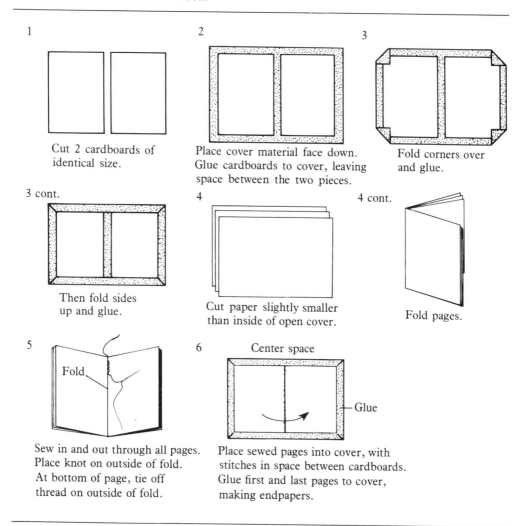

1

Cut 2 cardboards of identical size.

2

Place cover material face down. Glue cardboards to cover, leaving space between the two pieces.

3

Fold corners over and glue.

3 cont.

Then fold sides up and glue.

4

Cut paper slightly smaller than inside of open cover.

4 cont.

Fold pages.

5

Fold

Sew in and out through all pages. Place knot on outside of fold. At bottom of page, tie off thread on outside of fold.

6

Center space

Glue

Place sewed pages into cover, with stitches in space between cardboards. Glue first and last pages to cover, making endpapers.

addition to the regular assignments. Wall charts could be used to show sports figures, people in the news, historical automobiles, or medieval costumes with written facts about each, but they should be changed every week or two before they become dull to the eye.

Letters students write to arrange a field trip can be copied and displayed on the wall, and the responses added as they come in. The same can be done with letters students write to authors of their favorite books, the president, astronauts, movie stars, and foreign embassies. Daily observations of the growth of classroom plants, of weather changes, and the numbers of recyclable aluminum cans students have collected can be written on charts and displayed on walls, doors, and the backs of bookcases.

In short, reading and writing in the classroom should serve functions for which adults value them: they record important events and facts and offer a means of communication with others across space and time.

Classroom Organization and Student Interaction

The climate of classrooms for reading instruction should encourage curiosity and risk taking (of course within the bounds of respect for others).

Language instruction often creates noise. The activities necessary for developing language ability cannot flourish in a silent classroom, but children need order too. They need at least enough order to feel secure, to know that their concentration will not be unduly interrupted when they are engaged in a task, and to be assured that the teacher is not silently seething and about to erupt because they are too noisy. One can usually tell when the activity level in the classroom is just right. There is neither an oppressive silence nor a brain-jarring din, and the individuals in that setting look intent on what they are doing, but not tense.

There are several ways to set up such a classroom. One is to make clear to children what is expected of them in the way of behavior and where the limits are. Many teachers have class meetings at the beginning of the year, when they allow children to suggest rules for conduct and discuss each one before the class either accepts it or rejects it. Those rules the class accepts (and that the teacher can live with) are written up on tagboard and posted on the wall. The teacher then reminds the children of these rules from time to time, and occasionally the class will revise one or more of them.

William Glasser's *Schools Without Failure* (1969) program extends the idea of the class meeting throughout the year. It is modeled on the old town meeting, a form of government in rural New England where all the people in the town came together regularly to discuss issues affecting life in the area. Glasser's class meetings are like that: once or more each week all the students sit in a big circle and, under the teacher's direction, discuss issues of importance to them. The classroom atmosphere, problems they are having, things they are excited about or frustrated about, new procedures they are going to try out, all are discussed calmly and openly in a setting where everyone is encouraged to participate.

A classroom atmosphere like this, where students and teachers interact and share responsibility for order and productivity, and where productive activity produces noise but not a din, may be called a "language-rich environment" (Auten, 1985). Such an environment is necessary for language development, both oral and written, to flourish. The teacher serves as a model for vocabulary usage and actively encourages language exchanges among students, not just with the teacher. Students interact in an error-tolerant environment that invites exploration, interchange, and growth through oral and written language.

Another important aspect of such a classroom atmosphere is that it encourages cooperation and interaction rather than primarily individual or competitive efforts. In a fascinating study of classroom organizations and achievement patterns Skon, Johnson, and Johnson (1981) concluded that cooperative interaction, as opposed to competitive or individualistic efforts, promoted higher achievement and the discovery of superior cognitive reasoning strategies in first graders, regardless of their ability levels or whether they were cooperating with others of like or different ability.

The ways classrooms are organized to promote or inhibit student interaction and cooperation are functions of the role reading plays in those classrooms. According to Bloom (1985) and others, reading is more than a process of learning to get meaning from print. It is also a social process that, by its role in classroom life and the ways it is taught and practiced, affects nearly every facet of how students perceive their own and others' abilities and weaknesses, the distribution of power and status among teacher and students, and the ways students associate reading with success and failure and social standing.

Bloom proposed that there were three aspects of reading as a social process: the social context of reading, reading as a cultural process, and reading as a sociocognitive process.

To determine the social context of classroom reading, Bloom proposed that teachers ask themselves questions like:

☐ How is reading used to form social groups and to separate individual from social groups? (Are reading groups static or dynamic? Are they based on any factor other than reading ability? Are their activities different from those of other groups?)
☐ What must students do to act appropriately in reading groups? (Correct each other? Help each other? Compete? Challenge, or avoid challenging, the teacher?)
☐ How is turn-taking during reading organized?
☐ How are resources like materials, teacher feedback, and library use distributed among students and groups?
☐ How are reading tasks distributed? (Who gets to do what, on what basis?)

To determine the nature of the cultural process of classroom reading, Bloom proposed these questions:

☐ In what ways do reading activities and materials reflect readers' cultures?
☐ In what ways do they reflect the culture of the school and community?
☐ What kinds or acts of reading are valued in the classroom and what kinds are overlooked or discouraged?

☐ In what ways do school reading events reflect certain values, beliefs, or ways of acting or feeling?

☐ In what ways are cultural differences recognized and identified, or overlooked and denied?

To determine the sociocognitive aspects of reading, Bloom proposed asking:

☐ What kinds of language and cognitive demands are consistently made during reading?

☐ What are the cumulative effects on language, cognition and social standing of these demands? (adapted from Bloom, 1985, pp. 139–140)

Bloom suggested that serious consideration of questions like these can help us determine how reading affects the social and cognitive development of all our students, and help us change or adapt practices that may be inhibiting success and achievement.

Developing Reading Attitudes

Another important aspect of classroom atmosphere is the direct attention given to fostering positive attitudes toward reading. According to a study by Heathington and Alexander (1984), teachers are very aware of the importance of positive reading attitudes, but spend little time directly promoting them and are largely unaware of ways of assessing attitudes other than by observation. Heathington and Alexander's subjects, most of whom taught in primary grades, ranked positive reading attitudes second only to comprehension in importance in reading activities for their grade levels, but indicated they spent more time on all other activities except study skills (which are rarely taught at the elementary level). No subject could name an attitude assessment device; most said they used simple observation, and a third of the subjects reported using no attitude assessment of any kind. Heathington and Alexander concluded that belief in the importance of a topic is no guarantee that much classroom time will be devoted to it, and that teachers need direct help in learning to promote positive attitudes.

How can positive attitudes toward reading be directly encouraged? We have already discussed maximizing the amount of time spent reading, making reading follow students' own interests and informational needs, making reading and writing a part of all activities, and displaying books and magazines invitingly. Fredericks (1982) and Heathington and Alexander (1984) also suggest these means:

☐ Develop or find an informal reading interest inventory (see Chapter Nine) to assess student interests and reading preferences. Supplement this with your own observation.

☐ Allow time daily for self-selected reading.

☐ Provide a variety of materials on subjects of student interest. Your librarian can help you with this.

☐ Guide students toward new materials and new topics.

☐ Choose monthly reading topics based on student interests. Encourage pleasure reading and library research, special events and presentations, and students' sharing of books and articles.

☐ Use creative ideas for book-sharing, such as art projects, dramatics, interpretive readings, puppetry, and writing activities instead of the "same old book reports."

☐ Help students design and produce their own books (see Figure 10.1) and ask your librarian to display and circulate them in the library.

☐ Produce a "reading newspaper" of student-written articles, reviews, biographies of authors, artwork and book-related puzzles and games.

Summary

It is our belief that reading assessment cannot end with the child; we must also look closely at the classroom. In order to have a good reading instruction environment, there are five major guidelines we ought to follow:

1. Instructional goals should be set by informed teachers, not dictated by commercial programs. Under this principle we noted that teachers should have an adequate understanding of how children learn to read, and they should be given the responsibility for making day-to-day instructional decisions consistent with their understanding of the reading process and the needs of their students.

2. Children in a reading class should spend their time doing profitable tasks. Careful examination has revealed that in many classes, children spend only a few minutes a day reading real text while most of their time is spent doing nonreading activities. The tasks we believe should occupy the most time are reading aloud to the students, having the students themselves read real text, and seeing to it that they read to satisfy inquiry. Integrating the language arts is also advised, if not during the same period, at least during the same day. Since reading development is interrelated with the development of oral language and with writing, teachers should see that all these communication skills go forward.

3. Interesting materials should be displayed in an eye-catching manner in the classroom library as well as in the school library. We cannot assume that the students will have sufficient interest in reading to go to the library and ask for a book by title, no matter how old or young they may be. The teacher and librarian must use every device they can think of to put interesting materials in the path of children, in such a way that they cannot be ignored. Setting up classroom libraries is most worthwhile, and books written and bound by the children themselves should be part of the collection.

4. The classroom should have a relaxed but businesslike atmosphere: open enough for students to pursue their tasks without undue pressure, yet sufficiently controlled for them to feel secure and free from distraction. Creating such an atmosphere involves the following. First, the teacher should give the guidelines for behavior, although they may also be set by the whole class after discussion. Second, the teacher should make sure all of the students understand the purposes of the tasks in which they are engaged. Third, the classroom should be a "language-rich environment" in which language in all its forms is modeled and encouraged and in which students engage in cooperative work and interaction. Fourth, the ways that reading activities are organized and presented should be thoughtfully examined in light of their social function and impact on students' perception of their own success or failure, strengths and weaknesses.

5. Systematic attention should be given to encouraging the development of positive reading attitudes, beginning with the assessment of student reading interests and habits and using activities that foster reading enjoyment based on these interests.

Extension Activities

1. If you are not yet teaching, visit a class in grades one through six during the reading instruction period. Pick a child at random and sit somewhere so that you can observe what the student is doing. Keep track of the amount of time spent on reading connected text during the period. If you are in a class, arrange to have three pupils visit one class, each to observe the reading time spent by students designated as good, average, or poor readers, respectively. Compare the results.

2. Locate an elementary reading program that uses a skills management system, one published by the basal system company or one bought to supplement the basal instruction. Look over the teacher's manuals. Without listing every skill, can you state in simple terms what competencies the system suggests students should have? Which seem to you to be readiness skills? Which deal with word recognition and analysis? Which with reading comprehension, especially comprehension beyond the literal level? How do these competencies compare with those we described in Chapters Three, Five, and Six?

3. Identify the activities that one child would typically carry out in the management system. Choose any skill level you wish. Try to calculate the total amount of time the student spends doing each activity each week (e.g., see Table 10.1).

4. Interview five teachers. Ask them to describe:
   a. four activities they feel are most effective for teaching word knowledge (recognition of words and their meanings)
   b. four activities they feel are most effective in developing reading comprehension

TABLE 10.1. Student activity time.

	TIME (IN HOURS OR FRACTIONAL HOURS PER WEEK)
ACTIVITY	
1. Listening to stories	_____
2. Listening to nonfiction material	_____
3. Reading fiction text (more than a paragraph)	_____
4. Reading nonfiction text (more than a paragraph)	_____
5. Workbook activities	_____
6. Duplicator sheet activities	_____
7. Discussions and dramatics	_____
8. Extended writing	_____
9. Watching television	_____
10. Word games, etc.	_____
11. Other	_____

Total time reading (3 + 4)   _____

Total time listening (1 + 2)   _____

Total time discussing (7)   _____

Total time on worksheets (5 + 6)   _____

Total time writing (8)   _____

If the teachers mention the use of commercial materials such as SRA kits, ask them to describe what the students *do* in such materials that is effective.

5. Interview four students of different ages. Ask them to describe:
   a. the activities they do in reading or language arts that *help* them the most in learning to read or improving their reading
   b. the activities they *enjoy* the most in reading or language arts
   How do their answers compare? How do they compare with the activities the teachers described as being most helpful?

6. Find an interest inventory (see Chapter Nine) or create your own for your grade. Ask students to complete it and discuss their reading interests and habits with them. Then examine the classroom to see how well the available materials reflect their interests. If there are too few materials in these areas, make some plans to improve the situation.

Suggested Readings

Calkins, Lucy McCormick. **Lessons from a Child: On the Teaching and Learning of Writing.** *Exeter, N.H.: Heinemann Educational Books, 1983.* The story of one child's growth in writing, and through it of how a school became immersed in writing.

George, Mary Yanaga. **Language Art: An Ideabook.** *Scranton, Pa.: Chandler Publishing Company, 1970.* Reading teachers will find valuable advice in language arts methods books. This one is short, and also especially thoughtful.

Graves, Donald H. **Writing: Teachers and Children at Work.** *Exeter, N.H.: Heinemann Educational Books, 1983.* The definitive work on helping children grow as writers and bringing print into every aspect of the school day.

Griffin, Peg. **"How and When Does Reading Occur in the Classroom?"** *Theory into Practice XVI, No. 5 (December 1977): 376–*383. A study conducted at the Center for Applied Linguistics that examines the reading occurring in classrooms outside of the reading circle.

Guthrie, John T., Martaza, Victor, and Seifert, Mary. **"Impacts of Instructional Time in Reading,"** *in Lauren B. Resnick and Phyllis A. Weaver, eds. Theory and Practice of Early Reading, Vol. 3. Hillsdale, N.J.: Lawrence Erlbaum Associates, 1979.* Explores the often neglected premise that the time the child spends interacting with print affects achievement more than the instructional method employed.

Temple, Charles, and Gillet, Jean Wallace. **Language Arts: Learning Processes and Teaching Practices.** *Boston: Little, Brown, 1984.* A language arts methods text with emphasis on integrating language arts with content areas, encouraging language growth, and enriching the writing program.

References

Allen, R. Van. *Language Experiences in Communication.* Boston: Houghton Mifflin, 1976.

Allington, Richard L. "Fluency: The Neglected Reading Goal." *The Reading Teacher* 36, No. 6 (February 1983): 556–561.

Auten, Anne. "Building a Language-Rich Environment." *Language Arts* 62, No. 1 (January 1985): 95–100.

Bloom, David. "Reading as a Social Process." *Language Arts* 62, No. 2 (February 1985): 134–143.

Barbe, Walter B. *Educator's Guide to Personalized Reading Instruction.* Englewood Cliffs, N.J.: Prentice-Hall, 1961.

Brown, Roger. *A First Language: The Early Stages.* Cambridge, Mass.: Harvard University Press, 1973.

Calkins, Lucy McCormick. *Lessons from a Child: On the Teaching and Learning of Writing.* Exeter, N.H.: Heinemann Educational Books, 1983.

Chomsky, Carol. "Write First, Read Later." *Childhood Education* (March 1971): 296–299.

Chomsky, Carol. "Reading, Writing, and Phonology," in Frank Smith, ed. *Psycholinguistics and Reading.* New York: Holt, Rinehart & Winston, 1973.

Clay, Marie M. *The Early Detection of Reading Difficulties: A Diagnostic Survey with Recovery Procedures,* 2nd ed., Exeter, N.H.: Heinemann, 1979.

Cramer, Ronald L. "Reading to Children: Why and How." *The Reading Teacher* 28, No. 5 (February 1975), 460–463.

Elbow, Peter. *Writing With Power: Techniques for Mastering the Writing Process.* New York: Oxford University Press, 1981.

Estes, Thomas H., and Johnstone, Julie P. "Twelve Easy Ways to Make Readers Hate Reading (and One Difficult Way to Make Them Love It)." *Language Arts* (November–December 1977): 891–897.

Fader, Daniel. *The New Hooked on Books.* New York: Berkley, 1976.

Fredericks, Anthony D. "Developing Positive Reading Attitudes." *The Reading Teacher* 36, No. 1 (October 1982): 38–40.

Gemake, Josephine. "Interactive Reading: How to Make Children Active Readers." *The Reading Teacher* 37, No. 6 (February 1984): 462–466.

Glasser, William. *Schools Without Failure.* New York: Harper & Row, 1969.

Goodman, Kenneth S. "Behind the Eye: What Happens in Reading," in Kenneth Goodman and Olive Niles, eds. *Reading: Process and Program.* Urbana, Ill.: National Council of Teachers of English, 1970.

Graves, Donald. "The Growth and Development of First Grade Writers." Paper presented at the annual meeting of the Canadian Council of Teachers of English, Ottawa, May 1979.

Graves, Donald H. *Writing: Teachers and Children at Work.* Exeter, N.H.: Heinemann Educational Books, 1983.

Heathington, Betty S. and Alexander, J. Estill, "Do Classroom Teachers Emphasize Attitudes Toward Reading?" *The Reading Teacher* 37, No. 6 (February 1984): 484–488.

Hipple, Marjorie L. "Journal Writing in Kindergarten." *Language Arts* 62, No. 3 (March 1985): 255–261.

Huck, Charlotte S. *Children's Literature in the Elementary School,* 3rd ed. New York: Holt, Rinehart & Winston, 1976.

Huus, Helen. "Teaching Literature at the Elementary School Level." *The Reading Teacher* 26, No. 8 (May 1973): 795–801.

Kean, Michael, Summers, Anita, Raivetz, Mark, and Irvin Farber. *What Works in Reading?* ED 176 216. Arlington, Va.: ERIC Document Reproduction Service, 1979.

Loban, Walter. "Relationships Between Language and Literacy." *Language Arts* 56, No. 5 (May 1979), 485–486.

Martin, Bill Jr., and Brogan, Peggy. *Bill Martin's Instant Readers, Teacher's Guide.* New York: Holt, Rinehart & Winston, 1971.

Martin, Bill Jr., and Brogan, Peggy. *Sounds of Language.* New York: Holt, Rinehart & Winston, 1974.

Merritt, John. *Reading, Writing and Relevance.* London: Open University Press, 1978.

Moffett, James, and Wagner, Betty. *Student-Centered Language Arts and Reading, K-13: A Handbook for Teachers,* 2nd ed. Boston: Houghton Mifflin, 1976.

Morris, R. Darrell. "Some Aspects of the Instructional Environment and Learning to Read." *Language Arts* 56, No. 5 (May 1979): 497–507.

Nessel, Denise D. "Storytelling in the Reading Program." *The Reading Teacher* 38, No. 4 (January 1985): 378–381.

Roney, R. Craig. "Background Experience is the Foundation of Success in Learning to Read." *The Reading Teacher* 38, No. 2 (November 1984): 196–199.

Sarason, Seymour B. *The Culture of the School and the Problem of Change.* Boston: Allyn and Bacon, 1971.

Skon, Linda, Johnson, David W., and Johnson, Roger T. "Cooperative Peer Interaction Versus Individual Competition and Individualistic Efforts: Effects on the Acquisition of Cognitive Reasoning Strategies." *Journal of Educational Psychology* 73, No. 1 (February 1981): 83–92.

Stallings, Jane. "Allocated Academic Learning Time Revisited, or Beyond Time on Task." *Educational Researcher* 9, No. 11 (December 1980): 11–16.

Stauffer, Russell G. *The Language-Experience Approach to the Teaching of Reading,* rev. ed. New York: Harper & Row, 1980.

Veatch, Jeannette. *How to Teach Reading with Children's Books,* 2nd ed. New York: Citation Press, 1968.

Index